Endc

'What is a Sikh' is teeming with knowledge, references and answers hundreds of frequently asked questions concerning Sikhi and its socio-religious and politico-economic affairs. Gian Singh Sandhu has depicted Sikh philosophy, theology, ideology, and relevance to the temporal life most effectively and efficiently. Besides, he has also exhibited how susceptible and uncharted trails (such as abortion, test-tube babies, surrogate mothering, artificial insemination, etc.) can be approached and strategized over through Gurbani (Hymns in the Sikh scripture) medium.

- Dr. Gurnam Singh Sanghera
Visiting Professor' Centre for Studies on Sri Guru Granth Sahib
Guru Nanak Dev University, Amritsar

Who are the Sikhs? is a captivating read that encapsulates scholarly and socio-cultural research work. The author's perceptive mind has been able to find answers to many of the challenges facing humanity today. His depth of knowledge on each question and his analytical approach to presenting answers in a common phraseology make it easier for the average reader to comprehend it.

- Prof. (Dr) Dharam Singh
Former head of Encyclopedia of Sikhism,
Punjabi University, Patiala, Punjab.

"*Who Are the Sikhs?* is a monumental effort by Gian Singh which fills a gap in public accessibility for well-researched information regarding the Sikh tradition. Written in a dialogic manner with no question left unasked, there is simply no better amalgamation for all people and the global caretakes of diversity.

- Dr. Harjeet Singh Grewal,
Dept. of Classics and Religion
University of Calgary, Canada

WHO ARE THE SIKHS?

Previous Books by the Author

20-Minute Guide to the Sikh Faith (2020), Bhalaee Foundation, Surrey, British Columbia, Canada

Angahe Raah (2019), (Punjabi translation of *An Uncommon Road*), Unistar Books, Chandigarh, India

An Uncommon Road: How Canadian Sikhs Struggled Out of the Fringes and Into the Mainstream (2018), Echo Storytelling Agency, Vancouver, Canada

Previous Books to Which the Author Contributed

Guru Nanak Darshan: Philosophy of Guru Nanak (2019), Sri Guru Singh Sabha, Surrey, Canada

Guru Nanak: Revealer of Truth (2019), India Cultural Centre of Canada, Richmond, Canada

Guru Nanak Sahib: Jagat Guru—Founder of New World Order (2019), Akali Singh Sikh Society, Vancouver, Canada

Other Translations/Transliterations of the Author's Books

Śīkha dharma māṭē 20 miniṭanī Pustikā (2022), (Gujrati translation of *20-Minute Guide to Sikh Faith*), Bhalaee Foundation, Surrey, Canada

Sikh Dharam Baare 20 Mintaan Di Jaankaari (2022), (Shahmukhi translation of *20-Minute Guide to the Sikh Faith*), Sanjh Publications, Lahore, Pakistan

Un-Gahe Rah (2021), (Shahmukhi transliteration of *Punjabi Angahe Raah*), Sanjh Publications, Lahore, Pakistan

WHO ARE THE SIKHS?

AN EXPLORATION OF THE BELIEFS, PRACTICES, & TRADITIONS OF THE SIKH PEOPLE

GIAN SINGH SANDHU

ARCHWAY
PUBLISHING

Archway Publishing books may be ordered through booksellers or by contacting:

Archway Publishing
1663 Liberty Drive
Bloomington, IN 47403
www.archwaypublishing.com
844-669-3957

Cover design by Davinder(Ravi) Deo of STUDEO
Design, Surrey, British Columbia, Canada.

1. Sikh 2. Sikhi 3. Sikhism 4. Sikh History 5. Sikh Gurdwara 6. *Sikh Rehat Maryada* 7. Sikh Marriage Ceremony 8. Sikh Culture 9. Sikh Articles of Faith 10. Guru Granth Sahib 10. SGGS 11. Guide to Sikh Faith. 12. Guru Nanak 13.Title

ISBN: 978-1-6657-3952-8 (sc)
ISBN: 978-1-6657-3951-1 (hc)
ISBN: 978-1-6657-3953-5 (e)

Library of Congress Control Number: 2023903745

Print information available on the last page.

Archway Publishing rev. date: 03/28/2023

To *Sri Guru Granth Sahib*, the eternal Guru,
for spiritual wisdom and guidance.

CONTENTS

Part VII: Organization and Administration

Chapter 21: Governance

Chapter 22: Gurdwara—Place of Congregation and Learning

FOREWORD

When Gian Singh Sandhu, the author of *Who Are the Sikhs?*, approached me to review this manuscript, I was unsure whether I would be reading a scholarly researched work or a general sociocultural book. To my surprise, it turned out to be a combination of both. As I read it, I was captivated by his depth of knowledge on each question and his analytical approach to presenting answers in a common phraseology, making it easier for the average reader to comprehend it. The author is a devout and committed Sikh who has spent a major part of his life in North America. He is well aware of the difficulties Sikhs have faced in gaining acceptance in an entirely alien culture and the questions about Sikh religion and culture that many, who are not familiar with it, ask. This book is a highly appropriate and appreciable attempt at answering many of these questions.

The author has competently taken up questions dealing with almost all aspects of Sikh religion, community, culture, and identity. These questions might appear to be simple at first glance, but answering them in a concise but comprehensive, simple but satisfying manner is never easy. The author has prepared a detailed list of questions and put them under different headings to help readers consult the sections and chapters that most interest them. These questions relate to Sikh metaphysics, philosophy, social thought, history, tradition, institutions, beliefs, practices, and so on, thus justifying the book's subtitle, "an exploration of the beliefs, practices, and traditions of the Sikh people."

Sikhism is only a little more than five centuries old, and it can well be called one of the youngest among major religions of the world. It is a distinct religion with its own scripture, philosophy, and theology; its own holy places and practices; and its own history and tradition. In this sense, it represents the latest stage in the evolution of the religious consciousness of humankind. That is perhaps the reason why the author's perceptive mind has been able to find answers even to many of the challenges facing humanity today: the sanctity of life, including in vitro fertilization, genetic engineering, and euthanasia; ecology, spiritual unity, and ethnic equality for all; religious plurality, and so on. Of course, the Gurus did not perceive these issues as we do today because these existed only in a very minuscule form then, but the author has tried to respond to these issues based on his overall understanding of the Sikh ethos. Articulating a Sikh response to questions relating to these issues adds to the book's relevance and value.

According to the author, the Sikh God is the one and only entity, the cause of all causes, and the ever-present essence. God, the Primal Lord, is self-created and ever existent, but everybody and everything else is His creation. Since the latter is the manifestation, as Spirit, of God, it becomes relatively real—divine in essence though evanescent, unlike the Creator. This lends spiritual character to the entire material reality—this world is declared the abode of God.

With the help of several scriptural sabads, the author explains that the soul, which acts as a life force in each human body made of the same five perishable elements, is a particle of the same Real One. This shows that all human beings are, in essence, the same and equal among themselves. All differentiations on the bases of caste, creed, class, gender, and race are rejected. All of humankind, says the author, is one society; all are children of one God. At several places, the author uses this premise to emphasize the Sikh view of a just and equitable social order, gender equality, mutual love, philanthropy, and acceptance of religious plurality.

The author is well aware of "the unique relationship between humans and the environment, and the need to respect all species, including vegetation," and highlights the Sikh concern for the environment by saying, "The divine light resides within creation and, therefore, the environment must be respected." He holds that protection of the environment is "not only a social responsibility but also a religious commitment for the Sikhs," as Guru Nanak, in one of his sabads, said, "Air is the Guru, water is the father, and earth is the great mother." As a result, Sikhs across the world celebrate March 14 as Sikh Environment Day and engage in activities such as tree plantings and community cleanups.

In sum, the book attempts to explain almost all aspects of Sikh religion, philosophy, and life in the question and answer form. Herein is explained a Sikh's daily routine through the three principles of *Naam Japna* (remembering the Name Divine), *kirat karna* (working hard and being honest), and *vand shakna* (sharing with the needy whatever he or she earns). The true nature and character of a Sikh are explained through one's *inner rehat* (spiritual and moral values one must uphold) and *outer rehat,* which gets manifested in their social behaviour and outward identity, generally recognized by men's neatly tied or flowing beard and a dastaar (turban) and women wearing a dastaar or scarf. Questions relating to the Sikh holy places, scripture, and philosophy have all been cogently articulated and explained.

Through the author's courtesy, I feel privileged to have had the opportunity to read through the typescript and introduce the book, which, in my mind, will help in forging cordial intercommunity relations based on mutual understanding and also remove any misconceptions about the Sikh identity. I congratulate the author for his labor of love, his comprehensive knowledge, and his effort in successfully testing all of his formulations at the touchstone of the scripture, which makes the account genuinely authentic.

While the author is always humble, saying "he is not an academician or a scholar," he has authored and coauthored several books listed on the previous publication page. In addition, he has written more than two hundred scripts for weekly radio shows "Sikhi Virsa: The Sikh Heritage" on FM Radio CISK 94.3, Williams Lake, British Columbia.
—Professor (Dr.) Dharam Singh
Former head of Encyclopedia of Sikhism
Punjabi University, Patiala, Punjab

PROLOGUE

[When] I unlocked it, viewed, and examined the treasures of
my father and grandfather [ancestors], I was filled with joy
and content. The repository is limitless and invaluable.
—Guru Arjan Ji, *Sri Guru Granth Sahib*

This encyclopedic book, *Who Are the Sikhs?* By Gian Singh Sandhu, is
fundamentally based upon the Holy Sikh scripture (*Sri Guru Granth
Sahib*). It is an invaluable reference work offering answers to many of life's
questions—complex situations, practices, traditions, and ceremonies—
and helps sort out doubts and indetermination surrounding decision-
making in general. Nonetheless, this educational volume is written in
common parlance, and it facilitates guidance and further discussion.

The question and answer format makes it easy for a reader to cherry-
pick a question and find a quick answer. This book embodies both
simplicity and detail.

Before I delve into this insightful book, allow me to make a general
remark on migration and Sikh philosophy. Migration from one place
or region to another in search of a better life is fundamental to human
nature. Guru Nanak Ji, the first Guru of the Sikhs, undertook long
intercontinental walking odysseys in the later part of the fifteenth and
early sixteenth centuries, not in search of a better life in a material sense,
but to engage in discourse with religious leaders of other faiths and
share his divine message with the masses. No encounter could impede
his mission.

The author writes about one of the many thought-provoking stories of Guru Nanak Ji's travels when the Guru and his companion, Mardana, were shunned by a village populace and asked to leave. On departing, the Guru blessed them, saying, "*Vasde Raho*" ("May you prosper and stay here forever"). In contrast, as they moved on to another village whose residents were kind and gracious and received them with open arms, he blessed them and said, "*Ujarh Jao* ("May you be displaced from here"). The moral lesson was clear: kind people should spread out since their goodness and positivity are needed everywhere, while callousness and negativity anywhere need to be curbed and curtailed.

True to Guru Nanak Ji's benediction, Sikhs have migrated globally, and North America is home to more than 1.5 million. In addition to improving their socioeconomic conditions, they have implanted their charitable values of the common free kitchen for all, irrespective of their social status and faith. They have adopted the inclusive philosophy of Guru Nanak Ji that has won their adopted countries' admiration. They have set up meaningful social relationships with the mainstream societies they live in and proudly call their home. Through appropriate adjustments and accommodations in the West's multifaceted environments, and without compromising their identity and salient socioreligious culture, Sikhs have carved out spaces for themselves without alienating others.

The Gurudwara "institution" established by Guru Nanak Ji for the teaching and preaching of philosophy, ideology, and spirituality inscribed in *Sri Guru Granth Sahib* has played a pivotal role in the establishment, development, and advancement of the Sikh community in the diaspora countries. Shabad Guru's essence is said to lie in the blood and hair follicles of a Sikh. Every Sikh tries to discharge his or her socioreligious duties and perform Sikhi-related customs and ceremonies (birth, matrimony, marriage, death, etc.) by the scripture and the Sikh code of conduct.

Since 1708, *Sri Guru Granth Sahib* has been the "eternal Guru" of the Sikhs. The wisdom, spiritual philosophy, salvific ideology, and holistic life-redeeming *gyaan* (spiritual knowledge) contained within is the foundational fountainhead that guides a Sikh's life in all spheres: life's acts, deeds, activities, and even thoughts.

Who Are the Sikhs? Is teeming with knowledge, references, and answers to hundreds of frequently asked questions concerning Sikhi and its socioreligious and politico-economic affairs. The Sikhs' eternal truth, Gurbani, is noted to guide various ceremonies, practices, and their origin. The author and his family are practicing Sikhs. He is immersed in the most significant aspects of Sikhi. I have never found him dodging challenges. He offers candid answers to three hundred questions, based upon Gurbani, Sikh history, authentic traditions, and *Sikh Rehat Maryada* (code of conduct), alongside evidence-based and validated Sikh literature, including that of Bhai Gurdas, Bhai Nandlal, and of prominent and well-recognized academic scholars and intellectuals.

The author depicts Sikh philosophy, theology, ideology, and relevance to contemporary life most effectively and efficiently. He also shows how susceptible and uncharted trails (such as abortion, test-tube babies, surrogate mothering, artificial insemination, etc.) can be approached and strategized through Gurbani's medium.

Nothing is static except the universal laws of nature and the fundamental truths described in the Sikh Holy Scripture. Changes occur at all times and in all aspects of life. Humankind must have the knowledge and ingenuity to cope with them. In response to "Sikh community challenges for the twenty-first century" the author highlights distinct challenges; the Sikh population in India has to always be on guard for fear of annihilation by the majority religion and masterfully reminds diaspora Sikhs that their responsibility extends beyond the Sikh people: "To be a Sikh is to recognize the bond of peoplehood—the tie of community that knows no geographical boundaries."

Finally, Sikhs are not free to believe or practice just anything they want. They are to live following the teachings of *Sri Guru Granth Sahib*. The new eternal vision expressed through Guru Nanak's Bani, infused in the spiritual and temporal aspects of Sikhi and Sikh culture, is to be implemented in the worldly life since Shabad Guru is God-centric and time-centric. All Guru Nanak Ji's efforts and the Bani of His word, originating from the primordial reality/Waheguru, were devoted to providing the salvific Shabad Guru. His other most forceful and articulate pronouncement of the attestation/intent is evident in this verse:

> I am the lowest of the lowly, the lowest of the low born.
> Nanak seeks their company and does not emulate the
> rich, the great. For where the poor and weak are cared
> for, there doth Thy Mercy reign. (*SGGS*, 15)

Guru Nanak Ji saw Waheguru pervading everywhere and residing in everyone. The ultimate objective of a Sikh is not worldly riches or to reach "heaven" but to seek an eternal union with Waheguru. This is to be kept front and centre at all times. Guru Nanak advises, "Listen, listen to my advice, O my Mind. Only good deeds shall endure, and there will not be another chance" (*SGGS*, 287).

This is the first Sikhi book of this size written in a question and answer format. The writing style captivates the reader and furnishes straight and undeviating answers within Gurbani's perimetres (*Sri Guru Granth Sahib*). Though subjectivity cannot be banished entirely, the objectivity of ethical values has been ensured by rooting answers in Waheguru (the Absolute). Any answers sought can be acted upon or realized by the reader at will.

The author has skillfully and eloquently interwoven Gurbani's philosophy, teachings, and theology to answer hundreds of pressing questions. The entire book exhibits unparalleled creativity and adroitness, and it is replete with facts, insights, and Sikh doctrines. Its erudition will be extremely valuable in any home or library. This will prove to be a boon for Sikhs and non-Sikhs alike.

—Dr. Gurnam Singh Sanghera
Former principal and visiting professor at the Centre for Studies on *Sri Guru Granth Sahib*
Guru Nanak Dev University, Amritsar

PREFACE

On May 30, 2018, I was on an Air Canada flight from Winnipeg to Ottawa. As I settled down in my aisle seat, a polite male voice said, "Excuse me. I have the window seat." I rose to let my seatmate in. As we buckled up, we exchanged greetings. Sitting stone-faced for hours is not my personality, so I initiated a conversation, asking the young gentleman, whose name I later learned was David, whether he was going on a business trip to Ottawa or returning home from vacation. This broke the ice, and we inquired about each other's background.

As the flight reached cruising altitude, he asked if I was born in Canada, perhaps noticing the absence of an Indian accent. "No," I said, and I gave him my capsule biography. As it happened, David was a professor of Christian theology. We delved into an ethical, social, and political discussion. From my *dastaar* (turban) to my beliefs and Sikh customs, his questions kept pouring in, and I really had to think hard to answer some of them. Three hours slipped by quickly, and we began our descent into Ottawa. Before we landed, I handed David a copy of my recently released book *An Uncommon Road: How Canadian Sikhs Struggled out of the Fringes and into the Mainstream.*

As I was deplaning, something dawned on me. I thought, *If this professor was unaware of who Sikhs were, then what about the millions of other Canadians and people around the world who have never met a Sikh? Might they have formed their own opinions or concluded "what a Sikh is" from social media?* Suddenly, the light went on. I remembered reading *What Is a Jew?* Back home a week later, I looked for that book in my library and reread it. Rabbi Morris N. Kertzer and Rabbi Lawrence A.

Hoffman had done an excellent job explaining the beliefs, traditions, and practices of Judaism. Their book and the chance encounter with David became my inspiration to write *Who Are the Sikhs?*

Some of the questions in the book are similar to the ones in Kertzer and Hoffman's book. However, there are hundreds more questions that have been asked of me by Sikhs and non-Sikhs alike over the years, including children as young as five. In addition, I have included a few questions raised by the *Ottawa Citizen* for its column "Ask Religious Experts" in the early 2000s. The World Sikh Organization of Canada (of which I was the founding president) was a regular contributor to this column for almost fifteen years. The Sikh viewpoint was published under three different bylines: Kiran Kaur Bhinder, Ajit Singh Sahota, and Balpreet Singh. I have expanded upon some of those in the following pages using specific quotes and references from the *Sri Guru Granth Sahib* and other central texts.

Disclaimer

This book is a resource written to help the public better understand Sikh beliefs and practices (Sikhi). My goal in writing this book is not to provide an academic treatise on Sikhism but to familiarize readers with the Sikh worldview. I am neither an academician nor a scholar, but I have based the book on knowledge I gained as a leader in the Sikh community, countless interactions with learned Sikh scholars, and insights I gleaned over decades of practicing, studying, and living Sikhi.

This book is meant for everyone, regardless of their religious beliefs or where they may be on their personal spiritual journey. Its aim is to provide a resource for Sikhs and non-Sikhs alike, whether they are curious to learn more about their faith or simply wish to have a better understanding of their Sikh neighbours.

Tips for Reading This Book

First, a basic tip. Having lived in Canada for more than half a century, I have heard various pronunciations of the word *Sikh*. The correct one is *Sickh*, with a short *i*. *Sikhi* (the Panjabi term for the Sikh faith) is pronounced "Sickh-ee," with slightly more emphasis on the first syllable.

The book is divided into eight parts, which are further divided into twenty-seven chapters answering more than 260 questions. The question and answer format is intended to make it easier for a reader to choose a topic and find a quick answer rather than reading the complete text to extract information. Part I lays out the origins of the Sikh faith, providing a road map of the Sikh community. Part II defines the Sikh identity, including being and becoming a Sikh. Part III delves into the evolution of Sikhi and its practices. Parts IV and V cover the Sikh view of the Creator and the Creation respectively. Part VI highlights Sikh beliefs and ethics. Part VII captures how Sikh faith is organized and administered. Part VIII peers into the Sikh psyche.

In the footnotes and the text, you will see an abbreviated reference to *SGGS*, which stands for *Sri Guru Granth Sahib*, the sacred Sikh scripture. The *SGGS* is a 1,430-page compilation of the teachings of the Sikh faith. The compositions contained in the *SGGS* are the original writings of six of the ten Sikh gurus, and thirty divinely inspired bhagats and faqirs hailing from other faiths. The writings are in poetic form and appear as separate poems or stanzas, which are called "*sabad*" (also spelled "*shabad*"). In some instances, I have referred to a particular sabad from the Sikh scriptures. In so doing, I have included an English translation of the sabad, a footnote with its phonetic spelling in English, and the sabad as it appears in the *SGGS*, using the original Gurmukhi script (the original language of the *SGGS*) and page number.

In reading this book, you will also notice a prefix or suffix added to certain names. The most common prefix, "Sri," is a title of respect. Sikhs also use the suffixes "Sahib" and "Ji," or the combination "Sahib Ji," after a name or title.

There are other terms that I will use that are not common to the

English reader as they are terms unique to Sikhs. When doing so, I will provide their most common phonetic spelling and define the term. These words or terms are also included in the glossary, along with any notable variations in the English spelling.

A Note about Terminology

In the past, scholars, including practicing Sikhs, used Christian or Western terminology to explain Sikhi to non-Sikhs. Rather than using, for example, the Sikh words *"granthi,"* *"Sri Guru Granth Sahib,"* "Waheguru," or *"dharam,"* they would opt for "priest," "Bible," "God," or "religion." These terms do an injustice to the reader as well as to the Sikhs since they do not impart the same meaning. There are many concepts in Sikhi that have no equivalent in Christian theology or Western religious discourse, and vice versa. To give readers a more consistent and accurate portrayal of the Sikh worldview, I use the original Sikh term and explain its meaning. Wherever possible, I also name and discuss important Sikh concepts that arise from the different terminology. For instance, I use the word "dharam" (an overarching ethical order), which is how Sikhs refer to their faith, rather than the word "religion." I also use the Sikh or Panjabi term "Sikhi" in place of the word "Sikhism." Finally, I have also made a conscious effort to transcribe words as they are used in Panjabi rather than Hindi or Sanskrit. This is in keeping with the Sikh worldview, a decolonizing practice that I hope clarifies and familiarizes rather than confuses.

Now that you have the basic tools to guide you on your adventure, let's begin our journey into Sikhi.

—Gian Singh Sandhu

PART I

Origins: Road Map of the Sikh Faith

Introduction

Before discussing the Sikhs or their faith, allow me to introduce the Sikh community. Despite having more than twenty-eight million adherents who live in every corner of the earth, the Sikhs remain among the least understood faith communities in the world in terms of their beliefs, practices, and values. In writing this book, I hope to fill a gap in knowledge about the Sikhs.

Being Sikh reflects a way of thinking, accepting the human place in creation, and having a relationship with an all-pervading Creator. Sikhi does not endorse active proselytization and conversion. Rather, the focus is on personal growth and development, toward the betterment of the self and all humanity. Sikhs emphasize their own individual practice in connection with learning together and acting collectively for the betterment of society. By combining inward growth with outward action, one can ensure consistency between beliefs and behaviour. This preoccupation with personal development and social welfare has meant that Sikhs, as a group, have not spent as much time trying to explain their sacred teachings and way of life to others.

Sikhs are united in their firm belief in the *Sri Guru Granth Sahib* as a living embodied expression of oneness. For a Sikh, the outcome of living a spiritually inspired life is the end of duality (the idea of the self being separate than the whole) and the realization of oneness. Sikhs believe that by reading, reflecting, and acting on the teachings of the Sikh gurus, they can end this sense of duality and achieve oneness. Sikhs recognize that we are each at our own place along a life in oneness. There is no single absolute way of knowing the truth in which all of creation resides and participates. Such absolutism, for Sikhs, is tyrannical and disrupts our capacity to intuit our place in oneness. Rather, for Sikhs, the goal is learning to act in ways that are consistent with the order of creation in every moment of one's time in this world. This is in keeping with central ideas about individual and collective knowledge such as the idea of "diversity in oneness" (*eka-aneka*).

The followers of the Sikh path are students of life and students for life. They are but travelers on their own uniquely personal journeys. Like any human, they are fallible. This means that sometimes our cultural practices or traditions may diverge from established Sikh philosophy and teachings. Where that is the case, I endeavour to point this out. I approach this task with both joy and trepidation. Joy because I feel privileged to share my knowledge about Sikhi—who I am and why I am. Trepidation because nothing I write can fully explain what it really means to be a Sikh. Sikhs are not a homogeneous group, ethnically or genealogically. They do not agree on everything. Sikhs have divergent views, and it is the goal of this book to acknowledge that diversity and explain the things that unite all Sikhs.

CHAPTER 1

Before We Begin

Let's say a proper hello, shall we? Sikhs greet each other with folded hands. Two greetings that are commonly used among Sikhs are listed here. These greetings are the same regardless of the time of day, occasion, or event and whether you are coming or going:

- *Sat Sri Akaal!* This is the most commonly used greeting among all Sikhs. It is the second part of the full slogan (or jaikara) introduced by Guru Gobind Singh[1] as a call to victory, triumph, or exultation: Jo Bole So Nihal, Sat Sri Akaal! The full slogan means "Whoever utters Sat Sri Akaal shall become exalted!" The term *akaal* used here means "bereft" or "outside of time." Sikhs use this greeting when meeting another to remind each other that truth (satt or Sach) is with the Timeless One through which all exists. It is a reminder that humanity's existence is always within the Timeless One's embrace.
- *Waheguru ji ka Khalsa, Waheguru ji ki Fateh!* This greeting literally means "The Khalsa belongs to the Creator, and Victory belongs to the Creator!" It is commonly used among *amritdhari* Sikhs and by anyone speaking publicly in a *gurdwara* (Sikh place of worship) or at any other religious gathering hosted by Sikhs.

---

[1] The tenth Sikh Guru (1666–1708).

This greeting is expected to start and end a speech. Employing this greeting recognizes the importance of the Khalsa Order to Sikh identity and beliefs.

As this description of Sikh greetings already shows, readers will learn some important terms in this book. Many Sikh concepts found here require a definition or an explanation. I will discuss them as necessary in order to provide detailed answers to the questions this book contains; they are also collected in a glossary at the end of this book for quick reference. There are some words that are critical to the reader's ability to understand this book and are explained here by way of introduction to the Sikh worldview.

- Sikh: a student of divine knowledge.
- Gursikh: another term for Sikh, with particular reference to a practicing or amritdhari Sikh.
- Guru: a teacher of divine knowledge.
- Gurmat: the Sikh way of life as taught by the gurus.
- Waheguru: the wonderful and wondrous Teacher; the Divine Creator.
- Bhagat: a spiritual teacher other than a Guru who is revered by Sikhs.
- Sri Guru Granth Sahib: the living embodiment of the Sikh gurus, which contains the gurus' teachings and guides the Sikhs worldview.
- Gurbani/Bani: the sacred teachings of the Sikh gurus and of other spiritually enlightened individuals, as contained in the *SGGS*.
- Sabad: a specific passage or teaching that is found in the *SGGS*.
- Dharam: a spiritual discipline that guides one's daily actions toward living a life of awareness and intention; the ethical order of operation throughout creation and given by the Creator.
- Sikhi: the Sikh doctrine, philosophy, and practices associated with teachings of the Sikh gurus that enable a Sikh worldview.

- Panth or Sikh Panth: the collective body of Sikhs who engage in Sikhi and work for the well-being of humanity.
- Gurdwara: the Sikh place of congregational worship.
- Amrit: the nectar of immortality, which forms a key part of the Sikh initiation ceremony.
- Amrit Sanchar: the Sikh initiation ceremony, where one commits themselves to following the teachings of the Sikh gurus and living the Sikhi way of life.
- Amrithdari: a person who has been initiated into the Khalsa order and abides by its code of conduct, including keeping the five articles of faith.
- Naam: the name(s) of the one Creator; Naam is both one and many and, therefore, represents holistic vision of oneness.
- Naam Japna: the act of attentively reciting Naam; a Sikh form of meditation.
- Paath: the reading of Gurbani or recitation of Sikh prayers.

CHAPTER 2

The Foundation

Since the founding of Sikhi in the fifteenth century by Guru Nanak, Sikhs have grown to be a strong community of twenty-eight million and make up about 0.4 percent of the world's population. Roughly 57 percent of the Sikh population lives in the state of Punjab, India; 20 percent lives in the rest of India, and the remaining 23 percent lives outside of India. Globally, the Sikh diaspora is the most populous in Canada, the United States, the United Kingdom, and Australia. Each of these countries has between two hundred and seven hundred and fifty thousand Sikhs with the larger numbers residing in Canada and the United Kingdom.

Below is a timeline of where Sikhi fits in among other major world religions:

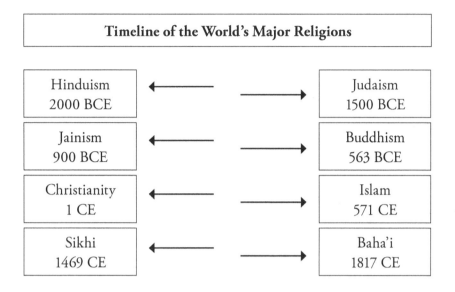

Timeline of the World's Major Religions	
Hinduism 2000 BCE	Judaism 1500 BCE
Jainism 900 BCE	Buddhism 563 BCE
Christianity 1 CE	Islam 571 CE
Sikhi 1469 CE	Baha'i 1817 CE

1. When was Sikhi founded?

Sikhi was established during the late fifteenth century by Guru Nanak, who was born in 1469. He lived in a region called Panjab, which straddles modern-day Pakistan and India. Guru Nanak was a beacon for Gurbani's expression. He began imparting knowledge of Gurbani through a classical form of music known as *dhrupad* and traveling to establish *dharamsalas*, a precursor to modern Gurdwaras. These were places where Gursikhs helped each other learn and practice Sikhi. Late in life, Guru Nanak established a centre of learning at a town he founded called Kartarpur. Guru Nanak passed on the mantle of guruship to Bhai Lehna, who became known as Guru Angad, the second Sikh Guru. In total, Sikhi evolved over a period of two hundred years, through ten gurus. The successive gurus passed on the Sikh teachings and expanded on the practices, compositions, and forms of musical accompaniment. These compositions were incorporated into the Sikh scriptures. In 1708, Guru Gobind Singh passed on the mantle of guruship to the *Sri Guru Granth Sahib.*

2. What is Sikhi?

Sikhi refers to the doctrine, philosophy, teachings, and practices of the Sikh faith. Sikhs do not consider their faith a religion in the commonly understood meaning of the word. The *Oxford Languages Dictionary* defines *religion* as "the belief in and worship of a superhuman controlling power, especially a personal God or gods."

Contrary to the above, Sikhi is not about worship of a supreme being or controlling power. It is about following a daily practice to enable one to attain self-enlightenment. This occurs by studying Gurbani, singing and meditating upon Naam, and selfless service of others. The goal of Sikhi is to help bring one's actions in harmony with all of creation. It is about learning to be human without harming existence or the order established in nature by the one Creator.

Sikhi is about finding one's place in the created order, coming to knowledge of oneness, acting in accordance with this knowledge, and seeing that one light reflected in everyone and everything around us. Sikhi teaches about becoming a truthful being (*sachiara*) and realizing that everything else is just an illusion (*kurha*).

3. What are the basic tenets of Sikhi?

The core of Sikhi is found in the *Mool Mantar*, a composition written by Guru Nanak, which is found at the beginning of the *SGGS*. It begins with the phrase *Ik-Oangkar* (pronounced Ikk-au-ang-kaar), which is commonly understood by Sikhs as meaning "there is one God, the Creator of all the universes, who resides within all creation." Oneness is considered a tenet in Sikhi.

Among its many teachings, Sikhi promotes the unity of creator and creation, grasped through universal love and the practice of equality among humans and all created things. Sikhi also promotes truthful conduct and categorically rejects social hierarchies like the caste system. It denounces idol worship and superstitious beliefs. The three golden rules, elsewhere referred to as principles of Sikhi, are meditating on the

Creator's wonders (*Naam Japna*), earning an honest living (*kirat karna*), and sharing one's earnings with others (*vand shakna*).

4. What was Guru Nanak's vision of the Creator?

The first symbolic entry in the *Sri Guru Granth Sahib* is "ੴ"— pronounced *Ik Oangkaar* ("One universal Creator"). It is the first word of the *Mool Mantar*—the root verse in Gurbani. The *Mool Mantar* sets out the Sikh vision of the Creator. The *Mool Mantar* states, "*Ikoangkaār saṯ nām karṯā purakẖ nirbẖao nirvair akaāl mūraṯ ajūnī saibẖang gur parsāaḏ.*"

This stanza encompasses the entire theology of the Sikh faith, making it an incredibly complicated and intricate verse to interpret. There are many opinions about the *Mool Mantar*'s precise meaning, but in an everyday sense, its meaning can be expressed in the following way:

Ik Oangkaar—There is one timeless all-embracing being
Satnam—whose name is "the one that exists"
Karta—the Creator of the universe
Purakh—the consciousness which permeates through all of creation
Nirbhau—that which has no fear
Nirvair—that which has no enmity
Akaal mūraṯ —that form which is not bound by time
Ajūnī—that which is unborn
Saibhang—that which came into existence on its own
Gur parsaad—that which can be realized with the grace of the true Guru

The *Mool Mantar* captures Guru Nanak's vision of Waheguru, and by extension, of the self. It is at once the vision statement and the mission statement for a Sikh. The remaining writings in the *SGGS* are considered an elaboration of the *Mool Mantar*.

5. What are Sikh virtues?

Virtues are characteristics or capabilities attained that impact how we act. The Sikh religion identifies five virtues or qualities for a Sikh: compassion (*daiya*); truth (*satt*); contentment (*santokh*); humility (*nimrata* or *gareebi*); and love (*pyaar*).[2] These are deemed fundamental to human development, ethical living, and transcendence.

Sat, or truth, is the virtue of truthful living, which means practicing righteousness, honesty, justice, impartiality, and fair play:

> The Waheguru's humble servants are true—they practice truth and reflect upon the spiritual Word [Sabad] of the Gurus.[3]

For Guru Nanak, living an honest life was more important than even truth itself: "Truth is high, but higher still is truthful living."[4]

Santokh, or contentment, is freedom from ambition, envy, greed, and jealousy. Contentment in life is the primary source of peace of mind: "Practice true contentment and kindness, that is an excellent way of life," says Guru Arjan.[5]

Daiya, or compassion/benevolence, involves considering another's difficulty or sorrow as one's own and helping to relieve it as much as possible. Being compassionate means that you overlook the imperfections and errors of others. "Be kind to all beings. This is more worthy than bathing at the sixty-eight sacred shrines of pilgrimage and the giving of

---

2   *SGGS* 51: sat sa(n)tokh dhiaa kamaavai eh karanee saar. ਸਤੁ ਸੰਤੋਖੁ ਦਇਆ ਕਮਾਵੈ ਏਹ ਕਰਣੀ ਸਾਰ॥

3   *SGGS* 600: har jan saache saach kamaaveh gur kai sabadh veechaaree—ਹਰਿ ਜਨ ਸਾਚੇ ਸਾਚੁ ਕਮਾਵਹਿ ਗੁਰ ਕੈ ਸਬਦਿ ਵੀਚਾਰੀ॥

4   *SGGS* 62: Sachahu orai sabh ko upar sach āchār—ਸਚਹੁ ਓਰੈ ਸਭੁ ਕੋ ਉਪਰਿ ਸਚੁ ਆਚਾਰੁ॥

5   SGGC 51: har jan saache saach kamaaveh gur kai sabadh veechaaree. ਸਤੁ ਸੰਤੋਖੁ ਦਇਆ ਕਮਾਵੈ ਏਹ ਕਰਣੀ ਸਾਰ॥

charity," reminds Guru Arjan.[6] Here, the Guru challenges the ritual of pilgrimage as a means of attaining salvation. Rather, the Guru enjoins Sikhs to focus on the virtue of compassion.

Nimrata or *Gareebi* refers to "humility" or "humbleness." Guru Arjan says, "The Divine-conscious being is steeped in humility. They take delight in benevolence and serving others."[7]

Pyaar, or love, the fifth virtue, is fundamental to human spiritual growth and requires Sikhs to be filled with the love of Waheguru and creation. Such love is unconditional. "Divine love flows through a natural process," says Guru Amar Das. Using the metaphor of husband and wife, Guru Arjan explains the virtue of the phenomenon as follows:

> People are awed [by] seeing Waheguru's creation around them. They talk and hear a lot about it yet are unable to taste and feel its presence. Why? Because the tongue does not have feet, hands, or eyes, how can it run and hug the Beloved One? Let the awe [presence] of Waheguru be your feet; let love be your hands; let understanding be your eyes. This way, O wise-soul-bride, you shall be united with your beloved Spouse, Waheguru.[8]

6. What are the core Sikh practices?

Guru Nanak emphasized the equality of all—irrespective of their origin, faith, gender, and social status. He outlined a three-pronged path in the conduct of daily living, thoroughly intertwined and integrated

---

[6] *SGGS* 136: aThasaTh teerath sagal pu(n)n jeea dhiaa; jis no dhevai dhiaa kar soiee purakh sujaan—ਅਠਸਠਿ ਤੀਰਥ ਸਗਲ ਪੁੰਨ ਜੀਅ ਦਇਆ ਪਰਵਾਨ ॥ ਜਿਸ ਨੋ ਦੇਵੈ ਦਇਆ ਕਰਿ ਸੋਈ ਪੁਰਖ ਸੁਜਾਨੁ॥

[7] *SGGS* 273: braham giaanee kai gareebee samaahaa; braham giaanee paraupakaar umaahaa—ਬ੍ਰਹਮ ਗਿਆਨੀ ਕੈ ਗਰੀਬੀ ਸਮਾਹਾ ॥ ਬ੍ਰਹਮ ਗਿਆਨੀ ਪਰਉਪਕਾਰ ਉਮਾਹਾ॥

[8] *SGGS* 139: dhisai suneeaai jaaneeaai saau na paiaa jai---bhai ke charan kar bhaav ke loin surat karei—ਦਿਸੈ ਸੁਣੀਐ ਜਾਣੀਐ ਸਾਉ ਨ ਪਾਇਆ ਜਾਇ ॥ ... ਭੈ ਕੇ ਚਰਣ ਕਰ ਭਾਵ ਕੇ ਲੋਇਣ ਸੁਰਤਿ ਕਰੇਇ॥

with one another: (1) *Naam Japna*—embarking on a quest for internal purity through meditation and prayer; (2) *kirat karni*—earning an honest living; and (3) *vand shakna*—sharing one's earnings with others, particularly the needy.

7. What things should a Sikh refrain from?

According to Sikh teachings, there are five key vices that impede spiritual development: *kaam* (lust), *krodh* (anger), *lobh* (greed), *moh* (attachment), and *ahankar* (ego). Guru Amar Das referred to them as the "five thieves."[9] They are considered to be the chief impediments to spiritual growth and harmony with the Divine. Sikhs are taught to subdue these five inner vices. Meditation helps render them inactive and turn their negative energy into a positive force to achieve the ultimate goal of self-realization. According to Sikhi, defilement of the body and mind occur when we are afflicted with any of these five vices. Such defilement can manifest as mistreatment of the self (mind or body) and/ or the mistreatment of others.

---

9   *SGGS* 600: eis dhehee a(n)dhar pa(n)ch chor vaseh kaam karodh lobh moh aha(n)kaaraa—ਇਸੁ ਦੇਹੀ ਅੰਦਰਿ ਪੰਚ ਚੋਰ ਵਸਹਿ ਕਾਮ ਕ੍ਰੋਧ ਲੋਭ ਮੋਹੁ ਅਹਕਾਰਾ॥

CHAPTER 3

A Spiritual Revolution

A *sabad* (verse) by Guru Arjan, the fifth Sikh Guru, eloquently describes Nanak's birth:

> God blessed humanity with Guru Nanak to dispel the darkness. Guru Nanak is the source of light (lamp) in the dark age. Through the Guru's thought-provoking spiritual message of realizing God in all of creation, the whole of humanity can easily transcend this ocean of life.[10]

8. Who is Guru Nanak?

The Sikh journey begins in 1469 in the village of Rai Bhoe Di Talwandi, where Guru Nanak, the founder of Sikhi, was born. The village was later renamed in his honour and is now known as Sri Nankana Sahib. It is in East (Lehnda) Punjab,[11] Pakistan, about sixty-five kilometres

---

[10]   *SGGS* 1387: balio charaag andhayeaar meh sabh kal udharee ik naam dharam; pargat sagal har bhavan meh jan nanak gur paarbraham—ਬਲਿਓ ਚਰਾਗੁ ਅੰਧਾਰ ਮਹਿ ਸਭ ਕਲਿ ਉਧਰੀ ਇਕ ਨਾਮ ਧਰਮ ॥ ਪ੍ਰਗਟੁ ਸਗਲ ਹਰਿ ਭਵਨ ਮਹਿ ਜਨੁ ਨਾਨਕੁ ਗੁਰੁ ਪਾਰਬ੍ਰਹਮ ॥

[11]   Punjab is pronounced "pan-ja-b." It literally means the land of five (panj) rivers (ab). After the partition of India in 1947, the Punjab province of British India was split between India and Pakistan.

from Lahore. Guru Nanak's father was Kalian Chand Bedi, but he is popularly referred to as Mehta Kalu. Mehta Kalu was a small landowner and worked as a *patvari* (land registrar or accountant) for Chaudhry Rai Bular Bhatti, the local Muslim chief. Guru Nanak's mother, Mata Tripta, is said to have been a woman of humble character, and she tried to strike a balance between her husband's concerns that young Nanak learn his father's trade and Guru Nanak's own spiritual inclinations. Guru Nanak's sister, Nanaki, (respectfully known as Bebe Nanaki) was five years his senior, and she was influential in his upbringing and development. Guru Nanak married Sulakhani at the age of fourteen. He and his wife had two sons: Sri Chand and Lakhmi Chand. Following four odysseys undertaken over twenty plus years, Guru Nanak settled with his wife and two children in the village of Kartarpur, now in Pakistan.

During his four odysseys, Guru Nanak traveled extensively on foot and by sea. His travels took him throughout India and the Middle East, where he spread his message of a universal Divine Creator and a spiritual practice aimed at elevating human existence. He expressed his teachings in poetic verses that were set to music. His teachings cover diverse topics and are designed to invoke thought and self-reflection. "Guru Nanak's communication style is in tune with modern academia, where the aim is to provoke thought. He does not preach. He does not give a belief system to follow," writes Nikki-Guninder Kaur Singh, a Sikh scholar.[12]

Guru Nanak's life was documented and passed on to succeeding generations through *janamsakhis* (life stories or allegories) that chronicle the development of his thought and revolution against the status quo. One such *janamsakhi* recounts how, at the age of nine, Guru Nanak refused to wear the *janeu,* a sacred religious thread worn by upper-caste Hindu males at their initiation into the religious order and to distinguish themselves from the lower castes. In doing so, Guru Nanak sought to challenge systematic and institutional oppression that caste represented during his time. He also rejected the violence and aggression that the

---

12   Singh, Nikky-Guninder Kaur. Sikhism *(I. B. Tauris Introductions to Religion,* 20). Bloomsbury Publishing. Kindle edition.

upper castes directed at lower castes by depriving them of access to goods as well as common human dignity. He proclaimed that people should be known for their qualities and their deeds rather than by their symbolic threads, rituals, or blind faith.

Guru Nanak's vision of creating a community of socially responsible and spiritually aware individuals was informed by the political turmoil and social division of his time. He was a visionary genius, centuries ahead of his time. During a period when women were treated as mere chattel and considered subhuman, he advocated against female infanticide, widow burning (*sati*)[13], and the veiling of women's faces. He maintained that all religions were equal and sought to unify people of different faiths. Guru Nanak encouraged a radical transformation in how individuals lived their lives, promoting self-awareness and truthful living, which are integral to the Sikh path.

9. How did Guru Nanak achieve self-realization?

Toward the end of the fifteenth century, Guru Nanak had a profound spiritual experience that led to his vision of the true nature of human existence and relationship with the Creator. He saw the Creator as a benevolent and "wondrous teacher" (*Waheguru*), accessible to all (*sarb-sanjha*), regardless of gender, race, ethnicity, or religious belief. He viewed himself as a student (the literal translation for the word "Sikh") of this wondrous teacher. Guru Nanak was a revolutionary who challenged socioreligious practices of his time. He declared that everyone was granted equality, an ethical right given by the Creator. Guru Nanak created a system of knowledge and practice that is available to everyone without any rituals.

According to Guru Nanak, Waheguru could be experienced by earning an honest living (*kirat karna*), embarking on a quest for self-realization through meditation (*Naam Japna*), and sharing one's earnings

---

[13]   The Indian practice of "sati," where widows were compelled to immolate themselves on their husbands' funeral pyres.

with others, particularly those less fortunate (*vand shakna*). These three principles have become the pillars of the Sikh way of life. They require a real and practical commitment to life and its ethical obligations. If practiced daily, Guru Nanak believed they would lead to a holistic and fulfilling life, leading one to become spiritually aware and socially responsible.

10. Was there more than one Sikh Guru?

There were a total of ten Sikh gurus—nine of whom were human successors to Guru Nanak. Prior to his *joti-jot* (passing), the tenth Sikh Guru, Gobind Singh, bestowed the guruship to the sacred Sikh scriptures, the *Sri Guru Granth Sahib*.

#	Name	Lifespan	Guruship
1	Guru Nanak	1469–1539	1469–1539
2	Guru Angad	1504–1552	1539–52
3	Guru Amar Das	1479–1574	1552–74
4	Guru Ramdas	1534–1581	1574–81
5	Guru Arjun	1563–1606	1581–06
6	Guru Hargobind	1595–1664	1606–44
7	Guru Har Rai	1630–1661	1644–61
8	Guru Har Krishan	1656–1664	1661–64
9	Guru Teg Bahadur	1621–1675	1664–75
10	Guru Gobind Singh	1666–1708	1675–1708
11	Sri Guru Granth Sahib	1708–	

Sikhi evolved over a period of two hundred years. Each subsequent Guru established new towns, expounded upon and reinforced Guru Nanak's spiritual teachings, and helped develop institutions to put these teachings into practice. This included maintaining—and if needed, evolving—the central concepts of *sangat* (congregation), *gurdwara* (true Guru's court), *langar* (humanitarian kitchen), *pangat* (sitting together and dining without any distinction based on social status), and *keertan* (singing of devotional sabads). This lineage was seen as not simply a lineage of mystics or gnostics—but of sovereign representatives of the one true Creator. Their spiritual compositions were also referred to as the Guru because they imparted divine knowledge and wisdom.

Shortly before he passed away, Guru Nanak selected Bhai Lehna to be his successor. Bhai Lehna was given the name Angad, meaning "of my own body." This name was chosen to signify that there was no distinction between Guru Angad and Guru Nanak. The practice of naming a successor Guru continued until Guru Gobind Singh stopped the lineage of human gurus.

Guru Gobind Singh was the last Guru in human form for the Sikhs. Before his *joti jot* (immersion with the Creator),[14] Guru Gobind Singh proclaimed the *Sri Guru Granth Sahib* as the eternal Guru for the Sikhs, to whom Sikhs should turn for spiritual guidance. He bestowed the temporal authority for the conduct of Sikh affairs on the *Khalsa panth* (the collective body of Sikhs who accept *amrit*).

11. What happened to the Sikhs after the tenth Guru?

The intense and fearless expressions of a profound ethical truth in Guru Nanak's message empowered the downtrodden and emboldened them to fight for social equality. As more people embraced the Sikh way of life, the Sikhs were increasingly viewed as a threat to the existing social structure and became targets of persecution by the state. Guru Arjan, the fifth Sikh Guru, was tortured and martyred for his refusal to bow to the demands of the Mughal Emperor Jahangir. The sixth Guru, Guru Hargobind, was also imprisoned for challenging the emperor. Guru Teg Bahadur, the ninth Guru, was beheaded for standing up for the freedom of Hindus to practice their faith free of interference and intimidation by

---

[14]   Sikhs do not use the word "death" to describe the passing of a Guru.

the Mughal rulers. Guru Gobind Singh was fatally stabbed by a Mughal mercenary in 1708.

One of Guru Gobind Singh's generals was a highly regarded woman named Mata Bhag Kaur (1670–1720), who led Sikh soldiers in a famous battle against the Mughals in 1705. Mata Bhag Kaur was raised in a devout Sikh family. Her father, Malo Shah, served in Guru Hargobind's army and taught her martial arts from a young age. She was a renowned warrior, and she eventually became one of Guru Gobind Singh's bodyguards. After Guru Gobind Singh's passing, Mata Bhag Kaur continued to lead the Sikhs. She eventually retired and settled in Karnataka, where she taught gurmat (the Guru's way).

In September 1708, Baba[15] Banda Singh Bahadur (1670–1716) raised a Sikh army to battle the Mughal oppression. In the following two years, he carved out a sovereign Sikh state in northern India. However, this first Sikh state fell apart following Banda Singh Bahadur's execution in Delhi in 1716. Bounties were given for killing Khalsa Sikhs, and innumerable numbers of them were imprisoned and executed publicly such as in the markets of Lahore. The continuing oppression of Sikhs along with pressures from numerous areas of the kingdom signaled the downfall of the Mughal Empire.

The persecution of Sikhs led to the battle known as the *Vadda Ghalughara* (major holocaust). On February 5, 1762, it was estimated that thirty thousand Sikhs were killed (martyred) in battle in one day. Instead of becoming demoralized, the Sikhs banded together, and the disparate independent *misls* (confederacies) eventually amalgamated in 1799 to create the Sikh *raaj* (empire) under the leadership of *Maharaja* (head king) Ranjit Singh (1780 to 1839).

Maharaja Ranjit Singh's empire extended from the Khyber Pass in the west (northwest frontier province of Pakistan), the river Satluj in the east, Mithankot in the south, and Kashmir in the north. Though many of his personal life choices fell far short of Sikh teachings, Maharaja

---

[15]   Baba means grandfather, or wise elder, and is an honourific used to refer to someone who is deeply respected for their knowledge and leadership, regardless of their age. The female term is Bibi or Mata, meaning mother.

Ranjit Singh was appropriately regarded as a fair and impartial ruler. In Ranjit Singh's kingdom, all faiths were given equal opportunity, and capital punishment was abolished. He appointed Sikhs, Muslims, Hindus, Christians, and people of other faiths to authoritative positions in his administration. His army had generals from France, Italy, and America.

Ranjit Singh's kingdom began to crumble after his death. Having conquered the rest of India some fifty years earlier, the British annexed what remained of Ranjit Singh's empire in 1849, merely ten years after his death. However, it was an uneasy reign, with many Indians, including Sikhs, openly rejecting British rule.

The movement to be free of British rule escalated in the 1920s and was finally successful twenty-five years later. In 1947, the people of India gained independence from the British—but not before losing millions of lives during Partition. The British agreed to split the country into three, creating the Muslim-majority countries of East and West Pakistan and the Hindu majority country of India.

The Sikhs, who had their own empire before British occupation, and who lost the most lives during the movement to end colonial rule, were given the option of their own independent state. Relying on promises made by the Indian political leaders (Jawaharlal Nehru[16] and Mohandas Karamchand Gandhi) that their distinct identity would be protected in a newly independent India, the Sikhs opted not to seek an independent country of their own. Sadly, Nehru and Gandhi failed to keep their word. This betrayal of the Sikh community led to many needless challenges in postcolonial India.

Modern Indian history has been marked by border disputes with Pakistan and China, as well as internal sectarian conflict as religious minorities (such as Christians, Sikhs, and Muslims) seeking to protect

---

[16] "The brave Sikhs of Punjab are entitled to special consideration," vowed Nehru, a year before India was granted independence and he became the nation's first prime minister. "I see nothing wrong in an area and a set-up in the North wherein the Sikhs can also experience the glow of freedom," reported *The Statesman* on July 6, 1946.

their own identities. For the Sikhs, this came to a head in 1984 when the government of India launched a full-fledged military assault (code-named Operation Blue Star) against the Sikhs who were advocating for greater rights for all states (including Panjab).

Operation Blue Star resulted in the loss of thousands of innocent lives. The Indian government's orchestrated attack on the *Darbar Sahib* (Golden Temple), the destruction of the *Akal Takhat Sahib* (the seat of Sikh temporal authority) and Sikh archives, and a simultaneous attack on thirty-eight other historical gurdwaras reverberated around the Sikh diaspora. This direct attack on Sikh places of worship has been the focal point of continuous Sikh disillusionment with postcolonial India.

Though some Sikhs have favoured the creation of a distinct state where Sikhs could live, flourish, and experience the glow of freedom (commonly referred to as Khalistan), Sikhs remain a vital part of India. Today, there are more than twenty-eight million Sikhs in the world, and more than five million are living outside of India.

PART II
Identity

CHAPTER 4

Defining a Sikh

Some would say that defining a Sikh is the most favourite pastime of Sikh scholars. Numerous scholarly articles, debates, and arguments have been had on this topic. Some like to focus their attention on the outward identifiers of a Sikh, others on whether the person is initiated into Sikhi, and still others on what lies beneath (i.e., the personal characteristics and values of an individual). Shakespeare summed up eloquently what many of us have a hard time grasping: "What's in a name? That which we call a rose by any other name would smell as sweet."[17] This simple yet beautiful statement should be kept in mind as you read this section. It is a reminder that even labels, and definitions have limitations.

12. What does the word "Sikh" mean?

The word Sikh comes from the Panjabi verb *sikhna*, meaning "to learn" and is derived from the term *śiṣya* in Sanskrit, meaning learner or student. Every student needs a teacher, and for Sikhs, the teacher is their Guru. The ultimate teacher is the Divine Creator, or Waheguru.

For many Sikhs today, the word "Sikh" essentially means someone who is learning to embody the true knowledge of oneness. Sikhs attempt to align their consciousness and actions with oneness as it already exists

---

17   William Shakespeare, "Romeo and Juliet."

throughout creation. This is done through individual and communal practices. A Sikh, therefore, is one who seeks to rise above their material existence through a regular discipline grounded in regular study (self-reflection and discipline), keertan, katha, and seva. These are all essential aspects of the daily routine of practicing Sikhs.

13. How does Sikhi define a Sikh?

The collective definition of a Sikh is contained in the *Sikh Rehat Maryada* (Sikh code of conduct), which has been adopted by most Sikh gurdwaras. The *Sikh Rehat Maryada* defines a Sikh as any human being who believes in one Immortal Being; the ten gurus, from Guru Nanak to Guru Gobind; the *Sri Guru Granth Sahib* (Sikh scriptures); the *amrit* initiation ceremony bequeathed by the tenth Guru; and who does not owe allegiance to any other religion. This definition is broad and inclusive and not limited by gender, geography, or ethnicity. All Sikhs are brought under the same umbrella, provided they acknowledge that they are bound together by a single unifying force (the One Creator), and that they commit their lives to follow the teachings of the Sikh gurus as reflected in the *Sri Guru Granth Sahib*.

Gursikhs take the *SGGS* as their authoritative teacher. For them it represents the true knowledge the oneness of creation and Creator. The *SGGS* defines Sikh in several places. For instance, a Sikh is one "who walks in the way of the Guru's Will."[18] This refers to living under the Guru's teachings and following the will of the Waheguru. The *SGGS* dispenses light and removes the darkness of ignorance for Gursikhs. For Guru Nanak, the One Creator is the only true teacher. Hence, Guru Nanak's name for the One Creator was Waheguru, meaning Wondrous Teacher. Guru Nanak emphasized the attributes of a Sikh, and wrote, "One who deliberates on the Guru's teachings and follows them faithfully

---

[18]   *SGGS* 601: so sikh sakhaa ba(n)dhap hai bhaiee j gur ke bhaane vich aavai. ਸੋ ਸਿਖ ਸਖਾ ਬੰਧਪੁ ਹੈ ਭਾਈ ਜਿ ਗੁਰ ਕੇ ਭਾਣੇ ਵਿਚਿ ਆਵੈ ॥

crosses the ocean of worldly temptation under the watchful eye of the Benevolent One."[19]

14. Is there a relationship between Sikhi and Hinduism and Islam?

Sikhi came out of Guru Nanak's experience of the Divine. Guru Nanak and all the subsequent Sikh gurus expressly stated that the message within the *Sri Guru Granth Sahib* was based upon an unmediated encounter with the One. There is no other source of inspiration for Sikhi than the possibility of this connection with oneness.

Many Western scholars have attempted to explain Sikhi as a by-product of the contact between Hinduism and Islam. This is a gross mischaracterization and oversimplification that arises from a lack of understanding of Sikhi and its core principles. Sikhi arose as a new religion in Panjab at the beginning of the sixteenth century, when Islam and Hinduism were the prominent doctrines in the region. As Balwant Singh explains in *Gurmat*, "Guru Nanak, the founder of Sikhism, and his successors used the terminologies of other religions to express and explain Sikh philosophy, but their meanings are not necessarily the same as in the parent religions." Indeed, the meanings were radically altered.

While some overlaps exist between these faith traditions, these overlaps can also be seen with Buddhism, Christianity, and Judaism. Indeed, Sikhi acknowledges these overlaps by teaching that every religion, at its core, reflects a different pathway to the same destination.

Those who endeavour to authenticate their claim equating Sikhism to Hinduism highlight Guru Nanak's birth to a Hindu family. They forget that Guru Nanak challenged many Hindu beliefs and practices and refused to wear a Hindu sacred thread (*janeu*), the most identifiable mark for Hindus. Guru Nanak believed that there was a profound disconnect between the spiritual teachings of Islam and Hinduism (the

---

[19] *SGGS* 465: sikhee sikhiaa gur veechaar; nadharee karam laghaae paar. ਸਿਖੀ ਸਿਖਿਆ ਗੁਰ ਵੀਚਾਰਿ ॥ ਨਦਰੀ ਕਰਮਿ ਲਘਾਏ ਪਾਰਿ ॥

dominant religions of the time) and the practices of the adherents. He felt these practices were oppressive toward women and perpetuated injustice against the marginalized. Guru Nanak's revolution challenged what he perceived to be ritualistic and non-egalitarian practices from both faith traditions, and he "articulated a distinct and new metaphysics and then made it the basis of his social philosophy."[20]

Subsequent gurus and the Sikh panth continued to challenge the status quo and desired to build a more humane society. The Sikh gurus bluntly rejected simplistic notions of religious identity that were meant only to preserve domination of the masses, extract wealth, and oppress humanity. "We are neither Hindu, nor Muslim," said Guru Arjan.[21] This gave rise to political tensions with powerful groups of elites who identified as Muslim or Hindu. The common human aspiration for a just society established bonds across religious identities as well as mutual recognition of the Sikh role in the struggle to create a free and just world.

---

[20]   Singh, *Guru Nanak*, 54.

[21]   *SGGS* 1136: naa ham hi(n)dhoo na musalamaan. ਨਾ ਹਮ ਹਿੰਦੂ ਨਾ ਮੁਸਲਮਾਨ ॥

CHAPTER 5

Being a Sikh

It should already be apparent that, fundamentally, Sikhi is a unique worldview with its own beliefs, values, thoughts, and ethics. This is not to state that there is no way to compare or objectively describe Sikhi; on the contrary, it is to recognize that comparison cannot begin without recognizing Sikhi's basic principles. This chapter explores the wide spectrum of people who affiliate themselves with the Sikh faith. The focus here is not on whether someone "qualifies" as a Sikh from the perspective of Sikh doctrine. Rather, it is my intention to give you a closer look at the Sikhs.

15. Are Sikhs an ethnic group or a cultural group?

Sikhi is a universal worldview that has distinct practices and teachings that inform a common culture among Sikhs. The Sikh community and its identity arise from the teachings and practices of the ten Sikh gurus as well as the *Sri Guru Granth Sahib*. Since its inception, Sikhi has transcended ethnic, racial, and cultural boundaries, and has attracted people from diverse socio-ethnic backgrounds. Thus, it is common to see Sikhs living in every corner of the world, and it is not at all unusual to see Sikhs of European, African, or Asian origins.

While there is no historically identifiable ethnic or cultural group known as "the Sikhs," over time, Sikhi gained greater popularity and adoption among certain demographic communities in northwestern South Asia. Sikhs also developed a specific set of cultural practices drawn pluralistically from these groups that are consistent with Sikh teachings. Important historical events have also developed a common bond among Sikhs that strengthens the shared cultural consciousness among them.

In modern times, the overwhelming majority of Sikhs either hail from, or are descended from, the inhabitants of the north Indian state of Panjab. They share a common language, clothing, food, music, culture, and social traditions. Yet there are also unique cultural differences between diaspora Panjabi Sikhs and those still living in India. Quite often, Sikhs will meld cultural practices from their families of origin with the traditions and cultures of the countries to which they have migrated. It is in the context of migration that the appearance and label of an ethnic group is ascribed to Sikhs. In multicultural secular countries, "ethnic" is a governmental administrative category to manage diversity; however, it is one that often erases internal diversity in the eyes of the majority population. The category "ethnic" also produces governmental pressure to homogenize internal group diversity. Thus, while it is important to acknowledge the common linguistic, cultural, and social bond shared by the majority of Sikhs, it is necessary to recognize each Sikh as a unique individual.

16. Are Sikhs a nation?

The *Oxford Language Dictionary* (online) defines a nation as a large body of people united by common descent, history, culture, or language, inhabiting a particular country or territory. In that sense, there is no doubt that Sikhs are a nation. Sikhs overwhelmingly hail from the same geographic region, and their connections to each other run deep— irrespective of their domiciles. Sikhs are united by their shared language, history, culture, and spiritual beliefs.

Sikhs also see themselves as a nation. The Sikh word for their community is *panth*. The word *panth* has its origins in the Sanskrit words *patha, pathin,* or *pantham*. These words literally mean "a way, passage, or path" and refer to a way of life or a religious creed. Unlike European understandings of nation as based on ethnicity or race, it is this sense of pluralistic notion of community that creates the Sikh nation (*qaum*). This national identity is not limited by geography or language. Rather, it encompasses the entire diaspora of Sikhs, wherever they reside, who share the same culture, values, and beliefs.

17. Do Sikhs speak a common language?

The Sikhi originated in the fifteenth century in the Panjab region, but that geographical definition has changed over time. Panjabi is the predominant language spoken by people of the region. There are more than 125 million Punjabi-speaking people around the world. The name Punjab is the compound of two Persian words, *Panj* ("five") and *ab* ("water,") referring to the five major eastern tributaries of the Indus River. So, Punjab is known as the "land of the five rivers," and the language of Punjab is Punjabi.

In the sixteenth century, Guru Angad, the second Guru of the Sikhs, standardized the Gurmukhi script to write the Sikh scripture. Until then, Punjabi was written in the Shahmukhi script, a Perso-Arabic alphabet used by Muslims in Punjab. Even today, in Pakistan, Urdu script is used to write Punjabi. The word *Gurmukhi* means "from the Guru's mouth." While the *Sri Guru Granth Sahib* contains many languages and dialects, the most common is Punjabi, written in Gurmukhi script.

In contrast to the twenty-six letters of the English alphabet, the Gurmukhi script has thirty-five *akhars* or consonants, identical to the Punjabi alphabet, including three vowel holders and thirty-two consonants. Each character represents a phonetic sound. The alphabetical order of the Gurmukhi script is entirely different from the English alphabet. A Gurmukhi *akhar* (alphabet) is based on groupings with certain similarities arranged in a grid of five horizontal and seven vertical rows with specific pronunciation properties. Each letter has a combination of characteristics depending on its horizontal and vertical position. Some letters are pronounced with the tongue touching the back of the upper teeth or curled back to touch just behind the ridge on the roof of the mouth. Letters may be pronounced with a puff of air or require holding the breath again. Some characters have a nasal sound. Gurmukhi is the official standard script for Punjabi. It is the official language of Punjab.

18. What is the Khalsa?

The term "Khalsa" is translated as both "sovereign and free" and "the pure." It is used in multiple senses. In common parlance, it denotes an *amritdhari* Sikh. The word also refers to the collective body of *amritdhari* Sikhs,[22] though it can also be used in the singular sense as a form of endearment. The term Khalsa appears in Sikh sacred writings in this way: "Those who know Waheguru's loving devotional worship and are humble become sovereign and free—they become Khalsa."[23] To create a sense of self-respect, spiritual awakening, and strength in the people, Guru Gobind Singh formally created the Khalsa on Vaisakhi day in 1699,[24] when the first *amrit sanchar* (initiation ceremony) was held.

19. What is an amritdhari Sikh?

The word amritdhari is combined from the words "amrit" (the Sikh initiation ceremony), and "dhari" (the one who embodies). Amritdhari thus refers to someone who has taken amrit and formally committed themselves to following the Sikhi way of life. Amritdhari Sikhs are expected to abide by a code of ethics, which includes:

---

[22]   Sikhs who have received the initiation of Khanda, the double-edged sword.

[23]   *SGGS* 654: kahu kabeer jan bhe khaalase prem bhagat jeh jaanee—ਕਹੁ ਕਬੀਰ ਜਨ ਭਏ ਖਾਲਸੇ ਪ੍ਰੇਮ ਭਗਤਿ ਜਿਹ ਜਾਨੀ॥

[24]   Madanjit Kaur, "The Creation of the Khalsa and Prescribing of the Sikhism," in *Advanced Studies in Sikhism: Papers Contributed at Conference of Sikh Studies Los Angeles* (195–213), edited by Jasbir Singh Mann and Harbans Singh Saron (Irvine, CA: Sikh Community of North America, 1989), 201.

- Keeping all five articles of faith (*panj kakars*): kesh (unshorn hair); kangha (wooden comb); kara (an iron or steel bracelet); kashera (a cotton undergarment); and kirpan (a small sword).
- Daily meditation and recitation of the same five banis (divine utterances) that are recited at their amrit sanchar (initiation) ceremony.
- Refraining from four transgressions: (1) dishonouring their hair; (2) eating meat that has been ritualistically slaughtered and caused suffering to the animal (kutha);[25] (3) adultery; and (4) using tobacco, alcohol, or other intoxicating substances.

This code of ethics is enshrined in the *Rehat Maryada*. An amritdhari Sikh is easily identifiable by their unshorn hair and keeping of the *panj kakars* (five articles of faith).

Becoming an amritdhari Sikh is considered the aspirational goal for all Sikhs. However, not everyone is ready to, or desirous of, committing themselves to initiation. The Sikh community has developed terms to refer to non-amritdhari Sikhs. Before turning to these terms, it is important to note that Sikhi does not recognize any formal hierarchy or category of Sikhs. The concepts of amritdhari, *sahijdhari*, and *kesdhari* relate to a particular individual's outward adherence to the established Sikh identity rather than their value or worth as a Sikh.

20. What is a kesdhari Sikh?

The word *kesh* means unshorn hair. A *kesdhari* Sikh is someone who does not cut their hair. Their hair is most often covered by a *dastaar* or other head covering. They have full faith in the Sikh teachings, but they have not

---

25   There are different interpretations of "Kutha." Those who prefer eating meat refer to Bhai Kahn Singh Nabha's *"Gur Shabad Ratnakar Mahankosh"* definition (meat of an animal slaughtered through Muslim way) and the clarification issued by the Akal Takhat (Sikhs' highest authority) Jathedar Sadhu Singh Bhaura on February 15, 1980. A significant segment of the Sikh community believes that the word "Kutha" means all meat, irrespective of how an animal was killed.

taken the final step of formalizing their commitment to living the Sikhi way of life. A kesdhari Sikh may keep some or even most of the five Sikh articles of faith. However, a *kesdhari* Sikh will normally not wear a kirpan. A kirpan is sanctioned for those Sikhs who have become *amritdhari* or are practicing keeping the panj kakars prior to taking amrit.

21. What is a sahijdhari Sikh?

The word *sahijdhari* is a combination of the two terms *sehaj* (gradual or evolving) and *dhari* (the one who embodies). Thus, it refers to someone who is slowly growing in their Sikhi practice. *Sahijdhari* refers to someone who is on the Sikh path but has not committed to taking amrit. It denotes a person who embraces Sikhi gradually first by being *kesdhari* and then taking amrit at a later point in time.[26] A sahijdhari Sikh can be identified by the kara (bracelet), but they will rarely wear any of the other articles of faith.

22. What is a cultural Sikh?

A cultural Sikh is someone who was born into a Sikh family. They have a strong emotional bond to the Sikh community and culture. They regard the teachings of Sikhi, and Sikh ethics, traditions, customs, and literature, as their own, but may not practice Sikhi in any observable way. They will likely wear a kara—and they may even keep their unshorn hair—but they will not be *amritdhari*.

23. What is a mona Sikh?

Mona means clean-shaven. The term *mona* applies to men or women of Sikh heritage who cut the hair on their heads. Sometimes, such an

---

[26]   Bhai Kahn Singh Nabha, comp., *Gurshabad Ratankar Mahan Kosh*, the Sikh Encyclopedia in Punjabi (1930).

individual is called *rodah* (bald) though that is an offensive term. The term *mona Sikh* is often used pejoratively and is perceived by many as carrying negative connotations.

24. What is a gora Sikh?

Many who convert to Sikhi from different faiths and regions of the world find that the association of colour or geographical terms common in the Panjabi vernacular. The term *gora* means white and refers to people of European descent. Since the middle of the twentieth century, many people of European descent have adopted Sikhi. In general conversation, they may be referred to as *gora* Sikhs. The term is not intended to have any negative connotations, but it may be perceived that way.

25. What is a sanatan Sikh?

Sanatan Sikh refers to someone who, from outer appearance, looks like any other practicing Sikh but "continues to follow the customs and traditions of Hindu society."[27] This includes practices that are expressly against Sikhi teachings, such as maintaining caste hierarchy and rituals or beliefs associated with coding human behaviour within the caste system.

26. Are there moderate or fundamentalist Sikhs?

In the 1980s, the Sikh community went through intense turmoil and crisis as a result of politics in Panjab. The Indian government's attack on Darbar Sahib (the Golden Temple) and thirty-nine other historical gurdwaras in Panjab split the Sikh diaspora. Mainstream media

---

[27] Singh, Gurharpal and Giorgio Shani. 2022, 42. *Sikh Nationalism: From a Dominant Minority to an Ethno-Religious Diaspora,* Cambridge University Press, United Kingdom.

journalists who lacked knowledge about Sikhs started using the terms *moderate* and *fundamentalist* to describe members of the Sikh community. To them, "moderates" were clean-shaven, "modern," and "assimilated" Sikhs. "Fundamentalists" were the kesdhari or amritdhari Sikhs, who were cast as being "backward" in their practices and thinking. The Sikhs who supported the Indian government's actions in Panjab seized on this terminology and adopted the term "moderate" to describe their own political views. Further, amritdhari Sikhs take offense at being labeled fundamentalist. In fact, moderate and fundamentalist Sikhs do not exist, and it has taken the Sikh community decades to shake off this labeling.

CHAPTER 6

Becoming a Sikh

Anyone can become a Sikh. You do not need to be born into a Sikh family or be able to speak Panjabi to become a Sikh. Many people from European, Asian, African, and South American backgrounds have adopted the Sikh faith. Becoming a Sikh has internal (personal) and external (societal) implications. All Sikhs are expected to learn the teachings in the *Sri Guru Granth Sahib*, learn and perform the daily *nitnem*, regularly participate in the congregation, and join the Khalsa through the amrit sanchar ceremony. They would then adopt the five *kakars* (articles of faith), which visually identify a practicing Sikh. Although some Sikhs may need time to adopt them, the *kakars* are an integral part of their spiritual and social identity. For a Sikh who has entered the Khalsa, the kakars cannot be compromised under any circumstances. This chapter explores the process for formally adopting the Sikh faith.

27. How do you become a Sikh?

Any individual who wishes to be formally initiated into the Sikh faith must undergo amrit sanchar (an initiation ceremony). Initiation ceremonies are held at every gurdwara, and usually at multiple times per year, in major cities around the world. Details about where the nearest gurdwara (Sikh place of worship) is and how to contact them are found through the World Sikh Organization of Canada at www.worldsikh.org.

28. Do you have to take amrit to become a Sikh?

Taking *amrit* is very much a personal decision. The Sikh gurus taught a way to living an ethical life based on affirming in one's everyday life that there is one Creator who brought forth a oneness of all creation. Taking amrit and committing to follow the practices given to Sikhs directly by the One is understood as being a way for Sikhs to unswervingly react to natural events or organize in their societal worlds humbly and with regard for values that benefit and defend everyone. This level of commitment is why the Khalsa is held in high esteem by all Sikhs. It is also why many who are Khalsa understand it as the only way to practice Sikhi in a way that is consistent with the teachings. There are Sikhs who believe that one can only fully call oneself a Sikh if one has taken amrit. However, as noted above, the Sikh code of conduct does not define a Sikh so narrowly. Recognizing that the spiritual journey is an intensely personal one, the *Rehat Maryada* emphasizes that a Sikh is someone who believes in the taking of amrit as part of the goal of fully adopting Sikhi.

29. Do all Sikhs use the names Singh and Kaur?

All amritdhari Sikhs share the name Singh or Kaur. Sikh males take *Singh* (lion) as their middle or last name, and Sikh females take *Kaur* (princess or lioness) as their middle or last names. The names Singh and Kaur are used to emphasize equality, sovereignty, and a sense of belonging. By adopting these names, Sikhs become part of the Sikh nation. There is no expectation that a Sikh woman will take her husband's name at marriage. Rather, a *Kaur* is encouraged to always remain a *Kaur* and to maintain her independence publicly and privately.

A Sikh does not have to be amritdhari to use these names. The name Singh or Kaur is usually bestowed to a child at birth, by their parents, if they are born into a Sikh family. However, when one formally becomes initiated into Sikhi, they will be given the name Singh and Kaur if they do not have it already. Some Sikhs may also choose a new first name when they take amrit, although that is very much a personal choice. There is no requirement to change one's first name.

30. What is amrit sanchar?

Amrit sanchar refers to the initiation ceremony that one has to undergo to be formally inducted into the Sikh faith. The taking of *amrit* is the public declaration by a Sikh of their decision to commit themselves to following the Sikh teachings in order to achieve self-realization. It is the formal marking of the beginning of a journey of self-discovery through Sikhi. Amrit sanchar is an intensely personal and sacred ceremony and is not to be taken lightly. The decision to take amrit can be taken at any age and by any person, and no one can be forced to take amrit against their own will. The decision must be made freely and voluntarily.

Once a person has taken *amrit*, they have joined the Khalsa and are known as an *amritdhari* Sikh. They are required to abide by a certain code of conduct and to live in accordance with Sikh teachings and values.

31. When was the first amrit sanchar?

The first amrit sanchar (initiation ceremony) was held on March 29, 1699,[28] by the tenth Sikh Guru, Gobind Singh. On that day, more than eighty thousand people, hailing from many different faiths, assembled in the city of Anandpur, located in the foothills of the Himalayas in Punjab. They were there to celebrate Vaisakhi—the spring harvest festival. Guru

---

[28]   Purewal, Pal Singh: moolnanakshahicalendar.wordpress.com. The Mool Nanak Shahi calendar has fixed April 14 as Vaisakhi Day. However, the calendar published by SGPC continues to promote April 13.

Gobind Singh chose this occasion to hold his first amrit sanchar in the midst of this gathering.

Traditional accounts state that after holding a morning meditation and *keertan* (singing of devotional sabads), Guru Gobind Singh suddenly stood up with his drawn sword in hand. He asked the gathered crowd if any devoted Sikh was willing to give their head to the Guru. The crowd fell silent. Daya Ram (1661–1708), a shopkeeper from Lahore, arose and offered himself. The Guru took Daya Ram inside a tent and came back with his sword dripping with blood. A chilled silence fell over the crowd. The Guru demanded a second head, and Dharam Das (1666–1708), a farmer from Hastinapur from Uttar Pradesh (near modern-day Delhi), bravely stepped forward. The Guru entered the tent with Dharam Das. A short while later, the Guru exited the tent alone for a second time, his sword still covered in blood. This pattern was repeated three more times. Next came Himmat Rai (1661–1705), a water bearer from Jagannath Puri (in present-day Odisha state); then came Mohkam Chand (1661–1705), a calico printer/tailor from Dwarka, Gujarat; and finally, Sahib Chand (1663–1705), a barber from Bidar, Karnataka. Each time a volunteer stepped forward, the silence over the crowd deepened. On the final occasion, the Guru remained in the tent for a very long time.

Unknown to the gathered assembly, the Guru had taken each of the five volunteers into a tent where he held a private initiation ceremony called amrit sanchar or *khande di pahul*. A special nectar called *amrit* was prepared by Guru Gobind Singh. As the water was being stirred, the Guru recited compositions from Guru Granth Sahib, and his wife, Mata Ajeet Kaur (some write Mata Sahib Kaur), added *patasey* (sugar puffs) to sweeten the nectar.[29] Once the recitation of prayers was complete, each of the five initiates was given the nectar (or amrit) to drink. Each Sikh was also bestowed five articles of faith. To eradicate any caste distinctions

---

[29]   Many writers write that Patase were added by Mata Sahib Kaur. A renowned Sikh scholar, Giani Pinderpal Singh, in his discourse at Gurdwara Dukh Nivaran Sahib, Surrey, BC, Canada on September 12, 2022, stated that the patase were added by Mata Jeeto (Ajeet Kaur). The initiation was held in 1699, and Mata Sahib Kaur did not come to the family until 1701.

denoted by their previous last names, each initiate was given the common last name, Singh (lion). This name signified internal strength, courage, and sovereignty that their spiritual transformation entailed.

Once the amrit sanchar was over, the Guru exited the tent with his initiates, and they were all dressed in resplendent saffron and blue attire. The five initiates were then presented to the entire congregation and declared to be the *panj pyare* (five beloved ones). They were addressed with the honourific "bhai," meaning brother. These five men from different walks of life, belonging to different castes and arriving from different parts of India, had all been moved to follow Sikhi. They became role models for all Sikhs. In this way, the Guru created a family of committed Sikhs, called the Khalsa (pure and sovereign), who were bound by common identity and discipline. Coincidentally, each of the panj pyare's birth names represent the attributes that a Sikh is expected to exemplify: daiya (compassion), dharam (righteous living), himmat (courage), mohkam (strength or determination), and sahib (masterful or divine).

Since 1699, any Sikh aspiring to join the Khalsa goes through an amrit sanchar similar to the one administered by Guru Gobind Singh Sahib. Those who accept *amrit* commit to becoming protectors and custodians of the universal truth contained within the *Sri Guru Granth Sahib* and which pervades all creation. The *amritdhari* Sikhs are obligated to practice the spiritual way of life that the Sikh gurus taught and modeled. By taking *amrit*, they are expected to surrender their bodies (*tan*), minds (*man*), and worldly wealth (*dhan*) and dedicate themselves to living a Sikhi-inspired life.

32. Did Guru Gobind Singh take amrit?

There is a famous poem sung by Sikhs in remembrance of Guru Gobind Singh: *"vaho Gobind Singh, apay gur-chela."* It means, "wondrous, wondrous is our teacher Gobind Singh, who was at once the Guru, and also the disciple." This poem references another remarkable thing that occurred on April 13, 1699. In an extraordinary show of humility and equality, after initiating the *panj payare*, the Guru knelt before them and asked panj payare to bestow the *amrit* to him. By so doing, he at once elevated the panj payare, and he also cemented the importance of the amrit sanchar as the path toward living a meaningful and fulfilled life.

After receiving the *amrit*, the Guru changed his name from Gobind Rai to Gobind Singh. Guru Gobind Singh's wife, Mata Jeeto, and his mother, Mata Gujri, also took *amrit*, and each woman assumed the last name Kaur (lioness or princess). As Kaurs, they too were expected to exhibit personal strength, courage, and sovereignty. Thus, Jeeto became Ajeet Kaur, and Mata Gujri became Mata Gujar Kaur.

33. Did Guru Gobind Singh really behead the panj pyare?

There are some Sikhs who take literally the story regarding the Guru's call for volunteers to give up their heads on that Vaisakhi Day in 1699. They believe that when the Guru entered the tent, he actually beheaded each of the panj payare, and with his miraculous and mystical powers, he brought them back to life. However, many Sikhs understand this story to be an allegory told as a tool to teach about the level of commitment and courage needed to follow the Sikhi way of life. For this latter group of Sikhs, the bloody sword is a metaphor for relinquishing one's ego-driven existence and following the spiritual teachings of the Guru. They see the Guru's call for volunteers who would be willing to die for the one truth as exemplifying the highest qualities developed through Sikhi.

The Sikh concept of "saint-soldier" follows from this ideal. It is the vision of a person who is brave, but whose bravery is tempered by humility and compassion. A saintly soldier acts bravely but without ego, tries to eschew the trappings of a material existence without ignoring their duty to honour all living beings, and is willing to put their own life on the line to stand up to injustice.

34. Who are the current panj pyare?

Today, the term *panj pyare* refers to an ad hoc group of five amritdhari Sikhs who are recognized by the congregation for their commitment to Sikhi and are asked to perform certain functions. The *panj pyare* are given the honour of conducting the amrit sanchar (initiation ceremony) and may also be called upon to perform other important services, such as laying the cornerstone of a gurdwara or leading a religious procession. They may also assist in dispute resolution, such as deciding issues confronting a family, the local Sikh sangat (community), or the greater Sikh panth as a whole. They must be of the highest moral standing and adhere strictly to Sikh principles and values. The *panj pyare* are all volunteers, and they are selected when the need arises. They maintain this status until the duty they were asked to perform has been fulfilled.

At crucial moments of Sikh history, the panj pyare have collectively acted as supreme authority for the Sikhs. For example, during the battle of Chamkaur, the last five surviving Sikhs constituted themselves into the Council of Five, and they commanded Guru Gobind to leave the fortress and save himself to reassemble the Sikhs. Before Guru Gobind Singh passed away, he ended the line of living gurus. Through the institution of the panj pyare, the Guru envisioned a continuing society that would conduct itself democratically and choose its leaders based on merit.

35. What happens in a modern amrit ceremony?

The modern-day amrit sanchar takes place in a Gurdwara or another designated place in the presence of *Sri Guru Granth Sahib*. The initiation ceremony takes about two to three hours. It is presided over by the *panj pyare*—five practicing Sikhs who are highly regarded by the local congregation as being persons of high moral character. These panj payare represent the first five beloved ones who became initiated by Guru Gobind Singh. The amrit sanchar is held in private, and only those who are partaking in it are permitted to be present. All initiates arrive wearing the five articles of faith. Before they are allowed to enter the initiation room, each initiate is asked if they have come of their own volition. Each initiate is asked a series of questions to ensure that they are taking amrit willingly and not under compulsion or threat by anyone.

The ceremony starts with an *ardaas* (prayer). The initiates then sit cross-legged and meditate in unison with the *panj pyare*. Each one of the *panj piaray* takes a turn to recite one of the five *Banis*, select spiritual utterances of the gurus (*Jap, Jaap, Chaupaiee, Tav Prasad Savaiye, and Anand*) that are

Iron bowl with Khanda

part of an *amritdhari* Sikh's daily meditation routine. Concurrently, the panj payare prepare the *amrit* by stirring water with a *khanda* (double-edged sword) in an iron bowl, and they add *patasey* (sugar puffs) to create the sweet nectar.

Once the prayers are complete, the *amrit* is ready to be administered. The initiates are reminded of their ethical, moral, and spiritual obligations. Once each initiate has indicated their willingness to abide by their duties to themselves, to the Sikh panth, and to all of humanity, they are each given a sip of the amrit. All of the initiates drink *amrit* out of the same bowl to symbolize their equality regardless of age, gender, race, or socioeconomic status. From henceforth, the initiates are referred to as the Khalsa, the way of the saint-soldier. While they may enter the ceremony as strangers, they leave as brothers and sisters who are united in their commitment to following Sikhi.

36. Who Can Take Amrit?

Any person—regardless of gender, race, ethnicity, prior religion, or age—can take amrit as long as they believe in one Immortal Being; the teachings of the Sikh gurus and the *Guru Granth Sahib*; commit to keeping the five articles of faith; and do not owe allegiance to any other religion. The initiate must also agree to refrain from dishonouring their hair, eating meat that has been ritualistically slaughtered and caused suffering to the animal (kutha), engaging in adultery; and using tobacco, alcohol, or other intoxicating substances.

Amrit must be a personal choice, and it cannot be forced on anyone. There is no prescribed age at which a Sikh can be initiated. Sikhs can choose to take *amrit* whenever they are ready and understand the obligations of being an *amritdhari* (initiated) Sikh. According to the *Sikh Rehat Maryada* (code of conduct), only those who understand the significance of the ceremony and carry its discipline with sincerity should be initiated. Thus, it is generally frowned upon to give amrit to a young child.

37. What are the Sikh articles of faith?

The five articles of faith for Sikhs are known colloquially as the panj kakaars (the "five Ks," referring to the letter of the alphabet that they all start with):

- Kesh (pronounced "Case"): unshorn hair
- Kangha: a wooden comb
- Kara: an iron or steel bracelet
- Kashera: a cotton undergarment
- Kirpan: a small sword or dagger

All initiated Sikh males and females are required to wear these articles of faith as an outward identifier of their commitment to following Sikhi.

Each of the five Ks has profound religious meaning for Sikhs since each is imperative to the spiritual and temporal identity of the individual who honours the wisdom and courage of the Sikh teachings. The articles are not symbols, nor can they be construed as mere "apparel." Instead, they are the outwardly identifiable markers of an initiated (*amritdhari*) Sikh.

38. What is the significance of the Sikh articles of faith?

The five articles of faith, the *kakaars*, form part of the initiation ceremony for a Sikh. They manifest Sikh beliefs and are a core part of the Sikh identity. They represent the values that guide a Sikh, and they align with the five vices that a Sikh is to detach from: *kaam* (lust), *krodh* (anger), *lobh* (greed), *moh* (attachment), and *ahungkar* (ego). The significance of each article of faith is as follows:

- *Kesh:* Unshorn hair represents the acceptance of Waheguru's   will. One's hair is to be kept covered at all times with a *keski* or *dastaar* (turban). It is socially acceptable for Sikh women or young boys to wear a smaller dastaar (*keski*) or other head covering if they do not wish to wear a full dastaar. For most Sikhs, keeping of the kesh is inseparable from the dastaar. The dastaar signifies dignity, responsibility, gender equality, spiritual wisdom, and humility. The unshorn hair and the dastaar, together, signify the antithesis of *ahungkar* or ego.

- *Kangha:* The wooden comb represents cleanliness and self-  discipline. It is carried in the hair and used to keep the hair neat and tidy. As Sikhs comb their hair, they are also reminded to comb their mind of impurities and detach themselves from material things (*moh*).

- *Kara:* The iron or steel bracelet is worn on the initiate's dominant hand as a sign of commitment to following a spiritually informed life. The bracelet's circular shape represents the continuum of the universe and the oneness of Waheguru. This article of faith serves to remind the bearer to lead an honest, ethical, and compassionate life; to use their hands for the benefit of humanity; and to shed greed (*lobh*).

- *Kachera:* This uniquely sewn cotton undergarment serves as a  reminder to maintain high moral character and discipline. It enjoins a Sikh to keep their sexual desires or lust (*kaam*) under control and to live a life of commitment and fidelity to their life partner.

- *Kirpan:* This small personal sword is worn sheathed and held in  a cloth sash (*gathra*) next to the body. The word "ki*rpan*" is a composite word; *kirpa* means "grace" or "compassion," and *aan* means "honour." The *kirpan* signifies the responsibility of a Sikh to stand up against injustice. The kirpan reminds a Sikh to act out of compassion rather than anger (*krodh*). The size of the *kirpan* varies according to one's age or preference. Younger persons usually wear *kirpans* with a blade of two to eight centimetres (one to three inches), while adults typically wear a kirpan with a blade ranging in size from fifteen to twenty-three centimetres (six to nine inches).

These five articles of the Sikh faith are not mere symbols. As Jasbeer Singh, a colleague from Edmonton, wrote to me in a note in 2019: "Symbols can be arbitrary and changed to suit times or convenience; articles of faith are embedded in the foundations of faith; and thus, meant to withstand the challenges of [the] times."

39. Why do Sikhs carry a kirpan?

The *kirpan* has deep religious significance for Sikhs, and it is not intended to be used as a weapon. To understand its purpose, one must appreciate its historical context.

As Sikhi grew in popularity, Sikhs became a threat to the establishment. The fifth Guru, Arjun, was tortured and martyred for refusing to give up his faith. The sixth Guru, Guru Hargobind, resisted cruelty and faced tyrant Mughal rulers head-on. He began to wear two *kirpans* (swords) over the traditional dress: the sword of *miri* (temporal power) and the sword of *piri* (spiritual power). The sword of miri was used for self-defence, while the sword of piri was worn to remind himself to never raise his sword out of violence or as an instrument of oppression. When Guru Gobind Singh incorporated the kirpan as an article of faith, it was the sword of *piri* (spiritual power) that became part of the Sikh articles of faith.

40. What was the inspiration for the Sikh articles of faith?

Guru Tegh Bahadur, the ninth Guru of the Sikhs, was beheaded by order of Mughal Emperor Aurangzeb in 1675 for defending the right of Hindus to freely practice their faith. Bhai Jaita (Jeevan Singh) recovered the Guru's dismembered head and carried it more than three hundred kilometres to his family in Anandpur Sahib, Panjab. Guru Tegh Bahadur's son, Gobind Rai (Guru Gobind Singh) complimented Bhai Jaita for this courageous act and asked if there were no other Sikhs to assist him. Bhai Jaita responded that it was challenging to identify Sikhs since there was nothing distinguishing them from the other people that were present from different faiths. This incident is often considered the impetus for Guru Gobind Singh creating a Sikh who could be easily identified from a distance. However, though this may have been the triggering point in history, many Sikhs believe that the creation of the Khalsa was a fulfillment of Guru Nanak's mission of *Nirmal Panth* as a distinct way of life.[30]

Like the uniform of a police officer, the Sikh physical appearance and attire of a Sikh provides a signal to others that the distinctly identifiable Sikh is someone they can turn to for help. For a Sikh, it serves as a

---

[30] Bhai Gurdas Vaar 1: Maariya sika jagat vich Nanak nirmal panth chalaaya—
ਮਾਰਿਆ ਸਿਕਾ ਜਗਤ ਵਿਚ ਨਾਨਕ ਨਿਰਮਲ ਪੰਥ ਚਲਾਇਆ॥

constant reminder of the ideals that a Sikh strives to live up to. It is an outward reflection of an inward identity.

41. Should Sikh articles of faith be appropriated for advertising?

Advertising campaigns of major brands and the entertainment industry have tried responding to calls for greater inclusivity for more than a decade now. While their efforts are commendable, there have been occasions for debate within the Sikh community about cultural appropriation, misunderstandings around the articles of faith, and whether presence in campaigns for capitalistic consumption should be considered progress. Based on what the Sikh articles of faith represent, the sacrifices made to retain them, and the Sikh vision of an egalitarian society, many feel strongly that the articles of faith should not be appropriated for commercial profiteering.

The Sikh articles of faith hold profound spiritual importance for a Sikh. Countless Sikhs have been killed in many parts of the world, including India, North America, and Europe, simply because of their outward identifying articles of faith, particularly the dastaar. Other Sikhs have been tortured or faced unspeakable hardships to maintain these articles. In consideration of these things, some Sikhs are offended when their articles of faith are appropriated for advertising. Other Sikhs recognize the initial attempts have been offensive in various ways but suggest that dialogue and education will help make inroads. These Sikhs argue that representation and visibility in cultural productions and public spaces may be difficult and fraught at first but will help ensure that future generations of Sikhs do not face the same level of discrimination and exclusion. There are still other Sikhs who consider the recent attempts to give presence to Sikhs in advertising as something to celebrate. It should be mentioned that outside of this debate, the economic prospects and employment challenges faced by amritdhari Sikhs have only increased.

One example of a recent debate occurred in 2019. Italian fashion house Gucci advertised an "Indy Full Turban" depicting a European model wearing a turban that was listed for sale on Nordstrom's (luxury department store) website for a hefty price tag of $790. The Sikh community was outraged. Eventually, Gucci and Nordstrom both apologized and withdrew the ad and the product from stores. There are several issues that can be raised with this example that show general lack of awareness and culturally insensitivity. "When companies like Gucci appropriate articles of faith, like the turban they are trying to capitalize on, they do not take into consideration the discrimination that Sikhs face while adhering to the tenets of their faith," the Sikh Coalition [USA] wrote in a Facebook post on May 16, 2019.[31] It is notable also that the display of the turban on non-Sikh models, when there are practicing Sikhs who could have modeled the attire in a respectful way, reinforces the exclusion of Sikhs in public spaces.

42. Who can wear Sikh articles of faith?

The five articles of faith are mandatory for all *amritdhari* (initiated) Sikhs. Sahijdhari Sikhs who are on their journeys toward taking amrit may wear the various articles of faith depending on where they are on their spiritual journeys. The kara is usually the first article of faith adopted by a Sikh and is worn almost universally by anyone with an affinity to Sikhi. Other kakaars, including a dastaar, may also be commonly worn by Sikhs at different levels of adherence. Provided that they are worn out of respect and not at a costume party or to otherwise mock the faith, there is no bar to them being worn by anyone. The only exception is the kirpan. It is generally regarded to be reserved only for amritdhari Sikhs and are not sanctioned to be worn by anyone who has not taken amrit or is preparing to take amrit. This is because of the kirpan's significance to the Sikhs. The kirpan is not a weapon and is not to be used for violence. It is crucial that the person who is wearing

---

[31]   CNN, May 18, 2019: "Here is why Sikhs were offended by this $790 Gucci turban," by Harneet Kaur.

it have high regard for the kirpan and to understand the restrictions against its use. On the other hand, no one suggests restricting access to kirpans completely as that would be against basic Sikh principle of human freedom. Sikhs who want to wear a kirpan are encouraged to take amrit and learn the associated practices and knowledge so that they do not misuse such a significant symbol.

43. Are Sikhs allowed to wear the kirpan anywhere?

Prior to 9/11, many countries, including Canada, permitted Sikhs to wear a *kirpan* in any public spaces, including on domestic and international flights, although the size was limited to a four-inch blade (ten centimetres). Following the events of 9/11, security protocols were changed, and Sikhs were required to remove their kirpans before boarding an airplane.

Current policy on wearing kirpans on domestic and international flights varies. In Canada, the UK, New Zealand, and the EU, Sikhs can fly with a small *kirpan* (with a blade length of six centimetres or less than 2.5 inches) on domestic as well as international flights. This policy is followed by most member states of the International Civil Aviation Organization, except the United States of America. India presently allows Sikh passengers on domestic flights to wear a *kirpan* with a total maximum length of nine inches (22.9 cm), subject to the requirement of a public order (BCAS Circular 14/2005). However, India does not permit *kirpans* on international flights.

CHAPTER 7

Outward Expression of Sikh Identity

Clothing is a symbol of our place in society as well as our character. We express ourselves to others in the way we dress. And, as mentioned, the dress can also be a visual religious identifier. It can also be a window into the social world, which is bound by an unspoken set of rules, customs, conventions, and rituals that guide face-to-face interactions. Holistically, dress functions as an effective means of nonverbal communication. For Sikhs, clothing plays an important role and can be a reflection of deeply held spiritual beliefs.

44. Why do Sikhs tie a dastaar (turban)?

The spiritual significance of the dastaar for Sikhs harkens to Guru Nanak. Guru Nanak was a strong advocate for the rights of women. He was vehemently opposed to the veiling of a woman, which was an endemic practice during his time in both the Muslim and Hindu traditions. Rather than a symbol of modesty and humility, Guru Nanak saw the veil as a tool of oppression of women. He condemned the forceful veiling of women, whether through a burka (as in the Muslim tradition) or *chuni* (as in the Hindu tradition). Guru Nanak believed that women were equal to men and that the only supreme being was the Divine

Creator. To enshrine the ideal of gender equality, Guru Nanak lifted the veil. To instill the virtue of humility, he enjoined all persons, male and female, to cover their heads as a sign of respect to the omnipresent Divine Creator. The covering of choice for Guru Nanak was the dastaar.

Since Guru Nanak's time, the dastaar has been part of the Sikh identity, but it was not formally adopted as part of the Khalsa dress until the first amrit sanchar in 1699. Guru Arjan, the fifth Guru, invokes us to "keep the Divine-given form intact with a dastaar donned on your head."[32] Guru Gobind Singh says, "He who lives up to the Sikh form is my Sikh—he is my master, and I am his disciple, [or] follower. Comb your hair twice, both in the morning and evening; wear your dastaar neatly."[33]

In Sikh philosophy and practice, the keeping of unshorn hair means that Sikhs live in and resign themselves to the will of Waheguru. The dastaar meets both practical and spiritual purposes. To keep the long hair intact and tidy, and to maintain spiritual sanctity, the dastaar has been prescribed by Sikh tenets. Balpreet Singh, legal counsel for the World Sikh Organization of Canada, writes:

> It is inconceivable that Sikhs who keep their unshorn hair would not cover it with a turban. As the turban is such an integral part of the Sikh identity, being forced to remain without it is tantamount to asking Sikhs to do something which is completely against their beliefs. Sikhs believe that Waheguru is everywhere, and as a sign of respect for Waheguru, and a reflection of their humility and belief in equality between men and women, Sikhs wear the turban everywhere [and all the time]. Just as an individual would be extremely embarrassed in having to appear in a state of undress, a Sikh would feel

---

[32] *SGGS* 1084: "Napaak paak kar hadoor hadisaa sabat surat dastaar sira"— ਨਾਪਾਕ ਪਾਕੁ ਕਰਿ ਹਦੂਰਿ ਹਦੀਸਾ ਸਾਬਤ ਸੂਰਤਿ ਦਸਤਾਰ ਸਿਰਾ॥

[33] Khalsa *Rehat Maryada*. For additional information, go to https://www.worldsikh.org.

a similar level of humiliation in being forced to remove the turban, tantamount to a strip search.[34]

Here is a further quote on the religious significance of dastaars from SikhWomen.com:

> The dastaar, as the Sikh turban is known, is an article of faith that has been made mandatory by the founders of Sikhism. It is not to be regarded as mere cultural paraphernalia. When a Sikh man or woman dons a turban, the turban ceases to be just a piece of cloth and becomes one and the same with the Sikh's head. The turban, as well as the other articles of faith worn by Sikhs, have an immense spiritual as well as temporal significance.[35]

Wearing a dastaar is a personal decision that symbolizes many things, such as sovereignty, equality, humility, dedication, self-respect, courage, and piety. For some Sikhs, it is as simple as acting "out of love and obedience to the wishes of the founders of their faith."[36]

45. Is it ok to touch a Sikh's dastaar?

Sikhs consider it inappropriate and offensive when others try to touch their dastaars. Intentionally knocking off a Sikh's dastaar or asking them to remove it in public is dehumanizing, and some consider it equivalent to stripping them naked. Sikhs are very protective of their dastaars or head coverings, and there is a history of trying to destroy Sikhi by targeting the dastaar and committing genocide of Sikhs who refused to stop wearing it. A dastaar is not just a piece of cloth that one wraps

---

[34]   Significance of Turban—www.worldsikh.org.
[35]   SikhWomen.com, "Why Do Sikhs Wear a Turban and What Does It Mean?" 1–2, http://www.sikhwomen.com/turban/sikhs.htm.
[36]   .Ibid., 2.

around one's head. Instead, it is an integral part of Sikh identity, and it holds sacred significance for a Sikh.

In Canada, Britain, and the United States of America, all police forces, border security agencies, and airport security screening staff have been trained to respect Sikh dastaars and follow respectful security search procedures in a private room, if warranted. There is almost no instance where one would need to handle or touch a Sikh's dastaar. When absolutely necessary, one must seek permission from a Sikh. However, this should always be preceded by a conversation with the individual where all options to the contrary that maintain the Sikh's bodily integrity have been considered and informed consent is given.

46. Can a Sikh wear a safety helmet or hard hat over a dastaar?

Most Sikhs object to wearing any item on top of their dastaar. This is particularly true for hats and caps, but it also includes safety helmets and hard hats. Many Sikhs object to wearing a hat over their dastaars because they consider it an affront to their Sikh identity. This includes safety helmets. Even if a helmet is made that can properly be fitted over a dastaar, most Sikhs would find wearing it objectionable for reasons of personal conscience.

Historically, Sikhs have sacrificed their lives for the sake of their faith and the right to wear their dastaars. The issue of helmets arose during the Second World War and is instructive of how this can be dealt with. Alarmed at the number of incidents of insubordination as Sikh soldiers refused to wear helmets, many senior British officers, who had served with the Sikhs, started to educate young British officers on the dastaar issue, supporting the Sikh soldiers' refusal wear helmets. Consequently, by the middle of 1940, orders were passed not to force Sikh soldiers to wear helmets. During the twentieth century, more than eighty-three thousand Sikhs died, and 119,000 plus were injured defending freedom for all during World Wars I and II. It is difficult to ascertain how many of those lives may have been spared or whether the extent of injuries would have been different if Sikhs wore helmets, but we do see from the example that Sikhs made an informed choice to risk their lives rather than compromise maintaining the articles of faith.

Helmets became an issue again as more and more Sikhs migrated to the United Kingdom. In the mid-1970s, a Sikh was fined five pounds for riding a motorcycle without a helmet. This started a debate in the British Parliament. On June 23, 1976, during a committee hearing, Winston Churchill MP (grandson of wartime Prime Minister Sir Winston L. S. Churchill) eloquently spoke in favour of exempting Sikhs from wearing helmets:

> British people are highly indebted and obliged to Sikhs for a long time. I know that within this century, we needed their help twice, and they did help us very well. As a result of their timely help, we are today able to live with honour, dignity, and independence. In the war, they fought and died for us, wearing the turbans. At that time, we were not adamant that they should wear safety helmets because we knew that they were not going to wear them anyways, and we would be deprived of their help. At that time, due to our miserable and poor situation, we did not force it on them to wear safety helmets, [so] why should we force it now? Rather, we should now respect their traditions, and by granting this legitimate concession, win their applause.[37]

Sikh motorcyclists were exempted from wearing safety helmets in the United Kingdom after interventions like this. There have been ripple effects in countries like Canada, where starting in 1999, Sikhs received a similar exemption in four provinces (British Columbia, Alberta, Manitoba, and Ontario) where there is a significant Sikh population. Subsequently, Britain extended the exemption to work sites. In Canada,

---

[37]   House of Commons official report, Standing Committee hearing June 23, 1976, Columns 11, 12, 20.

Sikhs received case-by-case exemptions, and efforts are underway for a blanket exemption through legislation. However, many corporations and businesses around the world respect the Sikh identity and exempt dastaar-wearing Sikhs from wearing hard hats.

47. Do colours have any significance for Sikhs?

The Sikhi stance against ritualism applies equally to colours. There is no specific colour prescribed for Sikh clothing. However, social customs or historical precedent may result in Sikhs wearing some colours more frequently than others. Also, Sikhs have periodically worn specific colours in support of political causes.

Blue, white, saffron, yellow, and black dastaars are ubiquitous among Sikhs. Blue signifies that the mind of a Sikh should be as broad as the sky and as deep as the ocean. Black is often worn when protesting against oppression, particularly during a protest or a march. Saffron or yellow dastaars or clothes are often worn on days of religious observance or for special commemorative events, such as Vaisakhi. The yellow represents the commitment to stand up against injustice. White is associated with the purity of the physical body and the consciousness. White used to be a traditional colour worn at Sikh funerals, though are no specific colour requirements. It has slowly been replaced by black among many diaspora Sikhs, due to loss of cultural fluency and pressure to assimilate dominant Western norms. The symbolic association of the colour white with death is why you will rarely see Sikh brides wearing white at their weddings. Sikh brides still have an overwhelming preference to wear different shades of red or pink on their wedding day. The colour red is associated with vitality, life, youthful vibrancy, and fertility. It is a favourite among brides in many Eastern cultures where the symbolism is shared.

48. Do Sikhs wear special clothes?

Initiated Sikhs are required to wear their articles of faith. This includes the kashera (special cotton underwear signifying chastity and fidelity) and the dastaar or keski (turban or similar head covering). There are no other restrictions on what kind of clothes a Sikh can wear. That said, practicing Sikhs generally tend to dress conservatively (not revealing too much flesh). The simplicity of the dress is emphasized in the Sikh scripture. "O Baba (revered), the pleasure of other (trendy) clothes are false," says Guru Nanak.[38]

Sikhs may often be seen wearing non-Western clothing, especially when attending Gurdwara. Most commonly, it is the salwar-kameez for women (colloquially referred to as the "Panjabi suit") and kurta-pajama for men. This attire for both men and women consists of a long tunic and narrow-legged pants. This clothing has cultural but does not have religious significance.

---

[38]   *SGGS* 16: baba hor pehnal khushee khuar. ਬਾਬਾ ਹੋਰੁ ਪੈਨਣੁ ਖੁਸੀ ਖੁਆਰੁ॥

CHAPTER 8

Eating for the Body and the Soul

No one can deny that food can be a great unifier. Whether it is the consumption of food in their homes or in their places of worship, for Sikhs, food plays an important role in nourishing the body and the soul. Sikhi encourages temperance and moderation in matters of food.

49. Is food a part of the religious service?

Sikhs are encouraged to eat simple and nourishing foods that aid and improve daily life. Healthy food keeps the body and soul together and helps to prevent excessive sleep and inactivity. One can more easily meditate and be proactive in life with a healthy body and mind.

Food is an integral part of the Sikh worship experience. Within the *darbar* (prayer hall) itself, *prashad* (a sweet, buttery pudding) is served to all worshippers. The prashad symbolizes equality. Every gurdwara also has a langar (food) hall where free vegetarian food is served to anyone who enters. Even when Sikhs perform religious functions in their own homes, a vegetarian meal will always be served to guests.

50. Are there any dietary requirements or restrictions for Sikhs?

Sikhism stresses healthy and moderate eating. Sikhs serve lacto-vegetarian food in gurdwaras. It includes vegetables, pulses (*daals*), fruits, dairy products (such as milk, cheese, yogurt, butter, and cream), nuts, and fruits. Sikhs do not serve eggs, seafood, or meat in gurdwaras. Most amritdhari and many non-amritdhari Sikhs are lacto-vegetarian in their daily diets.

In this vein, the Sikh code of conduct (*Rehat Maryada*, 1945) prohibits the eating of meat from an animal killed by ritual slaughter (halal or kosher). This is considered one of the four transgressions that Sikhs are required to avoid. The Panjabi word for this restriction is *kutha*, literally meaning *carrion*. Some Sikhs interpret *kutha* as permitting them to eat meat (except that killed by halal or kosher means). Others say that *kutha* instructs Sikhs to avoid falling prey to the rituals of other religions.

The argument about eating meat has been going on since Guru Nanak's days. He specifically addressed this argument in one verse where he says, "Those who argue about eating or not eating meat are fools. Rather than wasting time in these petty eating arguments, they should concentrate on meditation and spiritual wisdom."[39] Recognizing health concerns, in another verse, Guru Nanak advises, "One should avoid eating food (including drinks) that increases health risks, causes harm to the body, and gives rise to wickedness and corruption."[40]

Most practicing Sikhs believe that simple, wholesome, vegetarian foods are better for their health. Some believe that a vegetarian diet also helps them concentrate during meditation. Many practicing Sikhs view meat eating as permissible in a matter of necessity, i.e., the life of an animal (or fish) should only be taken if you need to eat it for your

---

[39]   *SGGS* 1289: maas kar moorakh jhagaRe giaan dhiaan nahee jaanai—ਮਾਸੁ ਮਾਸੁ ਕਰਿ ਮੂਰਖੁ ਝਗੜੇ ਗਿਆਨੁ ਧਿਆਨੁ ਨਹੀ ਜਾਣੈ॥

[40]   *SGGS* 16: baabaa hor khaanaa khusee khuaar. jit khaadhai tan peeReeaai man meh chaleh vikaar—ਬਾਬਾ ਹੋਰੁ ਖਾਣਾ ਖੁਸੀ ਖੁਆਰੁ ॥ ਜਿਤੁ ਖਾਧੈ ਤਨੁ ਪੀੜੀਐ ਮਨ ਮਹਿ ਚਲਹਿ ਵਿਕਾਰ॥

survival. Otherwise, one should maintain a vegetarian lifestyle out of respect for all life.

51. Do Sikhs have any meal preparation or consumption rituals?

In food preparation, the emphasis is on purity and cleanliness of the kitchen, utensils, mind, body, and hands. Most Sikhs say a prayer before eating, whether individually or collectively. The prayer may vary from person to person, but it generally includes an expression of gratitude: "We owe thanks to the Creator for providing us with abundant food and good health."

While preparing *meal* or *prashad*, it is expected that Sikh cooks will meditate and avoid gossip or negative thoughts. Anyone working in the gurdwara kitchen is also required to keep their heads covered. For hygiene reasons, they are also enjoined to refrain from eating or nibbling on food while cooking.

52. Do Sikhs practice fasting?

Fasting has no religious merit for Sikhs. Sikhs believe that the human body is a gift from the Creator. As the temple of the soul, one's body must be nourished and cared for. Fasting as an austerity, as a ritual, or as a mortification of the body by means of willful hunger is forbidden in Sikhi. Guru Nanak, the founder of Sikhi, says, "Penance, fasting, austerity, and alms-giving are inferior to 'The Truth;' right action is superior to all."[41] Guru Nanak also stated, "The mind is not softened by fasting and austerities. Nothing else is equal to the worship of the Creator's name."[42]

The bottom line is Sikhi does not believe fasting aids in our

---

[41] *SGGS* 75: teerath varat such sa(n)jam naahee karam dharam nahee poojaa—
ਤੀਰਥ ਵਰਤ ਸੁਚਿ ਸੰਜਮੁ ਨਾਹੀ ਕਰਮੁ ਧਰਮੁ ਨਹੀ ਪੂਜਾ ॥

[42] *SGGS* 905: a(n)n na khaeh dhehee dhukh dheejai; bin gur giaan tirapat nahee
theejai. ਅੰਨੁ ਨ ਖਾਇ ਦੇਹੀ ਦੁਖੁ ਦੀਜੈ ॥ ਬਿਨੁ ਗੁਰ ਗਿਆਨ ਤ੍ਰਿਪਤਿ ਨਹੀ ਬੀਜੈ ॥

path toward the truth. Nonetheless, fasting for reasons of health is understandable when done on medical advice. Therefore, for Sikhs, fasting is only accepted when done in the interest of one's health. Hunger strikes are suicidal and are not acceptable in Sikhi.

PART III

Practices

CHAPTER 9

Traditions and Art

Tradition can be defined as the "transmission of customs or beliefs from generation to generation" (*Oxford Languages Dictionary*). Traditions help communities maintain a sense of unity and continuity. They can include customary practices related to eating, dressing, worshipping, and marking major life events. Traditions may also develop or be reflected through the fine arts, such as music, art, and artifacts.

Music is an essential part of human life. It is a way of expressing one's passions as well as one's emotions. Visual art, meanwhile, influences society by changing opinions, instilling value, and translating history and experiences across space and time. Art is a method of communication that allows people of different cultures and historical times to communicate with each other via images, sounds, and stories. Painting, sculpture, music, literature, and the arts represent the repository of a society's collective memory.

This chapter explores some of the traditions and customs practiced by Sikhs and the roles that the fine arts, particularly music, play in our lives.

53. Why are customs important?

The imparting of customs and beliefs is important for preserving a particular culture and communicating it to future generations. Customs also help add stability and certainty to people's social lives, bring people together, and develop social relationships among them. Customs provide a feeling of security in human society generally.

Customs are often followed because they resonate with people's personal belief systems and values. Thus, Sikh customs are generally those that are consistent with Sikhi teachings as contained in the *SGGS*. Though Sikh customs are often infused with Sikh values, they may also be reflective of the larger society or culture in which Sikhs live. They may not always be consistent with Sikh teachings, or they may clash with Sikhi values and principles. I have therefore distinguished between the two by calling the former *religious customs* and the latter *social customs*.

54. Is there a priest or clergy in Sikhi?

There is no priestly class in Sikhi. Nor is there a clergy as commonly understood in other faith traditions. There are, however, persons in a Sikh gurdwara (*granthis*) who will lead prayer and worship or perform other religious duties. Sikhs also have religious leaders, *jathedars*, who serve as the heads of the five Takhats (seats of temporal authority) in Sikhism. These Takhats are all located in India—as are the jathedars who act as administrators or governors. As a collective, they have the power to make religious ordinances or assist in otherwise managing the affairs of the Sikh community.

It is important to note here that while granthis and jathedars are respected by Sikhs, they are not ordained into the religion in some special way distinct from others. People often achieve these roles based on their knowledge of Sikhi and their personal adherence to Sikh ethics. However, the selection of a jathedar can also become politicized, and there are many within the Sikh community who question the selection process and argue that the role itself is antithetical to Sikhi values, which do not support a hierarchical religious order. A glimpse into Sikh history explains the ambivalent relationship that Sikhs often have with religious "leaders."

Guru Nanak traveled extensively throughout Southeast Asia and the Middle East, teaching his message of one Creator and the unity of humanity. He built the first *Dharmsaal* (religious gathering place) in 1521, in a newly established town called Kartarpur (located in Pakistan), for the congregation of Sikhs. The practice of developing new congregation centres continued with the second Guru, Guru Angad. During Guru Amar Das's guruship period (1552–1574 CE), Sikhi took a strong foothold, due primarily to the Mughal ruler Akbar's accommodation and admiration of the Sikh religion.

The Mughal Empire was divided into twenty-two provinces. Guru Amar Das decided to establish Sikh teaching and practice centres, *Manjis,* in all twenty-two provinces, headed by devout men and women committed to the three-pronged life (kirat karna, Naam Japna, and vand shakna) propagated by Guru Nanak. To break with patriarchal culture and to promote gender equality, he appointed women to head some of the *Manjis* (Matho Murari for the Lahore region, Mai Seva for the Kabul region, and Mai Bhago for the Kashmir region).[43] Their role could be loosely compared to that of a Catholic diocese bishop. To strengthen the organizational structure, Guru Ram Das, the fourth Guru, and Guru Arjan, the fifth Guru, increased the reach and expanse of spiritual teachings by appointing *mahants* (head priests or clerics). The responsibilities of *mahants* could be loosely compared to those of bishops. They were responsible for teaching the threefold Sikh discipline of *Naam, daan,* and *ishnaan* (divine name, charity, and purity), corresponding to their relation to the Divine, to society, and to the self and acting as liaisons between the Guru, the local community, and the regional governance of Sikh Dharmsaals.

Unfortunately, over time, this system became corrupt and immoral. Instead of empowering Sikhs, some *mahants* encouraged Sikhs to worship them. Guru Gobind Singh, the tenth Guru, disbanded this system. In 1699, he created the order of the Khalsa, thus empowering women and men to initiate each other into Sikhi. Each initiated Sikh thus becomes

---

[43] Satbir Singh: *Sada Ithas (Our History)*, 191–192, Twelfth Edition (2011), New Book Company, Jalandhar, India.

their own minister, needing no intermediary between them and the faith.

55. What is Parbhat Pheri?

In some villages in Panjab—and even in some major urban centres—one may see a group of Sikhs walking and singing religious songs and sabads early in the morning. The early-morning rounds of sabad singing before sunrise are called Parbhat Pheri. *Parbhat* (also spelled *prabhat*) means "early morning," and *Pheri* means "round." So, together, the phrase literally means "early-morning rounds." This ritual of a morning procession of singing sabads was widespread in India among Hindus, mainly to commemorate certain religious events. The tradition was for people from the villages to get up before sunrise and walk rounds of the village while singing sabads or folk songs, praising God, and playing percussion instruments such as the *dholki* (small drum) and bells. This ritual was believed to invoke the good spirits and welcome the morning with good vibrations.

In Sikhi, the Parbhat Pheri tradition started with Baba Buddha (1506–1631), a contemporary of Guru Nanak, when he led sabad-singing processions to Gwalior Fort, where Guru Hargobind, the sixth Sikh Guru, was incarcerated (1617–19) by the Mughal emperor, Jahangir. Though the practice started as a protest, it became an uplifting spiritual experience for the Sikhs. The procession was a precursor to more massive Nagar Keertan processions that were promoted by dedicated Sikhs like Baba Attar Singh Mastuana Wale at the beginning of the twentieth century.

Lately, this tradition of Parbhat Pheri has been lost in the face of modernization, but it still continues in India on a smaller scale. With industrialization and people working on different shifts, such a noisy procession would not be allowed in the Western world. Some gurdwaras in Canada have revived this tradition on a much smaller scale, holding these rounds within the premises of a gurdwara.

56. What role does music play in Sikhi?

For Sikhs, music, and more particularly *keertan*, is an essential aspect of spiritual communion with the Divine. While the Naam (the divine message or Sabad), is of primary importance, keertan is the vehicle through which the Naam can be expressed. Keertan is the singing of compositions from the *SGGS* with musical accompaniment. The gurus taught that by singing and listening to *keertan,* the mind can be awakened and uplifted out of a material existence. Sikhs use keertan as a form of meditation rather than entertainment. Music speaks to the soul, and when it is paired with the wisdom of the gurus as expressed in Gurbani, keertan can have a transformative effect.

The gurus believed that music could transcend cultural and linguistic barriers and open one up to experiencing the Divine. Thus, Guru Nanak shared his wisdom through his poetic compositions, which were put to music. Through all his travels, Guru Nanak was accompanied by his friend Bhai Mardana, who played the *rabab*, a stringed instrument similar to a lute. Together, the two would lead others in devotional singing and meditation.

Keertan continues to play a central role in the lives of Sikhs. The Sikh sacred teachings in the *Sri Guru Granth Sahib* are composed in thirty-one *raags* (traditional musical measures or scales). The *raag* creates a particular atmosphere and mood, which has the power to elevate consciousness. Each *raag* is thus associated with a different time of the day when it is considered optimal to be played or sung. There were six *raags* before the time of the Sikh gurus, who created twenty-five additional *raags* and were skilled in playing various instruments. Guru Teg Bahadur, the ninth Guru of the Sikhs, composed *raag jaijawanti* and said, "Waheguru ji, please bestow the blessing of your *Naam*, that this soul may continue to sing your glorious praises."[44]

Although, traditionally, instruments such as the *rabab* and *taus* (a bowed string instrument) accompanied Sikh music, the most common apparatus used today is the harmonium (pump or reed organ), which was

---

[44]   *SGGS* 1186: deejay naam rahai gun gai. ਦੀਜੈ ਨਾਮੁ ਰਹੈ ਗੁਨ ਗਾਇ॥

introduced into India by British missionaries and was initially created in France. Usually, a keertan jatha (group) will consist of two persons on the vaja (harmonium) and a third person who plays the *tabla* (a pair of hand drums). However, it is not uncommon to see other musical instruments being incorporated, such as a guitar, sitar, or flute.

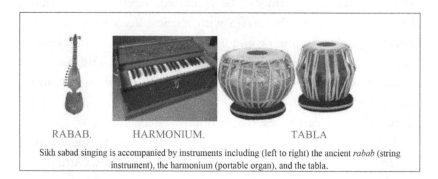

RABAB.   HARMONIUM.   TABLA

Sikh sabad singing is accompanied by instruments including (left to right) the ancient *rabab* (string instrument), the harmonium (portable organ), and the tabla.

Gurdwaras will often host keertan classes and competitions to encourage and engage children. During special occasions, gurdwaras will also hold keertan darbars, where congregants gather to sing together and listen to keertanis (the singers of keertan) who may hail from other cities or even countries.

At major Sikh gurdwaras, the singing of Gurbani keertan begins before dawn and continues throughout the day. At smaller centres, keertan may be limited to set times during the day or week. In addition to Sikh households having their own selection of *keertan* video/audios, there are live internet and television broadcasts of *keertan* from gurdwaras around the world, including Darbar Sahib in Amritsar.

57. Can anyone do Gurbani keertan?

There is no restriction on who can learn or do Gurbani keertan. Parents often put their children in keertan classes so that they can learn how to play classical musical instruments or sing Gurbani. There are also classes for adults who wish to learn how to do keertan. Punjab universities offer graduate degrees. Guru Nanak Institute of Global Studies, a Canadian nonprofit institute offers gurmat music diplomas (www. gurunanakinstitute.ca).

Keertan can be performed in a variety of settings, including one's home, a gurdwara, an auditorium, or even a park. However, regardless of whether the keertan occurs in a private or public setting, some basic protocols are expected to be followed. It is part of Sikh tradition to always cover one's head and remove one's shoes while doing keertan. The singing of verses from the *SGGS* is considered a sacred act, and anyone participating in the keertan, whether alone or with others, is expected to cover their head as a sign of respect and reverence to the Divine Word. It is also against Sikh tradition to drink alcohol or have any other intoxicants present in a setting where keertan will occur. Most Sikhs also consider it inappropriate to serve or consume meat in the same location. Though keertan is almost always performed while seated cross-legged on the ground, there may be instances when a person will perform keertan standing up. There is no bar to this occurring—as long as the head is covered and shoes are removed.

Every gurdwara service involves the singing of keertan, which can be performed by the resident *granthi*, congregants, or professional *raagis* (trained musicians). Smaller gurdwaras usually rely on the resident granthi and members of the congregation to do keertan during the gurdwara service. The larger gurdwaras will usually have a professional raagi jatha (group) perform keertan during the service. The raagi jatha may be local or may hail from another country (quite often India). Traveling raagi jathas usually take up residence for a period of one to six months. Most of the gurdwaras located in urban centres have Gurbani keertan being sung twice each day—once in the morning and once in the evening.

Though keertan can be performed by anyone, the practice with respect to who is permitted to sing keertan from a public gurdwara stage varies regionally, and it also depends on each local gurdwara. The *Sikh Rehat Maryada* stipulates, "Only a Sikh is allowed to perform keertan

(Spiritual sabad singing) in a congregation."[45] Some gurdwaras interpret the *Rehat Maryada* liberally and permit anyone to perform keertan from the stage, regardless of whether they are practicing Sikhs. Others interpret it more restrictively and will only permit an amritdhari Sikh to sing keertan from the stage. Gurbani is meant to be shared and enjoyed universally, and the *SGGS* does not provide any restriction with respect to who can perform keertan publicly.

Below is a youth keertini jatha performing keertan at Sri Guru Singh Sabha Gurdwara in Surrey, British Columbia, Canada.

L-R: Rabia Kaur, Japleen Kaur, Kartar Singh and Harkirat Singh

58. Is there someone who interprets or helps explain Gurbani?

Sikhs believe that the spiritual journey is an intensely personal one. Thus, the best way to understand what is written in the *SGGS* is through personal reflection. Guru Amar Das explains: "Through the Guru's teachings, the devotees intuitively taste the sublime, exquisite and ambrosial teachings of Waheguru."[46]

---

[45]   *Sikh Rehat Maryada,* section III, chapter 5 (sgpc.net).

[46]   *SGGS* 87: har amrit katha saresat utam gur bachani sehaje chaakhee—ਹਰਿ ਅੰਮ੍ਰਿਤ ਕਥਾ ਸਰੇਸਟ ਉਤਮ ਗੁਰ ਬਚਨੀ ਸਹਜੇ ਚਾਖੀ॥

The writings in the *SGGS* are written in many different languages and dialects, and they utilize various styles and techniques of poetic expression. Thus, they are not always easy to comprehend. To enhance our understanding of Gurbani, most gurdwaras feature a weekly (or daily) exposition by a *katha vachik*. Katha refers to the verbal explanation of Gurbani, Sikh history, and religious traditions. It is usually delivered in Panjabi, but some katha vachiks are well versed in English or other languages. They may deliver part or all of their presentation in a language other than Panjabi.

A Sikh scholar delivering such a discourse is a *katha vachak*. They are often referred to as "*Giani Ji*" (one who has spiritual wisdom). Either a male or female can perform this role, although katha vachiks have generally been male. Though there is no formal training required for a katha vachik, but many have spent years studying Gurbani. The most well-known katha vachik, Giani Sant Singh Maskeen (1934–2005) was the most respected Sikh scholar, theologian, and philosopher. Many gurdwaras commemorate his life by hosting annual *akhand path* and *katha darbars* (events). Currently, Giani Pinderpal Singh appears to be a leading katha wachak in Panjabi discourses on Gurbani.

59. Are there written translations available of the SGGS?

In addition to katha vachiks, Sikhs turn to written translations of the *SGGS* to help them understand the teachings of the gurus. More than two dozen translations are available. However, fifteen of them provide complete translations, each with some variation.[47]

---

[47]   SGGS Punjabi Translations: 1. ਸ਼ਬਦਾਰਥ (4 ਭਾਗ), ਸ਼੍ਰੋਮਣੀ ਗੁਰਦੁਆਰਾ ਪਰਬੰਧਕ ਕਮੇਟੀ। 2. ਫਰੀਦਕੋਟੀ ਟੀਕਾ (4 ਭਾਗ), ਗਿਆਨੀ ਬਦਨ ਸਿੰਘ। 3. ਦਰਪਣ (10 ਭਾਗ), ਪ੍ਰੋ. ਸਾਹਿਬ ਸਿੰਘ। 4. ਗੁਰਬਾਣੀ ਸੰਥਯਾ (7 ਭਾਗ), ਭਾਈ ਵੀਰ ਸਿੰਘ। 5. ਨਿਰਣੈ (13 ਭਾਗ), ਗਿਆਨੀ ਹਰਬੰਸ ਸਿੰਘ। 6. ਸਿਧਾਂਤਕ (8 ਭਾਗ), ਗਿਆਨੀ ਮਨੀ ਸਿੰਘ। 7. ਸਟੀਕ (8 ਭਾਗ), ਗਿਆਨੀ ਬਿਸ਼ਨ ਸਿੰਘ। 8. ਅਰਥ ਬੋਧ (5 ਭਾਗ), ਡਾ. ਰਤਨ ਸਿੰਘ ਜੱਗੀ।
SGGS English Translations: *Gopal Singh* (four volumes), *Manmohan Singh* (eight volumes), *Talib* (four volumes), *Sant Singh Khalsa* (online), Darshan Singh (five volumes), *Chahal* (five volumes), *Jawa* (eight volumes), etc.

Two key source books written in Panjabi (*Bhai Gurdas Varaan* and *Sri Guru Granth Sahib Darpan*) by Professor Sahib Singh are highly regarded. The first is written by a Sikh who lived during the gurus' time and is often referred to as the key to understanding Gurbani. The second source is a ten-volume interpretation of the *SGGS*, which is commonly used and referred to by most katha vachiks.

The first English translation of the *SGGS* was done by a German Indologist named Dr. Ernest Trumpp (1828–1885). He was commissioned in 1869 by the British India Office to translate the *SGGS* into English. His translation of the SGGS was completed in 1877. The Sikh community rejects Trumpp's translation as being incomplete and highly biased:[48]

Subsequent attempts by Sikhs to translate the *SGGS* into English have been more successful, though the translations are still considered to be flawed. For example, the four volumes (initially two) translation by Dr. Gopal Singh and eight volumes by Dr. Manmohan Singh (not the former prime minister of India) were published in 1960 and 1962–69 respectively. While they were both well received by the non-Sikh scholars, they are heavily influenced by colonialism, and they mostly use Christian language and terms to explain concepts in Sikhi that have no equivalency in Christianity.

Online translations of *SGGS* are available in English, including "Sikhi to the Max" and "iGurbani." Though they are useful tools, the user is advised to approach them with a significant degree of caution since these translations are not considered to be entirely accurate. Many of them repeat the errors of using Christian terminology and concepts that originate in other translations. Others oversimplify the *SGGS* and fail to capture the essence of Sikhi teachings. For example, the translation of the following line from Jap Ji Sahib "sochai soch na

---

[48]   See for example, the following passage from the preface to Trumpp's book: "The Sikh Granth is a very big volume, but as I have noted…incoherent and shallow in the extreme, and couched at the same time in dark and perplexing language in order to cover these defects." Ernest Trumpp, *The Adi Granth* (London, 1877), pg. vii.

hova-ee jay sochee lakh vaar" has been translated into English by many including Sant Singh Khalsa (srigurugranth.org) as "by thinking, He cannot be reduced to thought, even by thinking hundreds of thousands of times."[49] In contrast, Prof. Sahib Singh says that the word "soche" does not refer to "thinking" but rather the act of purification "sucha karna." Thus, Prof Sahib Singh translates this passage to "Ritualistic washing will not cleanse your soul, even if you do it a hundred thousand times."

To address the challenges faced by differing interpretations of Gurbani (riddled with numerous typographical errors), Guru Nanak Institute of Global Studies, a Canada based nonprofit educational institute (gurunanakinstitute.ca), has twenty-three Sikh scholars working on compiling one digitized compendium of fifteen translations to provide a single source for research scholars to compare existing translations.

60. Is any other type of music sung in a gurdwara besides keertan?

The focus of a gurdwara is to disseminate the teachings of the gurus. In addition to Gurbani keertan, most gurdwaras will also feature music from *dhadis* (bards). The dhadis explain Sikh history, teachings, and traditions through the performing of ballads. The ballads are usually original and performed through a mixture of discourse and signing.

Dhadis sing in a group of three or four, called a *dhadi jatha*. Dhadi jathas can be comprised of men and women. The leader of the jatha, the chief orator, explains the significance or

Bibi Parminder Kaur Khalsa Jatha

---

[49] iGurbani, a Gurbani search engine, has a similar translation as *Sant Singh Khalsa*. And sikhitothemax.com translates it as "Even if one bathes hundreds of thousands of times, the mind does not become cleansed."

relevance of the ballad. The ballad is then sung in stanzas by the other performers, and they sing and play traditional musical instruments. These consist of a *sarangi*, a bowed short-necked string instrument, and a *dhadd*, an hourglass-shaped drum. Both these folk instruments are native to Panjab.

61. What is the origin of dhadi vaars in Sikhi?

Guru Hargobind (1595–1644) fostered and promoted the art of singing ballads about Sikh warriors. During his guruship (1606–44), he transformed the tradition from one of singing the praises of landlords or rulers to singing the praises of Waheguru. Minstrels or bards called *dhadis* mainly emerged during this time, when Guru Hargobind, who had established the Sikh temporal court Akal Takhat, also put in place *dhadis* to sing the previously composed Gurbani from the *Sri Guru Granth Sahib*. The repertoire of contemporary *dhadis* has broadened to include ballads of Sikh history (*vaars*).[50]

The word *dhadi* appears several times in the *SGGS*; it means "humbleness." In his own compositions, Guru Nanak calls himself a *dhadi* of Waheguru. The word *dhadi* also appears in the writings of Bhagat Namdev, who lived in the thirteenth century. This would suggest that *dhadis* have more than a seven-hundred-year history.

62. What is a performer of poetry called in Sikhi?

A *kavishar* is someone who writes and sings poetry (*kavashari*). The title *kavishar* is a compound of two words, *kavi* and *shayar*, meaning, respectively, singer and writer. A *kavishar* does not use any musical instruments; instead, they sing a cappella. Their poetic lyrics and singing style form the basis of their dynamic performance. A group of three or four *kavishar* singing together is known as *kavashari jatha*. Guru Gobind

---

50   This information about *dhadis* relies on "Dhadi (Music)," Wikipedia, https://en.m.wikipedia.org/wiki/Dhadi_(music) (accessed June 2, 2019).

Singh, the tenth Guru, initiated the *kavashari* format to energize Sikhs, acquaint them with their history, and build confidence in turbulent times. Similar to *dhadis* and *dhadi jathas*, kavishari jathas perform in gurdwaras as well as in public forums called "Dhadi/Kavi Darbar," celebrating historical events.

63. Are non-Sikhs permitted to read the Sikh scripture?

There is no restriction for non-Sikhs to read the *SGGS*. Electronic copies are easily available on the internet for anyone wanting access. Physical copies can be accessed through any gurdwara. An interested person can read the *SGGS* in a separate room in the gurdwara or take a copy home and read at their own pace. However, a person who wishes to access or have a physical copy of the sacred *SGGS* must follow certain protocols. The *Sri Guru Granth Sahib* must be accorded proper respect. Shoes must be removed, the head must be covered, and one must wash their hands and feet before starting to read. This tradition is followed regardless of whether the *SGGS* is being read at home or at the gurdwara.

The *Rehat Maryada* prescribes that a person wanting to read the *SGGS* in a public gurdwara function must be a Sikh. This is important because of the sacred nature of the *SGGS* to the Sikhs and the important role that Gurdwaras play in providing role models for others.

64. Are there any bars to women reading the SGGS?

Women have equal status in the Sikh faith, and there is no bar to women reading the *SGGS* either privately or in a public gurdwara setting during a service. Some people, especially those who have been raised in India, believe that a woman should not read the *SGGS* during menstruation or after childbirth. Such a practice is against Sikh teachings and has arisen due to the influence of other faith traditions where menstruating women are ostracized.

Menstruation is a natural biological process that women experience for a significant part of their lives, but this natural process has led to cultural and religious purity-based taboos and constraints. According to the scholar and activist Janet Chawla, founding member of the nongovernmental organization Matrika, in many parts of India, "menstruation is still considered to be dirty and impure. The origin of this myth dates back to the Vedic times (1500–500 BCE) and has often been linked to Indra's slaying of Vritras. For it has been declared in the Veda that [the] guilt, of killing a brahmana-murder, appears every month as [the] menstrual flow as women had taken upon themselves a part of Indra's guilt."[51] Elias E. Mazokopakis quotes Mosaic Law (Leviticus 11:1—15:3), which states that a woman undergoing menstruation is perceived as unclean for seven days, and whoever touches her shall be unclean.[52] Mazokopakis claims, "Almost all major religions of the world have placed restrictions on menstruating women."

While Sikh women should enjoy equal access to the religion, some Sikh leaders are still using this unclean or polluted theory of other faiths to restrict women from performing *keertan* in Darbar Sahib (the Golden Temple), which is contrary to Guru Nanak's edict. Guru Nanak, the founder of Sikhi, stood alone in the fifteenth century to speak of gender equality, declaring women equal in status, power, and participation in all social and religious activities. In Sikhi, menstruation is not considered a pollutant or hindrance to performing religious duties, reading scripture, or participating in social activities. Guru Nanak condemns the practice of treating women as impure while menstruating or after childbirth. He says, "Impure are those who suck the blood of human beings."[53] Further, "The actions of those who do not meditate on Waheguru's name are polluted."[54]

---

[51]   Janet Chawla: "The Mythic Origins of the Menstrual Taboo in the Rig Veda," Matrika (1992), http://www.matrika-india.org/Research/MythicOrigins.html.

[52]   https://www.ncbi.nlm.nih.gov.

[53]   *SGGS* 140: jo rat peeveh maanasaa tin kiau nirmal cheet—ਜੋ ਰਤੁ ਪੀਵਹਿ ਮਾਣਸਾ ਤਿਨ ਕਿਉ ਨਿਰਮਲੁ ਚੀਤੁ॥

[54]   *SGGS*, M3, 229: man kaa sootak doojaa bahaau—ਮਨ ਕਾ ਸੂਤਕੁ ਦੂਜਾ ਭਾਉ॥

65. What is Sikhi's most significant architecture?

The Darbar Sahib, also called *Harmandar Sahib*, or the Golden Temple, is widely considered to be one of the most significant works of Sikh architecture. With some similarities to Mughal architecture, Darbar Sahib is the most striking example of the hybridity of Sikh art, bringing together the most prominent aspects of contemporary arts and architecture. The construction of Darbar Sahib was begun by Guru Arjan in 1581. To exemplify the Sikhi values of honouring the practitioners of all faith traditions, the foundation stone was laid not by a Sikh, but by a Muslim Sufi mystic Hazrat Mian Mir. The massive complex was completed in 1589. In 1604 Guru Arjan, named it Harmandar ("The Creator's Abode") when he placed the first handwritten copy of *Aad Granth* in the centre of the building. Since that time, the Darbar Sahib has become the centre of spiritual life to devotees of the Sikh faith. Accessed by a walkway that juts into the "Pool of Nectar," a stunning rectangular water feature around which the complex is built, the Golden Temple comes by its nickname honestly: its dome, splendid and awe-inspiring, is gilded with nearly a ton of gold.

Darbar Sahib continued to be called Harmandar until 1708, and the suffix Sahib was added by Sikhs after the gurus' times. The present-day gurdwara was rebuilt in 1764 by the leader Jassa Singh Ahluwalia with the help of other Sikh *misls* (sovereign states of the Sikh Confederacy). When Maharaja Ranjit Singh established the Sikh Empire in the early nineteenth century, he had the upper floors of the gurdwara covered with tons of gold leaf, which gives it its distinctive appearance. The British translated Harmandar as "Golden Temple," and thus the gurdwara became known by this name. Sikhs call it Darbar Sahib—not the Golden Temple.

The exterior is entirely covered with marble and several tons of gold leaf. The interior is covered with fresco paintings and detailed

Darbar Sahib Amritsar, Punjab,
photo taken by the author in 2018

designs inlaid with marble of varying textures, colours, and hues. The *SGGS* remains in the middle of the building, resting under a fully and gorgeously decorated *palki* (canopy), and attracts devotees and visitors. In addition to the spectacular architecture of Darbar Sahib, the layout of the *sarovar* (pool) and the architecture of the surrounding buildings are just as impressive.

In recent decades, there have been attempts to have the Darbar Sahib—and the entire complex within which it is housed—to be declared a UNESCO World Heritage Site. However, the Sikh community, including SGPC, opposed this designation because it would mean that the Sikhs would lose control over a place that has deep spiritual significance for them rather than just historical significance. In 2015, UNESCO finally put this issue to rest and confirmed that "there was no consideration or any application for considering adding the Sikhs' holiest shrine in the list."[55]

66. Is there such a thing as Sikh art?

Sikhi is the fifth largest organized religion in the world, with more than twenty-eight million adherents. Not surprisingly, then, during five hundred years of history, Sikhs have developed their own expressions of art and culture, which are influenced by Sikhi and adapt artistic styles Sikhs have been exposed to. Nikki-Guninder Kaur Singh wrote about Sikh art in *The Oxford Handbook of Sikh Studies*:

> Sikh art is aniconic, for it does not exhibit images of any deities, and even the pictures of the historical Gurus are not displayed in the presence of the sacred scripture. The symbol *IkOagkaar* shown below is used extensively by the Sikhs as a form of ornamentation in arts, crafts,

[55] Yudhvir Rana, May 1, 2015, article in the *Times of India* (timesofindia.com).

and architecture. It expresses Guru Nanak's theological construct of the One transcendent reality.[56]

Other Sikh art and literature, including illustrated *Birs* (volumes) of the *Sri Guru Granth Sahib* and Janamsakhis, span more than five centuries of the Sikh religion. From early paintings depicting the gurus' period to the dazzling treasures of the Sikh Empire (founded 1799), the romantic artwork of visiting European dignitaries, and the serenity of Sikh architecture, these creations provide a doorway to this heroic and revolutionary faith. Every country where Sikhs live has a Sikh art gallery.

Perhaps the most famous Sikh artist was Sobha Singh, a twentieth-century painter who created many of the iconic paintings of the Sikh gurus on display in many Sikh homes. Jarnail Singh, a renowned artist, has painted many frescos in Sikh gurdwaras and has an art gallery in Surrey, British Columbia. The Singh Twins (sisters Rabindra and Amrit Singh) are contemporary British artists who have won international acclaim for their work and have exhibitions of their art all over the world. Their paintings often draw on both the Sikh tradition and Western pop culture.

Many art galleries around the world display Sikh art. From the Victoria and Albert Museum in England to the Surrey Art Gallery in British Columbia, Sikh art has been exhibited in many curated collections. Virasat-e-Khalsa Museum at Anandpur Sahib, Punjab, is a prominent tourist attraction. On the topic of Sikh art, the American professor I. J. Singh wrote in 2012:

---

[56] Nikki-Gunider Kaur Singh, chap. 34, "Sikh Art," in *The Oxford Handbook of Sikh Studies*, edited by Louis E. Fenech and Pashaura Singh (New York: Oxford University Press, 2014).

We have taken another giant step in the art world that has rightly surpassed the calendar art that is so common in India. Since 1999, several quality exhibits on Sikh art have been mounted: a collection on Sikh immigrant history at the Wing Luke Asian Museum in Seattle, and excellent displays of art at the Victoria & Albert Museum in London, the Smithsonian in the capital city of the United States, San Francisco's Asian Art Museum, the Royal Ontario Museum in Toronto, and one that ran very successfully in 2008 at the Rubin Museum in New York.[57]

In Canada, we have a unique Sikh historical site, the Gur Sikh Temple [Gurdwara], in Abbotsford, British Columbia. This gurdwara, built in 1911, was designated a national historic site in 2011. We also have the Canadian Sikh Heritage Museum (CSHM) in Mississauga, Ontario. In 2018, the Canadian government provided a $380,000 grant to the CSHM to develop the Canadian Sikh Heritage Trail and a traveling Canadian Sikh timeline exhibition.

67. Why do some Sikhs bow before paintings of the Sikh gurus?

The custom of bowing before an artist's rendering of the likeness of a Sikh Guru is inconsistent with Sikh beliefs and practices. As a matter of record, Guru Nanak especially forbade his followers from performing any traditional worship rituals toward him. Guru Gobind Singh was equally clear and instructed Sikhs not to call him Lord and instead "treat him as a servant of Waheguru."[58]

For the gurus, what was important was to preserve their message and not their likeness. Their message is contained in their writings in

---

[57]   I. J. Singh, *Sikhs Today: Ideas and Opinions* (Ethnicisland.com, 2012), Kindle edition, location 1970.

[58]   *Dasam Bani* 57: mo ko daas tavan kaa jaano—ਮੋ ਕੋ ਦਾਸ ਤਵਨ ਕਾ ਜਾਨੋ॥

the *SGGS*. The paintings that we often see of the gurus on display in people's homes are largely nineteenth- and twentieth-century artistic renderings made through the imagination of an artist. They are not actual depictions of the gurus, who were against self-glorification and did not commission paintings of themselves. Sikhs believe that all humans are blessed with a "soul" that can connect and communicate with the Supreme Soul, the Creator. "Your soul and the Supreme Soul become one, when the duality of the inner mind is overcome," says Guru Nanak.[59] Sikhs are required to reflect on sabads from *SGGS* and not on any person, figure, idol, or photograph.

Society, however, holds holy people in high esteem and strives to learn from the messages delivered by them and the righteous lives lived by them. Many Sikh homes have paintings of the gurus. Some Sikhs will adorn these images, place incense before them, bow before them, or touch the image before embarking on tasks. Whatever the reasoning may be, these practices are against Sikhi's philosophy and teachings. It is also inconsistent with Sikhi to give them a place of prominence in gurdwaras since this may further confuse Sikh congregations. The worship of images and idols—as well as the practice of rituals for one's material gain or to harm another—is spoken against in *SGGS*. It leads to the opposite of what a Sikh is trying to achieve through *simran*. Satish Dhillon writes, "When we worship God it is not necessary to deify pictures or statues. By doing this we are not worshipping God, because God is formless."[60]

68. Do Sikhs have a tradition of martial arts?

The simple answer is yes. The Sikh martial art is called *Gatka* or *Gatakbazi*. According to the scholar Kahn Singh Nabha (1999:38), *gatka* dates to the time of the gurus (1469–1708).

---

[59] *SGGS* 661: aatmaa paraatmaa eko karai—ਆਤਮਾ ਪਰਾਤਮਾ ਏਕੋ ਕਰੈ ॥ ਅੰਤਰ ਕੀ ਦੁਬਿਧਾ ਅੰਤਰਿ ਮਰੈ॥

[60] Dhillon, Harish. *The Sikh Gurus*. Hay House. Kindle edition, location 77.

Traditionally, it is believed that the gurus taught its theory and techniques. It has been handed down the unbroken lineage of *ustads* (teachers) and taught in many *akharas* (arenas) around the world [Kahn Singh Nabha, 1999:38].

The word *gatka* is derived from the Sanskrit root *satayas* or motion, but the Panjabi word *gatka* refers typically to the wooden stick utilized for the practice. Gatka is a style of stick fighting during which wooden

2019 Vaisakhi Nagar Keetan Gatka Team

sticks are intended to simulate swords used in training.[61] However, gatka can also include a wide variety of materials, such as metal swords or chakars. The chakar is a circular disk with a handle in the middle. The outer edges of the disk have chains like a web with iron or plastic balls at the end of each chain. It looks beautiful when rotated rhythmically. Nabha describes a *gatka* as a three-hand-span stick (with a basket hilt) that is used to teach the first part of *gada yudh* (club fighting). The *gatka* is held in the right hand, and a *phari* (small shield) is held in the left, and two people spar against each other.

Gatka continues to be a favourite martial art among Sikh youth around the world. You can witness this in every Nagar Keertan and other religious festivals.

69. What are the folk dances of Panjab?

Devotional dancing is not a part of the Sikh faith, which emphasizes inner devotion through love. However, the Panjabi culture has a rich tradition of folk dancing, and specific cultural dances originate from this region and are meant for social occasions or festivals. Though they

---

[61]   Kahn Singh Nabha (1999), 395.

have no religious significance, these dances are important aspects of Panjabi Sikh culture. Dances have been part of many ceremonies, rituals, celebrations, and entertainment since the dawn of the earliest human civilizations. Many present-day dance forms can be traced back to the ancient period's old-fashioned ceremonial and ethnic dances.

There are several folk dances of Punjab, but two have gained international prominence:

- *Bhangra:* Iqbal Singh Dhillon writes in *Folk Dances of Panjab*: "Like many other cultural folk dances, Bhangra is an energetic folk dance and music form that originated in Punjab, long before the partition of India and Pakistan. Today, it's the newest dance, music, and fitness phenomenon spreading all over the world. Bhangra has made its way to America's Got Talent, the London Olympics, and even the White House and the Canadian Parliament."[62] While bhangra used to be the exclusive dance of men, in recent decades, it has been embraced by Panjabi women, who participate in either all female or mixed-gender teams. One of the primary musical instruments of *bhangra* is the *dhol* (see photo), an oval-shaped drum played with bamboo sticks from both sides. Although many new musical instruments have been introduced into *bhangra*, the *dhol* remains the central feature.
- *Giddha:* This is a popular Panjabi folk dance performed by women that exhibits teasing, fun, and the exuberance of Panjabi life. Derived from the ancient ring dance, *giddha* is just as energetic as *bhangra*. At the same time, it manages to creatively display feminine grace, elegance, and elasticity. *Giddha* is generally danced either in circles, or within a circle. The women or girls form a ring. Seated inside the ring is a dancer who plays the *dholki* (see photo), a smaller version of the *dhol*,

---

[62] Iqbal Singh Dhillon, *Folk Dances of Panjab* (National Book Shop, 1998).

which is played by hand, not with sticks. The dancers often work in pairs, clapping their hands to produce a rhythm, and they sing couplets called *boliyan*, which represent folk poetry.

70. Are some Sikh customs just superstitions?

It is human nature to fall prey to superstitions, says Colonel Gurnam Singh, a psychiatrist. "There are many factors that are responsible—cultural and family learning, anxiety related to the important things of life, fear about the untoward, and basically the fact that everything in life is not in our control."[63]

But let me make it perfectly clear that Sikh religious philosophy does not believe in superstitions. "Let understanding be the anvil and spiritual wisdom the tool," says Guru Nanak.[64] However, due to the cultural influence of other communities in India, Sikhs have adopted some customs that are purely superstitious. The diaspora Sikhs living in the Western Hemisphere are no exception. They are caught up in the web of society's superstitious customs.

To give one example, some Sikhs look for "auspicious" days. Guru Amar Das, the third Guru of the Sikhs, addressed this question:

> Everything happens by Waheguru's Will. Concerns with omens and some days are better than others, lead one to duality. Without the True Guru, there is only pitch darkness. Only morons and fools worry about those omens and days (good or bad); those imbued with faith in God obtain understanding and realization.[65]

In another instance, many Sikhs, even some born in Canada or the United States, following the Hindu custom of tying a red "protection"

---

[63] Col. Gurnam Singh, blog posting; speekingtree.in.

[64] SGGS 8: bhau khalaa agan tap taau. ਭਉ ਖਲਾ ਅਗਨਿ ਤਪ ਤਾਉ ॥

[65] SGGS 843: aape pooraa kare su hoi. eh thitee vaar dhoojaa dhoi. ਆਪੇ ਪੂਰਾ ਕਰੇ ਸੁ ਹੋਇ ॥ ਏਹਿ ਥਿਤੀ ਦੂਜਾ ਦੋਇ ॥

thread on their wrist, called *kalava* or *mauli*. Ask any one of them, and the answer would be the same: "It is a ritual, and my parents or siblings asked me to wear it."

71. What is kalava?

Kalava is the sacred Hindu thread, which is also called *mauli* or *charade* in Hindi (and sometimes *Raksha)*. It is tied by a Hindu priest or an older family member, typically grandparents or parents, on the wrists of all the people attending the prayer ceremony. The *kalava* is tied on the right wrist of men and unmarried women and on the left wrist of married women. Red cotton strings are most common—as is red with small bits of yellow—but other dye combinations exist. This thread sometimes has knots that are tied while reciting sacred mantras to invoke the *satvik* (virtuous) state of human nature.

The *kalava* is worn to protect its wearer from evil. A stylized form of the *kalava* has become common for *rakhi* or *rakhri,* as Punjabis call it, when a sister ties this thread on her brother's wrist to ward off evil and seek protection. Sadly, India, a country that is a hub of rituals and superstitions to ward off evil, is unable as a society to protect women from real harm. A recent survey by the Thomson Reuters Foundation of 550 experts on women's issues found "India to be the most dangerous nation for sexual violence against women, as well as human trafficking for domestic work, forced labor, forced marriage and sexual slavery, among other reasons."[66] Superstitious rituals such as *kalava* have no place in Sikhi, though they might hold meaning for the persons who follow them.

---

[66] Angela Dewan, "India the Most Dangerous Country to Be a Woman, US Ranks 10th in Survey," CNN, June 26, 2018, para. 2, https://www.cnn.com/2018/06/25/health/india-dangerous-country-women-survey-intl/index.html.

CHAPTER 10

Men, Women, and Sexuality

This chapter endeavours to address some of the questions surrounding gender and sexuality in the Sikh faith. Tragically, inequality between men and women has existed for ages. There was a time when men produced all knowledgeable material and textbooks for men. This was true from the physical and social sciences to the canons of music and literature.

Professor Catherine Littleton (University of California) argued in 1987 that women's biological and cultural differences from men, regardless of whether they are "natural" or constructed, are real and significant.[67] Women's inequality, she contended, results when society devalues women because they differ from the male norm.

Although there are physiological differences between males and females, the Sikh faith teaches that, in essence, both sexes are created equal and carry the same light (*jot*), thus possessing a corresponding right to lead an independent, fulfilling life and cultivate their spirituality. Sikh doctrine and ethics are clear on the equality of men and women before Waheguru. On that basis, according to Sikhi, everyone should have equal access to every level of privilege, leadership, and responsibility regardless of their gender or sexuality.

---

[67] Catherine A Littleton: "Restructuring Sexual Equality" (1987), California Law Review [vol. 75:1279]

72. Are women equal to men in the Sikh faith?

Sikhi not only supports gender equality but also actively encourages it through numerous institutions and social structures implemented over the two-hundred-year development of the Sikh faith. Guru Nanak's first public stance against gender inequality occurred when he was eleven years old. During a religious ceremony marking a Hindu rite of passage, the young Nanak refused to wear a sacred thread *(janeu)* that would initiate him into the Hindu religion. When he questioned why his older sister, Nanaki, was not entitled to wear one, he was told it was reserved only for boys of higher castes. Gender discrimination and the stratification of humankind into high and low was not acceptable to Guru Nanak. Guru Nanak's stance against gender discrimination also resulted in his condemnation of female infanticide, widow burning (sati), the giving of a dowry, and the veiling of women in the presence of men. Guru cautions women "to not immolate 'sati' on their husband's pyres, instead immerse in Waheguru's name to become true Sati."[68] Using a bride's metaphor, Guru defines dowry in another sabad and says, "O my father, bless me with Waheguru's Name as my wedding gift and dowry, rather than material things."[69]

Sikhs widely accept that Guru Nanak's sister, Bebe Nanaki, was the first Sikh. She is portrayed through Sikh lore as an intelligent and insightful woman who inspired and guided Guru Nanak throughout his life. Sikh *sakhis* (life stories of gurus) are filled with the names of other powerful women who exemplified Sikhi values.

The *SGGS* emphasizes gender equality and the importance of women to the entire social order. Sikh religious practices actively encourage the participation of women. The Sikh gurus were precise that men and women—in fact, all human beings—irrespective of caste, religious

---

[68] *SGGS* 787: Slok Mahala 3. Satian eh na aakhian jo maRiaa lag jala (n) ni (h). Nanak satian jaanian birhe chot maranh. ਸਲੋਕੁ ਮਃ ੩ ॥ ਸਤੀਆ ਏਹਿ ਨ ਆਖੀਅਨਿ ਜੋ ਮੜਿਆ ਲਗਿ ਜਲੰਨ੍ਹਿ ॥ ਨਾਨਕ ਸਤੀਆ ਜਾਣੀਅਨ੍ਹਿ ਜਿ ਬਿਰਹੇ ਚੋਟ ਮਰੰਨ੍ਹਿ ॥

[69] *SGGS* 7੮: Siriraag Mahala 4. Har prabh mere babula har devoh daan mai daajo. Har kapro har sobha devo jit savray mera kaajo. ਸਿਰੀਰਾਗੁ ਮਹਲਾ ੪ ॥ ਹਰਿ ਪ੍ਰਭ ਮੇਰੇ ਬਾਬੁਲਾ ਹਰਿ ਦੇਵਹੁ ਦਾਨੁ ਮੈ ਦਾਜੋ ॥ ਹਰਿ ਕਪੜੇ ਹਰਿ ਸੋਭਾ ਦੇਵਹੁ ਜਿਤੁ ਸਵਰੈ ਮੇਰਾ ਕਾਜੋ ॥

belief, and social status, are born equal and have the same rights and responsibilities.

73. What does Gurbani say about gender equality?

The concept of gender equality is enshrined in the sacred teachings of the gurus and appears throughout the *Sri Guru Granth Sahib*. Guru Nanak reminds Sikhs in one composition found in the "Aasa ki Vaar," (Ballad of Hope) that:

> Through woman, man is born; within woman, man is conceived, and to the woman, he is engaged and married. A woman is befriended, and by a woman, the civilization is continued. When a woman (his wife or partner) dies, he seeks another woman. It is by a woman that the entire social order is maintained. Then why call her evil of whom are great men born? From woman, a woman is born; without woman, there would be no one at all. O Nanak, only the Creator, is without a woman.[70]

It is also noteworthy that the only living person who was not a Guru or a contributor to the *bani* (spiritual writings), specifically mentioned in the *Sri Guru Granth Sahib*, is Mata Khivi. She was the wife of Guru Angad, the second Guru, and implemented the *langar* (free kitchen) that is at the heart of every gurdwara. Balwand, one of the four Sikhs whose mystical poetry has been included in *Sri Guru Granth Sahib*, says, "Khivi, the Guru's wife, is a noblewoman, who gives soothing, leafy shade to all. She

---

[70]   *SGGS* 473: bhand jameeaai bhand nimeeaai bhand mangan veeaahu. Bhandahu hovai dostee bhandho bhando chalai raahu. Bhand muaa bhand bhaaleeaai bhand hovai bandhaan. So kiau mandha aakheeaai jit jameh raajaan. Bhandahu he bhand upjai bhandai baajh na koi. Nanak bhandhai baahraa eko sachaa soi— ਭੰਡਿ ਜੰਮੀਐ ਭੰਡਿ ਨਿੰ ਮੀਐ ਭੰਡਿ ਮੰਗਣੁ ਵੀਆਹੁ ॥ ਭੰਡਹੁ ਹੋਵੈ ਦੋਸਤੀ ਭੰਡਹੁ ਚਲੈ ਰਾਹੁ ॥ ਭੰਡੁ ਮੂਆ ਭੰਡੁ ਭਾਲੀਐ ਭੰਡਿ ਹੋਵੈ ਬੰਧਾਨ ॥ ਸੋ ਕਿਉ ਮੰਦਾ ਆਖੀਐ ਜਿਤੁ ਜੰਮਹਿ ਰਾਜਾਨ ॥ ਭੰਡਹੁ ਹੀ ਭੰਡੁ ਉਪਜੈ ਭੰਡੈ ਬਾਝੁ ਨ ਕੋਇ ॥ ਨਾਨਕ ਭੰਡੈ ਬਾਹਰਾ ਏਕੋ ਸਚਾ ਸੋਇ॥

distributes the bounty of the Guru's langar—the kheer, the rice pudding, and *ghee* (butter) are like sweet ambrosia."[71]

74. How did the gurus practice gender quality?

The Sikh gurus are clear about gender equality: all genders have the same divine light within; in the eyes of the Creator, they are equal. The Sikh gurus rejected the subordination of women and introduced several revolutionary social reforms. These social reforms were designed to "walk the talk." The gurus taught that women were no different from men in their ability to have a relationship with Waheguru and therefore had the same right to participate in and lead congregations.

The practice of sati, where widows were compelled to immolate themselves on their husband's pyres, was condemned and rejected by the Sikh gurus. The social practice of killing baby girls at birth because of a preference for boys was deemed deplorable. Later, Guru Amar Das, the third Sikh Guru, appointed women as religious leaders to head *manjis*.[72] As mentioned earlier, the gurus dismissed the idea that women were impure during menstruation as an untenable myth. Enshrined in the Sikh code of ethics is the specific denunciation and social shunning of those who continue this practice.

Both genders share the same rights and obligations in the Sikh faith. The amrit sanchar (Sikh initiation) was offered by Guru Gobind Singh to both men and women, and they equally wear the Sikh articles of faith. The first initiation ceremony involved the active participation of Guru Gobind Singh's wife, Mata Jeeto (Ajeet Kaur), who helped prepare the sweet nectar that was given to each initiate. Guru Gobind Singh, Mata Ajeet Kaur, and the Guru's mother, Mata Gujar Kaur (Gujri), all took amrit from the panj pyare after they had become Khalsa. Mata Ajeet

---

[71] *SGGS 967*: Balwand khivi nek jan jis bahutee chhaau patraalee. Langar daulat vandeeai ras amrit kheer ghiaalee—ਬਲਵੰਡ ਖੀਵੀ ਨੇਕ ਜਨ ਜਿਸੁ ਬਹੁਤੀ ਛਾਉ ਪਤ੍ਰਾਲੀ ॥ ਲੰ ਗਰਿ ਦਉਲਤਿ ਵੰਡੀਐ ਰਸੁ ਅੰਮ੍ਰਿਤੁ ਖੀਰਿ ਘਿਆਲੀ ॥

[72] Goindwal De Sunaihree Patray Soochi (ਗੋਇੰਦਵਾਲ ਦੇ ਸੁਨਹਿਰੀ ਪਤਰੇ ਸੂਚੀ): Matho Murari (Lahore), Mai Sevan (Kabul), and Mai Bhago (Kashmir).

Kaur took the last name Kaur, rather than her husband, Guru Gobind Singh's, name (Singh), further emphasizing her individuality and distinct personality. Guru Gobind Singh also had immense respect for women in the battlefield. Mai Bhag Kaur, known affectionately as Mai Bhago, became one of Guru Gobind Singh's bodyguards and also served as a general in his army. On December 29, 1705, when the Mughal army ambushed Guru Gobind Singh at Khidrana/Mukstar, Mai Bhag Kaur was appointed to lead the Khalsa army into the battlefield.

In the years following the joti jot of Guru Gobind Singh, Sikh women continued to play important leadership roles. Sahib Kaur (1771–1801) became prime minister of the Patiala State in 1793 and fought against the forces of George Thomas, forcing him to withdraw from Jind, a town in northern India. Maharani Jind Kaur (1817–1863) was regent of the Sikh Empire from 1843 until 1846. Her granddaughter, Princess Bamba Sophia Duleep Kaur Singh (1869–1957), was a well-known leader of the suffragette movement in Britain and a passionate advocate for self-rule and independence from colonial rule. More recently, Inderjit Kaur (1923–2022) became the first female vice chancellor of a Northern Indian university, serving at the Panjabi University in Patiala.

75. Do modern-day Sikhs practice gender equality?

In 1945, the Sikh community adopted the *Rehat Maryada* (code of conduct) to help regulate Sikh temporal life. The document is a remarkably forward thinking one, and it is informed by the Sikh values of gender equality. The gurus' vision of complete equality between men and women was well ahead of their time. Women were appointed as spiritual and social leaders, heading both *manjis* (similar to dioceses) and armies. However, modern Sikh women have had to struggle to regain the respect afforded them by the Sikh gurus.

In 1999, Bibi Jagir Kaur, a controversial person, was chosen to head the Shiromani Gurudwara Parbandhak Committee (Supreme Gurdwara Management Committee, or SGPC). She served in that role in 1999–2000, 2004–2005, and 2020–2021). Ironically, women are still not permitted to perform keertan in Darbar Sahib (Golden Temple). Notably, too, none of the Akal Takhat jathedars have been women, and it is rare to see a woman serving as part of the panj payare. Similarly, though the role of a granthi is open to men and women, it is rare to find a woman serving in that capacity. Despite gurdwara executive positions being available to women—and some committees openly recruiting women to sit on them—men dominate virtually all executive committees.

Sadly, modern-day Sikhs have failed to "walk the talk" and to live up to the ideals of gender equality that were role-modeled by the gurus. Panjabi culture, to which many Sikhs ascribe, remains patriarchal and male-oriented. Men dominate the political, academic, and religious scenes, and women are often relegated to background roles. Tragically, the harmful practices the gurus denounced centuries ago, such as female infanticide, the dowry, and intimate partner violence, continue to plague the Sikh community. It is undeniable that despite Sikhi teachings advocating complete gender equality, the Sikh community has failed to put these ideals fully into practice. The obligation remains on every Sikh to translate these essential social mores into our reality so that our wives, daughters, sisters, and mothers can live their lives to the fullest.

76. What is the Sikh view on women's face coverings?

During Guru Nanak's time, women from both the Hindu and Muslim faith traditions veiled their faces in the presence of men as a sign of deference, respect, and humility. The practice of *pardah* acted to subjugate women, severely limited women's mobility, and restricted them mainly to the home. Guru Nanak rejected the notion that men were superior to women, and he enjoined women to remove their veils as a display of their independence and autonomy. The dastaar became the outward expression of this belief in gender equality and the supremacy of the Divine Creator before whom all are equal. The Sikh tradition of males and females covering their unshorn hair with a dastaar or other head covering (such as a *chunni* or scarf) is an expression of gender equality. It goes hand in hand with the lifting of the *pardah* (veil covering the face), which women were forced to wear by social customs that demanded their subservience to men.

The Sikh code of conduct states, "It is not proper for a Sikh woman to wear a veil or keep her face hidden by veil or cover."[73]

77. Do we walk the talk? What is Sikhi's perspective on celibacy?

Sikhi does not teach celibacy as a way of achieving spiritual enlightenment. Instead, living a family life is encouraged. The *SGGS* teaches that to nurture one's spiritual relationship with Waheguru, one does not have to run away from family life. Instead, one needs to control lust, anger, greed, emotional attachments, and ego, which are the impediments to spiritual growth and a relationship with Waheguru. The ego is the biggest of all hurdles, and Guru Arjan cautions, "The celibate practices celibacy, but his heart is filled with ego."[74]

During his travels, Guru Nanak went to many spiritual centres. He confronted priests and talked them out of blind rituals in favour of an honest longing for the Creator. In one of his dialogues with Hindu yogis (ascetics), he was told that to complete his spiritual journey, he must renounce the world. To this, Guru Nanak replied, "You [yogis] have not renounced the world. Instead, you have run away from life. The world is on fire, and you have the knowledge to put it out. What kind of spirituality is this that leaves humanity to suffer? Renounce the world while being in it; that is what is intended for us by our Creator."[75]

The gurus elevated the marriage relationship to the level of spiritual practice. It is the practice of becoming one soul in two bodies and taking two individuals of their own distinct identities, working together to become one mind, one spirit, and one thought. Sex is part of Waheguru's creative power and should be enjoyed within the confines of a respectful

---

[73] *Sikh Rehat Maryada* (code of conduct), article 17.

[74] *SGGS* 1002: brahamchaar brahamchaj keenaa hiradhai bhiaa gumaanaa— ਬ੍ਰਹਮਚਾਰਿ ਬ੍ਰਹਮਚਜੁ ਕੀਨਾ ਹਿਰਦੈ ਭਇਆ ਗੁਮਾਨਾ॥

[75] *SGGS* 938–46: "Siddh Gost" ਸਿਧ ਗੋਸਟਿ ॥

and monogamous relationship. It should be experienced in a way that honours the sacred relationship between individuals.

Sikhs consider sex within marriage a natural expression of love and intimacy. Together, the couple expresses love and respect for each other, which helps them grow spiritually. The Sikh code of conduct denounces adultery. Extramarital relationships are considered a hindrance to the spiritual practice of the unity of two souls. Trust is the foundation of a happy marriage. Adultery and unfaithfulness to one's partner break that trust. Without an honest and sincere commitment to each other, it is impossible to become one soul from two, as advocated by the gurus.

Promiscuity and premarital relationships are also not condoned in Sikhi. Guru Amar Das says, "You may enjoy the pleasure of hundreds of women and rule the nine continents of the world. This shall not give you peace of mind, and you shall suffer in the pain of the cycle of continued transmigration repeatedly. Without following the spiritual and ethical teachings of the gurus, you will not find peace."[76]

However, enjoyment does not mean excessive indulgence. The downside of sexual energy comes in the form of lust (*kaam*). Like all major religions, the Sikh faith teaches that lust is a poison that clouds a person's mind. Unbridled sexual desire is considered a hindrance to achieving spiritual enlightenment. Like the other vices, such as anger, greed, attachment, and ego, one must learn to control one's sexual desires. This is where the significance of the Sikh articles of faith comes into play. One of the five articles of faith worn by an amritdhari Sikh is the *kashera*. The kashera is a loose-fitting pair of cotton underwear. The Sikh is reminded of their commitment to overcoming lust and honouring their vows and commitment to their life partner by wearing these every day.

---

[76] *SGGS* 26: je lakh istarian bhog karae nav khand kamaahe. ਜੇ ਲਖ ਇਸਤਰੀਆ ਭੋਗ ਕਰਹਿ ਨਵ ਖੰਡ ਰਾਜਿ ਕਮਾਹਿ ॥

78. What is the Sikh view on dating?

Though not traditionally practiced, dating has become much more common in the Sikh community. The discussion around dating is complicated—with many contentious areas when you start to examine it. While the term has many meanings, the most common refers to a trial period in which two people explore whether to take the relationship further toward a more permanent relationship called marriage. The dating concept is a twentieth-century phenomenon that has taken many shapes over the past hundred years. The new digital age has offered people dating apps.

Freedom of conscience and association are fundamental to Sikhi. Two people meeting to dialogue and assess compatibility for a lifelong relationship is not contrary to Sikh teachings. However, premarital cohabitation and a sexual relationship before marriage are not condoned. Marriage for a Sikh is a human journey that leads to self-discovery and guides us to understand who we are, what we are here for, what the purpose of life is, and finally how, by being together, two people can spiritually grow to connect with the Divine. The consummation of a relationship is considered sacred, and the community generally considers this to be something preserved for marriage.

79. What is the Sikh attitude on using beauty enhancement products or wearing jewelry?

As with many other topics relating to matters of personal choice, there is no consensus in the Sikh community on the wearing of jewelry or makeup. The cosmetic industry is edging close to a trillion-dollar business.[77] Sikh women (and, more recently, Sikh men) are as caught up in the artificial beauty web as other members of other communities.

The Sikh faith empowers women to make their own decisions. Concerning beauty, the *SGGS* does not condone egoism or excess

---

[77] loudcloudhealth.com.

ornamentation. Guru Nanak emphasizes inner beauty, and says, "Your mind is like a pearl, and make every breath your thread to string it. Having compassion in your heart will make qualities dwell in your heart, where Waheguru's name can reside."[78] In another verse, the Guru says, "The pleasures of fancy clothes and jewelry are false; why wear something [makeup] that ruins your body and gives rise to self-pity and imperfection or deterioration?"[79] Guru's teachings on this issue are directed toward the empowerment of women.

Sikhi is a way of life, and we are each at our own stage of life, hopefully, with the grace of God, improving day by day. Guru Amar Das sums up the Sikh attitude toward body ornaments beautifully: "Decorate yourself with the decorations that will never stain or fade and love the Lord day and night."[80]

Whether or not to wear makeup or jewelry is a choice that each person must make for themselves. The real question is not whether to wear makeup, but why a person (usually a girl or woman) may decide to do so. Insofar as she feels compelled to conform to social expectations of beauty, one must question the morals of a society that insists on placing greater value on how women look than on what they think or can do with their bodies. We must teach our daughters and sons to be proud of who they are and to feel comfortable in their own skin.

80. What is the Sikh faith's position on tattoos and body piercing?

Among uninitiated Panjabi Sikhs, nose and ear piercings are very common. As a reflection of the view that the human body is perfectly

---

[78] *SGGS* 359: man motee je gahanaa hovai paun hovai soot dhaaree—ਮਨੁ ਮੋਤੀ ਜੇ ਗਹਣਾ ਹੋਵੈ ਪਉਣੁ ਹੋਵੈ ਸੂਤ ਧਾਰੀ॥

[79] *SGGS* 16: baba jor khaanaa khusee khuaar. Jit khaadai tan peeReeaai man meh chaleh vikaar -ਬਾਬਾ ਹੋਰੁ ਪੈਨਣੁ ਖੁਸੀ ਖੁਆਰੁ ॥ ਜਿਤੁ ਪੈਧੈ ਤਨੁ ਪੀੜੀਐ ਮਨ ਮਹਿ ਚਲਹਿ ਵਿਕਾਰ ॥

[80] SGGS 785: aaisaa seegaar banai too mailaa kadhe na hoviee ahinis laagai bhaau—ਐਸਾ ਸੀਗਾਰੁ ਬਣਾਇ ਤੂ ਮੈਲਾ ਕਦੇ ਨ ਹੋਵਈ ਅਹਿਨਿਸਿ ਲਾਗੈ ਭਾਉ ॥

created and does not need enhancement, the Sikh code of conduct prohibits men and women alike from piercing their ears and noses.[81] At the time of the amrit sanchar ceremony, if the initiate is wearing a nose ring or earrings, they are asked to remove them. Most initiated Sikhs continue that practice and do not wear earrings or nose rings.

The earliest known evidence of tattooing was found on a mummified human body, about 5,300 years old, which was discovered in the Alps in 1991.[82] The history of nose piercing dates back some four thousand years in the Middle East. This practice was brought to India in the sixteenth century by the Mughals.[83] Ear piercing history traces back to Australia about five thousand years ago. Though these practices have strong cultural roots, there is no spiritual significance to them.

According to the Sikh code of conduct, tattoos and piercings are not permitted for Sikhs.[84] Many Sikhs who have piercings or tattoos have them because of cultural influences, but not by religious tradition. Tattoos served another function among the Panjabi community. Many Sikhs from the older generation (born in the early 1900s) would tattoo their names and/or the IkOngkaar symbol [ੴ] onto their forearms or the back of their palms. The tattooing of the name became a popular practice during Partition, when thousands of Sikhs were slaughtered as they were forced out of their homes in what is now called Pakistan. Many of these Sikhs were thrown in caravans. The practice of putting the name on the forearm was intended as an easy way of identifying the deceased, and the IkOngkaar indicated that they were a Sikh and should be cremated according to Sikh funeral rites.

---

[81] *Sikh Rehat Maryada*, sec. 16(k).

[82] William T. Kirby, "Tattoo Removal," in *Lasers and Energy Devices for the Skin*, 2nd ed., ed. Michael P. Goldman, Richard E. Fitzpatrick, E. Victor Ross, Suzanne L. Kilmer, and Robert E. Weiss (Boca Raton, FL: CRC Press, 2013), 74.

[83] Laura, "History of Body Piercings," Painful Pleasures, October 7, 2013, https://info.painfulpleasures.com.

[84] *Sikh Rehat Maryada*, sec. 16.

81. What are Sikh views on modesty?

The *SGGS* uses the term *nimrata* to discuss modesty. The importance of modesty is described in the Sikh scripture: "Modesty and righteousness both, O Nanak, are qualities of those who are blessed with true spiritual wealth."[85] In many cultures, the word *modesty* has been almost exclusively attached to women's dress. Similarly, there are many Sikhs who also cannot think past that. However, according to Sikhi, modesty is required equally of men and women. Modesty is the offspring of humility. The two words that define modesty for Sikhs are *nimrata*, one of the five virtues, and *saadgi*. Concerning *nimrata*, Guru Nanak dictates, "Sweetness and humility, O Nanak, are the essence of virtue and goodness."[86] In Sikhi, as I have explained, no distinction or limitation is made based on one's gender.

Guru Nanak talks of broader guidelines on the appropriateness of clothes. He says, "Oh my friend! Wearing clothes that provoke mistaken desires should be avoided—as they lead us to momentarily false pleasures and end up causing pain and ruining our lives."[87] The Sikh code of conduct does not restrict how Sikhs dress, except that they must wear *kashera* (drawer-type, cotton tie-able underwear) and a turban. A Sikh woman may or may not tie a turban. Women have the option of covering their heads with a scarf instead of a turban.[88]

---

[85]   *SGGS* 1287: saram dharam dhui naanakaa je dhan palai pai—ਸਰਮੁ ਧਰਮੁ ਦੁਇ ਨਾਨਕਾ ਜੇ ਧਨੁ ਪਲੈ ਪਾਇ॥

[86]   *SGGS* 470: moThat neevee naanakaa gun cha(n)giaaieeaa tat—ਮਿਠਤਿ ਨੀਵੀ ਨਾਨਕਾ ਗੁਣ ਚੰਗਿਆਈਆ ਤਤੁ॥

[87]   *SGGS* 16: baabaa hor painan khusee khuaar. Jit paidhai tan peeReeaai man meh chale vikaar—ਬਾਬਾ ਹੋਰੁ ਪੈਨਣੁ ਖੁਸੀ ਖੁਆਰ ॥ ਜਿਤੁ ਪੈਧੈ ਤਨੁ ਪੀੜੀਐ ਮਨ ਮਹਿ ਚਲਹਿ ਵਿਕਾਰ ॥

[88]   *Sikh Rehat Maryada*, article 16(t).

CHAPTER 11

The Sikh Wedding

Marriage is an important rite of passage in most cultures. For Sikhs, marriage is considered a crucial step on the spiritual journey, which helps unite two bodies into one soul, so that each partner can ultimately merge with the Divine. This chapter addresses the cultural, social, and religious aspects of Sikh marriage. Some of the ceremonies and practices explained have no direct bearings on Sikh matrimony. Still, they are highlighted to help you understand their historical background and how cultural traditions of the host country might find their way into Sikh practices.

82. What is the purpose of marriage in Sikhi?

The marriage ceremony, called the *Anand Karaj* (meaning "mystical experience," "spiritual bliss," "blissful union," or a "state of happiness") is a metaphor for life, the human journey, and self-discovery. As its name suggests, the Sikh wedding ceremony is a sacred occasion, where two persons create a lifelong bond born of mutual respect. It is considered a crucial step toward attaining the heights of worldly joy and spiritual bliss. It is a vehicle for the unity of mind and soul. It is a means to achieve spirituality and not an end in and of itself. The goal of marriage in Sikhi is the blissful union of both souls with Waheguru, the Creator. Marriage is a vehicle that carries us together to the highest form of love: the love for the Divine.

The Sikh marriage tradition has evolved since Guru Nanak's time. Guru Nanak introduced the original form of the Sikh wedding ceremony in 1487 when he refused to marry by the ancient Hindu rites (the Vedic marriage ritual) of circumambulating a fire. Instead, he wrote the *Mool Mantar* (original utterance) of *SGGS* on a piece of paper, placed the paper on a stool, and went around it four times with his wife while reciting the *Mool Mantar*. However, after Guru Amar Das composed "Anand Sahib"[89] (Song of Joy), this bani was used for solemnizing marriages. The practice became to recite the Anand Sahib, followed by *ardaas*, supplication or prayer.

The modern Sikh marriage is solemnized by the reading of the *lavaan* (vows), which were composed by Guru Ram Das. The *lavaan* remind a couple of their responsibilities and obligations to each other, to their families, to their community, and to the Divine Source. They focus on a spiritual union where both partners agree to walk the temporal and spiritual path together to achieve the ultimate goal of unity with the Creator.

83. Is there an appropriate age for marriage?

The Sikh faith does not set an age for marriage. However, recognizing that child marriage was a common practice within Panjabi society, the Sikh code of conduct expressly prohibits child marriage. It states that a wedding should take place only when an individual is "physically, emotionally, and by the maturity of character, suitable. Child marriage is therefore completely forbidden and taboo for Sikhs."[90]

The trend in the Sikh community mirrors that seen in Canadian society: young Sikhs are generally waiting longer to get married. Although some individuals may mature and be ready for marriage at a younger age, the current trend is for partners to hold off until they complete their educations and are financially secure. These are, however, individual choices based on sociocultural factors rather than religious

---

[89]   The bani is actually called "Anand." Sikhs often attach the suffix "Sahib" as a sign of respect.
[90]   *Sikh Rehat Maryada*, chapter XI, article XVIII.

doctrine. Whether and when to get married is a profoundly personal life decision, and individuals have the freedom to choose what is right for them and whom they marry.

84. Do Sikhs have arranged marriages?

The Sikh faith does not proscribe a particular method by which the couple is introduced to each other. The term *arranged marriage* refers to a practice that used to be very common in the Indian subcontinent and other parts of the world. Arranged marriages were prevalent throughout the world until the eighteenth century. As in many other cultures, arranged marriages have been a tradition for Sikhs for centuries and certainly during the gurus' times. They were common in Russia until the early twentieth century; most of these marriages were endogamous (the custom of marrying only within the limits of a local community, clan, or tribe).[91] China had this practice until the middle of the twentieth century, and it continues to be a common practice in many parts of India. Also, marriage arrangements were standard in the United Kingdom, Europe, United States, and Canada among immigrant families of different backgrounds through the first half of the twentieth century.

The Sikh code of conduct provides the following guidance on marriage:

- A Sikh man and woman should enter wedlock without giving thought to the prospective spouse's caste and descent.
- A Sikh's daughter must be married to a Sikh.
- A Sikh's marriage should be solemnized by Anand marriage rites.
- Child marriage is taboo for Sikhs.
- When a girl becomes marriageable, physically, emotionally, and by virtue of maturity of character, a suitable Sikh match should be found, and she should be married to him by Anand marriage rites.

---

[91]   Wikipedia, s.v. "Arranged Marriage," https://en.m.wikipedia.org/wiki/Arranged_marriage.

It's important to note that while the reference in the *Rehat Maryada* is to a daughter, it is commonly interpreted to include sons. In a society where caste, race, and class still play enormous roles in selecting marriage partners, Sikhs are taught not to have any regard to the person's racial, ethnic, or caste characteristics. The only appropriate consideration should be the person's faith. Since the Sikh marriage ceremony is intensely spiritual and centres on the uniting of two souls into one, it is believed that sharing the same spiritual path is essential for maintaining a successful marriage. Thus, the requirement that a Sikh should marry a Sikh.

The *Rehat Maryada* does not expressly comment on arranged marriage. A segment of the community is of the view that the Sikh code of conduct literally talks about parents' responsibility to find a suitable match for their children. The liberal interpretation is that a proper match should be found jointly by parents and young people—and that adult children should have the freedom to choose their partners. There is no unanimity on this subject. There are instances where some parents have forced their children to marry someone of the parents' choice. This is not a Sikh way of life and is viewed very negatively by the community at large. Currently, especially in Western countries, Sikh children choose their own marriage partners, though it is not uncommon for the young couple to seek the blessing of their parents before they firm up their commitment to get married.

85. Are there any Sikh pre-wedding traditions?

In contrast to the elaborate pre-wedding ceremonies explained elsewhere, there are two pre-marriage events that many Sikh families participate in. These are associated with a conventional Sikh wedding, and are unencumbered by much more costly and extraneous celebrations:

- *Sehaj Path* or *Akand Path:* Generally, about a week or two before the fixed date for the Anand Karaj, families thank Waheguru by holding a religious ceremony. Some hold these ceremonies at home, and others hold them at the gurdwara. The *Sri Guru Granth Sahib* (Sikh scripture) is read either intermittently in a week or two, which is called Sehaj Path, or it is read uninterrupted in approximately forty-eight hours, which is called Akhand Path. Usually, the bride's and the groom's families individually hold this religious ceremony at their respective places.

- *Keertan darar:* Some couples or families prefer to have a keertan darbar, either hosted at home or at the gurdwara. During this function, invited guests gather to sing sabads from the *SGGS*.

86. Are there nonreligious pre-marriage customs followed by Sikhs?

Most non-Sikhs and many Sikhs may not be aware that Sikh customs and traditions are different from general Panjabi cultural ones. The Sikh code of conduct describes in detail how a marriage ceremony must be performed, and there is no mention of pre-marriage rituals. However, many Sikhs are caught up in wedding rituals, songs, dance, food, and dress that have evolved over the centuries. They seem to be following traditions that are a combination of Hindu and Muslim rituals and traditions that are commonly dubbed "Panjabi culture." Lately, pre-wedding customs have also been influenced by Western mainstream practices and trends. Some of these wedding practices followed by many Sikh families, are described here:

- *Engagement:* There is no requirement for an engagement in the Sikh tradition. The Sikh code of conduct, chapter 9, article 18, states: "Marriage may not be preceded by an engagement ceremony. But if an engagement ceremony is sought to be held, a congregational gathering should be held, and after offering the Ardaas (prayer) before the *Guru Granth Sahib*, a kirpan [sword], a steel bangle, and some sweets may be tendered to the boy [groom]."[92] Most practicing Sikhs follow this directive, but the numbers are dwindling. Instead, the recent trend among many families is to hold an elaborate engagement ceremony in banquet halls, where hundreds or thousands of guests are in attendance for the evening. Before the engagement ceremony, a few more ceremonies have cropped up (see *rokka* and *chunni*, below), which are part of Panjabi traditions.

- *Roka:* Some argue that this wedding "announcement" tradition has its roots in the arranged marriage norm, where the parents would announce that they had found a suitable match for their daughter or son. Its origin lies with the Hindu customs that many present-day Sikhs have adopted it as their own. True, at one time, the tradition was for parents and grandparents to arrange the matrimony of their children. But these days, most couples decide when to declare their commitment publicly. The roka is an unofficial engagement ceremony where the groom's family and friends come to bless the bride-to-be and give her gifts.

  In some cases, the glamour associated with this ceremony has gone too far, particularly in India, where the bride's parents pay a large sum of money to the groom's family to arrange their daughter's marriage. In September 2016, Delhi High Court Justices Pardeep Nadrajog and Pratibha Rani, in a family dispute decision, said, "Roka is a social evil that needs to be condemned. It entails useless expenditure and, in many cases, becomes the source of bickering."[93]

- *Chunni:* This is not a Sikh matrimony requirement. However, those who undertake this ceremony announce the official engagement or cement the relationship. The groom's family visits

---

92 *Sikh Rehat Maryada*, chapter 9, article 18.

93 ·*Express News Service*, "'Roka' Is a Social Evil Which Needs to Be Condemned: Delhi High Court," *Indian Express*, September 6, 2016, para. 4, https://indianexpress. com/article/india/india-news-india/roka-is-a-social-evil-which-needs-to-be-condemned-delhi-high-court-3015663.

the bride's house or venue (arranged to accommodate guests) with gifts (sweets, fruits, and a complete outfit for the bride-to-be). Some families opt to bring many more gifts, depending upon what arrangements both sides have made. The mother-in-law and other female guests dress the bride. The engaged couple is seated together, which is when the ritual is performed. The groom's mother places a red *chunni* (scarf) on the bride's head. This usually matches the outfit she is wearing. Then the mother-in-law and other close relatives on the groom's side of the family adorn the bride with different gifts, including cash. The groom's parents feed the bride a whole dry date or some sweets. Then both parents, families, and friends drop money in the couple's *jholi*. These monetary gifts help recover the cost of this event. Some families are opting to have this ceremony *along with* the engagement ceremony.[94]

- *Bridal and wedding showers:* The Western culture of bridal or wedding showers has influenced the Sikh community. A bridal shower is considered a fun, celebratory occasion, a way for the bride's close friends and family members to spend time together before the big day. It is also a practical way of "showering" the bride-to-be with gifts to help her establish her new home successfully with her future spouse. A bridal shower is typically hosted by a woman close to the bride and is often held at a venue chosen to accommodate female family and friends. On the other hand, a wedding shower is held for both the bride and the groom, and guests from both families and genders are invited. Another fun party!

- *Maayian:* There is no such "preparation" ceremony in the Sikh faith. Despite that, many Sikh families still go through this pre-wedding practice because their parents, grandparents, and great-grandparents did it. The old Panjabi tradition was that

---

[94] Raj Kaur Bilkhu-Sohal, "A Guide to Punjabi Weddings—Chunni Ceremony" (blog post), June 16, 2012, https://epicevents.org.wordpress.com/2012/06/15/a-guide-to-punjabi-weddings-chunni-ceremony/amp.

each family would hold a ceremony for the bride or groom in their respective homes three days before the wedding. The ceremony involved applying a paste made from turmeric powder and mustard oil on the prospective bride and groom's faces, arms, and legs in the presence of all relatives and friends. It was accompanied by the singing of festive songs. The justification was that the turmeric paste is healthy for the skin and brings a glow to the surface, particularly on their faces. It is similar to having a "spa day" with one's entire extended family! Since most young people nowadays do not relish the idea of a turmeric facial, the application of turmeric is often superficial and more of a prop for the photoshoot than an actual spa-like experience. Some Sikh families have taken this ceremony to its extreme, holding it in banquet halls with hundreds or thousands of guests.

- *Ladies' sangeet:* The *sangeet* function is hosted by the bride's family, and usually only a few close members of the groom's family are invited. The bride's family plays the *dholki* (small drum) and sings songs to tease the groom and his family. Lately, this function has been expanded to a more elaborate event. Most of these events have become dinner and dance parties with DJs playing modern bhangra music. These singing parties were traditionally held for the bride and her bridesmaids, but the latest trend is to invite both genders.

- *Henna* or *mehndi party:* The Mughals brought *mehndi* (body art with henna paste) to India in the fifteenth century. Gradually, the use of *mehndi* spread, and its application methods and designs became more sophisticated. The tradition of henna or *mehndi* originated in North Africa and the Middle East. It is believed to have been in use as a cosmetic for the past five thousand years. According to the professional henna artist and researcher Catherine Cartwright-Jones, PhD, the elaborate patterning prevalent in India today emerged only in the twentieth century.[95] Most women from that time in India

---

[95]   Catherine Cartwright-Jones, The Henna Page, https://www.hennapage.com.

are depicted with their hands and feet hennaed, regardless of social class or marital status. This practice is firmly embedded in the Hindu pre-marriage ritual. The future mother-in-law sends *mehndi* to her prospective daughter-in-law in a beautifully decorated basket. The *mehndi* artist (about a week prior to the wedding) uses the paste to decorate the hands of the bride and her female family members and friends (including teenagers) with temporary tattoos. The bride has tattoos drawn on both sides of her hands and on her feet, but the other guests have them only on their hands (one or both). This ceremony is perhaps another excuse to have a party. Henna tattoos started to be used socially outside of weddings and are now catching on in Europe and North America as an alternative to painful and permanent needle-puncture tattoos. At least the *mehndi* does not appear to have any side effects.

- *Jaggo party:* This "wake-up" dance, full of energy and celebration, is designed to humour family and friends and put them in a jovial mood for the wedding day. Usually, the night before the wedding, a maternal aunt takes the lead for this wake-up dance. Accompanied by family and friends, she goes to the bride/groom's home or other place where the families have gathered for the evening, carrying a decorated copper or brass vessel, a *gharha* ("pot"), with flashing lights on top of her head. One of the women carries a long stick with bells to produce a musical sound to the tune of songs and dance. At the bride's home, which has been beautifully decorated with flowers, streamers, and lights, family and friends receive their guests by singing and dancing as well and welcome them into the home with sweets and drinks. Other than being a loud party—sometimes to the irritation and inconvenience of neighbours—this dance ceremony has no religious significance. The custom of *jaggo* is also practiced in Pakistan.

These extravagant pre-wedding ceremonies can cost several thousands of dollars and are a matter of debate and discussion among the Sikh community.

87. What happens when the bride and groom arrive at the gurdwara?

The cultural practice for a Panjabi Sikh wedding is for it to be hosted by the bride's family. The gurdwara at which it is held is traditionally selected by the bride's family and may be located in her hometown or elsewhere convenient to the bride's family and their guests. There are two distinct things that happen on arrival at the gurdwara for the wedding:

> *Milni ceremony:* Though the Sikh code of conduct does not mandate this ceremony, it has become a traditional part of most Sikh wedding ceremonies. On the wedding day, the groom comes to the gurdwara escorted by family and friends. The wedding party is received by the bride's family and friends. An *ardaas* (prayer) is conducted by a *giani*, followed by the formal introductions of parents, grandparents, and close relatives from both sides. Only the groom is present during this event; the bride is inside the Gurdwara, getting ready for her grand entrance for the start of the wedding ceremony. However, even this simple tradition is mired in controversy. More often than not, only the male members of the family are introduced during the milni, though more brides are insisting that their mothers, aunts, and sisters be given the same honour. In addition, there has been a traditional practice of the bride's parents giving expensive gifts to the groom, his father, grandfathers, close relatives, and some dignitaries identified by the groom's family. This practice is also waning in popular support. The public show of giving

gifts is disappearing, and family members may instead present each other with a garland of flowers.

After the milni, the entire wedding party is invited to have *chaah* (tea) and snacks before the wedding ceremony begins.

88. What is proper conduct inside the gurdwara at weddings?

All guests and visitors to the gurdwara follow the required protocol of covering their heads and removing their shoes. Separate shoe racks are provided for men and women. No alcohol or drugs (including cigarettes and marijuana and other intoxicants) are permitted inside the gurdwara premises (including the parking lot).

Guests walk in and sit in the main *darbar* hall, where the *keertan* (devotional singing) is in progress, and they wait for the bride and groom to enter. The groom, escorted by his parents and/or siblings, enters the prayer hall first, and they all take a seat in the congregation. Once all guests are seated, the groom is asked to sit in front of the *Sri Guru Granth Sahib* and wait for the bride to join him. The bride, escorted by her parents and/or siblings, then enters the darbar hall (hall where the *SGGS* is housed) and sits beside the groom on his left. Though it has now become common practice among many Sikh families, a flamboyant entry with a procession of couples or attendants (such as flower girls or bridesmaids and groomsmen) walking in front of the groom and bride is against both the Sikh code of conduct and Sikh tradition.

89. Are there special rules of behaviour for a bride and groom during the marriage ceremony?

In virtually every culture, the bride and groom take precedence on their wedding day. We have all come to expect that the couple will be given deference and special treatment as they publicly announce their commitment to each other.

However, in a gurdwara, the bride and groom must give way to the *SGGS*, which alone holds special status and centre stage. The sacred commitment they are making in a gurdwara is to each other, their Guru, and their entire community. As such, it is expected that the bride and groom will conduct themselves with humility and decorum while in the gurdwara. In a gurdwara, all are equals, regardless of social or marital status. Thus, the bride and groom are expected to follow all gurdwara protocols, such as:

- Seating: As a show of equality and humility, the bride and groom are expected to sit on the carpet with the rest of the congregation. They are not permitted to have any special seating, including padded carpets, chairs, or stools.
- Conversation: The bride and groom should not converse with each other during the marriage ceremony. Their focus is expected to be on the sacred ceremony, their vows, keertan, and the teachings of the gurus as explained by the persons officiating the marriage ceremony.
- Affection: It is inappropriate for the bride and groom to display any physical affection while in the gurdwara. This includes holding hands or kissing each other.
- Clothing: Clothing worn by the bride and groom is expected to be modest and in accordance with acceptable gurdwara attire. They are required to cover their heads with either a dastaar (turban) or chunni (scarf). They are not permitted to wear hats as head coverings inside the gurdwara. The bride cannot have her face veiled.
- Photographs: While photographs and videos are permitted during the ceremony, they cannot interfere with the wedding ceremony itself. The photographers and videographers are expected to respect all gurdwara protocols, such as covering their heads and not facing away from the *SGGS*. It is strictly

forbidden for the photographers and videographers to interfere in the sacred vows taken by the bride and groom as they walk around the *SGGS*. Thus, the camera operators are not permitted to walk in front of the bride and groom as they take their vows and walk around the scriptures or engage them in conversation. The bride and groom are expected to remember that they are in a sacred place of worship; the gurdwara and *SGGS* are not props for a photo shoot.

- Family: The bride and groom are considered autonomous individuals. As a reflection of their autonomy and free will, it is expected that they will walk around the *SGGS* unaided by friends or family. The Panjabi cultural practice of having the bride's brothers escort her around the *SGGS* is antithetical to Sikh teachings and actively discouraged in the Gurdwara setting.

- In-law escorts: Lately, another practice appears to have creeped in. Toward the end of fourth *lav* (vow), when the groom and the bride are circling the *Sri Guru Granth Sahib*, the groom's parents join in escorting the bride. This is not part of the *Sikh Rehat Maryada* (code of conduct) and is also discouraged.

- Music: The only music permitted during a marriage ceremony is keertan (the singing of sabads from the scriptures), and *dhadi vars* (bards who sing about the social significance of the wedding). Dance music and love songs are not permitted to be played in the gurdwara.

90. Does a Sikh wedding ceremony require exchange of rings?

The exchange of wedding rings is a part of Western marriage traditions. The Sikh marriage ceremony does not require a couple to exchange rings to complete the wedding. Sikhs consider the *palla* to create the physical bond that symbolizes the union between the bride and groom. The palla is a long cotton or silk scarf that the groom wears at the wedding. At the commencement of the marriage ceremony, one or both of the bride's parents will take one end of the palla and hand it to their daughter, while placing the other end in the groom's hands. This palla signifies the sacred union that they are about to embark on. The palla must be held continuously by the couple until the marriage ceremony has been completed in its entirety. Many couples embellish the palla with ribboning or a fringe sewn along the edge. While this is permissible, it is not acceptable to have a palla that is made of material other than fabric. Thus, a palla made from garlands of flowers, or a chain of beads, is inappropriate for the solemn ceremony.

The familiarity with Christian norms, unfamiliarity with fading cultural practices, and subtle assimilative pressures do mean that some couples choose to exchange wedding rings while in the gurdwara. The *Sikh Rehat Maryada* does not prohibit the exchanging of wedding rings. The practice is also permitted in the gurdwara, but only after the official Anand Karaj ceremony has been completed.

91. Who can get married in a gurdwara?

With the increase of interfaith and cross-cultural marriages, couples face an additional dilemma of which faith tradition to get married in. Many feel pressured by their families to participate in a religious ceremony even if they—or their partners—have no emotional affiliation toward Sikhism and do not understand or place any value on Sikh traditions.

Sikhs believe in freedom of faith and do not restrict anyone from coming to the gurdwara or participating in the services. However, it is expected that persons participating in an Anand Karaj ceremony have some level of spiritual, emotional, or cultural connection to Sikhi. The gurdwara ceremony is sacred for Sikhs. It is expected that only those people who affiliate with Sikhi and the Sikh way of life will participate in it. If a bride or groom does not have any understanding of the Anand Karaj ceremony—or any emotional affiliation toward Sikhi—they are expected to learn about Sikhi, the meaning of the vows, and what they are committing themselves to prior to participating in the Anand Karaj ceremony.

92. What does the marriage ceremony entail?

As humans, we are constantly searching for happiness and fulfillment. A critical step toward accomplishing this goal is marriage, which brings together two souls in spiritual union. As Guru Amar Das says, "Merely sitting together does not make them husband and wife. Instead, henceforth they must become one—make all decisions jointly, acting like one soul in two bodies, and contemplate on Waheguru."[96]

Most people get married for social acceptance, emotional gratification, economic security, or legal legitimacy. Marriage for Sikhs, however, far exceeds these bounds.

A Sikh couple wanting to marry attends the gurdwara on a prearranged date and presents themselves before the *Sri Guru Granth Sahib* for spiritual guidance. It is this part of the human journey that leads them to self-discovery and guides them to understand who they are and what their purpose is in life. Here is the process in more detail:

- At a predetermined time, the congregants start filing into the main darbar hall where the Anand Karaj will be held, and a ragi jatha sings sabads from the *SGGS*. The groom is expected to arrive early with the wedding party, and he will sit in the congregation and listen to the keertan. When the granthi is ready to begin the ceremony, the groom will stand up and move to a place immediately in front of the *Sri Guru Granth Sahib*. The ragi jatha will continue singing sabads until the bride arrives.
- When the bride arrives, she sits down to the left of the groom. The wedding ceremony begins shortly thereafter.
- A couple's connection with the *Sri Guru Granth Sahib*, with each other, and with the community at large starts with a silent prayer

---

[96]   *SGGS* 788: Ek Jot Doay Murti—ੲੇਕ ਜੋਤਿ ਦੁਇ ਮੂਰਤੀ॥

led by a giani, and the bride, groom, and their parents stand with hands folded in prayer. The rest of the sangat (congregation) remains seated.

- A *vaak*, also called *hukam* (divine directive for the event), follows the prayer. The giani randomly selects a verse from the *Sri Guru Granth Sahib*, and this random stanza read from the top left-hand corner of the page is literally taken as the Guru's command for the couple.

- The next step in the ceremony is for the bride's parent or guardian to take one end of the palla (sacred scarf) from around the groom's shoulders and hand it to the bride.

- While this is happening, the keertani jatha (sabad singers) sing a specific sabad: "O Waheguru, all relationships are false and tough to shoulder; hence we have jointly grasped the hem of your robe and implore your blessing."[97]

- The most significant part of the marriage is the performance of four vows called lavaan (lav singular and lavaan plural). These vows are prescribed in the *Sri Guru Granth Sahib*; they are intended to help guide the couple as they grow on their spiritual path and connect with the Divine. As the giani recites each lav (stanza), the couple stands with hands folded and listens attentively. At the end of each recitation, the couple circles the *Sri Guru Granth Sahib* in a clockwise direction while the keertani jatha sing the same lav in their blended voices. Upon completion of each circle, the couple bows in respect, kneeling and touching their foreheads to the floor, to demonstrate that they do accept this commitment" The four *lavaan*, or vows, briefly translate to the following:

1. *First lav:* The couple commits to letting go of the past and embarks on a new journey. This includes a commitment to the spiritual teachings of the *Sri Guru Granth Sahib* as

---

[97] *SGGS* 963: habhe saak kooRaave ddiThe tau palai taiddai laagee—ਹਭੇ ਸਾਕ ਕੂੜਾਵੇ ਡਿਠੇ ਤਉ ਪਲੈ ਤੈਡੈ ਲਾਗੀ॥

well as an acknowledgment of the couple's duty toward one
another, their families, the community, and humanity at
large.[98]

2. *Second lav:* During the recitation of this lav, the couple
    commits to putting aside their egos and other materialistic
    attachments and replacing them with a desire for internal
    peace through the singing of Waheguru's praises.[99]

3. *Third lav:* The third lav signifies the couple's detachment
    from the past and their profound desire to never be apart
    from each other and to join with Waheguru as one.[100]

4. *Fourth lav:* The final lav describes the state of harmony and
    union experienced in married life during which human love
    blends into the love for the Divine.[101]

At the end of the ceremony, a congregational prayer is held, and
another *hukam* or *vaak* is taken from the *Sri Guru Granth Sahib* for

---

[98] *SGGS* 773: Har pahldi lav par virti karam dridaya Bal Ram jio. Dharam
drirr-ahu har naam dhi-aav-hu simrit naam drirr-aa-i-aa. Satigur gur pooraa aa-
raadh-hu sabh kilvikh paap gavaa-i-aa. Sehaj anand hoaa vadd-bhaa-gee man har
mee-thaa laa-i-aa. Jan kehai naanak laav peh-lee aa-ranbh kaaj rachaa-i-aa.

[99] Ibid.: Har dooj-rree laav satigur purakh milaa-i-aa bal raam jeeo. Nirbho bhai
man hoe houmai mail gavaa-i-aa bal raam jeeo. Nirmal Bho paa-a-aa har gun
gaa-i-aa har vekhai raam haddo-rae. Har aatam raam passer-o-aa su-aa-mee sarab
reh-9-aa bhar-poo-rae. Anatar baaahar har prabh ko mil har jan mangal gaa-ae.
Jan naanak doo-jee naanak doo-jee laav cha-laa-ee anhad sabad vajaa-ae.

[100] *SGGS* 774: har teejrhee laav man chaa-o bha-i-aa bairaagee-aa bal raam
jee-o. sant janaa har mayl har paa-i-aa vadbhaagee-aa bal raam jee-o. nirmal har
paa-i-aa har gun gaa-i-aa mukh bolee har banee. sant janaa vadbhaagee paa-i-aa
har kathee-ai akath kahaanee. hirdai har har har Dhun upjee har japee-ai mastak
bhaag jee-o. jan naanak bolay teejee laavai har upjai man bairaag jee-o. ||3||.

[101] *SGGS* 774: Har chou-tha-rree laav man sehaj bha-i-aa har paa-i-aa bal raam
jeeo. Gurmukh mil-i-aa su-bhaa-e har man tan mee-thaa laa-i-aa bal raam jeeo.
Har mee-thaa laa-i-aa mere prabh bhaa-i-aa andin har liv laa-ee. Man chind-i-aa fal
paa-i-aa su-aamee har naam vajee vaa-dhaa-ee. Har prabh thaakur kaaj rachaa-i-aa
dhan hir-dhai naam vi-gaa-see. Jan naanak bolae chou-thee laa-vai har paa-i-aa
prabh avin-aa-see.

successful completion of the marriage. Although it is not a religious requirement, Canadian law requires the couple to sign the marriage register maintained by a giani or an authorized executive member of the gurdwara. Some couples exchange rings, but that is not a Sikh religious requirement or a part of Panjabi marriage tradition.

93. Who can perform the marriage ceremony?

As discussed in other chapters, Sikhs do not have a class of clergy or priests. A *giani* or *granthi*, or for that matter any practicing *amritdhari* Sikh, man or woman, who is familiar with the responsibilities of conducting marriages, can perform the wedding rite. The Sikh code of conduct (*Rehat Maryada*), section 18, explains the process of solemnizing a marriage.

94. What happens after the marriage ceremony?

After the religious wedding ceremony in the gurdwara, guests are treated to a vegetarian meal prepared either by volunteers in the gurdwara or by caterers retained by the bride's family for this occasion. In India and Europe, particularly United Kingdom, it has become common for many people to hold the Anand Karaj ceremony in a gurdwara but serve food or snacks at a banquet or community hall where they are free to serve vegetarian or nonvegetarian food. However, this is not considered an acceptable practice for Sikhs living in Canada, and they tend to adhere quite closely to the tradition of having the langar at the gurdwara.

Following the langar, the couple departs the gurdwara with close family members for wedding photos, usually taken, weather permitting, in a park of their choice. After the photo shoot, the bride and the groom, along with close family members, go to the bride's home for the official departure of the bride, and she bids farewell to her parents and sibling(s) prior to a move to her new home. This ceremony is called *Doli* or *Vidai*:

- *Doli* or *Vidai—Departure of the bride:* Many Sikhs are still largely influenced by the wider patriarchal Panjabi culture within which they have grown up. Thus, at marriage, many families expect their daughters to move with their husbands and live with their in-laws. The ceremony of doli is the final farewell or send-off for the daughters, which is why it is often bittersweet and accompanied by a lot of tears. After departing the gurdwara—and either before or after the wedding pictures have been taken at a nearby park—the bride returns to her parents' home for the first time as a married woman. While the bride and her newly acquired in-laws enter the home, the bride's sisters and cousins will often play a game where they will only allow the groom into the home if he has passed some sort of test of his love. This could consist of singing a song or some other display designed to tease him. Only when the groom has satisfied the bride's sisters is he permitted into the home to join his bride and have tea and sweets. The bride then departs the home with her groom amid tears and farewells from her family and friends. The couple then departs the home of her parents in a decorated car arranged by the groom.

- *Reception—The final step:* While the bride's family hosts the Anand Karaj at their gurdwara of choice, socially, it falls to the groom's family to host the wedding reception. Lavish dinners are becoming the norm for Sikh families, costing thousands of dollars to host. Sadly, some families will even mortgage their homes to put on these fancy parties to please their kids and impress their relatives and friends. This trend is inconsistent with the Sikh principles.

95. Why does the bride sit or stand to the left of the groom during the wedding ceremony?

There is no definitive answer to this question. This tradition stems from the old days, when women were traded and sold for marriage or "marriage by capture." It is postulated that the reason behind the practice is twofold.[102] By standing or sitting on the left side, the bride is "under her groom's heart." Her position also keeps the groom's right hand ("fighting arm" or "sword arm") free to defend his bride, should any enemy try to steal her away at the last minute. The groom could hold his bride with his left hand while using his sword with his right hand against any oncoming attackers.

Another explanation was that men and women were split up before they entered the place of worship, with men usually sitting on the right side and women sitting on the left. Because of this, it made sense for the groom to sit or stand on the right-hand side, facing the *SGGS*, and his bride on his left. Yet another idea is that when newlyweds turn and face their friends and family at the end of the ceremony, the bride is standing or walking to the groom's right, symbolizing her spot as his "right hand" throughout the rest of their lives together.

Regardless of all these explanations, it is important to remember that the seating arrangements are not a religious requirement; they are a tradition. Traditions die hard! Sikhs rely on the *SGGS* and the Sikh code of conduct for guidance. For seating arrangements before the *Sri Guru Granth Sahib*, the *Rehat Maryada* states that the bride should sit on the left side of the groom.

96. How do Sikhs view intercultural marriage?

There is no bar in the Sikh faith to intercultural marriage. Marriage, as discussed earlier, is between two adults who have an inherent right to choose their life partner. The Sikh gurus demonstrated a life path that one could follow to meet the Divine. In Sikhi, the decision to marry should not be taken lightly. One must choose a partner with whom one shares similar beliefs. Since human life is an opportunity to meet God, choosing a life partner who shares similar beliefs helps both partners

---

[102]   Most of this explanation is from the website of "At Your Side Planning," a company based in San Diego, https://www.atyoursidesplannng.com.

strive for and reach this goal, regardless of the cultural background of the prospective spouse.

To live a peaceful, spiritual lifestyle to accomplish the purpose of human life, one should marry someone whose spiritual goal is similar to one's own. And for a Sikh, it would be following the teachings of the Sikh gurus. This enables a couple to carry on their journey to be one with God. To clarify, the teachings of the Sikh gurus are not focused on belonging to a particular religion; the focus is on enhancing one's existence so that one can achieve union with the Divine.

Like all other major religions, a marriage as per Anand marriage rites in the gurdwara can be performed only to unite two Sikhs: "A Sikh man and a woman should enter into matrimony without giving thought to the prospective spouse's caste and descent."[103] The Sikh code of conduct further goes on to explain that the Anand marriage should be between two Sikhs (a man and a woman): "A Sikh should be married to a Sikh" in the presence of the *Sri Guru Granth Sahib*.

The gurdwaras are welcome to wed all those who believe in the teachings of the ten Sikh gurus (from Guru Nanak to Guru Gobind Singh) and the *Sri Guru Granth Sahib*. Also, one must believe in the *amrit* bequeathed by the tenth Guru and not owe allegiance to any other religion to get married by Anand marriage rites. However, most gurdwaras around the world solemnize interfaith marriages, though there has been controversy on this issue in the United Kingdom.

Civil marriage is recommended for two people with different religious faiths.

97. Can Sikhs get divorced?

There is no bar to a Sikh getting a divorce. The Sikh code of conduct is silent on this subject, except for an article that says, "Under normal circumstances, no Sikh should marry a second wife if the first wife is

---

[103] *Sikh Rehat Maryada*, approved by the Shiromani Gurdwara Prabandhak Committee in 1945.

alive."[104] This is often interpreted to mean that polygamy is expressly forbidden rather than as a prohibition against divorce.

As explained earlier, the Sikh wedding (Anand Karaj) is a spiritual union. Both husband and wife are joined in equal partnership, make a religious commitment, and accept the *Sri Guru Granth Sahib* as their guide. For Sikhs, marriage is not a civil contract. Instead, it marks the start of a spiritual journey in which both partners help each other and grow together to experience the divine light.

The gurus regarded marriage as a spiritual state of life, and this institution is highly respected and considered sacred. Most Sikhs consider marriage to be for life—through good times and bad. Therefore, it is important to marry a partner whose social and moral values and spiritual goals are similar. The ideal family is one where there is mutual love and respect between the husband and the wife and their offspring. A Sikh couple is expected to reconcile their differences, including getting mediators involved. Of course, where extenuating circumstances exist, such as abuse, continuing infidelity, or a refusal to reconcile by one party, divorce may become unavoidable. In such cases, there is no religious divorce available—only a legal dissolution of the union. Divorce is considered a very grave matter and a last resort; it is not something that should be undertaken casually. However, for Sikhs, as in any other civil society, instead of enduring the pain of immoral and abusive relations, it is advisable to obtain a divorce under civil law.

There is no formal process set out in the Sikh faith for divorce, and every effort must be made to resolve marital issues and maintain the marriage. Couples can approach the congregation or seek guidance and assistance from the panj payare to request their intervention in confidence and assistance to help them overcome any severe conflicts.

---

[104]   *Sikh Rehat Maryada*, chapter 11, article 18.

98. Can Sikhs remarry?

The *Sikh Rehat Maryada* specifically provides for the remarriage of widows and widowers. The following paragraphs in section XVIII of the *Sikh Rehat Maryada* (code of conduct) clearly permits widows to remarry:

- Para 'n.' If a woman's husband has died, she may, if she so wishes, finding [find] a match suitable for her, [and] remarry. For a Sikh man whose wife has died, [a] similar ordinance obtains.
- Para 'o.' The remarriage may be solemnized in the same manner as the Anand marriage.
- Para 'p,' Generally, no Sikh should marry a second wife [spouse] if the first wife [spouse] is alive.

Guru Arjan, the fifth Guru, married Mata Ganga of village Mau (ਮਉ) in June 1579, after his first wife Ram Dayee of village Maur (ਮੌੜ) passed away.[105]

99. What is the Sikh view on polygamy or polyandry?

When a man is married to more than one wife at a time, the relationship is called *polygamy*. When a woman is married to more than one husband at a time, it is called *polyandry*. According to a post on the Sikh Philosophy Network:

> Polygamy is widespread among different cultures of the world. According to one study of "853" cultures, only 16 percent stipulate monogamy. Historically, most of the Sikh kings practiced polygamy in the 18th and 19th centuries. Guru Amar Das has clearly defined that [the]

---

[105] *Guru Arjan Dev: Jiwan Te Bani* (Punjabi), 2011 Dr. Mohinder Kaur Gill, formerly principal Mata Sundari College, Delhi University, New Delhi—ISBN 81-302-0196-8, Publication Bureau Punjabi University, Patiala, 56.

conjugal relationship has to be two bodies and one soul. It vividly conforms to monogamy [as] ideal.[106]

Polygamy was practiced in the Indian subcontinent and in many sections of Indian society in ancient and medieval times. Many people in modern Indian society consider it immoral, and like in Canada, it is illegal there today. Sikhi does not condone these practices either.

Several examples of support against polygamy and polyandry can be found in central Sikh text and historical precedents. Firstly, Sikhi stresses and preaches the significance of family or married life (*Grehsiti Jiwan*) and guides what a good marriage relationship is. In the words of the *SGGS*, "Merely meeting and sitting together does not make them [a couple] husband and wife. Instead, henceforth they must become One—make all decisions jointly, acting like one soul in two bodies, and contemplate Waheguru."[107] Bhai Gurdas, a central seventeenth-century Sikh intellectual, gives the most direct comment about the emphasis on monogamy, "Having one wife [or husband] is the religious commitment of a Sikh, which is equivalent to celibacy. Treat others like your children or siblings."[108] Fidelity to one's married partner is the essence of self-restraint and is conducive to a stable householder life. Monogamy is the rule.

Despite the widespread belief that polygamy is antithetical to Sikh teachings, many scholars write that Guru Hargobind and Guru Gobind Singh had multiple wives. Many books refer to Guru Hargobind marrying three wives (Damodari, Mahadevi, and Nanaki).[109] Similarly, Satish Dhillon writes about the three wives of Guru Gobind Singh

---

[106] Neutral Singh, "Polygamy and Sikhism," Sikh Philosophy Network (June 1, 2004), paragraph 4, https://www.sikhphilosophy.net/threads/polygamy-and-sikhism.534.

[107] *SGGS* 788: dhan pir eh na aakheean bhan ikaThe hoi. Ek jot dhui moorate dhan pir kaheeaai soi—ਧਨ ਪਿਰੁ ਏਹਿ ਨ ਆਖੀਅਨਿ ਬਹਨਿ ਇਕਠੇ ਹੋਇ ॥ ਏਕ ਜੋਤਿ ਦੁਇ ਮੂਰਤੀ ਧਨ ਪਿਰੁ ਕਹੀਐ ਸੋਇ॥੩॥

[108] Bhai Gurdas vaar 6, pauri 8: Eka nari jati hoi par nari dhee bhain vaikhanai—ਏਕਾ ਨਾਰੀ ਜਤੀ ਹੋਇ ਪਰ ਨਾਰੀ ਧੀ ਭੈਣ ਵਖਾਣੈ॥

[109] Dhillon Harish, *The Sikh Gurus* (130), thirteenth reprint 2015, Hay House Publishers India.

(Jeeto, Sundari, and Sahib Devan). He explains circumstances under which Guru ended up marrying three wives. [110]

This is a topic of passionate academic and not so academic discussions among Sikhs, particularly with Guru Gobind Singh's wives. Without getting into the foray of justification either way, I accept Guru Amar Das's (1479–1574) words in the *SGGS* (788), "Ek jot dhui mooratee dhan pir kaheeaai soi" (Acting like one soul in two bodies, and contemplate Waheguru)."

---

[110]   Ibid 195–196.

CHAPTER 12

Festivals and Holidays

Festivals and holidays are an expressive way to celebrate Sikhi's glorious heritage, culture, and traditions. They remind us of special moments and emotions in our lives that we acknowledge with our loved ones and the community at large. They play a significant role in adding structure to our social lives and connect us with our histories, families, and backgrounds. Sikhs do not believe that any particular day is more auspicious than another. However, some events have specific historical significance and are publicly commemorated by Sikhs on the dates the events occurred. Such dates often involve coming together to listen to Gurbani, keertan, and katha or to listen to dhadi *kavishars*. This chapter examines the historical importance of Sikh festivals and holidays.

100. Is there a particular day of the week when Sikhs gather for worship?

There is no set day that Sikhs are required to gather for worship and Sikhi does not teach that any particular day is more auspicious than another. When Sikhs congregate, worship is dictated by many things, such as the country's customs within which they reside and the work schedules of the congregants. Depending on the size of the congregation, most gurdwaras have twice-daily worship services (morning and evening). For Sikhs living in North America, Sundays have become the primary day for congregational worship because this is the day that most people were traditionally off from work in North American society. However, Sikhs living in Muslim countries have their main worship day on Fridays.

Gurdwaras around the world are open to the public for prayer and worship all day, every day; special congregational services are held both in the early morning and in the evening and in some major centres all day, starting early in the morning, usually around 4:00 a.m. and continuing till late in the evening.

101. What are the Sikh holidays and holy days?

As mentioned in the last question, Sikhs do not believe that any particular day is holier than others. However, some days have special commemorative significance. These are the days when Sikhs celebrate the birth anniversaries of the ten human Gurus, bhagats, and the martyrdom anniversaries of Guru Arjan, the fifth Guru; Guru Teg Bahadur, the ninth Guru; and the Chaar Sahibzaade (the four sons of Guru Gobind Singh, the tenth Guru). Sikhs also celebrate the day that the current Guru—the *SGGS*—was installed as the final Guru. These days serve to remind Sikhs of the importance of the daily rhythm of practicing Sikhi and the necessity of sacrificing for the greater collective good of humanity.

Please see appendix A for the details and dates of occasions that are celebrated and commemorated on a much larger scale.

102. When is the Sikh New Year?

For all intents and purposes, Sikhs follow the Gregorian calendar. They celebrate the new year on January 1, as well as the Sikh New Year, which falls on March 14. Until 2003, for all religious celebrations, Sikhs followed the Bikrami calendar, which is based on the lunar year, in contrast to the Gregorian calendar, which is based on the solar year. In 2003, the Sikh calendar, named the Nanakshahi calendar, developed by a Canadian Sikh, Pal Singh Purewal, was approved by the Akal Takhat (highest temporal authority for Sikhs) and the Shiromani Gurdwara Prabandhak Committee (SGPC). The Nanakshahi calendar is based on Earth's solar orbit of about 365 days, like the Gregorian calendar (in contrast to the lunar orbit of the Earth in about 354 days). The start of this calendar is the year 1469, the birth year of Guru Nanak, the founder of Sikhi. As per the new calendar, the Sikh New Year falls on March 14 in the Gregorian calendar.

103. What is sangrand?

The word *sangrand* has its origin in the Sanskrit word *sankranti*, meaning the first day of each month of the Indian solar calendar when the sun leaves one zodiac sign and enters a new zodiac sign. Hindus consider this an auspicious day. There is no concept of auspicious or inauspicious in Sikhi. Guru Arjan said, "Good and or bad omens affect those who do not keep Waheguru in their mind."[111] Sikhs in Panjab traditionally gathered in large numbers to listen to katha from prominent intellectuals for extended periods of time on these days, mirroring the pragmatic reasons why Sikhs living outside Panjab gather on Sundays. Unfortunately, there has been a continuation of the idea that sangrand is astrologically auspicious. Despite a clear message from the Guru, the association of sangrand's auspiciousness has not been sufficiently challenged by the intellectual and administrative groups. As a result, the cultural aspects of sangrand continue to impact the psyche of some Sikhs.

Gathering should provide an opportunity to read the Guru's pronouncement for each month and warnings against empty ritualistic behaviour. To quote, for the month of Chet (the first lunar month), Guru Nanak says, "The month of Chet is marked by *basant* (spring) and blossoming, but the human mind, even in such a season, will not effloresce without union with the Creator, achieved through meditation

---

[111]   *SGGS* 400: sagun upsagun tis kou lageh jis cheet na aavai—ਸਗੁਨ ਅਪਸਗੁਨ ਤਿਸ ਕਉ ਲਗਹਿ ਜਿਸੁ ਚੀਤਿ ਨ ਆਵੈ ॥

on [the] Divine name."[112] Similarly, Guru Arjan, in the stanza on Chet, reminds us to "not get caught up in meaningless rituals—the meditation on the name of Waheguru would bring unlimited bliss."[113] Both, in the end, say that each moment, day, or month spent in meditation on the Divine name brings bliss—and no other appeasement or worship of deities will help.

104. What is Vaisakhi?

For Sikhs, Vaisakhi (also spelled Baisakhi) is known as the Khalsa Sirjana (Creation of Khalsa) Divas. It falls at the beginning of the month of Vaisakh, the second month in the Indian lunar calendar (commonly known as the Vikrami or Bikrami calendar), which comes around the middle of April. The Sikh Mool Nanakshahi calendar, based on the length of the solar year, has the date fixed as April 14.

Vaisakhi has traditionally been a harvest festival in Panjab and across South Asia for centuries, but the day has a special religious significance for Sikhs. In the middle of the sixteenth century, this day was designated as the annual congregation day of all Sikhs by Guru Amar Das. Guru Amar Das also commanded his followers to assemble in his presence on the Hindu spring and autumn *mela* (festival) of Baisakhi (Vaisakhi), Diwali, and Hola Mohalla (to provide clarifications and guidelines on spiritual and social issues). This was clearly a way of implementing his policy of developing a distinctive Sikh identity. At these times, people had to choose where they belonged—with their Hindu kin or with the Guru. Festivals are essential in forging and expressing identity, as some of the comments above have implied, which Guru Amar Das successfully did. The Sikh melas combine religious purpose and sheer

---

[112]   *SGGS* 1107: chet basant Bhalla bhavar suhaavaRe—ਚੇਤੁ ਬਸੰਤੁ ਭਲਾ ਭਵਰ ਸੁਹਾਵੜੇ॥

[113]   *SGGS* 133: chet govindh araadheeaai hovai anandh ghanna—ਚੇਤਿ ਗੋਵਿੰਦ ਅਰਾਧੀਐ ਹੋਵੈ ਅਨੰਦੁ ਘਣਾ ॥

festive enjoyment in the prominent places where they are observed.[114] Following this Vaisakhi gathering tradition, in 1699, Guru Gobind Singh created the order of the Khalsa by creating a special ceremony for initiating Sikhs, including a specified code of conduct to adhere to.

The Sikh label Khalsa Sirjana Divas literally means "the day of the manifestation of the Khalsa."[115] The Khalsa are those Sikhs who have accepted the Sikh initiation or *khande di pahul* and commit to living their lives in the service of humanity and the spirit of equality and compassion. In addition to celebrating Vaisakhi in gurdwaras worldwide, Sikhs also celebrate Vaisakhi in the public domain with a procession.

105. What is a Nagar Keertan?

Many faith communities worldwide celebrate certain faith days in the public domain and hold parades or other public displays. Christmas is one example. Sikhs also hold public events to commemorate certain religious days. The most common format is a procession or march, called the Nagar Keertan. The word *Nagar* literally means "town" and *Keertan* (the singing of sabads from the *SGGS*). Combined, Nagar Keertan means "the singing of sabads in the public domain through a celebratory procession."

The Nagar Keertan is led by Panj Pyare ("the five beloved ones," who represent the first five Sikhs to have been initiated) and the *Sri Guru Granth Sahib* installed in a decorated float. Nagar Keertan will often include

Surrey, Canada Vaisakhi Nagar Keertan April 2019

displays of *gatka,* the Sikh martial art. Sikh congregations from other communities, human rights groups, and other community-oriented

[114] W. Owen Cole: *Understanding Sikhism*. Dunedin Academic Press. Kindle edition, location 2067.

[115] Ibid., location 432. For further details about Vaisakhi, go to the World Sikh Organization of Canada website: https://www.worldsikh.org.

organizations will often have their own decorated floats in the Nagar Keertan with their members or supporters following behind singing sabads.

In the Western Hemisphere, Vaisakhi celebrations have become a combination of religious and cultural displays. No Sikh celebration is complete without food. Hundreds of volunteers will set up food stalls along the route for the procession and serve Punjabi vegetarian delicacies such as samosas, pakoras, *chhole bhature* (chickpea curry and fried flatbreads), pizzas, nuts, fruit, tea, and soft drinks. Food is distributed free to anyone and everyone—irrespective of skin colour, caste, religion, gender, or nationality—enough to feed an army and more, in just about every major city in the world.

Outside of India, the Vaisakhi (Khalsa Nagar Keertan) celebration in Surrey, British Columbia, Canada, is the largest, and in pre-pandemic years attracted more than five hundred thousand attendees from all walks of life.

106. Do Sikhs celebrate Diwali?

Diwali is marked with the lighting of candles or oil lamps and has its origins in ancient India. Though it does not have any religious significance in Sikhi, many Sikhs follow the tradition. Thus, it is useful to briefly describe the broader connotations of Diwali before turning to discuss Sikhi. Many mythical stories are attributed to Diwali, and they vary regionally in India. They all point to elation and celebration with lights. More generally, this day is also seen as a victory of good over evil (light over darkness) by some.

Historically, during the Sikh gurus' times (1469–1708), there were two significant gatherings of Sikhs, at Vaisakhi and Diwali. These festivals fall six months apart and coincide with the celebrations of the dominant faith culture. The Gurus used these occasions to emphasize Sikh principles and teachings; they create unity and build knowledge within the Sikh community by providing Sikhs with an alternative way of celebrating. The Gurus took these public opportunities to try to explain the importance of living an elevated existence. Thus, the diva or lamp of Divali became synonymous with the lamp within one's soul, which must always be lit.

Bhai Gurdas (1551–1636), a Sikh scholar whose writings are labeled as key to the understanding of the Sikh scripture, explains Divali this way:

> On Divali, festival lamps are lighted in the night; stars of different varieties appear in the sky; in the gardens, the flowers are there, which are selectively plucked; the pilgrims going to pilgrimage centres are also seen. The ideal habitats have been seen coming into being and vanishing. All these momentary celebrations have no real meaning if one does not practice the virtues to combat vices.[116]

Guru Amar Das inspires us to recognize "our origin and turn on the divine light within us to enjoy Waheguru's blessing."[117] Thus, the lighting of lamps carries a different symbolic structure relate to connecting, or reigniting, that one light that is within us and pervades creation.

As Sikh history progressed, the day of Diwali came to take on its own historical significance for Sikhs. Since the time of Guru Hargobind Ji, the sixth Sikh Guru, the community began commemorating *Bandi Chhor Divas* ("Liberation Day"), which coincides with Divali. The association of Divali with Bandi Chhor Divas has been increasing ever since, and today Sikhs light candles in their homes, gather for elaborate fireworks displays, and congregate to hear the teachings from *Sri Guru Granth Sahib*. Those Sikhs who light a candle on Divali do not think of the Hindu association with this festival. Instead, they focus on the broader meaning of the light conquering darkness, or more specifically, the day of liberation.

---

[116]   Bhai Gurdas vaaran 19: divali ki raat deevai baaleean—ਦੀਵਾਲੀ ਕੀ ਰਾਤਿ ਦੀਵੇ ਬਾਲੀਅਨਿ॥

[117]   *SGGS* 440: mun tun jot sarooop hai aapnaa mool pachhaan—ਮਨ ਤੂੰ ਜੋਤਿ ਸਰੂਪੁ ਹੈ ਆਪਣਾ ਮੂਲੁ ਪਛਾਣੁ॥

107. What is Bandi Chhor Divas?

Bandi Chhor Divas ("Liberation Day" or "Freedom Day") is a Sikh celebratory day that coincides with Diwali. On this day, Sikhs commemorate the 1619 release of the sixth Guru, Guru Hargobind, from unlawful imprisonment in the Gwalior Fort by Jahangir, the Mughal ruler.

Any new social, spiritual, or philosophical movement is inevitably perceived as a threat to the status quo. This is particularly the case when the spiritual movement seeks to dismantle the existing social hierarchy that has legitimized the oppression of women and minorities and elevated this oppression to a spiritual practice (i.e., the caste hierarchy, which became equated with Hinduism). So, it is no small wonder that as Sikhi grew in popularity, the Mughal rulers of the time were anxious to quell the movement following the martyrdom of Guru Arjun for not accepting conversion to Islam. The last message that Guru Arjan sent to his son Guru Hargobind was to fight evil with all the might at his command. At his anointing, he set aside the *seli* (sacred headgear) tradition. Instead, Guru Hargobind opted for *kalgi,* an aigrette (the head plumes of the egret bird) on his turban and donned two kirpans (swords), one representing the Miri (temporal power) and the other representing Piri (spiritual power). The Mughals' hope of quelling the Sikhs had the opposite effect on people. They turned to Sikhi in greater numbers and were ready to lay down their lives to protect their religion. Finding a trivial excuse of nonpayment of fines imposed on his father, Guru Hargobind was imprisoned. The Sikh movement grew more robust, forcing the Mughal emperor to release the Guru.

History records that Guru Hargobind refused to leave the Gwalior Fort unless all fifty-two innocent Hindu princes, rulers of the mountainous regions of Punjab, who were also being held captive, were also released. Jahangir reluctantly agreed, but with a caveat: he would only allow the release of prisoners who could hold onto the corners of the Guru's robe. Guru Hargobind skillfully designed a robe tailored with fifty-two corners or strings and left the fort with all fifty-two rulers trailing behind him. When the Sikhs learned that their Guru had finally been released from captivity, they lit divas (lamps) in their homes. The release date coincided with Divali. Late in the twentieth century, this day was aptly named Bandi Chhor Divas or "Liberation Day" and was added to the Sikh calendar (Nanakshahi). It is celebrated by Sikhs the world over around the time of Divali.

108. What is Hola Mohalla?

Hola Mohalla, also called simply Hola, is a Sikh festival that is celebrated in March. The tradition was established by Guru Gobind Singh in the late seventeenth century to display and highlight Sikh martial arts through simulated battles. *Hola* means "the onset of an attack or frontal assault," and *Mohalla* implies an organized procession in the form of an army column.

Hola Mohalla is celebrated by Sikhs around the world. The celebration in Anandpur Sahib, Panjab, lasts for three days. In this city, Guru Gobind Singh initiated the first five Sikhs (Panj Pyare) and created the order of Khalsa in 1699 CE. This festival draws millions of Sikhs and non-Sikhs from around the world.

109. What is the festival of Lohri?

Folk festivals connect ethnic groups with significant events and become part of their seasonal festivities. Lohri is a popular wintertime Panjabi folk festival, which is primarily celebrated in the Panjab region of the Indian subcontinent.

Although Lohri has no relevance to Sikhs' history or religion, its link to Panjab is undeniable. Being inclusive is one of the traits of Sikhs—sometimes to their detriment. Despite this, they have eagerly adopted many such customs and festivals.

Many people believe that the festival commemorates the passing of the winter and the sugarcane harvesting time. It is celebrated a day after Maghi, the Sikh festival commemorating the sacrifice of forty Sikh warriors (Chali Mukte) who gallantly fought against the invading Mughal army for the Guru's cause in 1705.

Like most Indian festivals, Lohri has some legend and lore attached to it. The Sandal Bar region of Punjab between the Chenab and Ravi Rivers, now in Pakistan, is where a warlord named Sandal Bhatti put up the stiffest opposition to the Mughal ruler Akbar (1541–1605) in the sixteenth century. They refused to pay taxes. Instead, they looted royal caravans and distributed the booty among the poor. Sandal and his son Kabir were captured and executed to instill fear among the general population. One of Kabir's offspring, Abdullah or Dullah, as he is fondly called, continued rebellious activities unfazed, including nonpayment of taxes. Dullah Bhatti became known as the "Robin Hood" of Punjab. Supposedly, he used to steal from the rich and rescue poor Punjabi girls being taken forcibly to be sold in slave markets. He arranged their marriages to boys of the region and provided them with dowries from the stolen money.

At one time, he adopted an impoverished girl who was assaulted by the Mughal army general and arranged her marriage. He was unable to get a Hindu priest on short notice to chant Vedic hymns and sanctify the marriage according to Hindu rites. Instead, he composed an impromptu song, "Sundar Munderiye." As the bride and groom started to circumambulate around the fire, he started singing his hilarious song. The lyrics go something like this:

> Sunder munderiye ho!—O' you pretty lass.
> Tera kaun vicharaa ho!—Who is your protector, you pitiable one?
> Dullah Bhatti walla ho!—The man called Dullah from village Bhatti.
> Dullhe di dhee viayee ho!—Dullah is getting his daughter married.
> Ser shakkar payee ho!—Served a pound of brown sugar to guests.

Kudi da laal pathaka ho!—The girl is wearing a red suit.

He continued to add funny lyrics about those who were in attendance, including taunting the Mughal police.

In Punjab, on Lohri, children would go door to door, singing this song and asking for treats. In the evening, a large bonfire is held, and guests join in the festivities. Diaspora Sikhs who celebrate Lohri will book a large gathering in a banquet hall to mark the first birth anniversary of a child. In the past, only male children were celebrated this way, but increasingly both male and female children are given a Lohri party in current times.

110. What celebrations or commemorations are unique to the Sikh faith?

The history of festivals can be fraught with inaccuracies, which makes many historians wary. However, Sikh festivals and commemorative events accurately reflect the past and remain fresh because Sikhi is a relatively young dharam (religion). The following are among these celebrations:

- *Gurpurbs*: A *gurpurb* is an anniversary or a remembrance day associated with the lives of the Gurus (birthdays or deaths), including celebrations of the first installation day of *Aad Granth* and the Proclamation Day of *Sri Guru Granth Sahib* as the eternal Sikh Guru. Sikhs celebrate these in gurdwaras around the world.
- *Shaheedi purab:* This is a martyrdom anniversary that includes Sikh Gurus as well as other famous persons who died for their faith throughout Sikh history. The Sikhs remember all martyred Sikhs in their daily prayer and celebrate martyrdom anniversaries of many who lost their lives defending the Sikh faith. Sikhs commemorate the following four *shaheedi purabs* all around the world:

- *Guru Arjan (1563–1606):* During the tenure of the fifth Sikh Guru, Guru Arjan (1581–1606), Sikhi spread exponentially. The Guru undertook projects that the Mughal rules were unable to do. He established health centres to treat many people suffering from leprosy and expanded free food services. This attracted masses (Muslims and Hindus) to adopt Sikhi, which the Mughal emperor could not tolerate. Guru Arjan was arrested, tortured, and martyred on May 25, 1606.

- *Guru Teg Bahadur (1621–1675):* The ninth Guru's martyrdom occurred in November 1675. He had taken up the cause of Hindus being forcefully converted to Islam by the Mughal ruler Aurangzeb. The history relates that Kashmiri Pandits (learned Hindu Brahmins) sought the Guru's help to protect them, as hundreds of them were being slaughtered by the Mughal forces for refusing to convert to Islam. Guru Teg Bahadur told them to go and tell the emperor that they would accept conversion if he (the Guru) converted. But the Guru refused to abandon Sikhi. Hoping to instill fear, the Mughal emperor killed the Guru's three associates mercilessly in front of his eyes: Bhai Mati Das was sawed into two, his brother Bhai Sati Das was wrapped in cotton and burnt alive, and the Bhai Dyala was tied and dropped in a cauldron of boiling water. These killings did not deter Guru Teg Bahadur's commitment to Sikhi, and he was subsequently beheaded. He is remembered as the defender of the Hindu faith (Hind Di Chadar) and the defender of all religions (Dharam Di Chadar). The Sikhs and many Hindus commemorate his martyrdom on November 22.

- *Char Sahibzaade:* The four sons of Guru Gobind Singh (1666–1708) are called Char Sahibzaade ("four sons"). The two elder brothers (Ajit Singh and Jujhar Singh, barely eighteen and fourteen years old, respectively) were martyred in the Battle of Chamkaur (1704) while fighting Mughal forces. The two younger brothers (Zorawar Singh and Fateh Singh, eight and six years old) were bricked alive in a wall in Sirhind for refusing to convert to Islam.

- *Banda Singh Bahadur*: In 1708, after Gobind Singh's death, Banda Singh Bahadur, a devout Sikh, led the Sikh armed struggle against Mughal tyranny. They took control of Sirhind, and in 1710, they established the first independent Sikh Raj (kingdom), which only lasted for six years. He issued a coin in Guru Nanak-Guru Gobind Singh's name during this brief rule and brought significant agrarian reforms. Banda Singh was arrested, tortured, and killed in 1716. A century later, Maharaja Karam Singh of Patiala had gurdwaras constructed in Sirhind to commemorate the young martyrs and their grandmother.

- *Chhota Ghallughara (March 10)*: The word *chhota* means "small," and *ghallughara* means "holocaust" or "genocide," which took place on March 10, 1746. As mentioned earlier, Sikhs had had a fairly traumatic and conflict-ridden history since birth.

To exterminate Sikhs, in the early 1740s, the Mughal ruler put a bounty on their heads. All Muslims were encouraged to kill Sikhs and take their heads to the governor to receive a cash reward. The governor of Punjab (Yahiya Khan) and his premier, Lakhpat Rai, a Hindu, took personal charge of this heinous campaign. In Lahore, the capital of Punjab, hundreds of Sikhs were rounded up and killed. Copies of the *Sri Guru Granth Sahib* were burnt. In 1746, as Sikhs were retreating to the forests, their path was blocked, and more than seven thousand of them were massacred mercilessly. This episode is recorded in Sikh history as Chhota Ghallughara or "small holocaust."

- *Vadda Ghallughara (February 5)*: The *vadda* ("large" or "massive") holocaust occurred on February 5, 1762, a mere sixteen years after the Chhota Ghallughara. This was the time when the Mughal rule in India was waning. Ahmad Shah Durrani (Abdali) (1722–1772), the first ruler of Afghanistan, invaded India continually but had to face Sikhs en route to Panipat, near Delhi. On his sixth attempt, he decided to wipe out Sikhs from the face of India altogether. Sikhs were cognizant of this. They planned to get their wives and children out of Punjab to safe places in Rajasthan. However, Durrani learned of the Sikhs' plan and attacked them on February 5, 1762, near the village of Kup Rahira, before they could get their families out of harm's way. Miskin, a contemporary Muslim chronicler, estimates the death toll at twenty-five thousand, and Ratan Singh Bhangu, a Sikh historian, records the figure of thirty thousand men, women, and children.

Within three months, Sikhs consolidated their forces and started taking control of Punjab territories bit by bit through twelve independent confederacies (*misls*). They eventually established the consolidated Sikh Empire in 1799 under the leadership of Maharaja Ranjit Singh (1780–1839), conquering most of Afghanistan as well.

• *Saka Jalianwala Bagh*: The word *saka* also means "holocaust," and Jalianwala Bagh is a historic garden in Amritsar. The place has a well on one side of the 6.5-acre property. On April 13, 1919, more than fifteen thousand people gathered to celebrate Vaisakhi, one of the holiest festivities of the Sikh calendar, and protest against the Raj, or British rule.

On that day, Jallianwala Bagh became a killing field, the well itself a mausoleum filled with the bodies of men, women, and children who, harboring the faintest hope or filled with the most profound desperation, jumped into its depths to avoid the fusillade from British-led troops under the command of Brigadier General Reginald Dyer. Dyer ordered his men to shoulder their .303 Lee-Enfield rifles and shoot indiscriminately into the crowd, hoping to inflict a teachable moment on those who had the audacity to challenge their colonial overlords. He succeeded—but not in the way he had intended.

The massacre's official death toll was 379, but unofficial estimates put it closer to one thousand—120 bodies were pulled from the well alone. Although Muslims and Hindus also died that day, by far most of the casualties were Sikh—a particularly galling fact, considering the enormity of the sacrifices Sikh soldiers had made fighting for the British mere months before when the First World War still raged.

Although Dyer had his supporters in Great Britain, Secretary of State for War Sir Winston Churchill was outraged, and on July 8, 1920, clearly expressed his disgust in a speech to Parliament, calling it "a monstrous event, an event which stands in singular and sinister isolation." Although his umbrage was doubtless genuine, Churchill also likely viewed the massacre in strategic terms. He knew the carnage at Amritsar could ignite an opposition movement that might, in turn, threaten the primacy of British rule over South Asia. He was correct.

- *Saka Nankana Sahib (February 21):* Sikhs fought several wars against invaders, including two with the British, to maintain their sovereign kingdom for fifty years. However, within ten years of Maharaja Ranjit Singh's death, in 1849, the East India Company succeeded in annexing Punjab as part of the British Raj. The British studied Sikhs and learned that they draw inspiration and courage from their scripture, the *Sri Guru Granth Sahib*, as well as their holy places. To undermine Sikhs, the British administration decided to split them by supporting British sympathizer managers of historical gurdwaras. By the early 1920s, Sikhs were tired of these corrupt and immoral managers.

Nankana Sahib is the birthplace of Guru Nanak, the founder of Sikhi. On February 20, 1921, when a group of Sikhs entered the gurdwara there, eighty-five of them were murdered in cold blood, some burnt alive, including an eight-year-old child. "All indications point to the fact that the cruel and barbaric action is the second edition of Jalianwala Bagh massacre [April 1919] rather more evil and more invidious than even Jalianwala," wrote the renowned Sikh author Khushwant Singh in his two-volume history.[118] The Sikhs "remained peaceful and nonviolent from the start to the end," said M. K. Gandhi on March 3, 1921.[119]

- *Saka Akal Thakhat:* As mentioned, *saka* means "holocaust," and Akal Takhat, in the vicinity of the Darbar Sahib (the Golden Temple) in Amritsar, refers to the throne of the timeless and a seat of Sikh temporal authority. Sikhs commemorate the first week of June as "*Saka Akal Takhat.*" During this week in 1984, thousands of innocent Sikh pilgrims, including men, women, and children, were massacred by the Indian Army during an attack on Darbar Sahib (the Golden Temple) and thirty-eight other historical gurdwaras. The assault was code-named "Operation Blue Star" by the Indian government.

- *Sikh Genocide Week:* Sikhs designate the first week of November as Sikh Genocide Week to remember the November 1984 pogrom during which more than fourteen thousand Sikhs were killed in cold blood (the government of India's official number is only three thousand). They were burned alive with rubber tires around their necks, and women and girls were humiliated and gang-raped in front of their family members before being similarly tortured and killed.

111. Do Sikhs commemorate Remembrance Day?

The Sikh tradition of honourable military service can be traced back to the early seventeenth century, when the sixth Guru, Guru Hargobind (1595–1644), at his accession ceremony to guruship in 1606, decided to wear two *kirpans* (swords) representing Piri (spirituality sovereignty) and Miri (temporal sovereignty). The Guru wanted Sikhs to be both saint and soldier (*sant* and *sipahi*). This was the time when Guru Arjan, the fifth Guru, had been martyred for his refusal to convert to Islam. Some Sikhs

---

[118]   Khushwant Singh, *A History of the Sikhs*, vol. 2, *1839–2004*, 2nd ed. (Oxford: Oxford University Press, 2004; original work published 1963), 200.

[119]   Ruchi Ram Sahni, *Struggle for Reform in Sikh Shrines*, ed. Ganda Singh (Sikh Ithas Research Board, 1969), 81.

celebrate Remembrance Day today to commemorate the contributions of Sikh soldiers to the war efforts and the larger human costs. However, there are others who decry the practice because it is symbolic of a foreign imperialist war that defended an unjust system within which Sikhs had been yoked by the British. This debate is ongoing.

Sikh prowess in war is well documented. Prince Albert Victor of Wales, on his visit to Lahore (then the capital of Punjab) in 1890, referred to Punjab as "the soldiers' land," adding, "There is no province in India that can boast, as Punjab can, that it is the bulwark of defence against foreign invaders, or that can be termed with the same significance the guard-room of the Eastern Empire."[120] According to Katie Daubs, writing in the *Toronto Star* in November 2015, Sikhs' "reputation as fierce military men was a staple of Allied propaganda and even Kellogg's cereal box inserts."[121]

The British had recognized Sikhs' military skills and enlisted them in large numbers. Jagdeesh Mann wrote in a 2019 opinion piece in the *Toronto Star*:

Sikh soldiers in Paris in 1916 during WWI

> In the First World War, the Indian Army contributed a million combatants, of which half were from Punjab regiments to the war effort, and lost more soldiers—75,000—than Canada, Australia, or the other dominions. They suffered 9,000 casualties holding off the Germans in the First Battle of Ypres in fall 1914.[122]

---

[120]   Quoted in General Sir John J. H. Gordon, *The Sikhs* (Edinburgh and London: William Blackwood & Sons, 1904), 236.

[121]   Katie Daubs, "Celebrating Sikh Soldiers on Remembrance Day," *Toronto Star*, November 9, 2015, para. 7, https://www.thestar.com/amp/news/gta/2015/11/09/celebrating-sikh-soldiers-on-remembrance-day.html.

[122]   Jagdeesh Mann, "Race Politics Whitewashed Canadian History," *Toronto Star*, July 20, 2019.

And according to the Sikh Museum website:

> Over 65,000 Sikh soldiers fought in WWI as part of the British Army, and over 300,000 Sikhs fought alongside the allies in WWII. Over 83,000 Sikh soldiers died in [the] two World Wars fighting alongside their Canadian, British and American allies as part of the British Indian Army. These valiant fighters stood tall as friends in need at the darkest hour, winning more than 9,000 awards for gallantry (including 11 Victoria Crosses).[123]

The author with the oldest living (110 years in 2021) WWII veteran Reuben Sinclair in 2017.

Ten Sikhs out of a meagre population of 1,100 in the nation joined the Canadian Army to fight in World War I, and more than 125 served in World War II.[124] Canada is proud to have a Sikh defence minister, former Lieutenant Colonel Harjit Sajjan, who served in Bosnia and Afghanistan before being elected as an MP by the riding of Vancouver South in 2015. Thus, Remembrance Day has a special significance in the lives of Sikhs. The community pays homage to our fallen brothers and sisters because of whom we are enjoying our freedom today.

123   SikhMuseum.com, https://www.sikhmuseum.com.
124   Hugh Johnston, "Group Identity in an Emigrant Worker Community: The Example of Sikhs in Early Twentieth-Century British Columbia," *BC Studies*, no. 148 (Winter 2005–2006): 4, https://ojs.library.ubc.ca/index/php/bcstudies/article/view/1772/1817.

112. Does Sikhi advocate going on pilgrimages?

Sikhi places no value on pilgrimages or attending so-called holy sites in order to receive salvation. For the Gurus, the entire Earth is sacred, and no single place is "holier" than any other. As going on pilgrimages was an important religious tradition in the dominant religions of the time, the Gurus spent considerable energy trying to explain the importance of living a truthful existence rather than trying to seek salvation or expecting one's "sins" to be washed away simply by visiting and worshipping at a particular place. *SGGS* is replete with passages that explain how attending a pilgrimage will not result in spiritual salvation.[125]

Nevertheless, many Sikhs organize and go on tours or "pilgrimages" to historical sites. One such site is called Hemkunt Sahib gurdwara, situated at fifteen thousand feet above sea level, surrounded by the Himalayas in northern India. Dr. Jaswant Singh Neki, a leading Sikh scholar writes, "According to Bachitra Natak, the autobiographical account of the tenth Guru, Gobind Singh, it was at Hemkunt 'adorned with seven snow-dad peaks' that he meditated in his previous birth."[126] A gurdwara was built on the site allegedly referred to in the *Bachitr Natak* in the 1960s by Major General Harkirat Singh. It has become a tourist attraction since the 1970s. However, many Sikhs question the authenticity and authorship of the *Bachitr Natak*, and they do not believe that Guru Gobind Singh wrote it. They also do not ascribe any spiritual or historical significance to Hemkunt Sahib Gurdwara, and they view the idea of it being a site of pilgrimage as against Sikh teachings.

Some Sikhs believe that bathing at specific gurdwaras will cleanse their souls. For example, Goindwal Gurdwara has eighty-four steps leading down into a pool, which many Sikhs say equate to the 8.4 million species referenced in the *SGGS*. Some Sikhs think that bathing

---

[125] *SGGS* 473: a(n)dharahu jhooThe paij baahar dhuneeaa a(n)dhar fail. aThasaTh teerath je naaveh utarai naahee mail. ਅੰਦਰਹੁ ਝੂਠੇ ਪੈਜ ਬਾਹਰਿ ਦੁਨੀਆ ਅੰਦਰਿ ਫੈਲਿ ॥ ਅਠਸਠਿ ਤੀਰਥ ਜੇ ਨਾਵਹਿ ਉਤਰੈ ਨਾਹੀ ਮੈਲੁ॥

[126] Neki, Jaswant Singh Dr. *Pilgrimage to Hemkunt*, 2002, Singh Brothers, Amritsar.

at the gurdwara will free them from having to transmigrate through various life cycles. As they go down each step, they repeat the *Mool Mantar* in the fervent hope of freeing themselves from the cycle of birth and death. Other Sikhs believe it is important to bathe at Darbar Sahib to be a "complete" Sikh. These Sikhs take their inspiration from a sabad by Guru Ramdas:

> That person who is called a true Sikh, awakens every morning and meditates on the Divine Name. Such a person makes an effort each morning to bathe the body and immerse themselves into the pool of nectar.[127]

As the word employed in this sabad for the pool of nectar is "Amritsar," where the Darbar Sahib is located, and since Guru Ramdas started the construction of the pool surrounding the Darbar Sahib, many Sikhs have interpreted the sabad to mean that the Guru is enjoining them to make a pilgrimage to Darbar Sahib. However, most *katha vachiks* and translators of Gurbani, such as Professor Sahib Singh (1892—1977), believe that the reference is to the pool of nectar that accumulates in the mind when one meditates on the divine name. Guru Ramdas sabad "*Ramdas sarovar naate; sabh uatre paap kamaate*" literally translated in the "Sikhi to the Max" states that "bathing in the nectar tank of Ram Das, all sins are erased." This encourages many Sikhs to bathe in the pool surrounding the Darbar Sahib. Professor Sahib Singh's Panjabi interpretation of *SGGS* reads, "Those who enjoin sadh sangat (fellowship of the seekers of truth, the devout congregation), their past *paap* shall be erased."[128] This is consistent with the numerous teachings in the *SGGS* where the Gurus spoke out against ritualism and practices such as fasting and pilgrimage.

---

[127]   *SGGS* 305–306: "Gur satgur ka jo Sikh akaey…" ਗੁਰ ਸਤਿਗੁਰ ਕਾ ਜੋ ਸਿਖੁ ਅਖਾਏ ਸੁ ਭਲਕੇ ਉਠਿ ਹਰਿ ਨਾਮੁ ਧਿਆਵੈ॥

[128]   *SGGS* 625: "raamadhaas sarovar naate. sabh utare paap kamaat. ਰਾਮਦਾਸ ਸਰੋਵਰਿ ਨਾਤੇ ॥ ਸਭਿ ਉਤਰੇ ਪਾਪ ਕਮਾਤੇ॥

Guru Nanak says in Jap Ji Sahib, "Ritualistic washing will not cleanse your soul, even if you do it a hundred thousand times."[129]

Sikhi teaches that austerity and penance do not intrinsically connect with the soul or spirit. Guru Nanak visited various pilgrimage centres to spread his message that the true pilgrimage was to look inward and recognize Waheguru within the self and all of creation. According to the teachings of the Gurus, meditation on the divine name, which can be performed sitting at home or anywhere, is the true pilgrimage and the only purifying act.

---

[129] *SGGS* 1: "soche soch na hovee jai soche lakh vaar—ਸੋਚੈ ਸੋਚਿ ਨ ਹੋਵਈ ਜੇ ਸੋਚੀ ਲਖ ਵਾਰ ॥

CHAPTER 13

Pluralism in Practice

Plurality of religious traditions and cultures has come to characterize every part of the world today. But what is pluralism? Here are four points to contextualize this discussion, drawn from the interfaith Pluralism Project website established by Diana L. Eck, a Harvard professor.[130]

- First, *pluralism is not diversity alone but the energetic engagement with diversity.* Diversity can and has meant the creation of religious ghettoes with little traffic between or among them. Today, religious diversity is a given, but pluralism is not a given social reality; it is an achievement. Mere diversity without real encounters and relationships will yield increasing tensions in our societies.
- *Second, pluralism is not just tolerance but the active seeking of understanding across lines of difference.* Tolerance is a necessary public virtue, but it does not require Christians, Muslims, Hindus, Jews, and ardent secularists to know anything about one another. Tolerance is too thin a foundation for a world of religious difference and proximity.
- *Third, pluralism is not relativism but the encounter of commitments.* The new paradigm of pluralism does not require us to leave

---

[130] Diana L. Eck, "What Is Pluralism?" The Pluralism Project, Harvard University, https://pluralism.org/about.

our identities and commitments behind because pluralism is the encounter of commitments. It means holding our deepest differences—even our religious differences—not in isolation but in relation to one another.

- *Fourth, pluralism is based on dialogue.* The language of pluralism is that of dialogue and encounter, give and take, criticism and self-criticism. Dialogue means both speaking and listening, and that process reveals both common understandings and real differences.

Keeping these four points in mind, this chapter examines how Sikhs interact with the multi-faith world they live in.

113. How do Sikhs view other religions?

It is commonly and perhaps rightly said that "man will do anything for religion—wrangle over it, argue it, fight for it, die for it—except living for it."[131] To hate a person and to worship God seems to be both contradictory and perverse.

Sikhi teaches that the ultimate reality of Waheguru is to be attained through service to humanity. Guru Nanak taught equality and respect for all. As highlighted many times in previous chapters, he advocated a three-pronged approach to life: to earn an honest living (*kirat karna*); to share the rewards of life with others (*vand shakna*); and to do both—live every moment of life—with an awareness of the infinite within you (*Naam Japna*). In this concept of service to humankind, there is no mention that those served must only be Sikh. Sikhs are dedicated to the service of humanity without distinction of one's personal characteristics, race, religion, ethnic identity, sexual orientation, or socioeconomic status.

Sikhi defines God as love—but love that is not limited only to Sikhs. If God is love, then to be "furious" in the name of religion is to be

---

131   W. Gurney Benham, *The Book of Quotations* (Philadelphia: J. B. Lippincott, 1914).

genuinely irreligious. In speaking of the road to spiritual enlightenment, the Gurus spoke of the universality of the human condition:

> Of all religions, the best religion is to utter the holy name with love and do good deeds. Of all rites, the holiest rite is to purify one's soul in the company of the holy; of all efforts, the best effort is to meditate on Waheguru and sing the Divine Name; of all speech, the sweetest is that having heard it, to speak of Waheguru's glory; of all temples, the most sacred is, says Nanak, the heart in which Waheguru dwells.[132]

The *SGGS* starts with three words: "One Divine Source." This is interpreted to mean that there is only God—not a Hindu God, Jewish God, Christian God, or Muslim God, but one universal Creator from which all life emanates. Guru Arjan says, "There is one Father, and we are all his children."[133] Though this verse employs the word "father," the word is used as an analogy, Sikhs view the Divine Source as free of gender, form, caste, or birth and the embodiment of truth and love.

Sikhi teaches us to respect, and not just tolerate, other spiritual paths. This respect can only grow from an understanding of our common ground and common source. In every aspect of Sikhi, from the *SGGS*, which includes the spiritual writings of persons of different faiths, to the laying of the foundation stone for the Darbar Sahib (Sikhi's most revered historic site) by a Muslim saint, Sant Mian Mir, to the structure of the gurdwara itself (four doors but one entranceway, to indicate all are welcome from every corner of the earth, but enter as one), Sikhi teaches respect and equality of all faith traditions.

It is a small wonder that Sikhs take the right of others to practice their own faiths very seriously. It was this belief in the freedom of conscience that motivated Guru Teg Bahadur to defend the rights of

---

[132]   *SGGS* 272: Sukhmani, Asatpadi 3, Pauri 8.

[133]   *SGGS* 611: Ek pitaa ekas kai hum baarak tu mera gur haaeyk ਏਕੁ ਪਿਤਾ ਏਕਸ ਕੇ ਹਮ ਬਾਰਕ ਤੂ ਮੇਰਾ ਗੁਰ ਹਾਈ॥

Hindus to practice their faith freely. He put his own life on the line and was beheaded in 1675 for his stance against forceful conversion of Hindus. More recently, the World Sikh Organization of Canada has defended the rights of Muslim women to wear the niqab in public and have argued cases before the Supreme Court of Canada in order to defend the rights of Christians and Jews to practice their faith freely.[134]

114. Do Sikhs have theological or other objections to the celebration of Halloween?

There is no bar for a Sikh to participate in Halloween festivities. Though Halloween is not widely celebrated in Southeast Asia, most Sikh families living in North America have no issue with their children partaking in the fun. Although Sikhs do not believe in supernatural invaders like ghosts, sorcerers, witches, and beasts that are said to be roaming the streets on Halloween night, many Sikh children in North America take part in this festive occasion, dressing up in costumes and going door to door asking for treats with the phrase "Trick or treat!" Sikh families are happy to participate in this event and give out candies to children and money for UNICEF and other charities. Halloween helps bring out the playful, childlike qualities in all of us. It is enjoyable to have festivities during this harvest season for fun and community sharing.

115. Are Sikhs permitted to observe holy days in other faiths?

The Sikh faith was born in Guru Nanak's realization of the unity of humanity under one universal Creator, a Creator who favoured no particular religion, language, gender, race, caste, or social status. Instead, this omnipresent Divine exists within every human being (and indeed within every living creature), regardless of which faith one chooses to

---

[134] *Loyola High School v. Quebec (Attorney General)*, 2015, and *Syndicat Northcrest v. Amselem*, 2004. For more information, see https://www.worldsikh.org.

follow. Guru Nanak said, "One who sees divine light within each heart understands the essence of Guru's teachings."[135]

All religions have certain days that are more sacred to the faithful than they are to the community at large. The Sikh faith teaches us to respect all beliefs. However, there is a difference between respecting other faith traditions and celebrating them. We believe Christmas has a similar meaning for Christians as Guru Nanak's birth anniversary or Vaisakhi (the birth of Khalsa) has to Sikhs. Thus, Sikhs do not celebrate the birth of Christ, but rather, the births of their own Gurus.

However, even if they do not believe in the religious significance of Christmas, there are some Sikhs that will participate in the cultural aspects of Christmas, such as decorating their homes with a Christmas tree or exchanging gifts. Other Sikhs may take their children to have pictures taken with Santa Claus. Despite Christmas having a deep religious meaning for many Christians, it has been commercialized to the extent that many non-Christians celebrate the event as well. Rather than ascribing to its sacred significance, they consider it a time for family and friends to come together. Some remember the Creator for the bounties they continue to receive daily, including the gift of life. Though many Sikh families may partake in gift exchanges or holiday decorations, other practicing Sikhs refuse to participate in the commercial aspects of Christmas since they consider it a profound disrespect to Christianity.

These festive celebrations present vital opportunities for different faiths to come together through a dialogue that fosters a greater understanding of each other. Learning about the faith traditions of our neighbours is one step toward building a more harmonious and loving society.

---

[135] *SGGS* 20: ghat ghat jot nirantaree boojhay gurmat saar—ਘਟਿ ਘਟਿ ਜੋਤਿ ਨਿਰੰਤਰੀ ਬੂਝੈ ਗੁਰਮਤਿ ਸਾਰ ॥

116. Do Sikhs believe in proselytizing or converting people into Sikhi?

Sikhi places no value on converting people or having them change their belief systems. Rather, Sikhi encourages each person of faith to be true to the core teachings of their religion rather than being lost in the superficial and man-made religious structures of organized religion. Its emphasis is on being true to the core principles of whatever faith we have chosen to follow. Sikhi teaches that if one is a Christian, they should be a true Christian; if one is a Muslim, they should be a true Muslim, and if one is a Jew, they should be a true Jew.

117. Can a Sikh also believe in other religions?

Simply put, no. Sikhi teaches us to commit to a particular path and to ensure that we follow that path's core and true teachings rather than getting lost in the superficial trappings of religious dogma. Considering that Sikhi teaches that each religion is a different path to reach the same goal, Sikhs believe that success can only be attained if one follows a specific path. The danger of following different teachers—and different paths or religions—is that one will likely end up going around in circles and never reach one's ultimate goal.

Religions are akin to different routes to a common destination. Take the city of Paris, for example. There are many different routes that one can take to get to Paris. Some may arrive through Britain, using the Channel Tunnel, while others may come through Belgium. Some may travel on foot, while others choose to fly or drive. Some routes are shorter and more direct, and others may be more scenic but circuitous and take longer. Some routes are easy to follow, and others are covered in grass and mud and are difficult to see. Regardless of the route, if one commits to one path, one will eventually make it to Paris. However, if one keeps shuffling back and forth between different paths, and not committing to any specific one, they will most likely never arrive in Paris.

So, for Sikhs, what is more important is finding a trustworthy guide

(Guru or teacher) who you believe has achieved the spiritual goal that you are seeking and then committing to the spiritual path provided by your chosen Guru. The journey may not be a simple one, and the path may often be cluttered with debris that must be painstakingly removed to see the path more clearly, but if one is committed to following the way of their Guru, the path will surely lead the faithful to their ultimate goal. For a Sikh, the Guru is *Sri Guru Granth Sahib*.

118. What is Sikhi's perspective on interfaith dialogue?

Interfaith dialogue is encouraged in the Sikh faith—not to convert others but to help discover our unity. The Sikh faith encourages discussion that rises above the distinctions of religion, ethnicity, gender, and class. One of Guru Nanak's first lessons was that humanity is one and that the divisions we have created are artificial. Indeed, much of Guru Nanak's life can be seen as a model for interfaith dialogue and encounter.

Guru Nanak traveled throughout Southeast Asia and parts of the Middle East. He visited major centres of Islam, Hinduism, Buddhism, and Jainism, and he engaged in dialogue with people of all faiths. Initially, he was met with apprehension. Despite that, his ability to transcend the bounds of religion and language endeared him to all who attended his congregations. As a result, he had friends and admirers from every community. Each subsequent Guru continued in Guru Nanak's tradition and courted members of other faiths as close friends. Even where the Sikhi is not in agreement with a particular religious observance, the Gurus taught that all persons must be afforded the freedom to follow their conscience.

In today's world, religious barriers continue to be an obstacle to understanding—or to true pluralism. Reluctance to engage in theological discussions for fear of offending others keeps us apart. Creating a safe space for people of different faiths to talk and participate on a personal level is vital. Once we speak, we realize that while we may not share a religious identity, we have much more that connects us than separates us. In the end, we all share our humanity.

119. Should we teach our children about other religions?

Sikhi encourages us to learn about different faiths. That broadens one's horizon and brings communities together. The emphasis is to dwell on similarities and avoid criticism of others.

The world has become a global village. Most countries have diverse, multicultural, and multi-religious communities. Canada takes pride in being a multicultural country and credits its diversity as a strength. School playgrounds reflect the different faces of our global community. All of us have a responsibility to teach the next generation the core national values of respect for the beliefs and traditions of others and acceptance of the similarities and differences between all cultures and religions. Parents, clergy, teachers, and school administrators play an equally important role in fostering these attitudes.

School boards across Canada have responded to the needs of a diverse student body by embedding equity guidelines in educational policy, reinforcing how vital it is for staff and students to encourage an environment where children feel accepted and included. This is particularly vital to Sikh youths from one of the most visibly distinct religious communities. Throughout the world, more than twenty-eight million Sikhs practice a faith that requires adherence to a strict code of conduct and the maintenance of five articles of faith that are essential to the identity of each devotee.

Since anti-racism is a fundamental principle of provincial curricula, school classrooms are the primary venues for dispelling the ignorance that feeds hatred. A cursory examination of the foods and festivities of a particular culture should not be the primary aim of a course about religion; the aim should be to foster understanding and appreciation for diversity that moves beyond the superficial and equally recognizes the unique perspective and practice of each Muslim, Sikh, Hindu, Jewish, Christian, or atheist student.

Many Canadians who practice the Sikh faith have faced considerable hardship at schools across the nation, having to defend their rights guaranteed by the Charter of Rights and Freedoms. While some students have responded to these difficulties by launching human-rights complaints or asking family and friends to participate in educational programming, others have quietly endured hurtful remarks, physical and mental abuse, and violence. Mutual understanding (true pluralism) is the foundation for preventing such injustice.

Religious and cultural diversity does not have to be a source of contention or acrimony if all members of society are willing to learn about their fellow citizens. Regardless of our professional roles in society, all of us have a duty to foster awareness and appreciation for the beliefs, perspectives, and traditions of those faith traditions outside the dominant majority.

PART IV

Creator

CHAPTER 14

Waheguru (God)

Most humans have a deep-seated hunger to know who created this awe-inspiring universe, how it functions, and what our role on Earth is. The mystery of divine power intrigues us, whether we are religious or not. Sikhs are students of life and seekers of truth and divine knowledge. And our greatest teacher—Waheguru—is the life force itself. The *Sri Guru Granth Sahib* forms the basis of what we do and how we conduct our lives. Leading a spiritually informed life leads to joy and inexplicable peace as we achieve our true purpose: conscious union with our Divine Source.

The central focus of Sikhi is spiritual enlightenment: to know and become one with the Divine Source of all creation. Along the way, Sikh philosophy attempts to answer the big questions that every student of life wrestles with: who am I, where did I come from, and why am I here? Yet Gurbani also teaches that the answer to the ultimate question—who created me?—is elusive and ultimately knowable only by the Divine Source itself. Thus, while I have attempted to answer the below questions, they are imperfect attempts to explain the perfect. Waheguru teaches us that the unknowable will always remain a mystery to all but Itself.

120. What is Waheguru (God)?

Sikhs do not ascribe to pantheistic ideas of multiple gods or a personal supreme godlike being. God is the Creator *and* the creation. It is, at once, the form and the formless; the eternal and the temporal; the immaterial and the material. Transcendent and yet permeating through every atom of the universe, it is the composer, the singer, the song, and the audience. According to Sikhi, whatever name God is called, there is only one God, the ever-present essence. In the Sikh scripture, God is referred to by thirty-six different names, more than fifteen thousand times. "The creator created Itself; and assumed Its own Name," says Guru Nanak.[136]

Gurbani contains numerous sabads about the qualities of God. Yet none summarize it more exquisitely than this original symbol, *Ik-Ong-Kaar*, which marks the beginning of the Sikh scriptures:

Professor Sahib Singh, the foremost modern theologian on Sikhi, explains the Sikh vision of the Divine as "One Supreme Reality that permeates the whole universe—there is none like it."[137]

Guru Nanak explains his vision of all-encompassing and genderless Divine Creator, through the *Mool Mantar* (original utterance), which appears as the first writing in the Sikh scripture:

Ik-Ongkaar—There is one eternal being that is all-embracing
Satnam—Whose name is "the one that exists"
Karta—The Creator of the universe
Purakh—The consciousness which permeates through all of creation

---

[136] *SGGS* 463: aapeen(h)ai aap saajio aapeen(h)ai rachio naau—ਆਪੀਨੈ ਆਪੁ ਸਾਜਿਓ ਆਪੀਨੈ ਰਚਿਓ ਨਾਉ॥
[137] Professor Sahib Singh, *Sri Guru Granth Sahib Darpan*, volume 1, 44, Raj Publishers, Jalandhar.

Nirbhau—That which has no fear

Nirvair—That which has no enmity

Akal murat—That form that is not bound by time

Ajuni—That which is unborn

Saibhang—That which came into existence on its own

Gurparsaad—That which can be realized with the grace of the true Guru

Though God has infinite qualities, for Sikhs, God is best described as Waheguru, the wondrous teacher. The Sikh scripture describes Waheguru as *nirgun* and *sargun,* absolute and personal. "Manifesting Its power, it fascinates the entire world," says Guru Arjan, the fifth Guru.[138] Waheguru is truth and knowledge. "There is none other like Waheguru; It is Unique, Formless, and present all over (Omnipresent)," writes Guru Gobind Singh, the tenth Guru.[139]

121. Is Waheguru (God) male or female?

For Sikhs, Waheguru is genderless, beyond gender, yet existing in all genders. "God is at once mother and father," says Guru Arjan, the fifth Sikh Guru.[140] The One in Sikhi is considered as *jot saroop*, meaning "luminescence of light" or "intangible spirit." And the *jot* (light) has no gender.

Gurbani uses both masculine and feminine pronouns to refer to Waheguru. So why do so many Sikh texts refer to Waheguru using the masculine pronoun? There are several reasons for this incorrect attribution of a gender to the Sikh vision of Waheguru God.

One reason has to do with the difficulty that arises when translating concepts from a different language and frame of reference into English. The linguistic differences between Panjabi and English make a direct

---

[138] *SGGS* 287: nirgun aap sargun bhee ohee; kalaa dhaar jin sagalee mohee. ਨਿਰਗੁਨ ਆਪਿ ਸਰਗੁਨ ਭੀ ਓਹੀ ॥ ਕਲਾ ਧਾਰਿ ਜਿਨਿ ਸਗਲੀ ਮੋਹੀ॥

[139] Dasam Bani, Jaap Sahib, Slok 58: aanupe aarupe smustal nivasee—ਅਨੂਪੇ ਅਰੂਪੇ ਸਮਸਤੁਲ ਨਿਵਾਸੀ॥

[140] *SGGS* 103: tu mera pita tu hain mera mata –ਤੂੰ ਮੇਰਾ ਪਿਤਾ ਤੂੰਹੈ ਮੇਰਾ ਮਾਤਾ॥

translation of Gurbani impossible. Panjabi, like French, is a language that gives masculine or feminine characteristics to all objects, animate or inanimate. While a book in English has no gender attributes—in French, "le livre" is a male; in Panjabi, the "*qitab*" is female.

A second reason is that the Panjabi language does not exhibit a strictly binary view of the world. Rather, Punjabi has a gender-neutral pronoun, "the one," which could refer to male or female actors. The absence of this gender-neutral pronoun in common English usage has frequently resulted in mistranslations of Gurbani. Where Waheguru is referred to as the "One" in the Sikh scriptures, translators have used the word "He." This is particularly the case with male Sikh scholars who have often defaulted to the masculine pronoun—no doubt because it resonates more easily with them.

The third reason has to do with the way in which Gurbani refers to the relationship between the Creator and creation. It is often expressed in a similar manner to the yin and yang concepts in Taoism—the male and female energy of the universe. In passages in Gurbani that use this analogy, all of creation is described as a feminine energy, and the Creator is described as a masculine energy. Thus, while the Gurus were all male, they referred to themselves using female pronouns in their spiritual writings. In passages of Gurbani that express this concept of the female unifying energy within all of humanity, the attribution of a masculine pronoun to the Divine was intentional, and the usage of the pronoun "He" may be appropriate. Sadly, the profoundly important idea that all souls (regardless of gender) share the same positive female energy, has literally been "lost in translation" by the indiscriminate use of the pronoun "He" in reference to Waheguru (God).

The final explanation has to do with the influence of traditional Indic social hierarchy, which was reinforced during British rule. The male-centred social structures that the Gurus challenged were recombined and integrated into the institutional framework of Sikhi to make it resemble a "religion" modeled after Christianity. These, in turn, gained support from imperial rulers. Disallowing women roles and prominence in Sikhi's institutions has meant that the female voice, which dominates

Sikh scriptures, has been virtually absent in the interpretation of the same scripture.

122. Where did Waheguru come from?

Most philosophers have struggled to solve this dilemma. The simple answer—that God created God—is a paradox that does not fit within our comprehension, yet that is precisely what Sikh philosophy teaches. Guru Nanak explains the self-manifesting quality of God this way:

> The One created Itself, and It assumed Its Divine Name.
> Then, the One fashioned creation. Seated within the creation, It beholds the play of the universe.[141]

To express divinity using a physical metaphor, Guru Nanak talks about the place where one can see and experience the presence of Waheguru:

> I have no desire to compete with or seek the company of lofty ideologues and arrogant individuals. Instead, I long for the company of the destitute, the lowest of the low, rock-bottom people [those who have been overlooked by society] because I know that is where God's blessings are showered.[142]

123. How can you find Waheguru?

Waheguru, in the simplest sense, is an experience rather than a thing. According to Gurbani, the One is an entity completely devoid of forms and shapes. The following question was posed to Guru Nanak by the

---

[141]   *SGGS* 463: aapeen(h)ai aap saajio aapeen(h)ai rachio naau—ਆਪੀਨੈ ਆਪੁ ਸਾਜਿਓ ਆਪੀਨੈ ਰਚਿਓ ਨਾਉ॥

[142]   *SGGS* 15: neechaa a(n)dhar neech jaat neechee hoo at neech- ਨੀਚਾ ਅੰਦਰਿ ਨੀਚ ਜਾਤਿ ਨੀਚੀ ਹੂ ਅਤਿ ਨੀਚ॥

Hindu *yogis* (ascetics): "When the Lord has no form, colour, [or] garb, how can we know Him and see Him?"[143] Guru Nanak replied, "Those who are detached from worldly attachments (*moh*) and are imbued with Its name, and follow Its commands, can see Waheguru everywhere." Thus, for Sikhs, understanding Waheguru is finding (experiencing) Waheguru.

While some may believe that Waheguru can be understood or experienced through wisdom and a discerning intellect, the Sikh scripture does not support that view. "Intellect and wisdom are of no use," says Guru Arjan."[144] Waheguru can be realized through humble devotion and Waheguru's grace.

Self-realization is the key to experiencing Waheguru within yourself. Guru Nanak further says, "Without controlling the wandering mind, you cannot realize Its value. Only a controlled mind can have a dialogue with Waheguru. It [Waheguru] cannot be realized by cleverness."[145] Another verse reiterates this point. "Waheguru is not obtained through intellect, ritual recitation, scholarly research, or cleverness. Devotion and love of the divine is the medium through which we meet the Creator."[146]

As gold is purified and made more valuable by being heated and pounded on the anvil, so the soul's vision is refined and made clear by perseverance, suffering, and pain. The difference is that one is a physical process, and the other is a spiritual process. Waheguru is not found by reasoning or logical argument; it is found through meditation and love. One must also learn to control the five vices that Sikhi teaches are barriers to spiritual growth: lust, anger, greed, emotional attachment, and ego. Ego is the most significant barrier of all. Sikh philosophy teaches that perseverance begets grace, which begets the Beloved. One

---

[143]   *SGGS* 945: varan bhaikh us roop na jaapee kio kar jaapis saachaa- ਵਰਨ ਭੇਖ ਅਸ ਰੂਪੁ ਨ ਜਾਪੀ ਕਿਉ ਕਰਿ ਜਾਪਸਿ ਸਾਚਾ॥

[144]   *SGGS* 396: chaturaiee siaanapaa kitai kaam na aaieeaai—ਚਤੁਰਾਈ ਸਿਆਨਪਾ ਕਿਤੈ ਕਾਮਿ ਨ ਆਈਐ॥

[145]   *SGGS* 221: chaturaiee na cheenia jaae; bin maare kio keemat paae—ਚਤੁਰਾਈ ਨਹ ਚੀਨਿਆ ਜਾਇ ॥ ਬਿਨੁ ਮਾਰੇ ਕਿਉ ਕੀਮਤਿ ਪਾਇ॥

[146]   *SGGS* 435: budh paaTh na paieeaai bahu chaturaieeaai bhai milai man bhaane - ਬੁਧਿ ਪਾਠਿ ਨ ਪਾਈਐ ਬਹੁ ਚਤੁਰਾਈਐ ਭਾਇ ਮਿਲੈ ਮਨਿ ਭਾਣੈ ॥

can reach greater heights and realize their primal state when inspired by the presence and teachings of the Guru, says Sikh scripture. "One must pound out ego, and only then shall one meet Waheguru," says Guru Amar Das.[147]

To find Waheguru, we need to start changing our thinking about Waheguru, start regarding every thought of Waheguru as Waheguru, and practice believing that Waheguru dwells in everyone, including ourselves. *Seva* (selfless service) and *simran* (meditation) are two wings, or should I say sails, that help us sail through the ocean of life. Sikh scripture talks about a longing to be one with the Creator by remembering and having faith in Waheguru. Guru Arjan says, "With each breath, I remember Waheguru and keep that memory close; I never go in search of another anywhere else."[148] Rendering service in this world helps one attain a place in the Divine Presence.

124. Where does Waheguru dwell?

While searching for God, scientists have pointed to many different regions of the brain. Dr. Vilayanur Ramachandran, a neuroscientist at the University of California proposed that God resided in the temporal lobe.[149] According to the *Independent*, the late Dr. Michael Persinger of Laurentian University did further studies. He carried out a test with the so-called God helmet, which stimulated a subject's temporal lobes, and he "found that he could artificially create the experience of religious feelings—the helmet's wearer report[ed] being in the presence of a spirit or having a profound feeling of cosmic bliss."[150] Elsewhere Andrew Newberg from the University of Pennsylvania injected a radioactive

---

[147]   *SGGS* 491: nanak vichahu haumay maaray taan har bhaitay soiee—ਨਾਨਕ ਵਿਚਹੁ ਹਉਮੈ ਮਾਰੇ ਤਾਂ ਹਰਿ ਭੇਟੇ ਸੋਈ॥

[148]   *SGGS* 812: saas saas nah beesray un kathay na dhaavou—ਸਾਸਿ ਸਾਸਿ ਨਹ ਵੀਸਰੈ ਅਨ ਕਤਹਿ ਨ ਧਾਵਉ॥

[149]   Steve Connor, "Belief and the Brain's 'God Spot.'" *Independent*, March 10, 2009, http://www.independent.ca.UK/news/science/belief-and-the-brains.

[150]   Ibid., para. 11.

isotope into practicing Buddhists at the point where they achieved meditative nirvana (paradise—a state of perfect happiness). According to the same article in the *Independent*, "Using a special camera, he captured the distribution of the tracer in the brain, which led the researchers to identify the parietal lobes as playing a key role during this transcendental state."[151]

Not all brain scientists think alike about God. In a study published in 2009 in the *Proceedings of the National Academy of Sciences*, Dr. Jordan Grafman, a neuropsychologist, wrote, "Religion doesn't have a 'God spot' as such, instead it's embedded in a whole range of other belief systems in the brain that we use every day."[152]

Sikhs believe that Waheguru is infinite and not confined to a particular part of the brain or the universe. And we believe that the human body is equipped with the means to connect or communicate with the supreme soul. The Sikh scripture provides an answer to this question of where Waheguru is located. According to Ayurvedic thought, the body is made of five perishable elements—earth, wind, fire, water, and ether (space). The Sikh Gurus taught that there exists a sixth element which is the life force; it is called *joti* or soul. This element permeates the entire corporeal structure, and indeed, the whole physical universe. The *atma* is considered a particle of the Divine. It is this essential human self that one must realize.

"Waheguru is the life support of the mind and the master of each breath of life; the One is within your body, don't search for It anywhere outside," says Guru Nanak. [153] He goes on to affirm in another verse, "Don't wander around looking for Waheguru externally. Look inside, and the True One resides in your body and [your] mind carries the divine light."[154] Guru Arjan also says, "The Waheguru of unfathomable form

---

[151]   Ibid., para. 14.

[152]   Ibid., para. 9.

[153]   *SGGS* 598: mun kaa jeeo paanpat dehee dehee meh dheau saamagaa—ਮਨਿ ਕਾ ਜੀਉ ਪਵਨਪਤਿ ਦੇਹੀ ਦੇਹੀ ਮਹਿ ਦੇਉ ਸਮਾਗਾ॥

[154]   *SGGS* 686: tan meh manooaa mun meh saachaa—ਤਨਿ ਮਹਿ ਮਨੂਆ ਮਨ ਮਹਿ ਸਾਚਾ॥

has Its place in the mind."[155] Bhagat Kabir, a fifteenth-century Indian mystic poet and saint whose writings are included in the *SGGS* also addresses how to find Waheguru. "Look deeper in your heart of hearts; that is the home and place where Waheguru lives."[156]

Gurbani speaks of five realms or domains *(khands)* of spiritual awareness. The first stage of spiritual reality is the realm of righteous action *(dharam khand),* followed by the realm of knowledge (*gyan khand*), the realm of spiritual endeavour (*saram khand*), the realm of grace *(karam khand),* and finally, the realm of truth *(sach khand),* where the formless God abides.[157] The *sach khand* is not a geographical region; it is a state of mind. It is a stage in life when a devotee finds spiritual union with the Creator and achieves complete harmony with the divine order *(hukam).*

As for where Waheguru is, the simple answer is everywhere. Waheguru is in you, me, and everything we see around us. However, Waheguru is not visible to the human physical eye. Gurbani teaches that Waheguru is in all of creation. The whole universe, inside each living being, the place where the Word (*Sabad*) is loved and sung—these are the Divine Creator's gurdwaras, temples, churches, synagogues, mosques, palaces, and huts. Guru Teg Bahadur, the ninth Guru, says, "My beloved Waheguru abides in each heart; the saints [Gurus] proclaim this as true."[158] Waheguru is the One, and the universe is part of the One.

In another verse in the *SGGS*, Guru Angad says, "The world is the home of the True One, in which the True One resides—in all Waheguru's creation."[159] Guru Arjan says, "Those who attend the faithful congregation and collectively meditate on *Naam* [the spiritual

---

[155] *SGGS* 186: Agam roop ka mun meh thaanaa—ਅਗਮ ਰੂਪ ਕਾ ਮਨ ਮਹਿ ਥਾਨਾ ॥

[156] *SGGS* 1349: dhil meh khoj dhilay dhil khojho ehee thaur mukaamaa—ਦਿਲ ਮਹਿ ਖੋਜਿ ਦਿਲੈ ਦਿਲਿ ਖੋਜਹੁ ਏਹੀ ਠਉਰ ਮੁਕਾਮਾ॥

[157] *SGGS* 7–8: Pauri 35–37: dharam khand ka aiho dharam—ਧਰਮ ਖੰਡ ਕਾ ਇਹੋ ਧਰਮ॥

[158] *SGGS* 1427: ghat ghat main har joo kahio pukaar—ਘਟਿ ਘਟਿ ਮੈ ਹਰਿ ਜੂ ਬਸੈ ਸੰਤਨ ਕਹਿਓ ਪੁਕਾਰਿ॥

[159] *SGGS* 463: Eh jug sachay key hai kothree sachay ka vich vaas—ਇਹ ਜਗ ਸਚੇ ਕੀ ਹੈ ਕੋਠੜੀ ਸਚੇ ਕਾ ਵਿਚਿ ਵਾਸੁ॥

word] become friends and realize that the master of the universe resides in all. The Creator gives the gift to all beings and cherishes them."[160]

125. Why was the universe created?

Gurbani teaches that Waheguru created the universe for Its own enjoyment—to at once become the playwright, the director, the actor, and the audience. Guru Arjan says, "For the remembrance of Waheguru [the Divine], the One created the whole Creation."[161] Many more verses in the Sikh scripture provide clarification on this question. Take the following: "Waheguru created the creation; the One watches over it, and Its command is over all. The One formed the planets, the solar system, and the nether regions and brought out what was hidden. No one knows Its limits. This understanding comes from the true Guru," says Guru Nanak.[162]

126. Is the Sikh faith the only way to spiritual enlightenment?

If you take away the external trappings of every religion—the clutter— you reveal the faith in its pure form. According to the Sikh Gurus, each religion in its pure form teaches the same fundamental values and philosophy. Each religion is a pathway to the same Divine Source. Thus, there is no need to convert to a different faith. If one is a Christian, one should be a faithful Christian; if one is a Muslim or Jew, one should be a true Muslim or Jew.

Sikhism was born out of a desire to put an end to prevailing superstitious beliefs and discriminatory practices that supported oppression and persecuted certain sections of society on the grounds

---

[160] *SGGS* 379: sabh madhe raviaa meraa Thaakur dhaan dhet sabh jeea sam(h) aare—ਮਧੇ ਰਵਿਆ ਮੇਰਾ ਠਾਕੁਰੁ ਦਾਨੁ ਦੇਤ ਸਭਿ ਜੀਅ ਸਮਾਰੇ॥

[161] *SGGS* 263: har simaran keeo sagal akaaraa—ਹਰਿ ਸਿਮਰਨਿ ਕੀਓ ਸਗਲ ਅਕਾਰਾ॥

[162] *SGGS* 1035: kar kar dhekhai hukam sabaiaa—ਕਰਿ ਕਰਿ ਦੇਖੈ ਹੁਕਮੁ ਸਬਾਇਆ ॥

of caste and creed. The Sikh faith champions traditions that would exemplify a commitment to peace and equality for every member of humanity. Gurbani teaches about the fundamental equality of all people. It notes that all humans are inherently good and equal before Waheguru—and that all have the choice of following their own spiritual path. Each religious tradition has equal value as a legitimate path to the Divine Source, with no particular faith group having more importance than another. The key is the adherent's sincerity of faith and practice. The *SGGS* is explicit on this: "Don't say that Vedas (the Hindu scriptures) and *Katebs* (the Abrahamic scriptures—Torah, Bible, and Quran) are false. Those who do not contemplate them are false."[163]

For many, Sikhi provides a practical spiritual path that demonstrates how to remain in high spirits (optimistic) throughout one's life, despite all kinds of trials and tribulations. By living in divine will, all may experience Waheguru's blessings. Through the daily practice of meditation, selfless service, and honest living, we can maintain and increase our understanding of the One despite all the negative forces around us. It is a struggle, with daily tests of one's faith, but the *Sri Guru Granth Sahib* is always there as our ultimate guide and teacher to help us live in a state of faith and love. In Sikhi, faith is determined by the way devotees live their lives. The goal of a Sikh is always to have a steadfast belief and trust in Waheguru and Its will. Sikhi inspires its adherents to remain in the state of complete faith in the Creator.

The *Sri Guru Granth Sahib* is the living spiritual teacher for Sikhs in all aspects of their lives. It is through the Sikh scripture that Sikhs find the tools of the faithful: inspiration and love for Waheguru and all of Its creations.

---

[163] *SGGS* 1350: bedh kateb kahahu mat jhooThe jhooThaa jo na bichaarai—ਬੇਦ ਕਤੇਬ ਕਹਹੁ ਮਤ ਝੂਠੈ ਝੂਠਾ ਜੋ ਨ ਬਿਚਾਰੈ ॥

127. What evidence is there that Waheguru exists?

For Sikhs, the existence of the universe itself is evidence of the existence of Waheguru. Even the smallest and most mundane aspects of life—from the miracle of conception and birth to a glorious sunset or the many mysteries of daily life—are realities that evince the existence of the One. Natural phenomena such as evolution, DNA, and the multiplicity of creation, including humans, animals, plants, minerals, stars, planets, and galaxies are divine wonders. The divine ordinance, or hukam, regulates the function of the universe. It is flawless, and everything happens as per the Divine One's decree.

CHAPTER 15

The Role of the Guru

The term *Guru* is most commonly interpreted as "teacher" or "spiritual guide," and *Sikh* is seen as "student," "learner," and "disciple." However, these words fail to convey the meanings of Guru and Sikh as used in the *Sri Guru Granth Sahib*. In the words of Guru Ramdas, "The *bani* [spiritual utterances of the Gurus] is the Guru, and Guru is the *bani*. Within the *bani*, the ambrosial nectar is contained."[164] In this chapter, I explain the relationship between Waheguru and the Gurus as well as Sikhs' commitment to living an ethical life as taught by the Sikh Gurus. The essential spiritual writings in the *Sri Guru Granth Sahib* motivate Sikhs and form the basis of what they do and how they conduct their lives.

128. What is a Guru in the Sikh faith?

There are different etymological interpretations of the word *Guru*. The one generally accepted in Sikhi is the one derived from the syllable *gu*, standing for darkness, and *ru* ("light"), standing for the one who removes darkness. The word *Guru* thus means "deliverer or liberator from darkness (ignorance) to light (enlightenment)." The Sikh Gurus taught how to move from darkness to light, from ignorance to enlightenment, from fear to confidence, from hate to love, and from despair to joy. Guru

---

[164]   *SGGS* 982: baanee guroo guroo hai baanee vich baanee a(n)mrit saare—ਬਾਣੀ ਗੁਰੂ ਗੁਰੂ ਹੈ ਬਾਣੀ ਵਿਚਿ ਬਾਣੀ ਅੰਮ੍ਰਿਤੁ ਸਾਰੇ॥

also refers to the "living word" (Gurbani, or Sabad Guru), the spiritual writings in the Sikh scripture.

While Sikhs believe that the guidance of the Guru is essential to one's spiritual enlightenment, Sikhi rejects the notion that the human Guru is a mediator between the disciple and Waheguru. Rather, Guru Nanak emphasized a personal and direct relationship with the Divine. The Guru's role is to reveal how to establish that relationship but never to come between the seeker and Waheguru (the Divine).

Numerous references to Guru ("spiritual master") appear in the Sikh scripture. Guru Nanak says, "The true Guru is the one who implants the truth within you, and helps you to concentrate on Sabad, thus becoming one with the Divine."[165] Guru Ramdas mentions further qualities of a Guru: "The true Guru is a primal being who has conquered [the] five passions [lust, anger, greed, worldly attachment, and ego]."[166]

From Guru Nanak's time to Guru Gobind Singh's time (1469–1708), each Guru taught that a person's realization of the light of oneness is an individual journey with collective responsibility. While a Guru can show us the way, it is up to each person to walk the path or not. The sacred sabads of the *Sabad Guru* (the collection of sacred writings) embodied in the Sikh scripture are the key to self-awakening. Early on, I defined the word *sabad* as a sacred verse or stanza. Besides referring to the Divine Word as a whole (Sikh scripture), it also means "sound."

Guru Nanak, the revealer of Sikhi, says, "Sabad, the Word is the Guru, upon whom I lovingly focus my consciousness; I am the disciple of Sabad."[167] Therefore, the *Sri Guru Granth Sahib* is the Guru, and by that fact, the sabad enshrined in the *SGGS* is the Guru. Guru Arjan describes Sikhs' relationship in verse in the Sikh scripture: "The Divine Guru is my mother, father, Lord and Master, the Transcendent Lord. The Divine Guru is my companion, the destroyer of ignorance, my

---

[165] *SGGS* 686: so gur karau jay such drihraaway—ਸੋ ਗੁਰ ਕਰਉ ਜਿ ਸਚੁ ਦ੍ਰਿੜਾਵੈ॥

[166] *SGGS* 304: soiee satigur purakh hai jin panjay doot keetay vas chhikay—ਸੋਈ ਸਤਿਗੁਰੁ ਪੁਰਖੁ ਹੈ ਜਿਨਿ ਪੰਜੇ ਦੂਤ ਕੀਤੇ ਵਸਿ ਛਿਕੇ॥

[167] *SGGS* 942: sabad gur surat dhun chela—ਸਬਦੁ ਗੁਰੂ ਸੁਰਤਿ ਧੁਨਿ ਚੇਲਾ॥

relative, and my brother. The Divine Guru is the giver, the teacher of Waheguru's name."[168]

129. What is the connection between Waheguru and the gurus?

As defined earlier, Sikh simply means a "student of divine knowledge." In order to establish an enduring connection with Waheguru, the True One, a guide can undoubtedly show you the path, but it remains an individual responsibility to traverse that path. Imagine being blindfolded in a vast dark room and not being able to find the door to get out. If you try hard enough and long enough, you may find the door on your own. However, it will go much faster and easier if you let the Guru guide you. The Guru is a beacon of light in the dark room. "Without the Guru, there is utter darkness; without the Guru, understanding does not come," says the Sikh scripture.[169] Guru, the enlightener, has the ability to awaken you and transform your life.

130. How do you find a true Guru?

The Sikh Gurus continuously warn us to be wary of false gurus. There are numerous self-confessed god-men in every religion who claim to possess divine knowledge when they are as blind as you are. To find a true Guru, one needs to look at the message, its originality, and how it connects with the Divine source. Guru Ramdas, the fourth Guru, says, "You know you have met [a] true Guru when meeting them, your mind is filled with bliss; your illusions (double-mindedness) vanish, and you

---

[168] *SGGS* 262: gurdev mata gurdev pitaa gurdev suaami parmesuraa—ਗੁਰਦੇਵ ਮਾਤਾ ਗੁਰਦੇਵ ਪਿਤਾ ਗੁਰਦੇਵ ਸੁਆਮੀ ਪਰਮੇਸੁਰਾ॥

[169] *SGGS* 1399: Gur Bin Ghor Andhar Guru bin mukat nap away (Bhatt Nal)— ਗੁਰ ਬਿਨੁ ਘੋਰੁ ਅੰਧਾਰੁ ਗੁਰੂ ਬਿਨੁ ਸਮਝ ਨ ਆਵੈ ॥

feel connected to the supreme status of the Waheguru."[170] Bhagat Kabir uses the metaphor of an arrow to explain how you know you have met the true Guru. He says, "When Guru aimed the sabad at me, it hit me like an arrow. As it hit me, I fell to the ground with a hole in my heart."[171] The reference to a hole in the heart relates to the eradication of the ego (*haumai*). Bhagat Kabir emphasizes the transformative impact that the spiritual message had on him. As soon as he let his ego go and concentrated on the spiritual message (sabad), it helped him connect with the Creator within.

131. How can you get to know or perceive Waheguru?

Waheguru is not a physical entity that one can point to. The Divine can only be known through intuition, explains Guru Nanak: "Only those who taste it know its sweet taste, like the mute, who eats the candy, and only smiles."[172] Perception is awareness, comprehension, or an understanding of what is around us. Sikhi helps perceive Waheguru's presence everywhere and intuit it within our consciousness.

The Sikh doctrine highlights *Naam Simran* (focused recitation of versus from the *Sri Guru Granth Sahib*) as a vehicle to help with perception and refers to the reality of living in oneness with the Creator. The word *Naam* appears in the *SGGS* more than 2,500 times. If you talk to a dozen Sikhs, you will likely hear a dozen different definitions of *Naam*. Some call it "an instrument to help perceive and realize the unperceivable God in a limited and personal way; to the extent of our limited human faculties."[173] Others define it as "the sign and symbol and the song of God." According

[170]   *SGGS* 168: jis miliaai man hoi ana(n)dh so satigur kaheeaai; man kee dhubidhaa binas jai har param padh laheeaai—ਜਿਸੁ ਮਿਲਿਐ ਮਨਿ ਹੋਇ ਅਨੰਦੁ ਸੋ ਸਤਿਗੁਰੁ ਕਹੀਐ ॥ ਮਨ ਕੀ ਦੁਬਿਧਾ ਬਿਨਸਿ ਜਾਇ ਹਰਿ ਪਰਮ ਪਦੁ ਲਹੀਐ॥

[171]   *SGGS* 1372: kabeer saachaa satgur mai miliaa sabadhu ju baahiaa ek; laagat hee bhui mil giaa pariaa klejay shake—ਕਬੀਰ ਸਾਚਾ ਸਤਿਗੁਰੁ ਮੈ ਮਿਲਿਆ ਸਬਦੁ ਜੁ ਬਾਹਿਆ ਏਕੁ ॥ ਲਾਗਤ ਹੀ ਭੁਇ ਮਿਲਿ ਗਇਆ ਪਰਿਆ ਕਲੇਜੇ ਛੇਕ॥

[172]   *SGGS* 634: jin chaakhiyaa saiee saad jaanan jeeO gungey mithiaaee—ਜਿਨਿ ਚਾਖਿਆ ਸੋਈ ਸਾਦੁ ਜਾਣਨਿ ਰਜਉ ਗੁੰਗੇ ਮਿਠਿਆਈ॥

[173]   SikhiWiki: Encyclopedia of the Sikhs.

to SikhiWiki: Encyclopedia of the Sikhs, "Some scholars of Sikhi state that Naam is not just the reciting of God's name but the conceptualization of the reality that we call 'God' in one's psyche."[174]

The Encyclopedia of Sikhism volume 3, (160) states Naam is the "bringer of liberation—from the cycle of birth and death." *Naam Simran* or *Japna* includes recitation of the word "Waheguru," meaning "Wondrous Teacher" or "Hail to the Great Teacher." The point is to recite the word consciously and with understanding and appreciation of its meaning. *Naam Japna* is one of three aspects of a Sikh's life that are discussed in more detail in other chapters.

Those who have had routed the perceptual consciousness through Naam Simran to align with oneness can intuitively know that the One pervades the cosmos. They begin to engage with reality and the responsibility as created beings through that knowledge. They are coloured by the divine qualities of truth, compassion, and contentment. However, one of the realizations that comes with the experience of Waheguru is that the One is infinite and beyond the limits of comprehension. The Sikh scripture, when describing the knowledge of The One says, "Its sublimity cannot be described, It can only be seen and realized."[175]

132. How do you build a relationship with Waheguru?

Human beings are indeed capable of building a relationship with and experiencing the Divine. In that context, it is possible to know Waheguru. It is, however, impossible to fully understand the extent of Waheguru or to encapsulate the divine. Let us acknowledge that there is a marked difference between knowing *about* Waheguru and knowing Waheguru. The Sikh faith teaches that Waheguru is the One and all-pervading. All of creation is animated by Waheguru's light. Understanding Its' nature is very different than *experiencing* Waheguru. Just like knowing the

---

[174] SikhiWiki: Encyclopedia of the Sikhs, s.v. "Naam," https://www.sikhiwiki. org/index.php/Naam.

[175] *SGGS* 1370: kahibe kau sobhaa nahee dhekhaa hee paravaan—ਕਹਿਬੇ ਕਉ ਸੋਭਾ ਨਹੀ ਦੇਖਾ ਹੀ ਪਰਵਾਨੁ ॥

chemical composition and formula of sugar cannot provide the experience of tasting sweetness, Waheguru is something that must be experienced.

The goal of a Sikh is to merge their consciousness with the Divine Source. This is accomplished through meditation. But just as a droplet of water can become one with the ocean but never know the extent or limit of the sea, it is impossible to see the vastness and greatness of the Creator.

133. Are there any contemporary paintings of the Gurus?

There are no verified contemporary pictures or paintings of any of the Sikh Gurus. Many state that this is by design since the Gurus did not want people to focus on their physical existence but on their spiritual teachings. The ubiquitous image of Guru Nanak shows him wearing a long robe to his ankles, his shoulder draped in a shawl, and a dastaar tied in a simple wraparound style *dumalla*. On the other hand, the image of Guru Gobind Singh shows him wearing expensive and colourful attire (a long silk robe with a *kamarkasa* (waist sash) around his waist, tight pajamas, jewelry around his neck, and a bejeweled dastaar). He is dressed like a prince. These twentieth-century images painted by Sobha Singh (1901–1986) flow from an artist's imagination rather than a reflection of reality. There were earlier attempts to imagine the appearance of the Gurus during the eighteenth and nineteenth centuries, but their source, patronage, and inspiration are uncertain.

134. Do Sikhs have a current living Guru?

In September 1708, the tenth Guru anointed the *Sri Guru Granth Sahib*, the Sikh scripture, as the final, sovereign, and eternal living Guru and spiritual guide of the Sikhs. Since then, there have been no more human Gurus. The *Sri Guru Granth Sahib* is the only Guru that the Sikhs bow to; the gathered congregation that basks in its light—and the Khalsa in its capacity to lead the sangat—are considered aspects of the Guru.

135. What is Sri Guru Granth Sahib?

The *Sri Guru Granth Sahib* (is the only Guru of the Sikhs. The standard printed version of the *SGGS* comprises 1,430 pages of sacred spiritual teachings written in poetic verse. The *SGGS* comprises the writings of the first, second, third, fourth, fifth, and ninth Gurus—as well as thirty-six bhagats (spiritually enlightened persons of other faith traditions).[176] In the *SGGS,* none of the Gurus after Nanak used their personal names in their verses; instead, they all referred to themselves as Nanak, with the guruship succession number in the Guru lineage. For example, Guru Angad is the second Nanak, and Guru Arjan is the fifth Nanak.

In 1599, Guru Arjan, the fifth Guru, initiated the compilation of an anthology of sabads composed by himself and the preceding four Gurus and various bhagats.[177] This collection was called Pothi.[178] Later, the Sikhs referred to it as the *"Aad Granth"* or the first iteration to differentiate this original compilation from its final iteration, the *Guru Granth Sahib.* More than one-third of the 5,895 verses in the *Aad Granth* are from Guru Arjan's pen. In 1604, the first codex of the *Aad Granth* was installed in the Darbar Sahib (Golden Temple). Guru Arjan appointed Baba Buddha (1506–1631), a revered Sikh who was alive from Guru Nanak's time, as the first head *granthi* (curator and reader of the *Sri Guru Granth Sahib*) of Darbar Sahib (also known as Harmandar Sahib, referred colloquially as the Golden Temple). In 1706, Guru Gobind

---

[176] It's a compilation of 5,995 sabads of six Guru sahibs (Guru Nanak, Guru Angad, Guru Amar Das, Guru Ram Das, Guru Arjan, and Guru Teg Bahadur), fifteen *bhagats* or saints of different background (Kabir, Farid, Namdev, Ravidas, Tirlochan, Dhana, Baini, Bhikhan, Jaidev, Surdas, Sain, Pipa, Parmanand, Sadna, and Ramanand), seventeen *bhats* or learned *brahamins* (Bal, Bhal, Bhikha, Das, Gayand, Harbans, Jal, Jalap, Kaleh, Keerat, Mathara, Nal, Sadrang, Kalsahar, Sal, Tal, and Jalay), and four Sikhs (Bhai Mardana, Baba Sundar, Sata, and Balwand) who were learned Sikhs of the Gurus' time.

[177] Hari Ram Gupta (1984) *History of Sikhs, Vol. 1—The Sikh Gurus (1469–1708),* 135, Munshiram Manoharlal, New Delhi.

[178] *SGGS* 1226: pothi parmeshar ka than—ਪੋਥੀ ਪਰਮੇਸਰ ਕਾ ਥਾਨੁ॥

Singh added the sabads of his predecessor, Guru Teg Bahadur, to the
Aad Granth.

Three years later, in 1708, Guru
Gobind Singh ended the lineage of human
gurus, and reemphasized the guruship
of the Divine Word as contained in the
Guru Granth Sahib. He invoked the sacred

Sri Guru Granth Sahib

teachings as "Guru," hence the name *Guru Granth Sahib.* The prefix
"Sri" was added by the Panth as a sign of reverence or respect, henceforth
the *Sri Guru Granth Sahib.*

Guru Gobind Singh enjoined the Sikhs as such:

> Oh Beloved Khalsa, under orders of the Immortal
> Being, the Panth was created. All the Sikhs are enjoined
> to accept the Granth as their Guru. Accept the spiritual
> words in the Guru Granth as an embodiment of the
> Gurus. Those who want to realize God can find It in
> these sabads.[179]

Thus, the Word of Waheguru, which had manifested as Guru in Nanak,
and had passed through the ten personifications of Guru, was now
returned to its form as the Word, the Bani (spiritual utterances), the
Sabad.

The Sikh Gurus spread the message of a universal divinity and the
oneness of all humanity. They spoke out against blind ritualism and the
division of society on the basis of caste, creed, and human life into four
different *ashrams* (classes). These and many other Sikh teachings are all
contained in the *Sri Guru Granth Sahib.*

The *Sri Guru Granth Sahib* is written in poetic verse, composed to
thirty-one different *raags* (musical measures). *Raags* are very particular
melodies that are meant to be sung at different times of the day or in

---

[179]   Sarb Loh Granth —Aagiya Bhai Akal ki tabay chalayo panth, sabh sikhan ko
hukan hai Guru manao granth. ਆਗਿਆ ਭਈ ਅਕਾਲ ਕੀ ਤਬੀ ਚਲਾਇਓ ਪੰਥ ਸਭ ਸਿਖਨ
ਕੋ ਹੁਕਮ ਹੈ ਗੁਰੂ ਮਾਨਿਜੋ ਗਰੰਥ॥

different seasons. The spiritual means to awaken yourself to your inner divinity in the Sikh religion is to recite and sing the sabads in raags. The spiritual verses are considered to have a profound healing effect on the mind and body—whether one reads, recites or sings the verses in their original raag form.

136. Can the Sri Guru Granth Sahib be changed?

The *Sri Guru Granth Sahib* is the Guru for the Sikh community and is considered a living embodiment of knowledge about oneness. Historically speaking, the only individual who had the sanction to add contents or correct the text was the human line of ten Gurus. Indeed, much of the text remained as it was created by Guru Arjan with the exception of the revision and addition of Guru Tegh Bahadur's bani. When Guru Gobind Singh ended the line of human Gurus, there was effectively no one with the authority and sanction to alter the *Sri Guru Granth Sahib*. Its time of expansion ended with Guru Gobind Singh; its teachings were considered sufficient to impart the knowledge of oneness.

Thus, Gurbani/bani can never be changed. The *Sri Guru Granth Sahib* is the Guru for the Sikhs, and the sabads in it are to be maintained in their pure form. No editing is permitted. It is considered sacrilegious. Guru Har Rai shunned his son Ram Rai because he changed one word from a *sabad* in the *SGGS*[180] in deference to the Mughal Emperor Aurangzeb. The Guru considered this an act of dishonesty and cowardice, and he emphasized that a Sikh must always speak truth to power—no matter the consequence. The Guru ordered Ram Rai never to see him again and instructed Sikhs not to maintain any social or religious relationship with Ram Rai. Despite the passage of four hundred years—and Ram Rai gaining his own religious following—practicing Sikhs continue to follow Guru Har Rai's directive. The Sikh code of conduct instructs Sikhs to not deal with *Ram Raeeay* (the followers of

---

[180] *SGGS* 466: Mitti Musalmaan key perai payee kumihaar; ghar bhaanday itaan keeaa jaldheekare pukaar—ਮਿਟੀ ਮੁਸਲਮਾਨ ਕੀ ਪੇੜੈ ਪਈ ਕੁਮਿੑਆਰ ॥ ਘੜਿ ਭਾਂਡੇ ਇਟਾਂ ਕੀਆ ਜਲਦੀ ਕਰੇ ਪੁਕਾਰ॥

Ram Rai). Given the history of attempts to usurp or change the writings and the meaning of the *Sri Guru Granth Sahib*, Sikhs consider altering the *SGGS*, mishandling it, intentionally misquoting it, or changing the meaning to be disrespectful and one of the worst transgressions one can commit.

137. What language is the Sri Guru Granth Sahib written in?

The *Sri Guru Granth Sahib* is written in Gurmukhi script. The script was standardized by Guru Angad, the second Sikh Guru; today, it is the official script of the Punjabi language. The common language of the Sikhs is Panjabi. This is the predominant language in the *Guru Granth Sahib*. However, many passages in the *SGGS* are written in many other regional languages and dialects spoken in Southeast Asia and the Middle East. These include Lahnda (Western Punjabi), Braj Bhasha, Kauravi, Sanskrit, Sahiskriti, Sindhi, Sant bhasha, Marathi, Khari Boli (old Hindi), Hindi, Rajastani, Marwari, Bangu (Haryanvi), Bihari (Bhojpuri, Magahi, Maithili—Abdi), Sadukari (mostly spoken in religious places), Rekhta (Urdu), Gatha, Dogri, Pothohari, Chamiali (Pahari Boli), and Persian.[181] By including writings in all of these languages, the Gurus hoped to improve the accessibility of their teachings. Taken together as a single form of expression, as it is in the form of the *Sri Guru Granth Sahib*, the language is referred to as Gurbani—or the language (bani) of the Guru (the one who removes darkness and spreads light).

138. Can anyone read the Sri Guru Granth Sahib?

Anyone may read the *Sri Guru Granth Sahib*. However, knowledge of Gurmukhi and the Panjabi language is necessary if someone wants to read it in its original form. Though English translations are also

---

[181]   September 5, 2021, telephone conversation with Dr. Gurmail Singh, assistant professor of religious studies, Punjabi University, Patiala.

available—as well as translations in other languages—the *Sri Guru Granth Sahib* remains a challenging work to translate. There are several reasons for this, including its metrical compositions, structure, and conceptuality. To understand the deeper meaning of *sabads*, the reader should deeply study the *Sri Guru Granth Sahib* while referencing various exegeses and translations (see references in the bibliography).

139. Are there particular ways to read the Sri Guru Granth Sahib?

Since the colonial period, every Sikh has been encouraged to keep a copy of *SGGS* at home and read it daily. This is becoming more common in different spaces across the globe, including among diasporic Sikhs where the commonality of larger homes, such as in Canada and the United States, make it easier to dedicate room for *SGGS*. It is very important to treat *SGGS* with the utmost respect when reading from it.

Informally, one may read the *SGGS* in any manner they wish—at random or with focus on different *banis*—but there are also two formal ways of reading the *SGGS*. These are explained in the *Sikh Rehat Maryada*, as follows:

- *Akhand Path:* The continuous reading of the *Sri Guru Granth Sahib* from beginning to end is called an Akhand Path. To read the complete scriptures without interruption takes about forty-eight hours. An Akhand Path is typically undertaken for all significant life events, including births, marriages, funerals, new homes, and new businesses. These readings have turned into family and community events. An Akhand Path can be conducted by males or females, a group of friends and family, or a team of trained *paathis* or *granthis*. The paathis usually take one or two hours, and they take turns reading the *Guru Granth Sahib* out loud until its entire recitation is completed. Some Sikhs believe that the practice originated in 1706, which is when Guru Gobind Singh had the *Aad Granth* rescribed and then asked five Sikhs[182] to read it to him continuously. Another version of the Akhand Path practice's origin points to the middle of the eighteenth century, when the Mughal rulers were hunting Sikhs. During every opportunity they got to assemble, they would hold a continuous reading of the Sikh scripture.

- *Sehaj Path:* The reading of the *Sri Guru Granth Sahib* from beginning to end, but with no fixed time limit for completion— or a time limit that allows rest breaks from reading—is called Sahaj or Sadharan Path (gradual or slow reading). It can be done for personal enlightenment or in observance of a special occasion or family event. The *paathi* (reader) may read a few pages or several hours every day with no fixed intervals. They can be male or female. The Sehaj Path can be done by one person or by multiple persons.

The continuous reading of the *Sri Guru Granth Sahib* takes the reader and the listener on a spiritual journey that begins with Guru Nanak's *Mool Mantar* (first verse) and ends with the *Mundavani*, the epilogue, highlighting truth, contentment, and contemplation (*Sat Santokh Vicharo*),[183] and concluding with a gratitude statement, "Waheguru, I have no merits; You felt pity on me and made me worthy of this task."[184] However, there is a divergence in practice in the Sikh community; some prefer to end the reading of the *Guru Granth Sahib* after this passage, and others read the last page out loud. The last page, titled *Raag Mala* (literally meaning "garland of musical compositions"), is generally considered the table of contents, setting out most of the *raags* (musical forms) that much of Gurbani is written in. The *Raag Mala* is dedicated

---

[182]   Sikhiwiki.org lists Bhai Gurbaksh Singh, Baba Deep Singh, Bhai Dharam Singh, Bhai Santokh Singh, and Bhai Hari [Har] Singh as five Sikhs who first read it uninterrupted.

[183]   *SGGS* 1429: thaal vich tin vastoo paiO sat santokh vichaaro—ਥਾਲ ਵਿਚਿ ਤਿੰਨਿ ਵਸਤੂ ਪਈਓ ਸਤੁ ਸੰਤੋਖੁ ਵਿਚਾਰੋ॥

[184]   *SGGS* 1429: tera keetaa jaato naahin meinoo jog kitoee—ਤੇਰਾ ਕੀਤਾ ਜਾਤੋ ਨਾਹੀ ਮੈਨੋ ਜੋਗੁ ਕੀਤੋਈ॥

to describing the spiritual aspects of the different classical *raags* in Indian music, some of which are reflected in *Sri Guru Granth Sahib*.

140. How is Sri Guru Granth Sahib handled?

Sri Guru Granth Sahib is the eternal Guru of the Sikhs and is not replaceable by human gurus. Sikhs treat the *SGGS* as their living Guru, but they do not worship it as an idol. Thus, the protocols that have developed over time for handling the *SGGS* are there as a sign of respect. I have listed those protocols that are considered traditional norms, recognizing that there may be geographic or situational variation:

- *Touching or moving:* When the *SGGS* is not being read, it is kept covered at all times by a clean cloth (*rumallah*). Before touching or moving *SGGS*, one must remove their shoes, wash their hands and feet, and cover their heads with a dastaar or scarf. The handler then conducts *ardaas* (prayer) with folded hands, facing *SGGS*. If the *SGGS* is being opened for the first time in the day, the *Prakash* ceremony is followed (see below). If it is being closed for the day, the *Sukhasan* ceremony is followed (see below).
- *Sukhasan:* The *SGGS* is kept in a special resting place when it is not being actively read, such as at the end of the day or upon the completion of a spiritual ceremony. The *sukhasan* ceremony involves the closing of the *SGGS* while reading the *kirtan sohila* (bedtime prayer). The *SGGS* is wrapped in a clean fabric (rumallah), and an ardaas is completed. In most gurdwaras, and in some homes, there is a special room or resting space decorated with a canopy where the *SGGS* is kept for the night. If the *SGGS* is going to be moved to a different resting place, then the carrier places a clean towel or a piece of cloth over their head and places the *SGGS* on top of their head before carrying it to its location. There may be an attendant who accompanies them and waves a *chaur sahib* (whisk) over the *SGGS* while it is being carried. Everyone usually recites some meditative words such as "Satnam,

Waheguru" while the *SGGS* is being transported. Once it is put in its resting place, another short ardaas is conducted.

- *Parkash:* The daily opening of the *SGGS* is called *parkash.* An ardaas is conducted before moving the *SGGS* from its resting place. Whether the parkash is at Gurdwara or in the home, the carrier places a clean towel or a piece of cloth (usually kept nearby) over their head before carrying *SGGS.* If the transport involves a vehicle, the carrier or *giani/granthi* accompanying them usually sits on the front passenger seat. Once seated, the carrier lifts the *SGGS* over their head a few inches, so the second accompanying person can remove the towel or piece of cloth and place it on their lap. The carrier will then place the *SGGS* on their lap. While traveling, everyone in the vehicle recites some form of meditative *shabad,* such as "Satnam, Waheguru" until they reach their destination. Some carriers prefer to be barefoot during the entire journey with the *SGGS.* However, this is not necessary when the *SGGS* is being carried outside of the gurdwara or the home, particularly in subzero weather. The protocol for carrying the *SGGS* from the vehicle to the house is similar. The *parkash* is done on a pre-prepared *manji sahib* (a decorated platform with an overhead canopy). The carrier places the *SGGS* on a platform, removes the *rumallah* (clean cloth), and opens the *SGGS* while reciting some bani from the *SGGS.* The *SGGS* is then opened for a hukamnama (daily ordinance).
- *Hukamnama/Vaak:* See question 145.

141. What is a sabad?

Sabad literally means "word." However, in Sikhi, the term has two primary meanings, and both are related to spirituality. First, *sabad* refers to a sabad, stanza, paragraph, or section of the sacred writings in the *Sri Guru Granth Sahib.* The first sabad in the *SGGS* is the *Mool Mantar.* Second, sabad refers to the sacred name of Waheguru, the Creator of all and everything. *"Kiya khail bud mail tamassaa Waheguru taree sabh*

Rachna—You have formed and created this play, this great game (the universe). O Waheguru, this is all You, forever." [185]

In the *Sri Guru Granth Sahib*, sabad has many more meanings in different contexts, including "sound, holy word, lamp, light, speech, dialogue, religion, duty, obligation, message, advice, philosophy, and Guru."

142. What is the importance of Naam Simran?

The Sikh practice of *Naam Simran* or *Naam Japna* has to do with the recollection of the Creator's names by reciting passages from the *SGGS*. The literal meaning of the word *simran* is "to remember or recall."[186] *Simran,* in its essence, can be thought of as the art of gaining awareness of how to intuit oneness between Creator and creation. The importance of Naam Simran is that it brings you closer to the truth of oneness and enables individuals to act ethically in their lives.

143. Do Sikhs pray?

There are two interlinked but distinct concepts, Naam Simran and ardaas, that may look like prayer to those unfamiliar with Sikhi. Naam Simran has been addressed in the question above. Ardaas is used at the beginning or ending (or both) of the exercise of Naam Simran. The purpose of ardaas is to focus the mind to allow the individual to complete the intention behind doing Naam Simran. This is an opportunity to expunge oneself of material desires and to express good wishes for pursuits of gaining, or maintaining, intuitive awareness of oneness. Through ardaas, a Sikh will commonly express gratitude and appreciation for one's existence, health, wealth, and happiness for oneself

---

[185]   *SGGS* 1403: kiya khel bud mail tamaasaa Waheguru teri subh Rachna—ਕੀਆ ਖੇਲੁ ਬਡ ਮੇਲੁ ਤਮਾਸਾ ਵਾਹਿਗੁਰੂ ਤੇਰੀ ਸਭ ਰਚਨਾ॥

[186]   Bhai Kahn Singh Nabha, comp., *Mahan Kosh, Kosh, The Sikh Encyclopedia in Punjabi* (1930).

and all humanity. Ardaas is not meant for the fulfillment of a Sikh's wishes or desires in terms of material gain.

144. Is there a prescribed daily routine for Sikhs?

The *Sikh Rehat Maryada* (code of conduct) prescribes the daily recitation of a collection of sabads, performed three times during the day. This daily practice is called *nitnem* and involves doing Naam Simran of a specific group of sabads. Amritdhari (initiated) Sikhs are mandated to follow this daily recitation, many *sahijdhari* (non-initiated) Sikhs also recite partial or complete *nitnem*. The recitation has a foundational role in Sikh life. The morning nitnem is done early in the morning (ideally at dawn) prior to embarking on one's daily activities. The sabads recited in the morning include Jap Ji Sahib, Jaap Sahib, and Tavprasad Savaiye according to *Rehat Maryada*. However, amritdhari Sikhs are mandated at the time of amrit sanchar to recite five banis (three listed in *Rehat Maryada*, plus Chaupai Sahib and Anand Sahib). The second time for Naam Simran is in the evening or at dusk, at which time a bani known as "*So Dar*" commonly known as Rehras Sahib is read. The third time and last time of the nitnem, bani named "Sohila" is recited prior to bedtime. While these are the prescribed times for nitnem, the decision of when to do one's nitnem is ultimately personal and may be impacted by things such as work obligations (such as shift work).

145. What is a hukamnama?

A hukamnama is a message from the *SGGS*. Hukamnama means a command, or divine order from the Guru. It is also colloquially termed *vaaq*, meaning "words or messages from the Guru." Sikhs rely on a message from the Guru, the *Sri Guru Granth Sahib*, by randomly opening the scripture and reading the first *sabad* (verse or stanza) from the top left-hand side of the page. The hukamnama acts as a guide and inspiration for Sikhs to follow throughout their day. It is a message, dialogue, or communication that prompts actions in our day-to-day lives.

The practice began with Guru Arjan who installed *Aad Granth* (the premier Sikh scripture) in Darbar Sahib in 1604. The first Hukamnama, when the *Aad Granth Sahib* was installed in Darbar Sahib, was the following verse composed by Guru Arjan:

> Waheguru [God] has stood up to resolve the affairs of the saints; He has come to complete their tasks. The land is beautiful, and the pool is gorgeous; within it is contained the Ambrosial Water. It is filled with Ambrosial Water. My job is entirely complete; all my desires are fulfilled. Felicitations are pouring in from all over the world; all my sorrows are eliminated. The Vedas and the Puranas [sacred writings of the Hindus] sing the praises of the Perfect, Unchanging, Imperishable Primal Creator. The Supreme Waheguru has kept Its promise and confirmed Its nature; Nanak meditates on the Naam, the name of the Waheguru.[187]

This tradition has continued to this day. There are proscribed times when a hukamnama is taken—for example, after completion of each of the nitnem banis, or during the performance of religious ceremonies such as weddings or birth celebrations. However, a vaaq can be taken at any time or multiple times in a day. Traditionally, Sikhs went to the gurdwara to listen to the Hukamnama after completing their morning nitnem. Today, many read it at the gurdwara after it has been given on screens outside the main hall. Technology has revolutionized the way Sikhs take their daily hukamnama, turning to their laptops or handheld devices to read their own hukamnama.

---

[187] *SGGS* 783–84: Santaa ke kaaraj aap khaloiaa har ka(n)m karaavan aaiaa raam - ਸੰਤਾ ਕੇ ਕਾਰਜਿ ਆਪਿ ਖਲੋਇਆ ਹਰਿ ਕੰਮੁ ਕਰਾਵਣਿ ਆਇਆ ਰਾਮ॥

146. What is divine will?

For Sikhs, divine will is not some mystical order delivered by a distant God, but rather the natural consequences of one's actions. Abiding by the divine will means recognizing and accepting the choice one has made and being at peace with whatever consequences flow from it. A great example of abiding by divine will is when Guru Arjan sacrificed his life in torturous death to defy the Mughal rulers and champion the religious freedoms of the oppressed. As punishment for his defiance of the Mughal emperor (Jahangir), Guru Arjan was made to sit on a hot iron plate while burning sand was poured over his bare body. His only outcry was, "Sweet be Your Will, my Waheguru. Nanak [himself] begs the gift of your *Naam* [name of God]."[188]

Hazrat Mian Mir, a Muslim *sufi fakir* (ascetic) and friend of the Guru, asked why he would endure such agony. Guru Arjan simply replied, "Pain and pleasure come by Waheguru's Will; to whom should we go and complain. I bear all this torture to accept Waheguru's Will and set an example for Sikhs, not to lose patience or rail at Waheguru in affliction." [189]

The real test of any faith is in the hour of misery and pain. Accepting the divine will is acknowledging that there is a divine order to things that are beyond one's control and understanding. It also means letting go of one's attachment to the outcome, letting the journey lead wherever it is meant to.

147. Do Sikhs believe Guru Granth Sahib is the Word of God?

Guru Nanak composed and sang sacred verses in nineteen *raags*. He considered the verses to flow through him as an expression of the Divine

---

[188]   SGGS 394: teraa keeaa meeThaa laagai. Har naam padhaarath nanak maa(n) gai. ਤੇਰਾ ਕੀਆ ਮੀਠਾ ਲਾਗੈ॥ ਹਰਿ ਨਾਮੁ ਪਦਾਰਥੁ ਨਾਨਕੁ ਮਾਂਗੈ ॥

[189]   SGGS 431: such dhukh teree aagiaa piaare dhoojee naahee jai. ਸੁਖੁ ਦੁਖੁ ਤੇਰੀ ਆਗਿਆ ਪਿਆਰੇ ਦੂਜੀ ਨਾਹੀ ਜਾਇ॥

Grace, stating, "As the word of the Protector comes to me, so do I express it."[190] Guru Ramdas writes, "Know that the Word [the spiritual utterances] of the Guru is true, absolutely true, the Creator itself causes it to be recited."[191] Guru Arjan says, "The divine Sabad or word emanated from the primal Waheguru. It eradicates all anxieties."[192]

The most significant proof of the *Sri Guru Granth Sahib*'s divine origin is the experience of the sabad. Though in truth, Gurbani teaches that all creation and manifestation are from Waheguru, for many Sikhs, the *SGGS* holds special power because it provides knowledge and experience of the Divine. It focuses entirely on words that cleanse and rejuvenate our minds and souls and prepare the soil for the spiritual seed to sprout within us. It provides spiritual sustenance and inspiration that no ordinary words can match. It is the feeling of tranquility and joy and the experience of Waheguru one receives from the sabad, which is the real proof of its divine origin.

148. What is Dasam Granth?

Though Guru Gobind Singh was a prolific writer and renowned poet, he consciously chose not to include any of his own writings in *SGGS*. Another text, the *Dasam Granth*, contains compositions of Guru Gobind Singh. It was published after the death of Guru Gobind Singh in 1708 and does not rise to the importance given to the *SGGS*. The compositions were collected from various sources, and only some of them can be authenticated as being written by Guru Gobind Singh. Three of these *banis* (spiritual writings) have been universally attributed to Guru Gobind Singh. These are the Jaap, the Ten Swayias, and Chaupaiee.

---

[190] *SGGS* 722: Jaisee mein aaway khasam key bani taisaa kareen gyan way laloo—ਜੈਸੀ ਮੈ ਆਵੈ ਖਸਮ ਕੀ ਬਾਣੀ ਤੈਸੜਾ ਕਰੀ ਗਿਆਨੁ ਵੇ ਲਾਲੋ ॥

[191] *SGGS* 308: satgur kee baanee sat sat kar jaanahu gursikhahu har kartaa aap mahahu kaddaae—ਸਤਿਗੁਰ ਕੀ ਬਾਣੀ ਸਤਿ ਸਤਿ ਕਰਿ ਜਾਣਹੁ ਗੁਰਸਿਖਹੁ ਹਰਿ ਕਰਤਾ ਆਪਿ ਮੁਹਹੁ ਕਢਾਏ॥

[192] *SGGS* 628: dhur kee baanee aaiee, tin saglee chint mitaiee—ਧੁਰ ਕੀ ਬਾਣੀ ਆਈ॥ ਤਿਨਿ ਸਗਲੀ ਚਿੰਤ ਮਿਟਾਈ॥

They are part of the amrit sanchar (Sikh initiation ceremony) and are mandated in the *Rehat Maryada* (Sikh code of conduct) to be read as part of *nitnem*, the daily recitation by all devout Sikhs. The last section of *Dasam Granth* includes a spiritual victory letter called Zafarnama, which is widely believed to have been sent by Guru Gobind Singh to the Mughal emperor, Aurangzeb (1618–1707), after the martyrdom of the Guru's four sons: two of them in the battle of Chamkaur and the other two bricked alive in Sirhind. The language is Persian, which was the state language at that time, and the letter was purportedly hand-delivered by Bhai Daya Singh, one of the Panj Pyare (the first five initiated Sikhs).

However, there are other parts of the *Dasam Granth* for which the authorship is broadly questioned. This has resulted in three lines of thought regarding the *Dasam Granth*: 1) the entire *Dasam Granth* was authored by Guru Gobind Singh; 2) some of the writings are the genuine work of Guru Gobind Singh, and others are not; and 3) the authorship of the entire *Dasam Granth* is questionable. The first approach was endorsed by Bhai Randhir Singh and the *Report of the Gurmat Granth Pracharak Sabha*, among others. However, a significant group of Sikhs ascribe to the second approach. They point to portions of the *Dasam Granth* that relate tales from Hindu mythology that are antithetical to Sikh teachings contained in the *SGGS*. In addition, they take issue with a long composition entitled "Charitropakhyan," which tells numerous graphic stories about illicit liaisons between men and women. It is believed by many that this composition was authored by someone else and passed off as being the work of Guru Gobind Singh—either inadvertently or deliberately to malign the Sikh faith.

Controversy regarding the *Dasam Granth* also arises in relation to how the text is treated by some members of the Sikh community, who hold it at par with the *SGGS*. For many Sikhs, such treatment goes against the very wishes of Sri Guru Gobind Singh, who specifically chose not to include his writings in the *Sri Guru Granth Sahib*.

PART V

Creation

CHAPTER 16

The Universe and Creation

The Punjabi word for the universe is *Brahmand*. Sikhs believe that creation consists of a multitude of universes and that no one knows for sure how or when creation took place. The incomprehensible yet magnificent feat of creating the tangible (the universe and all life contained within it) from the intangible (the Divine Source from which all creation emanated) is why Sikhs refer to God as Waheguru (the wondrous teacher). In this chapter, we explore how Sikhi approaches the mysteries of the universe and the life contained within it.

Sikhs see the universe as a wondrous place of infinite possibilities and incomprehensible beauty. The fact that Earth has attributes that are suitable for life to flourish and grow causes Sikhs to believe that our existence was not a mere coincidence. Guru Nanak says, "Creating the rhythm of nights, days, weeks, and seasons. Making wind, water, fire, and subterranean regions. Amid all these, within the Earth a home for *dharm* (order) was established," [193] The earth is seen as a place where the divine play of creation unfolds. It is a sanctuary where union with Waheguru is attained through a discipline for living a purposeful existence aimed at betterment of one's own life and the lives of others. Sikhi imparts to us the knowledge that the universe, though transitory, allows for the pursuit of a meaningful and elevated existence so that the One in all of us can experience the wonders of being and the beauty of life in its purest form.

---

[193]   *SGGS* 7: raati ruthi thiti vaar; tis vich dharatee thaap rakhee dharam saal— ਰਾਤੀ ਰੁਤੀ ਥਿਤੀ ਵਾਰ ॥ ਪਵਣ ਪਾਣੀ ਅਗਨੀ ਪਾਤਾਲ ॥ ਤਿਸੁ ਵਿਚਿ ਧਰਤੀ ਥਾਪਿ ਰਖੀ ਧਰਮ ਸਾਲਾ॥

149. Where did the universe come from?

Included in the *Sri Guru Granth Sahib* is a unique bani called "Siddh Gost" (SGGS 938–946). This is a dialogue between Guru Nanak and mystic yogis (*siddhs*) where the Guru answers their spiritual questions. One of the siddhs poses a question about the origin of the world. Seeking clarification of the concept of *shunya* ("void"), he asked, "What can you tell us about the beginning? In what abode did the profound Lord dwell then?" Guru Nanak replied that before the creation of the world, there was no universe, yet it was not an empty void: "We can only express a sense of wonder about the beginning. The profound Waheguru abided deep within Itself then. When the world and the sky did not even exist, the light of the formless Waheguru filled the three worlds [sea, earth, and sky]."[194]

Sikhs believe that only the Creator knows the true origin of the universe. Guru Amar Das writes, "Waheguru, who created this universe, knows everything about it." Being created by the One, the universe tangibly expresses Waheguru's eternal truth (*Satt* or *Sach*), but since it arises and vanishes at the Creator's will, creation has no real or independent existence of its own. The Sikh faith is explicit that the One (true or truth) existed even when nothing else existed. Says Guru Nanak: "True in the beginning, True throughout the ages, True even now, Nanak Truth shall ever be."[195]

150. What is the universe made of?

Gurbani explains the composition of the universe in two ways: the tangible or material universe and its intrinsically intangible nature. The tangible, observable universe is said to be created out of five basic elements, all of which originated from the Divine Source.[196] Guru Ram

---

[194]　*SGGS* 940: aad kao kavan bichaar kathialay sunh kahaa ghar vasai—ਆਦਿ ਕਉ ਕਵਨੁ ਬੀਚਾਰੁ ਕਥੀਅਲੇ ਸੁੰਨ ਕਹਾ ਘਰ ਵਾਸੋ॥

[195]　*SGGS* 1: Aad sach, jugad sach, hapee sach, Nanak, hose be sach. ਆਦਿ ਸਚੁ ਜੁਗਾਦਿ ਸਚੁ ਹੈ ਭੀ ਸਚੁ ॥ ਨਾਨਕ ਹੋਸੀ ਭੀ ਸਚੁ ॥

[196]　*SGGS* 1038: pa(n)ch tat sun(n)nahu pargaasaa—ਪੰਚ ਤਤੁ ਸੁੰਨਹੁ ਪਰਗਾਸਾ [From the Primal Void, the five elements became manifest.]

Das writes, "After making the five elements, You have created the entire world. Let anyone try to make the sixth element, if they can."[197]

The five elements (*panj tatt*) are *mittee* (earth), *paanee* (water), *Aag* (fire), *havaa* (air), and *aakaash* (ether or space). In relation to the human body, these five perishable elements referred to are breath (air), blood (water), energy (fire), all bodily tissues, including bones and muscles (earth), and the space between each particle or atom (ether). These elements are similar to the basic elements of creation postulated in ancient Indian and Greek philosophy: earth, fire, water, air, and ether. Sikhs believe that when we die, the human body dissolves into these elements, balancing out the cycle of nature. [198]

However, Gurbani also teaches that the universe and all that is contained within it is ultimately an illusion—a fiction of the human mind. Just as Albert Einstein described the distinction between the past, present, and future as "a stubbornly persistent illusion,"[199] Gurbani describes the entire universe as being "like the shadow of a cloud" and a "flying dream of the night." Guru Teg Bahadur says, "This universe is just a mountain of smoke—what makes you think that this is real?"

151. Do Sikhs believe in evolution?

Guru Nanak says, "From the True One came the air, from the air came the water. From the water, the three worlds [sea, earth, and sky] were formed, and Waheguru infused life in every being."[200]

Evolution is a process that can be understood to be a part of the

---

[197] *SGGS* 736: panch tut kar tudh srisat sabh saaji koi sheva kario jay kichh keetaa hovai—ਪੰਚ ਤਤੁ ਕਰਿ ਸ੍ਰਿਸਟਿ ਸਭ ਸਾਜੀ ਕੋਈ ਛੇਵ ਕਰਿਉ ਜੇ ਕਿਛੁ ਕੀਤਾ ਹੋਵੈ॥

[198] Dr. D.P. Singh, "Panch Tattva: A perspective from Sri Guru Granth Sahib" https://www.sikhphilosophy.net/threads/panch-tattva-a-perspective-from-sri-guru-granth-sahib.40057/.

[199] Hawking, Stephen, *A Stubbornly Persistent Illusion: The Essential Scientific Works of Albert Einstein*, 2009, Running Press Adult.

[200] *SGGS* 19: saache te pawnaa bhaiya pawnai te jal hoi; jal te tirbhavan saajia ghat ghat jot smaae—ਸਾਚੇ ਤੇ ਪਵਨਾ ਭਇਆ ਪਵਨੈ ਤੇ ਜਲੁ ਹੋਇ ॥ ਜਲ ਤੇ ਤ੍ਰਿਭਵਣ ਸਾਜਿਆ ਘਟ ਘਟ ਜੋਤਿ ਸਮੋਇ॥

divine will. "The theory of evolution has posed no practical or moral issues for Sikhism.[201] Recognition of evolution and a belief in the one Creator are quite compatible for Sikhs. It was through Its will and infinite wisdom that creation took place. Guru Nanak says, "For eons and eons, there was nothing in the beginning but nebulous density. There was no earth or sky, there was only the infinite command of Its *hukam* (divine order). [202]

Like any other community, there are divergent views among Sikhs on the origin of the universe, its age, and the evolution of life on earth. However, life is seen as originating from a single Creator. Sikhs are open to scientific inquiries into the specific processes through which creation has evolved and exists now. Evolution or change over time in the genetic composition of populations is a scientific reality. The process has been observed and studied, and there is no doubt it occurs.

152. What is Sikhi's approach to modern technological advances?

While holding up Waheguru as the Creator of the universe, the Sikh faith does not conflict with science and the desire of humans to understand our material physical world. However, it is clear to Sikhs that nothing we humans can accomplish matches Waheguru's creation or challenges the One's existence. Scientists may manipulate or change the building blocks of life, but they cannot "create" in the same way Waheguru does. Recently, there has been news of the creation of "synthetic life" by researchers in the United States. Scientists have created a synthetic genome as a template based on an existing cell. Chemically constructed blocks of DNA were placed in living cells, which assembled them into a complete chromosome. Although this "creation" is a genuinely impressive scientific feat, it is the synthesis of a genome and not the creation of life.

---

[201]   Jhutti-Johal, Jagbir, *Sikhism Today (Relgion Today)*. Bloomsbury, London, 2011, Loc 364.

[202]   *SGGS* 1035: arbad narbad dhandookaara; dharan na gagna hukam apaaraa— ਅਰਬਦ ਨਰਬਦ ਧੰਧੂਕਾਰਾ ॥ ਧਰਣਿ ਨ ਗਗਨਾ ਹੁਕਮੁ ਅਪਾਰਾ॥

Rather than raising fears of "playing God," such developments raise questions about the potential use (or misuse) of the technology and about the ethical issues involved in patenting the building blocks of life.

Sikhs have divergent views about scientists making such breakthroughs. While any increase in our collective knowledge that can be used to improve our lives should be welcomed, there are some who challenge such endeavours. In *Ecology Resigning Genes: Ethical and Sikh Perspective* (14), Surjit Kaur Chahal argues, "The infinite God has not given any permission to man to modify or improve the earth. In fact, Sikhism clearly states [that] there is no scope [for] improvement. The entire universe (not merely the planet, Earth) is made by the Infinite God who has completed the process and has left nothing incomplete for man to complete it."

153. How do Sikhs regard the environment?

In Sikhi, a concern for the environment is part of an integrated approach to life and nature. Nature has intrinsic dignity and value. The *SGGS* states that the objective of life is harmony with the eternal (the Divine), which implies a life of harmony with all existence. The emphasis is on mastery and discovery of the self—not mastery over others and nature. Striving for a life of harmony also implies a growth of service, supporting individual rights and environmental causes.

The Sikh gurus refer to the earth as *Dharamsaal*, a religious sanctuary where union with the Divine is attained. In their daily morning prayer, Sikhs are encouraged to remember the sacred nature of planet earth. Guru Nanak explains this philosophy through a beautiful analogy: "Air is the Guru, water is the father, and earth is the great mother."[203] Elsewhere, Guru Nanak writes, "Amid the rhythms of Creation, the changing seasons, air, water, and fire, the Creator established the earth as the home for humans to realize their divinity in this world."[204]

In *Sikhi and Sustainability*, Susan E. Prill writes, "The Sikh tradition of seva, service to the community, is a prime motivator for ecological

---

[203] *SGGS* 8: Pavan guru paani pitaa mataa dharat mahat. ਪਵਣੁ ਗੁਰੂ ਪਾਣੀ ਪਿਤਾ ਮਾਤਾ ਧਰਤਿ ਮਹਤੁ ॥

[204] *SGGS* 7: raatee rutee thitee vaar- ਰਾਤੀ ਰੁਤੀ ਥਿਤੀ ਵਾਰ ॥

activism and is the basis for many of the most successful efforts."[205] Since 2010, Eco Sikh Group has been celebrating March 14 as the World Sikh Environment Day. On this day, Sikhs across the world engage in activities such as plantings trees and cleaning up their communities. Sikhi teaches that the natural environment and the survival of all life are intertwined in the rhythm of nature. The Sikh Gurus recognized that a beautiful environment is vital to the inspiration and pursuit of spirituality. Guru Har Rai, the seventh Sikh Guru, developed the town of Kiratpur in Punjab as a town of gardens and supervised the planting of different flowers and fruit-bearing trees.

154. Is there a heaven and hell?

The *Oxford Dictionary* defines heaven as a "place regarded in various religions as the abode of God (or the gods) and the angels, and of the good after death, often traditionally depicted as being above the sky."[206] The traditional conception of heaven is that it is some distinctive place where individuals are rewarded with afterlife comfort, pleasures, and happiness. By contrast, hell is defined as a "place regarded in various religions as a spiritual realm of evil and suffering, often traditionally depicted as a place of perpetual fire beneath the earth where the wicked are punished after death."[207]

Sikh philosophy does not adhere to the traditional views of heaven and hell. Rather, heaven and hell are viewed simply as states of mind. Balpreet Singh, writing in the *Ottawa Citizen*, expressed the Sikh view clearly this way:

---

[205]   Susan E.Prill, *Sikhi and Sustainability: Sikh Approaches to Environmental Advocacy* (2015).
[206]   *Oxford English Dictionary* (online), s.v. "heaven," https://www.lexico.com/definition/heaven.
[207]   *Oxford UK English Dictionary* (online), s.v. "hell," https://www.lexico.com/definition/hell.

The Sikh faith teaches that the true "heaven" is an awareness [of] and union with God. This heaven is only available through meditation on Naam or God's [Waheguru's] name and is possible while living here on Earth.

The Sikh faith accepts that God's creation is measureless and within it, there are countless realms and "heavens" and "hells." But for Sikhs, these are of no consequence. None of these places is permanent and a spiritual seeker should not desire such a heaven. Aiming for and desiring such a heaven is in fact considered a mental distraction. Guru Gobind Singh says that a noble person can go down as a devil and an evil person can earn the status of [a] god depending upon the kind of deeds they do; thus, heaven or hell represent one's state of mind.

The Sikh scripture, *Sri Guru Granth Sahib*, teaches that true and permanent happiness is only possible through being spiritually awakened and then realizing and experiencing God, both within the self and throughout creation. Spiritual awakening can only occur by meditation on Naam and living a spiritual lifestyle. When one attains the state of spiritual awakening, every place can become heaven if we attain mystically oneness with God through reflection on Naam. In Sikhi, heaven and hell do not represent distinct geographical places.

The Sikh faith has the concept of Sach Khand or the realm of truth, which is God's own realm and from which God's light shines into creation. Spiritually awakened individuals who realize and become one with God's light attain Sach Khand in life and reside there permanently after death. Rather than the traditional concept of heaven with gardens and rivers, etc., *Sri Guru Granth Sahib* teaches that describing this realm is beyond words. It is a place of light and spiritual bliss where the soul remains eternally immersed in God.

So, for Sikhs, heaven isn't a concept that requires much thought or worry. Rather than waiting for death to experience complete happiness and pleasure, if one meditates on Naam and lives a spiritual lifestyle, heaven is possible right here and right now.[208]

"We all come to this world by Waheguru's Will and leave this world by His Will," says Guru Nanak.[209] The Sikh faith believes that humans are given the freedom to choose between good and evil—and sometimes between two goods. Guru Nanak says, "According to one's action, one gets near to or distant from Waheguru."[210] The Sikh Gurus were more concerned about attaining one's spiritual goals in the present life and less concerned about notions of an afterlife. For example, Guru Arjan, referencing contemporary concepts of "salvation," writes, "I wish for neither kingdoms nor liberation, only that my mind be attached to Waheguru."[211] A Sikh strives to achieve liberation (*mukti*) while the soul is still embedded in the physical frame. The goal is not to go to heaven after death; it is to achieve union with our Divine Source while alive.

---

[208]　Balpreet Singh, "What Is Heaven?" Ask the Religious Experts, *Ottawa Citizen*, July 3, 2011, https://www.pressreader.com/canada/ottawa-citizen/20110703/281736971090139.

[209]　*SGGS* 472: jaman marnaa hukam hai bhaanay aavai jai—ਜੰਮਣੁ ਮਰਣਾ ਹੁਕਮੁ ਹੈ ਭਾਣੈ ਆਵੈ ਜਾਇ॥

[210]　*SGGS* 8: karamee aapo aapanee ke nairay kay door—ਕਰਮੀ ਆਪੋ ਆਪਣੀ ਕੇ ਨੇੜੈ ਕੇ ਦੂਰਿ॥

[211]　*SGGS* 534: raaj na chaahau mukat na chaahau man preet charan kamalaaray—ਰਾਜੁ ਨ ਚਾਹਉ ਮੁਕਤਿ ਨ ਚਾਹਉ ਮਨਿ ਪ੍ਰੀਤਿ ਚਰਨ ਕਮਲਾਰੇ॥

CHAPTER 17

Growing Up and Growing Old

It is nature's law that all who are born—if they are blessed with a long life—go through the process of growing up and growing old. "Whosoever has come shall depart, all shall have their turn," says Guru Nanak.[212]

With a focus on the beginning and the end of life, this chapter provides insights into Sikh family life and attitudes about procreation, raising children, and taking care of elders.

155. What is the significance of marriage and family?

The Gurus taught that the family unit is the foundation of a healthy society. Procreation ensures the continuation of humanity. Children are considered a blessing. They bring us joy, teach us how to love unconditionally, and help us learn patience and forgiveness. Ultimately, this process brings us closer to Waheguru. Contrary to many other religious and spiritual traditions, Sikhs do not value celibacy or the life of an ascetic. Rather, the Sikh Gurus extolled the life of a "householder." This was considered to be far more spiritually valuable and socially responsible than a life of "renunciation."

Family is considered a fundamental unit of cohesion and harmony.

---

[212] *SGGS* 474: jo aayaa so chalsee subh koee aaei vaariay—ਜੋ ਆਇਆ ਸੋ ਚਲਸੀ ਸਭੁ ਕੋਈ ਆਈ ਵਾਰੀਐ॥

Collectively, families form communities. The family has economic, educational, and social responsibilities to ensure the smooth and happy functioning of society. By contributing to social cohesion, the family also enables organizations and communities to prosper and flourish in a safe and secure environment. A robust family system ensures a prosperous biological, economic, and spiritual future for human societies.

156. What is the Sikh view on contraception?

There is no bar to the use of contraceptives in Sikhi. All life is celebrated, but the decision not to have children is respected. The birth of a child and each human life is viewed as being sacred. Social responsibility and individual autonomy mean that each parent should have the freedom to decide how many children (if any) they wish to raise based on their own resources and circumstances. They must have regard to economic considerations and, more importantly, the quality of time they can devote to raising and guiding their children.

Sikhi encourages basing the decision to have children, or how many to have, on a wider worldview, considering how best one can serve humanity and be a productive and responsible member of society. Sikhs must endeavour to take care of their own children and the children of the world whose basic needs are not met—needs that so many of us take for granted, such as daily meals, safe shelter, clothes, education, medical care, love, and protection from harm.

157. What does Sikhi teach about gender selection or male child preference?

Gender selection or gender preference is denounced in Sikhi—as are practices like female infanticide. In one sabad in the *Asa Ki Var* (*Ode to Peace*), which is dedicated to women, Guru Nanak writes: "From a woman a woman is born, without a woman there can be none. Nanak, only the true Lord is without a woman."[213]

Sadly in Panjab, the birthplace of Sikhism, statistics paint an alarming reality regarding the continuation of gender preference. A study conducted by Dr. Harshinder Kaur revealed that 78.8 percent of higher secondary school girls in urban areas did not want to give birth to a girl child.[214] "Son preference" is a harmful form of gender discrimination. It has led many people in different parts of the world to destroy female fetuses (female feticide). Since ancient times, and the early antecedents of our contemporary family system, historians have chronicled a preference for the male child across many cultures and faith communities. In Panjab, and elsewhere through India, the preference of boys over girls had to do with establishing lineage through paternity (not maternity), and it also involved economics. Traditionally, a daughter would leave her birth household upon marriage, taking with her a dowry (an outflow of goods and money). A son, on the other hand, brought his wife into his parents' household (an inflow of another set of hands, goods, and money). However, this cultural preference for a male was specifically denounced by the Sikh Gurus, who emphasized gender equality and the upliftment of women.

158. Is there a special procedure for naming a baby?

Second only to our gender identity, our names are labels that define us for our entire lives. Sikhs believe that the honour of naming their baby should be granted to their Guru. A few days or weeks after the child's birth, when the mother is once again mobile, the Sikh family will hold a naming ceremony. The ceremony is traditionally held in a Gurdwara, and it is called the *Naam sanskaar* (or *janam sanskaar*). Here, the *granthi* will sing a verse from the *SGGS* to thank Waheguru for blessing the

---

[213] *SGGS* 473: bha(n)ddahu hee bha(n)dd uoopajai bha(n)ddai baajh na koi; naanak bha(n)ddai baaharaa eko sachaa soi—ਭੰਡਹੁ ਹੀ ਭੰਡੁ ਉਪਜੈ ਭੰਡੈ ਬਾਝੁ ਨ ਕੋਇ ॥ ਨਾਨਕ ਭੰਡੈ ਬਾਹਰਾ ਏਕੋ ਸਚਾ ਸੋਇ॥

[214] Varinda Sharma article on April 16, 2010, article in *The Hindu*, India.

family with a child.[215] The *granthi* then does an *ardaas* (prayer) seeking
Waheguru's blessing to name the newborn. The *Sri Guru Granth Sahib* is
opened at random, and the first full verse to appear at the top left corner
is recited in its entirety. This verse is called a *hukam* (divine order) or
vaak (a message from the Guru). The name of the child is selected based
on the first letter of the first word of the verse. If a family is blessed with
twins, then the first child's name may start with the first letter of the
selected word, and the second child's name can start with the second
letter of the same word, or perhaps the second letter of the second word.

Sikh names usually have some spiritual significance or meaning attached
to them. All Sikh children are also given a second name, which can also be
used as a last name. Sikh boys are given the name Singh, meaning "lion,"
and Sikh girls are given the name Kaur, meaning "lioness" or "princess."
This practice was initiated by Guru Gobind Singh to signify gender equality
and break the barriers of caste and class. Sikh women are not required to
change their last names after marriage. My name, Gian, means divine
wisdom. My wife's name, Surinder, is composed of two Sanskrit elements:
"sura" (god) and "indra" (name of a Hindu god). Loosely translated, it means
the God of gods. Regardless of what name one chooses, the emphasis is on
following the Sikh code of conduct for the naming ceremony.

159. Is there a difference between male and female names?

In early Sikh history, male and female names *were* identifiable by the
first name, such as Gian for males and Giano for females. This practice
was dropped in the latter half of the twentieth century with a preference
for gender-neutral names. Most Sikh first names are now gender-neutral,
which means they can be given to boys or girls. Gian is now used to
name a male or a female child.

To avoid confusion, Sikhs turn to the second name—Singh or Kaur—to
determine the person's gender. However, there are some circumstances where

---

[215]   *SGGS* 396: Satgur Sache Diya Bhej—ਸਤਿਗੁਰ ਸਾਚੈ ਦੀਆ ਭੇਜਿ॥

women may have the last name "Singh." Some families have chosen to adopt the Anglo practice of the woman taking on the man's name after marriage or naming male and female children after their father. This practice was imported to India under British colonial rule, and though it is not common, one may still see it in usage. For example, the granddaughter of Maharaja Ranjit Singh (the last king of Panjab before British rule) was named "Princess Bamba Sophia Duleep Kaur Singh."[216]

160. Are there specific names that are associated with being a Sikh?

What's in a name? A name is what we are identified with and what we respond to when someone calls us. We are tagged with a name from the time we enter the world. Historically, a name, particularly a family name, was tied to a family's profession. In traditional Indian society, a family name identified one's "caste," part of a complex hereditary and discriminatory class system. Yet equality of all people is enshrined in the *Sri Guru Granth Sahib*. In 1699, at the time of the first amrit sanchar (initiation ceremony), Guru Gobind Singh removed any prior identification of "caste" attached to names and introduced two names:

- *Singh* meaning lion: used for all male Sikhs, a distinctive identity denoting equality. Even sahijdhari (non-initiated) Sikhs proudly use Singh as their middle name. Many non-Sikhs in India have had the name Singh for centuries. "It was adopted as a title by warriors in India."[217]
- *Kaur* meaning "princess," a name given to female Sikhs, which empowered them to be equal and independent. A Sikh woman

---

[216] Princess Sophia was also the goddaughter of Queen Victoria and a well-known leader in the suffragette movement in Britain. See for example, Lakhpreet Kaur, "10 Badass Sikh Women in History," online article for *Ms. Magazine*, March 17, 2015, https://msmagazine.com/2015/03/17/10-badass-sikh-women-in-history/.

[217] Angus Stevenson and Maurice Waite, eds., *Concise Oxford English Dictionary*, 12th ed. (Oxford: Oxford University Press, 2011), 1346.

is not obliged to take her husband's name upon marriage and is encouraged to maintain her own separate identity. Like men who use the name Singh, many sahijdhari (non-initiated) women proudly use Kaur as their middle or last name.

The same suffixes of Singh and Kaur for all male and female Sikhs, respectively, represent equality among men and women, a tradition set by Guru Nanak, the founder of Sikhi. Singh and Kaur remain common last names used by Sikhs. To be initiated, it is mandatory to include either Kaur or Singh in one's name. The tradition of last name usage for Sikhs was reintroduced by the British Raj in Punjab (1849–1947) so the colonial rulers could distinguish between people. However, this British tradition also brought with it the sexist practice of women taking on their husbands' last names. Sadly, this negative influence continues to this day, and many Sikh women will change their last names after marriage.

161. Are Sikhs given any honourific designations?

An honourific title is a word or expression used to convey respect or esteem.

Guru Nanak introduced the first honourific term, *Bhai,* meaning "brother," addressing his companion (a Muslim by birth) as Bhai Mardana and another Sikh as Bhai Lalo. This honourific title was given Gurdas, the sixteenth-century poet and exegete who inscribed the *Aad Granth* (the primal Sikh scripture) under the personal supervision of Guru Arjan, and Nand Lal, a poet in the *darbar* (court) of Guru Gobind Singh, whose writings are also highly revered. Out of respect, they were addressed as Bhai Gurdas and Bhai Nand Lal.

Since that time, the Sikh community has introduced a few new honourific designations, and you will notice many of them being used throughout the book:

- *Sri:* This is the most common prefix used as a title of respect before a name. For example, *Sri Guru Granth Sahib.*
- *Sahib:* This means sir or master, and it is an added term of reverence. Used alone, it can denote simple respect, such as "*Dr. Sahib*" when referring to one's doctor. When it is used in combination with other terms of reverence, it is understood to enhance the respect awarded to the named, such as *Sri Guru Granth Sahib.* The term *Sahib* derives from Arabic, meaning "companion." Its use became common during the British Raj in India when men in authority (Indians and non-Indians) were addressed as Sahib. To address women in authority, the English word *ma'am* was combined with *sahib* to create *memsahib.* India is still caught up in addressing all superiors and elders as sir and/ or madam.
- *Bhai Sahib:* (a title of veneration for learned and highly respected individuals). Lately, this honourific is used very loosely among Sikhs. When Sikhs, particularly women, use this term to address someone as Bhai Sahib, the form of address creates a sort of temporary, metaphorical brotherly kinship.
- *Singh Sahib:* an honourific designation meaning "Your Honour" or "The Honourable," generally given to the *jathedar,* head of a *takhat.* This is a twentieth-century term created out of respect for the heads of *takhats.*
- *Mata:* While the literal translation of mata is mother, it is an honourific prefix used to accord utmost respect, especially to an older woman. Guru Angad's wife, Kheevi, and Guru Gobind Singh's mother, Gujri, are addressed as Mata Kheevi and Mata Gujri (Gujar Kaur), respectively. Many other women in history have been given this honourific designation.
- *Bibi* is another honourific prefix used for women in respectable positions. Bibi Nanaki (Guru Nanak's sister), Bibi Bhani (Guru Amar Das's daughter) and Bibi Veero (Guru Hargobind's daughter) were honoured with this prefix. Sahib Kaur

(1771–1801), the prime minister of Patiala, was addressed as
Bibi Sahib Kaur.

- *Sardar*: The word has its origin in Persia and was introduced in
India during Mogul rule. It is a title of nobility that was originally
used to denote princes, noblemen, and other aristocrats. It was
also used to imply a chief, a head, or a leader of a tribe or group.
It also means "mister," and most Sikhs wearing dastaars are
commonly addressed as Sardar.

162. Are Sikhs required to raise their children as Sikhs?

Sikhi teaches that spirituality and religion are deeply personal. The
ultimate decision on which spiritual path to follow is an individual
one that must be made by oneself when a person feels ready. It cannot
be forced on anyone. At the same time, Sikhs are taught to raise their
children in a spiritual environment consistent with Sikhi values and
beliefs, so that they may have a strong foundation and the ingredients for
living a happy and fulfilled life. The *Rehat Maryada* (code of conduct)
instructs Sikhs to provide their children with a spiritual foundation and
education, to teach them Gurmukhi script (the script in which the *Guru
Granth Sahib* is written), and to refrain from cutting their hair.[218]

Parents have the responsibility to teach and pass on values to their
children. Spiritual values are an essential part of raising a well-rounded
child. Religion often plays a principal role in family life; it may influence
the way a family dresses, what foods they eat, which holidays they
celebrate, and how they view the world. It would be impossible (and
perhaps even irresponsible) to raise children in a religious family but to
isolate them from the family's religious views. Children would be deeply
confused to see a faith practiced in the home but not understand why.

Being a Sikh is not something that can be inherited through family
or bloodlines. Sikh teachings value independence of thought and

---

[218]   *Sikh Rehat Maryada* (Code of Ethics), section XVI, (g), (h) and (i).

personal autonomy. One must choose to be a Sikh. Although most Sikh parents strive to bring up their children with the faith's three critical values of remembering Waheguru, earning an honest living, and sharing with others, each child must make a conscious decision for themselves to live the Sikh lifestyle. Individuals choose to adopt the Sikh faith by receiving *amrit* or initiation formally, and this takes place whenever a person feels ready to make that commitment, whether as a youth or later in life. Each child must realize, on their own, the value of the living a spiritually informed life—whether it is in Sikhi or some other religion. Taking *amrit* is the starting point of a personal journey inside oneself. Only the person on that journey can decide when to begin it.

In many cases, children may choose to receive *amrit* even before their parents have made that choice. In other cases, a child may decide that they cannot live a Sikh lifestyle and may wish to cut their hair or take up other habits that are against Sikh ethics. Sikhi reminds us that our roles as parents are to love and guide our children—and not to behave as dictators. Parents must help their children make informed decisions about their spiritual identities. When a child is able to make their own decision, and understand the implications, parents must give their child the personal autonomy to choose their own spiritual identity and path and to continue to love them unconditionally.

163. Do Sikhs believe in sin?

The word "sin" is often loaded with meaning and has very specific application to teachings of particular religions. Sikhs do not believe in the traditional concepts of sin, i.e., that the commission of a sin will send someone to hell. The literal Panjabi translation for "sin" is *paap*. However, the word used in the Sikh scripture is *apraadh*, which carries a definition of the reason the conduct is considered objectionable. According to the Sikh faith, an *apraadh* is that which takes us away from the realization of the Divine and does not allow us to understand our true nature. An *apraadh* is committed under the influence of the "five vices" (lust, anger, greed, worldly attachment, and ego). These lead us away from Divine realization and trap us in materialism.

As in criminal law, an essential component of *apraadh* is the intention. Thus, children who may not be aware of the implications of their actions are not to be punished for their wrongful conduct; instead, they are to be educated with love and compassion. For adults, being unaware of one's "wrong" actions—even if under the influence of one of the five vices—is not an excuse for that action. Nevertheless, Sikhs consider it more important that one learns from their actions than dwelling on their mistakes.

Frankly, though, Sikhs do not spend a lot of time focusing on *apraadh*. As humans, we are prone to error. Sikhs believe that the key to uplifting one's life is *Naam Japna* (meditation on the Divine name or Divine remembrance). Meditation on *Naam* can help cleanse a soul and wash away all the negative energy accumulated through past actions and misdeeds. *Naam Japna* elevates our consciousness so that it is absorbed into the Divine, and we can be free from the lure of conduct that takes us away from this goal.

164. What responsibility do Sikhs assume for the care of elders?

Compassion, truth, and contentment are the basis of all faiths. For Sikhs, Waheguru resides in all beings, and respect for human dignity and protection of human rights are basic precepts of the Sikh faith. In the Sikh tradition, much respect is given to elders since their experience and wisdom can guide the family and the community. The Gurbani emphasizes respect for one's parents: "It is foolish to argue with your parents, who gave birth to you and raised you to be who you are today."

The majority of Sikh families prefer to take care of their elders at home, ignoring personal comforts. Many consider taking care of their parents an honour and an extension of their filial duty. Nevertheless, in our fast-paced lives today, due to work and child-raising obligations, it is becoming increasingly difficult for family members to solely provide compassionate care for their elders. Longer life expectancies and complications of dementia may mean that fragile elders need more care than families can provide. These are personal decisions that only a family can make for itself. However, in recent years, there has been an increased incidence of Sikh elders who reside in senior care facilities, at times distant from their families. Seniors, being isolated and also vulnerable in such homes, depending on the involvement of family members, may develop physical and mental challenges. This vulnerability has become even more apparent during the pandemic. Just as patience and love are needed in raising children, these virtues are also required in taking care of our elders who have become physically and sometimes mentally disabled. There is more need than ever for well-trained health care workers and special-needs services.

165. What are society's obligations to individuals who experience mental illness?

Society's obligations toward people with mental illness begin by acknowledging that it exists and is not uncommon. "About 15 percent of the world's population—some 785 million people—has a significant physical or mental disability, including about 5 percent of children," according to a 2011 report prepared jointly by the World Health Organization and the World Bank.[219] It has further been reported that approximately 20 percent of individuals in Canada will experience a mental illness during their lifetime, and the rest will be affected by mental illness in family members, friends, or colleagues.[220]

In the Sikh community, there have been ongoing efforts to address mental illness and eliminate the stigma around it. Because of the stigma

---

[219]   David Brown, "15% Worldwide Have Physical or Mental Disability," *Washington Post*, June 9, 2011, para. 1, https://www.cbsnews.com/news/15-worldwide-have-physical-or-mental-disability.

[220]   P. Smetanin et al., *The Life and Economic Impact of Major Mental Illnesses in Canada* (Toronto: RiskAnalytica for the Mental Health Commission of Canada, 2011).

associated with mental illness, it is an issue that has remained in the shadows, and those who suffer from mental illness often do not receive the assistance they need. Many who need help do not feel comfortable asking for it or are socially isolated. If they cannot ask for help, they suffer in silence. Workshops and seminars have taken place in partnership with Sikh organizations to create awareness, foster acceptance, and provide culturally appropriate support and resources so that those affected by mental illness can receive the support they need. Only through awareness can we work to remove the stigma associated with mental illness and aid those who need it.

166. What is death?

Gurbani discusses two types of death: death of the physical body and death of the ego.

Death of the body is considered a natural process of divine will or *hukam*. For a Sikh, birth and death are part of the human life cycle. This transition provides us with an opportunity for spiritual growth, liberation, and ultimate unity with Waheguru. Guru Nanak says, "Whoever has come, shall depart; all shall have their turn."[221] The body is like a guest house, and the soul is like the guest. While our relationships with our kith and kin end with our last breath, the soul, or divine light (*jot*) that is contained within each living being, does not extinguish. Guru Nanak writes, "Mortals come into this world with death already preordained; once their time is up, they cannot remain here. They have to move on to the world beyond."[222] Guru Arjan cautions us to focus our living days on what is important: "Your life-night is coming to its end. Don't get

---

[221] *SGGS* 474: jo aaya so chulsee subh koee aaee variae—ਜੋ ਆਇਆ ਸੋ ਚਲਸੀ ਸਭੁ ਕੋਈ ਆਈ ਵਾਰੀਐ॥

[222] *SGGS* 1022: maran likhaye mandal meh aaye kiau raheeaai chalanaa parathaae—ਮਰਣੁ ਲਿਖਾਇ ਮੰਡਲ ਮਹਿ ਆਇ ਕਿਉ ਰਹੀਐ ਚਲਣਾ ਪਰਥਾਏ ॥

entangled in lust, anger, greed, emotional attachment, and ego; these are the impediments to a sustainable, happy life and contentment."[223]

Sikhs are not concerned with physical birth and death but rather spiritual birth and death. Bhagat Kabir writes that most of the world is focused on the wrong kind of death: "The world is constantly dying, but not many have learned how to die truthfully. Those who know how to die (by giving up the five vices; lust, anger, greed, worldly attachment, and ego) indeed shall never have to die again."[224] Death is seen as the ending of the corporeal existence, but it is not the ending of the soul or divine light, which exists inside all of us, and is a part of the one Source. This divine light cannot be extinguished. The goal for every Sikh is to merge with their Divine Source while living. This occurs through the death of the ego, which is only possible when a Sikh makes it a daily practice to meditate, share their resources with others, and earn an honest living.

167. Is there life after death?

The *SGGS* provides multiple perspectives on what happens to us when our material existence comes to an end. But rather than dwelling on what happens after death, the Sikh scripture emphasizes honouring the life that we have been given. "The afterlife is not a primary concern [in Sikhi]," says Gurinder Singh Mann, a retired Sikh Studies professor. "It's a very life-affirming belief system."[225] Rather than looking for eternity after death, the Sikh scripture focuses on human duties while living on this earth.

The Sikh scripture contains a reference to 8.4 million life cycles (not necessarily all humans) by bard Bhatt Gayand, "You [God] created

---

[223] *SGGS* 43: lagha kit kuphukray subh mukdi chalee raiin—ਲਗਾ ਕਿਤੁ ਕੁਫਕੜੇ ਸਭ ਮੁਕਦੀ ਚਲੀ ਰੈਣ

[224] *SGGS* 555: kabeeraa marataa marataa jag muaa mar bh na jaanai koi—ਕਬੀਰਾ ਮਰਤਾ ਜਗੁ ਮੁਆ ਮਰਿ ਭਿ ਨ ਜਾਨੈ ਕੋਇ॥

[225] Quoted in Daniel Burke, "For Sikhs, the Soul Lives On Long after the Body Dies," *Washington Post*, August 9, 2012.

the 8.4 million species of beings and provide for their sustenance." [226]
Though some Sikhs believe this to be the exact number of species of life
forms on Earth, others consider this reference to be an acknowledgment
of ancient Eastern philosophy, which is not to be taken literally. Rather,
the term is used to emphasize the innumerable life cycles that the divine
light travels through until finally merging with the Creator.

Many Sikhs believe that if spiritual union with the Divine Source has
not been achieved during one's lifetime, one's soul will continue its journey
to another "guest house," whether that be human, animal, or insect. This is
commonly referred to as transmigration. However, this view is not shared
by all Sikhs. Some Sikhs believe that the reference to transmigration is an
analogy for the process of the birth and death of the ego.

The *SGGS* contains many teachings on the cycle of death and
rebirth and how to be released from it. Guru Nanak says, "Those who
meditate on Waheguru attain liberation. For them, the cycle of birth
and death has been completed."[227] There are other passages in *Gurbani*,
such as the following one written by Guru Amar Das: "Without the True
Guru, one cannot find peace [end the cycle of birth and death]; instead,
they wander lost through countless transmigration[s] of the soul like
crows in a deserted house."[228]

Many Sikhs take literally the reference to the soul migrating between
different life forms. Others believe that this is a metaphor used by the Gurus
to refer to the cycle that traps us in material joy and pain—the highs and
lows of life that cause us to die and be born over and over again. Regardless
of which interpretation one chooses, Sikhs are united in their understanding
that being free from the cycle of birth and death is fundamentally about
freeing oneself from the bondage of a material existence. The spiritual
aspirant learns that their relationship with the material world must transform

---

[226] *SGGS* 1403: chavaraaseeh lakh jon upaiee rijak dheeaa sabh hoo kau tadh
kaa—ਚਵਰਾਸੀਹ ਲਖ ਜੋਨਿ ਉਪਾਈ ਰਿਜਕੁ ਦੀਆ ਸਭ ਹੂ ਕਉ ਤਦ ਕਾ॥

[227] *SGGS* 11: se mukat se mukat bhe jin har dhiaaiaa jee tin tooTee jam kee
faasee—ਸੇ ਮੁਕਤੁ ਸੇ ਮੁਕਤੁ ਭਏ ਜਿਨ ਹਰਿ ਧਿਆਇਆ ਜੀ ਤਿਨ ਤੁਟੀ ਜਮ ਕੀ ਫਾਸੀ॥

[228] *SGGS* 30: bahu jonee bhaudhaa firai jiau su(n)n(j)ai(n) ghar kaau—ਬਹੁ ਜੋਨੀ
ਭਉਦਾ ਫਿਰੈ ਜਿਉ ਸੁੰਞੈ ਘਰਿ ਕਾਉ॥

from being attached to everything, and honouring nothing, to honouring everything but being attached to nothing.

168. Is deathbed conversion legitimate?

Is it ever too late to find Waheguru? Obviously not. Whether deathbed conversion is legitimate depends upon the circumstances under which that conversion takes place. Compared to Christian chaplains in hospitals who regularly encounter people who are on their deathbeds and lead them in prayer, bedside prayer is not a common practice among Sikhs. Now and then, however, someone on their deathbed may requests a prayer, or a family member makes such a request on their behalf. If a *giani* (someone learned in Sikhi) accedes to the request, their intention is not to convert the individual or encourage them toward initiation into Sikhi. Rather, it is to bring them solace and peace of mind and help them transition peacefully to the next part of their spiritual journey: "It is worthwhile to communicate with the Divine whether it is for an hour, half an hour or half of that," says Bhagat Kabir.[229]

Self-realization or self-reflection, even if it is in the last moments of one's life, can never be considered a waste of time. Indeed, if done with purity of thought and genuine intent, those moments can truly be liberating. "At the very last moment, one who thinks of the Divine, and dies in such a thought shall be liberated; the Creator shall abide in their heart," says Bhagat Tarlochan.[230]

All spiritual paths aim to help us become better human beings, at peace with ourselves, in harmony with nature, and respectful toward all of Waheguru's creations. While some especially blessed people may experience self-realization at an early age, most of us continue to seek the "eureka" moment throughout our lives. Anyone who makes such a

---

[229] *SGGS* 1377: Kabeer ek ghaRee aadhee gharee aadhee hoo(n) te aadh—ਕਬੀਰ ਏਕ ਘੜੀ ਆਧੀ ਘਰੀ ਆਧੀ ਹੂੰ ਤੇ ਆਧ ॥ ਭਗਤਨ ਸੇਤੀ ਗੋਸਟੇ ਜੋ ਕੀਨੇ ਸੋ ਲਾਭ॥

[230] *SGGS* 526: a(n)t kaal naarain simarai aaisee chi(n)taa meh je marai. Badhat tilochan te nar mukataa peeta(n)bar vaa ke ridhai basai -ਅੰਤਿ ਕਾਲਿ ਨਾਰਾਇਣੁ ਸਿਮਰੈ ਐਸੀ ਚਿੰਤਾ ਮਹਿ ਜੇ ਮਰੈ ॥ ਬਦਤਿ ਤਿਲੋਚਨ ਤੇ ਨਰ ਮੁਕਤਾ ਪੀਤੰਬਰੁ ਵਾ ਕੇ ਰਿਦੈ ਬਸੈ॥

discovery, even in their dying moments, should be considered fortunate. Legitimacy lies in their spiritual experience, and no one else should have any right to question its validity.

169. Do Sikhs have end-of-life prayers?

There is no particular prayer for the end of life. Prayer and meditation are part of the daily routine for a Sikh. They are spiritually uplifting and provide an excellent stress management technique.

Many Sikhs memorize their daily prayers and are able to recite them even when they are ill. But when someone is bereft with illness, they may wish to have the *Sukhmani Sahib* (*Song of Peace*) read to them or sung out loud. Some Sikhs prefer to recite *Keerten Sohila* (the pre-bedtime verses) when death is imminent. They suggest that doing so is beneficial to both the people reciting the bani and the terminally ill, but tradition seems to be less prevalent in modern Sikh practice. Prayers, whether done by the individual or by others, can provide the patient with a sense of peace, the will to fight their illness, and the strength to accept their pain and suffering if their illness is terminal.

170. Is it preferable to cremate or bury a dead body?

Sikhs accept death as the fulfillment of their journey on earth. How the body is disposed of makes no difference to the dead, but cremation is the preferred method of disposal for Sikhs and is recommended by the *Rehat Maryada* (Sikh code of conduct).[231] People from many different cultures or religious traditions consider cremation to be "more eco-friendly than burial."[232] Sikhs consider cremation to be the most natural way of returning the body to its elements and more economical compared to burial. However, when cremation is not a practical option, the person

---

[231] *Sikh Rehat Maryada*, Section 19(c).
[232] William Reville, "Which to choose, burial or cremation?" January 15, 2018, in Irishtimes.com.

may choose whatever suitable means are available and in accordance with their circumstances.

171. Is there any restriction on organ donation?

There is no bar to a Sikh donating their body or organs, whether for scientific research or to aid the living. Sikhs consider it their social duty to help others. What can be more helpful than using one's own body (even in death) to give someone else the opportunity to live?

172. What happens at a Sikh funeral?

The *Rehat Maryada* lays out certain religious rites that Sikhs must follow when someone dies. The body is washed and dressed in fresh clothes before cremation. If the deceased person was *amritdhari*, they must be adorned in all five articles of faith. As prayers will be conducted during the funeral, anyone in attendance is expected to cover their head during the ceremony. Most funeral homes that conduct Sikh cremations will have extra head coverings if an attendee does not have one with them. There are two prayers that are always said at a funeral. The *ardaas* is the Sikh prayer that is said at the commencement or end of major events to mark birth, death, and everything in between. This prayer is a supplication to the Divine Source to give the living the strength to move on with their lives after a loved one's passing. The second prayer is the *Keertan Sohila*, which is also the prayer read at bedtime. This prayer reminds all to accept death as the ultimate truth.

There are three aspects to Sikh funeral rites: one part occurs at the crematorium, the second at the gurdwara, and the third involves scattering of the ashes. The timing of these three steps varies, depending upon local customs and family traditions. In India, cremation usually takes place within a day or two of a person's death, although sometimes the funeral might be delayed while awaiting the arrival of close family members. Once the body has been cremated, the family will host a *Sehaj Path* (reading of the Sikh scripture).

Sikh funerals are usually public events and have evolved to suit different local needs and circumstances. Unless a family specifies that they wish to have a private event, it is common for anyone who was touched by the life of the deceased to attend. This includes family, friends, relatives, and even acquaintances—all of whom are welcome to gather at the funeral home to pay their last respects. Sikhs are encouraged to show respect to the deceased and their loved ones but try to maintain composure and serenity. Death is considered a necessary aspect of life; Sikhs believe that the focus at a funeral should be the celebration of the life of the deceased rather than the mourning of their loss.

Traditionally, in India, Sikhs wear white clothing at funerals. This colour is considered to represent peace and tranquility. However, there is no religious bar to wearing any other colour. Younger diaspora Sikhs, particularly those living in North America, have started to adopt the wider North American custom of wearing black at funerals mainly due to the impact of assimilation and loss of cultural fluency in Sikhi.

Following the completion of the religious part of the funeral rites, including *sehaj path*, close family members go to a nearby body of flowing water to scatter the ashes. Some Sikhs take a deceased relative's remains to a town called Kiratpur,[233] in Punjab, and dispose of them in the river there. This is not a religious requirement. Sikhs are recommended to dispose of remains in running water anywhere; if that is not possible, they can bury them anywhere, including in their backyards. Looking back historically, people took ashes to a place called Haridwar (one of the seven sacred cities of Hindus) where all family genealogy records were maintained. However, interning remains in a specific place and memorializing them is discouraged. Sikhs believe that once a loved one

---

[233]   Kiratpur was established by Guru Hargobind, the sixth Guru, and he immersed in eternal light there as well. Guru Har Rai and Guru Har Krishan, the seventh and eighth Gurus, were born there. The town is also the site where Guru Gobind Singh, the tenth Guru, received Guru Teg Bahadur's severed head from Bhai Jaita (a Sikh devotee), brought from Delhi after the ninth Guru was beheaded on Mughal ruler Aurangzeb's orders.

has passed on, it is important to let go of emotional attachment to them. The focus should be on living one's life in the present moment rather than being stuck in the past.

173. Are there mourning customs in the Sikh faith?

As discussed earlier, Sikhs believe in the cycle of life and transmigration of the soul from one life to another. Individuals' actions bind them to this cycle. The soul never dies, and it is not subject to death. Death is another aspect of the journey of life through the material universe. Sikhs try to continually be mindful of death so they can be sufficiently thankful and prayerful. This is part of the reason why Sikhs wear a kirpan (one of the five articles of faith for a Sikh, which resembles a stylized dagger). The kirpan reminds a Sikh to stand up against injustice and serves as a reminder of their own mortality—and as an enjoinder to make the most of one's life while alive.

Since the soul never dies, Sikhi discourages mourning at death. Sikhi teaches that a funeral should be a celebration of life. Guru Amar Das, the third Sikh Guru, says, "Let no one shed tears for me after I am gone. That would not please me at all... Sing *keertan* [sabads] in praise of Waheguru."[234]

But human nature being what it is, it is often very difficult to handle the passing of a loved one without feeling sorrow. The pain of loss varies from person to person, and depending upon the relationship and circumstances of death, it can be profound. In situations where loss is deeply felt, comforting the bereaved family members is important. This can happen in different ways. For Panjabi Sikhs, whether they live in India or abroad, the cultural tradition is to gather at the home of the deceased and sit with the loved ones left behind. In addition to encouraging them to pray and meditate, the family is also encouraged to share stories and shed tears. It is felt that rather than bottling up

---

[234] *SGGS* 923: mat mai pichhai koiee rovasee so mai mool na bhaiaa—ਮਤ ਮੈ ਪਿਛੈ ਕੋਈ ਰੋਵਸੀ ਸੋ ਮੈ ਮੂਲਿ ਨ ਭਾਇਆ ॥

emotions inside oneself, the process of open grieving will aid in letting go and moving forward.

Many families will also host a religious gathering on the one-year anniversary of the death of their loved one. The event allows an opportunity for closure and can be held at the gurdwara or someone's home. The religious part of the event usually involves reading from the *SGGS* and singing sabads that are intended to uplift and remind us of the purpose of our existence. The social part often involves the sharing of a meal, sharing stories, and reminiscing about the life of the departed.

174. Is there a concept of doomsday?

The question of doomsday, apocalypse, or the end of the world as we know it does not concern most Sikhs. We are born on this earth by divine will and leave by divine will. "Whatever pleases Waheguru, shall happen and that is a good deed, and it is futile to worry about it," says Guru Angad.[235]

The concept of doomsday is irrelevant in Sikhi because Gurbani teaches us to focus on what we do when we are alive. Guru Nanak says, "You created the creation and infused your power into it. You behold your creation, like the losing and winning dice of the earth. Whosoever has come, shall depart; all shall have their turn. Let's not forget Waheguru, the master of our minds, who holds our very breath of life. Let's avail [ourselves] of the opportunity to resolve our own affairs and meditate on Its name."[236]

---

[235] *SGGS* 1239: jo tis bhaavai naanakaa saiee bhalee kaar—ਜੋ ਤਿਸੁ ਭਾਵੈ ਨਾਨਕਾ ਸਾਈ ਭਲੀ ਕਾਰ ॥

[236] *SGGS* 474: aape hee karanaa keeo kal aape hee tai dhaareeaai—ਆਪੇ ਹੀ ਕਰਣਾ ਕੀਓ ਕਲ ਆਪੇ ਹੀ ਤੈ ਧਾਰੀਐ॥

175. What is the difference between spiritual death and physical death?

Sikhi concerns itself more with spiritual death than physical death. Physical death is an essential path in the journey of life and is not to be feared. Numerous verses in *SGGS* express the inevitability of death: "Whosoever is born, must perish, it's a matter of time."[237]

Guru Nanak has rightly said: "Death does not ask the time; it does not ask the date or the day of the week. Some are busy amassing worldly assets, and some who have amassed spiritual wealth are always ready to leave. Some are severely punished, and some are taken care of. When the time of death comes, they must leave all their worldly wealth, armies, and their beautiful mansions behind. O Nanak, the pile of dust, once again, will be reduced to dust."[238]

Physical death is permanent, but spiritual death is reversible and occurs by forgetting the Creator. A person who is so consumed by ego, anger, greed, lust, and worldly attachments that they cannot remember or connect with the divine in humanity and the universe is considered as good as dead. Sikhi teaches that to be truly alive, one must kill their ego. The killing of the ego permits the Sikh to be reborn and to be able to live a more complete life: "A devotee who dies by the Guru's sabads [lives a humble life] is truly dead. His death does not crush him, and pain does not afflict him."[239]

---

[237] *SGGS* 1429: jo upajio so binas hai paro aaj kai kaal—ਜੋ ਉਪਜਿਓ ਸੋ ਬਿਨਸ ਹੈ ਪਰੋ ਆਜੁ ਕੈ ਕਾਲਿ॥

[238] *SGGS* 1244: maran na moorat puchhiaa puchhee thit na vaar—ਮਰਣਿ ਨ ਮੂਰਤੁ ਪੁਛਿਆ ਪੁਛੀ ਥਿਤਿ ਨ ਵਾਰੁ॥

[239] *SGGS* 111: sabadh marai su muaa jaapai; kaal na chaapai dukh na suntaapay—ਸਬਦਿ ਮਰੈ ਸੁ ਮੂਆ ਜਾਪੈ ॥ ਕਾਲੁ ਨ ਚਾਪੈ ਦੁਖ ਨ ਸੰਤਾਪੈ॥

PART VI

Beliefs

CHAPTER 18

Unpacking Sikh Beliefs

Beliefs help us make sense of and interact with the world. They are also the way individuals develop a sense of who they are. Thus, they are central to our worldview. Beliefs can arise from a variety of sources. They can be shaped by environment, be grounded in scientific knowledge, or be based on personal experience. The important thing is that beliefs involve the brain's computation and reasoning abilities in ways that allow it to remain in a state of equilibrium in the face of constant sensory inputs. Sikhs draw on the teachings in the *Guru Granth Sahib*, the history of the Sikh faith, and their own lived experiences for their beliefs. In this chapter, I will dive a little deeper into the beliefs that guide our actions.

176. Is Sikhi the only true religion?

Major religions today differ significantly in some of their beliefs and practices. Despite this, Sikhi considers all these religious traditions to be means to the same end and cautions Sikhs not to criticize other religions. Religious labels have little meaning to Sikhs. The emphasis here is on individual practices that prepare the mind for changing its worldview and turning away from viewing the sensory world as distinct or separated from the Creator. Sikhs believe that the only truth is Waheguru, the Creator. All religions are simply pathways to the same destination:

conscious union with our Divine Source. Although Guru Nanak and his successors challenged existing religious practices and customs of the dominant faith traditions of the time (Hinduism and Islam), this was not done out of a sense of moral superiority. Bhagat Kabir writes in the *SGGS*, "Do not assume that the *Ved* (Hindu scriptures) and *Kateb* (Abrahamic scriptures—Torah, Bible, and Quran) are false. Instead, those who do not contemplate them are false."[240]

Guru Nanak denounced the caste system, mistreatment of women, ritualistic behaviour, and the religious leaders who sanctioned the oppressive regime that demoralized and marginalized the masses. He challenged those whose practice lacked *niyat* (intention) and genuine commitment to their faith. Guru Nanak believed that all people of faith should make a genuine effort to understand the true teachings of their faith traditions and put those teachings into action.

To further model their views about religious equality, the gurus included the writings of prominent exponents of oneness without considering how to "identify" them either as Hindu and Muslim or through caste associations. A Sufi saint, Mir Mohammad (also known as Mian Mir) was asked to lay the foundation stone of Darbar Sahib (the Golden Temple). Guru Arjan says, "Of all the religions, the best religion is to recite the name of Waheguru and maintain pure conduct."[241] Guru Teg Bahadur gave his life for the right for the upper-caste Brahmin and Kshatriyas to wear their sacred thread (*janeu*) and perform the ritual rites.

Through their actions, the Sikh gurus sought to challenge division and encourage people to see the commonalties between them on their path to oneness. Guru Gobind Singh says, "Listen, all of you, carefully, for I speak the truth—only those who are absorbed in true love will attain Waheguru."[242]

---

[240] *SGGS* 1350: baid kitaib kaho matt jhuthay jhuthaa jo na bicharay—ਬੇਦ ਕਤੇਬ ਕਹਹੁ ਮਤ ਝੂਠੇ ਝੂਠਾ ਜੋ ਨ ਬਿਚਾਰੇ॥

[241] *SGGS* 266: sarab dharam meh sresaT dharam; har ko naamu jap nirmal karam. ਸਰਬ ਧਰਮ ਮਹਿ ਸ੍ਰੇਸਟ ਧਰਮੁ ॥ ਹਰਿ ਕੋ ਨਾਮੁ ਜਪਿ ਨਿਰਮਲ ਕਰਮੁ॥

[242] Dasam Bani, verse 9 "Tav Prasad Saiaye": saach kaho(n) sun leh sabhai jin prem keeo tin hee prabh paio. ਸਾਚੁ ਕਹੋ ਸੁਨ ਲੇ ਹੋ ਸਭੈ ਜਿਨ ਪ੍ਰੇਮ ਕੀਓ ਤਿਨ ਜੀ ਪ੍ਰਭ ਪਾਇਓ॥

177. Do Sikhs believe in prophecy?

The idea that the future is predictable or set in stone goes contrary to Sikhi teachings such as free will. Gurbani emphasizes the need to focus on the present rather than dwelling on the past or the future.

178. Why is there suffering?

There are two forms of suffering according to Sikhi: physical or mental suffering and spiritual suffering. Gurbani addresses both forms of suffering—with a primary focus on alleviating spiritual suffering.

Sikhi does not pass judgment on physical or mental suffering as being good or bad—only that it occurs as a result of free will and the natural consequence of our actions. Many sabads in the *SGGS* emphasize that the Creator is without enmity or hostility and does not cause suffering. "I suffer because of my actions; thus, I cannot blame anyone else," says Guru Nanak."[243] However, cause and effect are not viewed here on a micro or individual level—but within a larger, holistic view of the self. The individual person may indeed seem to have suffered unjustly—for example, a young child stricken with cancer or abused by a parent. No one could fairly say that this child brought on their own suffering. However, when the child is seen through the lens of the larger whole of all humanity, their suffering is viewed as a natural consequence of the actions of the whole.

Part of the goal of living a spiritually informed life is learning to understand and accept the circumstances in which one finds themselves. This includes accepting physical or mental suffering. While Sikhs are encouraged to get medical or psychological assistance to alleviate physical or psychological pain, they are also taught to accept the situation within which they find themselves rather than railing against others or the Creator for causing them to suffer. According to Gurbani, everything

---

[243] *SGGS* 433: Jo mein keeya so mein paya dos na deejay avar jana. ਜੋ ਮੈ ਕੀਆ ਸੋ ਮੈ ਪਾਇਆ ਦੋਸ ਨ ਦੀਜੈ ਅਵਰ ਜਨਾ॥

happens in accordance with Waheguru's knowing—and that the Creator
is just, merciful, and loving. Guru Arjan writes, "Why do you waver,
O mortal being? The Creator shall protect you."[244] Thus meditation
becomes an important tool in order to reduce, if not eliminate, physical
and psychological suffering.

Suffering and joy are perspectives we have as humans due to
attachment to the material world. Sikhi teaches to go beyond these
perspectives. In Sikhi, spiritual suffering is the pain and torment we
experience because we are separated from Waheguru. In this way,
physical suffering and pain can serve a useful purpose. Guru Nanak
says, "So many endure suffering and pain. Even these are your gifts,
oh Great Giver! Liberation from bondage comes only by Your Will."[245]

At an individual level, the experience of pain can lead one to learn to
detach themselves from their corporeal existence and to accept the divine
will. On a global level, it can draw out great kindness and compassion.
The COVID-19 pandemic is a classic example, demonstrating most
of the population's empathy and resilience. Pain can also be a test, an
ordeal, to assess one's conviction and courage. Guru Nanak says, "Pain
is a remedy, and pleasure the disease." [246]

179. What is love?

The word *love* in Sikh philosophy refers to a spiritual state rather than
a physical, romantic relationship. The SGGS is full of verses expressing
love and devotion to Waheguru and all creation, but none is more
poignant than the following expression of true love between a seeker
of the truth (Sikh) and their Guru: "If you desire to play this game of

---

[244] *SGGS* 724: too kaahe dolay praania tudh raakhai gaa sirjanhaar. ਤੂ ਕਾਹੇ ਡੋਲਹਿ
ਪ੍ਰਾਣੀਆ ਤੁਧੁ ਰਾਖੇਗਾ ਸਿਰਜਣਹਾਰੁ ॥

[245] *SGGS* 5: ketia dukh bhug sudh maar. ਕੇਤਿਆ ਦੂਖ ਭੂਖ ਸਦ ਮਾਰ॥

[246] *SGGS* 469: Dukh daroo sukh rog bhaya ja sukh taam na hoee. ਦੁਖੁ ਦਾਰੂ ਸੁਖੁ
ਰੋਗੁ ਭਇਆ ਜਾ ਸੁਖੁ ਤਾਮਿ ਨ ਹੋਈ॥

love with me, then step onto my path with your head in your palm."[247] The reference to having "your head in your palm" is used in two senses here. First, it is an expression of true love. By removing the head from the body, one is showing the willingness to die for divine knowledge. However, the removal of the head from the body is also about the relinquishing of ego. In this way, the Guru is not talking about the death of the body but about the death of the ego and submission to divine will. In this verse, Guru Nanak therefore promises to guide those who show utmost devotion and give up their egos.

Love, benevolence, and kindness are the virtues of Waheguru that Sikhs are taught to concentrate on. Guru Gobind Singh says: "Listen, all of you! I declare the truth that those who become loving alone will realize Waheguru."[248] Guru Gobind Singh is talking about another dimension of love. This love is neither for a person nor a romantic type, as is immortalized in the legions of stories such as Romeo and Juliet or Heer and Ranjha. Instead, the love he refers to is the love for Waheguru, and by extension, all creation.

The Gurus have used this theme of romantic love, which is universally understood, as an analogy for spiritual love. Spiritual love is considered in Sikhi to be the highest form of altruistic love, surpassing any love for another human being. To explain the nature of the spiritual journey, the Gurus have used the analogy of the relationship between a bride and groom. The soul is described as the bride; her groom is Waheguru, the Divine creator, for whom she pines and longs to immerse within eternal union. The analogy of the soul-bride is the most frequently recurring theme in Gurbani and is expressed throughout the Sikh scriptures. Guru Arjan writes, "Oh my beloved Creator, I wait for you and adorn myself

---

[247]   *SGGS* 1412: jao tao prem khelan kaa chao; ser dhar tale galee mori aauo ਜਉ ਤਉ ਪ੍ਰੇਮ ਖੇਲਣ ਕਾ ਚਾਉ ॥ ਸਿਰੁ ਧਰਿ ਤਲੀ ਗਲੀ ਮੇਰੀ ਆਉ॥

[248]   Tav Prasad Savaee-ay—Guru Gobind Singh Ji—Jin prem kee-o tin hee prabh paaee-o—ਜਿਨ ਪ੍ਰੇਮ ਕੀਓ ਤਿਨ ਹੀ ਪ੍ਰਭ ਪਾਇਓ॥

with necklaces, eyeliner, beautiful clothes, and jewelry; sighing in the depths of my soul, I long for you and cannot sleep." [249]

Though the Sikh human Gurus were all male, they have written their spiritual poetry (sabads) using the feminine voice. This use of the female voice is an extension of the idea of the soul-bride. Guru Ram Das raises a question and then answers, "Tell me, my dear, where do I find my Beloved [Waheguru]? Oh, Saints of the Divine Creator, please show me the way that I can follow." He then replies, "The best way to find my Beloved, is to treasure the Words [spiritual utterances] of my Beloved Guru. A humble bride imbued in Naam Simran [meditation] is loved by her Beloved, even if she is physically disabled and [of] short stature." Guru Nanak emphasizes, "There is only the One Beloved—we are all soul-brides of our Husband, the Creator. She who is pleasing to her Husband immerses in the Divine light. What can poor and helpless Nanak do to walk on that path? Only endeared souls can walk the path that leads to becoming one with the Creator."[250]

The soul-bride analogy—and the feminine nature of the human soul—extends to all humanity as in the following verse by Guru Nanak: "We are all good in words, but bad in our deeds."[251] In this case, while the word "we" is written in the feminine tense, the Guru is speaking to all humanity and not just women. Many Sikhs who are not knowledgeable in Sikhi misinterpret these references to mean that the Guru is speaking to women about their misdeeds, but nothing could be

---

[249] *SGGS* 830: mohan needh na aavai haavai haar kajar bastar abharan keenay. Aaudeeni aaudeeni aaudeeni—ਮੋਹਨ ਨੀਦ ਨ ਆਵੈ ਹਾਵੈ ਹਾਰ ਕਜਰ ਬਸਤ੍ਰ ਅਭਰਨ ਕੀਨੇ॥ ਉਡੀਨੀ ਉਡੀਨੀ ਉਡੀਨੀ॥

[250] *SGGS* 527: Mero sundar kahoh melay kith galee. Har kay sant bataavoh marag hum peechhay lag chalee. Pria ke bachan sukhaane heearai eh chaal banee hai bhalee. Laturee madhuree thaakur bhai oho sundar dhul milee. Eko priau sakheeaa sabh pria key jo bhaavai pir saa bhalee. Nanak gareeb kiaa karai bichaaraa har bhaavai tit raah chalee. ਮੇਰੋ ਸੁੰਦਰੁ ਕਹਹੁ ਮਿਲੈ ਕਿਤੁ ਗਲੀ ॥ ਹਰਿ ਕੇ ਸੰਤ ਬਤਾਵਹੁ ਮਾਰਗੁ ਹਮ ਪੀਛੈ ਲਾਗਿ ਚਲੀ ॥੧॥ ਰਹਾਉ ॥ ਪਿਰਹ ਕੇ ਬਚਨ ਸੁਖਾਨੇ ਹੀਅਰੈ ਇਹ ਚਾਲ ਬਨੀ ਹੈ ਭਲੀ ॥ ਲਟੁਰੀ ਮਧੁਰੀ ਠਾਕੁਰ ਭਾਈ ਓਹ ਸੁੰਦਰਿ ਹਰਿ ਢੁਲਿ ਮਿਲੀ ॥੧॥ ਏਕੋ ਪਿਰਉ ਸਖੀਆ ਸਭ ਪਿਰਹ ਕੀ ਜੋ ਭਾਵੈ ਪਿਰ ਸਾ ਭਲੀ ॥ ਨਾਨਕੁ ਗਰੀਬੁ ਕਿਆ ਕਰੈ ਬਿਚਾਰਾ ਹਰਿ ਭਾਵੈ ਤਿਤੁ ਰਾਹਿ ਚਲੀ ॥

[251] *SGGS* 85: Galleen aseen changhian, acharee bureeyan—ਗਲੀ ਅਸੀ ਚੰਗੀਆ ਆਚਾਰੀ ਬੁਰੀਆਹ॥

further from the truth. As Dr. Nikki Guninder Kaur Singh writes, "The bride symbol in Sikh scripture exalts feminine love. Here, equality is the basis of the relationship. The bride, simply by loving, not by fearing or remaining in awe, or being totally dependent, senses the proximity of her Infinite Groom and is then able to share that feeling with her sisters and friends."[252]

180. Do Sikhs practice tithing?

The *Oxford Dictionary* defines *tithe* as a tenth of the goods that someone produced or the money that they earned, that was paid as a tax to support the church. Sikhs do not practice tithing. Instead, Sikhs ascribe to the principle of *dasvandh*. The word "das" means "ten" and the word "vand" means to share. It relates to the sharing of one-tenth of one's resources with others. The Sikh tradition of giving *dasvandh* can be traced back to the Gurus' time. [253] The concept of *dasvandh* is implicit in *SGGS*: "One who works hard and shares their earnings knows the path to spirituality and liberation."[254]

Sikhs are expected to share their time and their money for the betterment of society—and not just their own faith community. One's faith becomes a practical means of illustrating divine virtues like love, humility, compassion, and sharing. A gurdwara is one place where friends, families, and guests gather to practice these virtues. Congregants who attend the gurdwara donate whatever financial amount they are able to afford to be used toward the gurdwara's operations; they provide support for social causes the gurdwara is promoting; and they volunteer in the *langar* (community kitchen). However, sharing of one's

---

[252] Singh, Nikky-Guninder Kaur. *Sikhism (I. B. Tauris Introductions to Religion)* (110). Bloomsbury Publishing. Kindle Edition.

[253] Dr. Ganda Singh: *Hukamname*, 153, Punjabi University, Patiala. "ਹੁਕਮ ਲਿਖਿਆ ਹੈ ਦੇਖਦੇ ਸਿਤਾਬੀ ਹਜੂਰਿ ਤੇ ਜਟਾ ਜੋ ਗੁਰੁ ਕੇ ਨਰਵਤ ਹੋਵੈ ਗੋਲਕ ਦਸਵੰਧ ਮੰਨਤ ਸੋ ਹਜੂਰ ਆਪ ਲੈ ਆਪਣਾ॥

[254] SGGS 1245: ghaal khai kichh hathahu dhei. naanak raahu pachhaaneh sei. ਘਾਲਿ ਖਾਇ ਕਿਛੁ ਹਥਹੁ ਦੇਇ ਨਾਨਕ ਰਾਹੁ ਪਛਾਣਹਿ ਸੇਇ॥

resources with others also relates to service of humankind in general. The community, the family, and the individual are all responsible for the betterment of society. Many Sikhs understand *dasvandh* as a financial obligation or sharing from one's earnings, but for others, *dasvandh* can take many different forms. Though the term generally refers to financial wealth, it can also include the sharing of one's time, talents, nonfinancial capital, etc.

181. Is there a difference between charity and sharing?

Sikhi emphasizes the act of sharing rather than the act of charity. *Dasvandh* is not considered charity; it is sharing one's wealth with others for their benefit or the betterment of society as a whole. This is an important distinction. Charity envisions a hierarchical relationship between the donor and the recipient. Sharing envisions a relationship of equals. Each gives according to the resources they have at their disposal, in order to meet the needs of a fellow human being. Sharing one's wealth is an integral part of building a relationship with humanity, and by extension, the Divine Creator.

182. What is seva?

Seva means service. It refers to the act of helping others. To be truly considered "seva," one must do the act willingly (not because they were forced into it), selflessly (without any desire for personal glory), and indiscriminately (regardless of the other person's race, ethnicity, sexual orientation, etc.). I like to think of the word seva as an acronym for "serve everyone voluntarily and anonymously." Sikhs are encouraged to perform selfless service for others. This service can be as simple as volunteering one's time in the *langar*, the community kitchen that provides food free of charge to all visitors, or on other community projects.

Serving humanity is a duty for those trying to walk on the spiritual path since doing so helps us to recognize divine light in all of creation. Seva has two-dimensional value: it benefits the *lorhvand* (recipient), and it infuses humility and detachment in the *sevadar* (the person who serves). All of humanity is one giant family. Distinctions of nationality, ethnicity, and gender are superficial because, at our core, we all share the same divine light. For Sikhs, helping others in need is a duty that must be performed without any ego or desire for personal benefit. All our material belongings and wealth are a gift from Waheguru, and so the act of giving must be performed without pride.

183. What role does Sikhi play in physical healing?

Sikhi places a strong emphasis on healthy living (exercise), healthy eating (vegetarian diet), meditation, and *chardi kala* (a positive mindset) to maintain a healthy lifestyle and promote healing. The Sikh dharam does not subscribe to the notion of "miracle" cures, though people hawking such wares always seem to find a ready audience for their goods and services—even among Sikhs. Rather, conventional (proven) medical treatments are favoured, along with diet, exercise, and meditation as part of the essential regimen for maintaining one's mental, physical, and spiritual health.

Faith and meditation are considered essential ingredients for recovery from injury or illness. Having "faith" that one will recover if they follow a certain course of treatment is important because it helps create a positive mindset. Meditation helps calm the mind and spirit. Even in the case of incurable illnesses or diseases, meditation can aid in alleviating physical discomforts and allow people to live their last moments joyfully.

Many quotes from the *SGGS* underline the power of faith. By reciting and remembering Waheguru's name, all happiness and bliss are said to be obtained—and all suffering is destroyed. Meditation is seen as a cure for pain since it assists in changing the mindset. "Celestial peace and absolute bliss come when one meditates on Waheguru—suffering is dispelled," says Guru Arjan.[255]

For many Sikhs, reading, singing, or listening to Gurbani is calming and provides soothing relief from pain. The most commonly read bani for physical and mental healing is the *Sukhmani Sahib* (Song of Peace) written by Guru Arjan. Guru Arjan emphasizes: "Meditate, meditate, meditate in the remembrance of Waheguru and find peace. Worry and anguish shall be dispelled from your body."[256]

184. Do Sikhs believe in salvation?

Salvation refers to deliverance from sin and its consequences. This concept is often used in the Christian faith in conjunction with ideas like heaven and hell. As noted elsewhere, Sikhs do not believe in heaven or hell. Rather than deliverance, Sikhi concerns itself with liberation from the cycle of birth and death. This liberation focuses on freeing oneself from the trappings of the material world, where one lives and dies countless times a day, experiencing suffering and joy with the lows and highs of life. The Sikh concept of freedom from this cycle of birth and death is modified by the concept of Waheguru's *mehar* (grace). Guru Nanak states, "The body takes birth because of *karm*, but liberation is attained through Guru's mehar."[257]

Guru Nanak's teachings are founded not on a destination of heaven or hell but on a spiritual union with the Divine, which results in liberation or *jivanmukti* (liberation while alive). *Jivanmukti* means transcendence—becoming enlightened and emancipated in this life by being able to rise above material attachment to a deeper and more meaningful existence. *Jivanmukti* is equivalent to the concept of union

---

[255] SGGS 963: sookh sahaj aanadh ghanaa prabh japatiaa dhukh jai. ਸੂਖ ਸਹਜ ਆਨਦੁ ਘਣਾ ਪ੍ਰਭ ਜਪਤਿਆ ਦੁਖੁ ਜਾਇ॥

[256] SGGS 262: simarau simar simar sukh paavau. kal kales tan maeh miTaavau. ਸਿਮਰਉ ਸਿਮਰਿ ਸਿਮਰਿ ਸੁਖੁ ਪਾਵਉ ॥ ਕਲਿ ਕਲੇਸ ਤਨ ਮਾਹਿ ਮਿਟਾਵਉ॥

[257] SGGS 2: karamee aavai kapaRaa nadharee mokh dhuaar -ਕਰਮੀ ਆਵੈ ਕਪੜਾ ਨਦਰੀ ਮੋਖੁ ਦੁਆਰੁ॥

with Waheguru. Sikhs believe that the ten Gurus achieved this spiritual state through enlightenment. Thus, we refer to their departure from the earth as *Joti Jot samauna* (immersion in eternal light) rather than the Punjabi word for death, *marna*, which references death of a physical body that has not attained enlightenment. Sikhs believe that human birth is obtained with great fortune; therefore, this human existence is to be honoured and not wasted. Guru Arjan says, "I seek no power or liberation/salvation. My mind is in love with your Lotus Feet (sabad)—I may forever remain connected with Waheguru."[258]

Liberation is the closest translation of a concept called *mukti* in Sikhi, which means spiritual enlightenment. Sikhi does not claim a monopoly on enlightenment or the only path to *mukti*. The Sikh teachings emphasize leading a pious life so one can be deserving of Waheguru's grace. The Sikh gurus never claimed to be the only ones who have the key to enlightenment. What they did was show us a short and simple way to self-realization, which is exemplified by their own lives and based on practical experimentation. Sikhi is one way to liberation from the material world, and it is perhaps the simplest. And it is open to all. Guru Amar Das says, "The world is ablaze, oh Waheguru; save it in your mercy. Through whatever way they come, Waheguru, please pull them up to your bosom."[259]

185. Does the Sikh religion believe in miracles, divination, or magical powers?

Divination is another word for supernatural prophecy, but it also includes the word *divine*, so that is where my answer begins. One of the basic tenets of the Sikh faith is the acceptance of the divine will, which underlies everything we can see and perceive, and the wonderment at the miracle of life. Life—from conception to birth, through growth

---

[258] SGGS 534: raaj na chaahau mukat na chaahau man preet charan kamalaare—ਰਾਜੁ ਨ ਚਾਹਉ ਮੁਕਤਿ ਨ ਚਾਹਉ ਮਨਿ ਪ੍ਰੀਤਿ ਚਰਨ ਕਮਲਾਰੇ ॥

[259] SGGS 853: jagat jala(n)dhaa rakh lai aapanee kirapaa dhaar—ਜਗਤੁ ਜਲੰ ਦਾ ਰਖਿ ਲੈ ਆਪਣੀ ਕਿਰਪਾ ਧਾਰਿ ॥

and unto death—is our most common experience of divine will. In addition, the natural phenomena of day and night, the change of seasons, a cool breeze, fresh waters, or the natural provisioning of food are divine miracles to sustain life. The potential of a seed to grow into an enormous tree, and a tree producing its seed, is a wonder. The limitless natural creation of planets, stars, and galaxies, following a pattern of divine law in play, gives us to think that the Supreme Being is a puppeteer and all that exists is the divine puppet show.

The Sikh faith incorporates no notions of supernatural or magical forces within its ideology. Supernatural or magical occurrences that operate outside of natural events or forces are alluded to metaphorically in the *SGGS*, but aside from these metaphorical references, Sikhi is not concerned with their existence or nonexistence.

Given the mass appeal of magical powers and the widespread belief that religion and magical prowess were somehow intertwined, the founders of the Sikh faith made specific injunctions in their writings against either seeking out magical (supernatural) abilities or ascribing any kind of spiritual insight or awareness to those purporting to have magical powers. Guru Nanak describes the natural universe operating under the divine will with awe and describes it as magical in and of itself. Spiritually awakened individuals, according to Guru Nanak, aspire only to divine inspiration in their spiritual journey, rejecting even the desire for any other form of supernatural or magical occurrences within their lives.

The Sikh Gurus denounced those who claimed to possess predictive or supernatural powers as being no more than thugs who tried to deceive the masses for their own gain. Bhagat Kabir, in the *SGGS,* says, "Wearing religious clothes, carrying a rosary around the neck and glittering jugs in their hands, the pundits claiming to be godly and virtuous, are nothing but a façade. They are not saints of Waheguru, instead they are thugs of Benaras [one of the seven holiest cities in India for Hindus]."[260]

---

[260] *SGGS* 476: gaj saadde tai tai dhoteeaa tihare pain tag; galee jin(h)aa japamaaleeaa loTe hath nibag; oi har ke sa(n)t na aakhe'eeh baanaaras ke Thag. ਗਾਜ ਸਾਧੇ ਤੈ ਤੈ ਧੋਤੀਆ ਤਿਹਰੇ ਪਾਇਨਿ ਤਗ ॥ ਗਾਲੀ ਜਿਨ੍ਹ ਜਪਮਾਲੀਆ ਲੋ ਟੇ ਹਰਭ ਰਨਬਗ ॥ ਓਇ ਹਰਿ ਕੇ ਸੰਤ ਨ ਆਖੀਅਹਿ ਬਾਨਾਰਸਿ ਕੇ ਠਗਾ॥

186. Is evangelism or spreading the Word of God to nonbelievers a part of a Sikh's duty?

Sikhi does not advocate trying to convert others. Just as the decision to believe, or not believe, is a personal one, so too is the path one chooses to follow. Equality of all religions and freedom of religion are strong aspects of Sikh teachings. The message of the Sikh Gurus was for all humanity. They did not try to convert people to Sikhi; they simply shared their experiences to try to assist others in achieving the same state of enlightenment. Those who were inspired became followers and are known as Sikhs. Sikhs have continued with the Gurus' message of inclusivity and respect for all, irrespective of how they find inspiration and peace. In our daily prayers, we ask Waheguru for the uplifting of all humanity.

Sikhs do not try to convert others to Sikhi, but they do give information about Sikhi to educate others about their faith. Each Sikh's responsibility is to be an ambassador of the faith. If someone is inspired and wants to become a Sikh, they are welcome to join our way of life, which inspires the love of Waheguru and Its creation.

187. What are the benefits of living a Sikhi existence?

The key benefits of living a life in conformity with Sikh beliefs are twofold: self-realization and contentment. First, some fundamental questions beg answers. For example, "Who am I? Why am I here on Earth? What is the purpose of my life? How can I achieve it? Who will help me achieve my mission?" Answering these questions (thus self-realization) is critical for balance and contentment. By practicing the Sikh faith, Sikhs endeavour to comprehend the vast world around them. We, who are essentially divine beings, live in a material world. Our true nature is spiritual, and our desire for happiness and contentment cannot be fulfilled only through material pleasures. Just as the human body requires food, water, clothing, and shelter for its survival, the soul has needs as well. If we ignore the needs of the soul, balance in life and contentment are not possible. An experience of the divine and a relationship with Waheguru are food for our soul. Life is an opportunity to experience and unite with the Divine Creator, and only this union results in pure bliss. That becomes possible through meditation on *Naam* (the name of the One as revealed by our spiritual teachers).

The rewards and benefits of following a spiritual path, according to the Sikh faith, are available in the present and not in any distant future or the afterlife. Our current life is an opportunity for us to experience and unite with Waheguru. Meditation on *Naam* and reflection on sabad, or the word of the Gurus, as enshrined in the *SGGS*, provide a tangible experience of the Divine. A relationship with Waheguru and Guru is established, which is an eternal source of guidance and contentment. The Sikh faith offers a system for building this relationship and continually strengthening it. In short, our goal is to live in conformity with Sikh beliefs, which results in life's purpose becoming apparent and the experience of God becoming a reality.

188. Do Sikhs believe in angels?

Sikhs do not believe in angels. The Sikh faith believes in no mediators to connect a person with Waheguru. As with many other Judeo-Christian concepts, such as heaven, hell, or the devil, the *SGGS* uses the concept of angels as a metaphor. Bhagat Namdev says, "With Divine grace, a human can become an angel in an instant; the True Guru has given me such teaching. Born of human flesh, with the Guru's blessing, one attains the medicine [Divine Name] and ability to conquer the heavens and have no other desires."[261]

Though the Gurus did not believe in the existence of angels, they respected that angels may be a part of some people's religious beliefs. Rather than calling them foolish for believing in them, the Gurus taught that even celestial beings like angels are not above the laws of the

---

[261] SGGS 873: nar te sur hoi jaat nimakh mai satigur budh sikhalaiee: ਨਰ ਤੇ ਸੁਰ ਹੋਇ ਜਾਤ ਨਿਮਖ ਮੈ ਸਤਿਗੁਰ ਬੁਰਧ ਸਿਖਲਾਈ॥

universe. They still long for the opportunity to unite with Waheguru. The purpose of human life is to become one with the source that created us. Sikhs believe that meditation and living a spiritual life are the only ways to achieve that goal.[262] Human life is particularly precious because it is, in fact, the only life form that can achieve union with Waheguru. Thus, humans have the capacity to surpass angels through devotion and meditation on *Naam*. Guru Arjan says, "Shiva, Brahma [Hindu gods of destruction and creation], angels and demons, all burn in the fire of death [perish like all material things]."[263]

189. Do Sikhs believe in the devil?

There is no concept of Satan, the devil, demons, or any other evil power in Sikhi. We do not believe in a devil or evil spirit being the rival of God, since the Creator has no rivals or peers. Guru Nanak says, "Waheguru is devoid of fear and devoid of enmity [hostility]."[264] However, the concepts of Satan, the devil, and demons are an integral part of many faith traditions. The *SGGS* uses these concepts as metaphors to explain the importance of living a spiritually informed existence. Many references in the *SGGS* point to the real devil being the devil inside, our ego-centredness, which makes us stray from Waheguru. Ego supported by lust, anger, greed, and emotional attachment makes a person behave like a devil. Guru Nanak describes how immoral and unethical behaviour caters to evil: "Thieves, adulterers, prostitutes, and pimps befriend

---

[262] SGGS 674: prabh jee ko naam japat man chain—ਪ੍ਰਭ ਜੀ ਕੋ ਨਾਮੁ ਜਪਤ ਮਨ ਚੈਨ॥
[263] SGGS 1267: siv bira(n)ch asur sur jete kaal agan meh jarate—ਸਿਵ ਬਿਰੰਚ ਆਸੁਰ ਸੁਰ ਜੇਤੇ ਕਾਲ ਅਗਨਿ ਮਹਿ ਜਰਤੇ॥ In the Trimurti concept of Hinduism, the cosmic functions of creation, maintenance, and destruction are personified by the forms of Brahma the creator, Vishnu the maintainer or preserver, and Shiva the destroyer or transformer. These three deities have been called the "Hindu triad" or the "Great Trinity."
[264] *SGGS* 1: Mool Mantar: nirbhau nirvair—ਨਿਰਭਉ ਨਿਰਵੈਰੁ॥

immoral folks—they do not know the value of Waheguru's praise and as such, the Devil or Satan is always with them."[265]

Just as Sikhs do not believe in the devil or any other "anti-God energy," Sikhi also does not use the words "good" and "evil" to describe people or events. Instead, actions are considered positive or negative in the context of how they impact our relationship with the Divine—and ultimately, our true selves. Actions that take us closer to the Divine are desirable (good); actions that take us away from the Divine are undesirable (bad). Guru Nanak suggests the following remedy against evil: "Make Truth the knife. Let it be sharpened on the whetstone of Waheguru's name. Keep it protected in a sheath of virtue."

In daily prayers, the Sikhs invoke Waheguru's grace to keep them away from evil thoughts, words, and deeds. The *SGGS* notes that the most durable shield against negative deeds is to join the society of the right and pious (*sadh sangat*) where one is influenced positively by their words and deeds.

190. Do Sikhs believe in ghosts?

Though Sikhi does not ascribe to the concept of ghosts, as with other concepts like angels and the devil, the *SGGS* makes metaphorical reference to ghosts. These are referenced using words such as *bhoot* or *pret*.[266] Guru Arjan warns, "Without loving devotional worship of the Divine, and by forgetting Waheguru, you turn into a *pret*."[267] While describing the last moment of life, Bhagat Tarlochan says, "At the very

---

[265] SGGS 790: choraa jaaraa ra(n)ddeeaa kuTaneeaa dheebaan || vedheenaa kee dhosatee vedheenaa kaa khaan. sifatee saar na jaananee sadhaa vasai saitaan—ਚੋਰਾ ਜਾਰਾ ਰੰਡੀਆ ਕੁਟਣੀਆ ਦੀਬਾਣੂ || ਵੇਦੀਨਾ ਕੀ ਦੋਸਤੀ ਵੇਦੀਨਾ ਕਾ ਖਾਣੂ || ਸਿਫਤੀ ਸਾਰ ਨ ਜਾਣਨੀ ਸਦਾ ਵਸੈ ਸੈਤਾਨੁ ||

[266] *SGGS* 276: kiee koT bhoot pret sookar miragaach. ਕਈ ਕੋਟਿ ਭੂਤ ਪ੍ਰੇਤ ਸੂਕਰ ਮ੍ਰਿਗਾਚ || Guru Arjan says, "Many millions are the evil-natured spirits (bhoot pret) and animals (pigs and tigers)."

[267] SGGS 706: har bhagat bhaav heena(n) naanak prabh bisarat te pretateh—ਹਰਿ ਭਗਤਿ ਭਾਵ ਹੀਣੰ ਨਾਨਕ ਪ੍ਰਭ ਬਿਸਰਤ ਤੇ ਪ੍ਰੇਤਤਹੁ ||

last moment, one who thinks of mansions, and dies in such thoughts, shall be reincarnated repeatedly as a goblin."[268]

The Sikh faith teaches that although these souls or spirits may affect those who believe in them, those who meditate on Waheguru's name are not affected at all.

191. Do Sikhs believe in yugas (eras of time)?

The *SGGS* contains several references to *yuga* (meaning "era of time"), but these too are used as analogies and in reference to popular cultural concepts. In Hindu philosophy, a *yuga* is an epoch or era within a cycle of the four dharmic ages (Satya Yuga, Treta Yuga, Dvapara Yuga, and Kali Yuga). E. Burgess equates these ages with the Roman Golden, Silver, Bronze, and Iron ages, respectively.[269] According to Indian astronomy and Hindu mythology, the world is created, destroyed, and recreated every 4.32 million years (Mahan Yuga). These cycles repeat like the seasons, waxing and waning within a greater time cycle of the creation and destruction of the universe. Like spring, summer, autumn, and winter, each *yuga* involves stages or gradual changes around which the Earth and the consciousness of humankind revolves. The solar system's motion around a central sun is said to be causing a complete *yuga* cycle from a high Golden Age of enlightenment to a Dark Age and back again. The *Gursabda Ratnakar Mahan Kosh* breaks down the period of each *yuga* as follows: Satya Yuga (1,728,000 years); Treta Yuga (1,296,000 years); Dvapara Yuga (864,000 years), and Kali Yuga (432,000 years). These four *yugas* equal 4.32 million years or a Mahan Yuga. In turn, one thousand Mahan Yugas or 4.32 billion years equal one Kalpa.[270] It

---

[268] SGGS 526: a(n)t kaal jo ma(n)dhar simarai aaisee chi(n)taa meh je marai; pret jon val val aautarai ਅੰਤਿ ਕਾਲਿ ਜੋ ਮੰਦਰ ਸਿਮਰੈ ਐਸੀ ਚਿੰਤਾ ਮਹਿ ਜੇ ਮਰੈ ॥ ਪ੍ਰੇਤ ਜੋਨਿ ਵਲਿ ਵਲਿ ਅਉਤਰੈ॥

[269] Rev. Ebenezer Burgess: Translation of the Suriya—Siddanta—The Textbook of Hindu Astronomy, May 17,1858.

[270] Bhai Kahn Singh Nabha, comp., Gur Shabad Ratankar Mahan Kosh: The Sikh Encyclopedia in Punjabi (1930), 1009.

is commonly understood in Hindu teachings that humanity is currently living in the dark ages (*kal yug*).

Guru Nanak did not accept the divide of time as stated in the Puranas (Hindu scriptures):

> Those who are selfish and egotistical are living in Kal-yug. Thus, kal-yug is within your heart and mind and not defined by any epoch or period. In all these *yugs* there is the same moon, stars, sun, earth, and air. When those who act like tyrants are accepted and approved— recognize that this a sign of [the] Dark Age of Kal-yug.[271]

Guru Nanak did not accept that the *yugs* are a reason for our actions. Instead, the actions of a person influence the *yug* (era of time). For example, in a place where righteous and good people dwell, one can say that they are dwelling in a state of *Sat-Yug* (Golden Age). On the other hand, where people are causing others harm, those around them experience Kal-Yug (Dark Age). Guru Nanak says, "The Dark Age [Kal-Yug behaviour] is the scalpel, the kings are the butchers, and righteousness has taken wings and flown. In this no-moon night of falsehood, the moon of truth is not seen to rise anywhere. In this darkness of *haumey* [ego], this world is crying how to get rid of this."[272]

192. What are the limits to free will?

The Sikh faith teaches that individuals have the ability to act freely and make choices. Nevertheless, we are all subject to the divine will. The divine will is another way of saying that we are all subject to the laws of

---

[271] SGGS 902: soiee cha(n)dh chaReh se tare soiee dhineear tapat rahai. Saa dhratee so paun jhulaare jug jeea khele thaav kaise. Jeevan talab nivaar. hovai paravaanaa kareh dhin(g)aanaa kal lakhan veechaar. ਸੋਈ ਚੰਦ ਚੜਹਿ ਸੇ ਤਾਰੇ ਸੋਈ ਦਿਨੀਅਰੁ ਤਪਤ ਰਹੇ ॥ ਸਾ ਧਰਤੀ ਸੋ ਪਉਣੁ ਝੁਲਾ

[272] SGGS 145: kal kaatee raaje kaasaiee dharam pa(n)kh kar uddariaa. ਕਲਿ ਕਾਤੀ ਰਾਜੇ ਕਾਸਾਈ ਧਰਮੁ ਪੰਖ ਕਰਿ ਉਡਰਿਆ॥

nature; otherwise, must suffer the natural consequences of our actions. Guru Nanak proclaimed, "Always remember the Creator who owns our soul and our very breath of life; Yet, you have the ability to carve your own destiny with your hands."[273] Sikhs believe in the system of *karm* (karma), which is the law of action and reaction. Our past actions shape our present, and our present actions will shape our future. *Karm* acts like a web that binds us to the material world and results in an endless cycle of happiness and sadness and continuous transmigration until we are able to find everlasting peace.

The Sikh faith teaches that it is only through Waheguru's grace that one becomes aware of this cycle and develops the will to be free from it. Through meditation on *Naam* (Divine name), the process of reuniting the soul with Waheguru begins, and the earlier *sanskaars* (cumulative or residual proclivities of past births) of our *karm* are eliminated. An individual who is spiritually awakened accepts Waheguru's will and acts within that will. The distinction between the individual's "free will" and Waheguru's will is erased as they become one.

The Sikh approach to life is proactive as opposed to fatalistic. The Sikh faith teaches that one must not passively allow tragedy or injustice to continue by dismissing it as inevitable or as fate. The individual has to act. The *kirpan*, a Sikh article of faith worn by all initiated Sikhs, is a physical manifestation of the commitment each Sikh makes to serve humanity and uphold the principles of justice. The orientation toward service is the reason Sikhs actively organize and take part in activities such as blood donation drives and relief efforts for places affected by natural and other disasters.

---

[273] SGGS 474: jis ke jeea paraan heh kiau saahib manahu visaareeaai; aapan hathee aapanaa aape hee kaaj savaareeaai—ਜਿਸ ਕੇ ਜੀਅ ਪਰਾਣ ਹਹਿ ਕਿਉ ਸਾਹਿਬੁ ਮਨਹੁ ਵਿਸਾਰੀਐ ॥ ਆਪਣ ਹਥੀ ਆਪਣਾ ਆਪੇ ਹੀ ਕਾਜੁ ਸਵਾਰੀਐ॥

CHAPTER 19

Ethics and Sikhi

Ethics are a doctrine of values or a set of rules that govern individual conduct. Ethics reflect beliefs about how humans should react to and distinguish between right and wrong, just and unjust, and good and evil. "Sikhism is a profoundly ethical religion," writes W. Owen Cole.[274] To explore this statement, this chapter delves into the Sikh code of conduct and other ethical guidelines for Sikhs.

193. What are the most important ethical precepts in the Sikh faith?

Sikhs must live in the material world, fulfill their familial and societal responsibilities, and keep their head above worldly attachments. In short, one must learn to honour everything—but be attached to nothing. Sikhs cannot be so internally focused that they forget their responsibilities to others or become burdens to society. Sikhs are enjoined to be self-reliant. By working hard and earning an honest living, Sikhs fulfill their duty to provide for themselves and their families.

The cornerstones of the practice of the Sikh faith are meditation (*Naam Japna*), earning an honest living (*kirt karni*), and selfless service

---

[274] W. Owen Cole, *Understanding Sikhism (Understanding Faith)* (Edinburgh: Dunedin Academic Press 2004), Kindle edition, location 1485.

(*vand shakna*). Embedded in these are the duty to the self, a duty to one's family, and a duty to society. Duty to the self means that a Sikh must always strive to achieve self-realization. This is done through meditation and self-reflection. Duty to one's family means fulfilling one's familial responsibilities, including caring for one's elders and raising children with Sikhi values.

Duty to society is reflected in the principle of *vand shakna* (sharing one's wealth with others). It embodies the concept of selfless service. Whether it is donating one's time, expertise, or money, Sikhs are expected to spend a considerable portion of their lives dedicated to the betterment of the lives of others. By living one's life in accordance with these three ethical principles, a Sikh can achieve their life's purpose: conscious union with the Creator. This is the internal state of an enlightened individual.

194. What are the social ethics of Sikhs?

Sikh social ethics are guided by the singular phrase in the *Sri Guru Granth Sahib*: "Recognize ye all human race as One." As noted above, Sikhs have an ethical duty to work toward the betterment of all humanity. They must do so without discrimination and regard to a person's race, religion, gender, sexual orientation, caste, or economic or social status. Sikhi stresses the importance of positive moral actions. Guru Gobind Singh reflects: "Waheguru, grant me the courage and strength that I may never be deterred from performing positive and moral actions."[275]

In summary, the fundamental social ethics of the Sikhs are social equality, universal fellowship, seeking the good of all (altruism), and social service. All these principles are interrelated, and taken together, they form the basis of Sikh ethics in terms of social relations. I have called them fundamental, but the last two, namely altruism and social service,

---

[275] Dasam Bani 240: dheh sivaa bar moh ihai subh karaman te kabahoo(n) na Taro. ਦੇਹ ਸਿਵਾ ਬਰੁ ਮੋਹਿ ਇਹੈ ਸੁਭ ਕਰਮਨ ਤੇ ਕਬਹੂੰ ਨ ਟਰੋਂ ॥

are in fact practical measures to realize social equality and universal brotherhood and sisterhood.[276]

195. Does guilt serve any purpose?

As humans, we are imperfect by nature, and we will inevitably make mistakes. Disappointment, regret, and self-blame are all part of what we call guilt. Guilt arises from regret over past conduct. A person who has committed an act that violated their own personal ethics may have a hard time letting go and moving forward. Although painful, guilt reflects the workings of one's conscience and the presence of moral values. It provides an opportunity to reflect on the past, particularly our errors, and find ways to rectify and avoid them in the future.

Sikhi does not advocate dwelling on negative human emotions such as guilt, remorse, or self-blame because Sikhs are enjoined to focus on how we live in the present rather than what we did in the past. For a Sikh, guilt serves no purpose except as a motivator for change. If one truly regrets a past action, one's ethical duty is to fix one's mistake, learn from it, and not repeat it. Thus, where guilt inspires action and change for the better, it can be a good thing. But where guilt lingers for a prolonged period, and results in sadness, anguish, stress, and depression, action must be taken to address guilt and prevent it from becoming chronic.

For Sikhs, enduring happiness is only possible by traveling on the spiritual path and experiencing the ecstasy of oneness through prayer and meditation. Sikhi teaches that every moment offers an opportunity for renewal and change. Positive change should never be delayed because the greatest regret for most of us is looking back on our lives at the end and realizing we should have done things very differently. The guilt that arises from an unfulfilled life is the most tragic because, at that point, we cannot do anything about our past actions. The emphasis of the

---

[276]   Avtar Singh, Ethics of the Sikhs, reprint ed. (Patiala, India: Publication Bureau, Punjabi University, 2009; original work published 1970).

Sikh faith is on performing actions that result in enduring happiness and contentment.

196. What is ego?

The *Sri Guru Granth Sahib* does not discuss how to resolve guilt, remorse, or other personal problems because the gurus were more concerned with getting to the root of all discontent, the ego. The ego causes us to view the world in fragments. There is me, and then there is everyone else—the other. This fragmentation of the world is what we refer to as *duality*. Duality arises from viewing oneself as distinct from the rest of creation.

When we are in the grip of the ego, we perceive upsetting events from the frame of reference of "victim" and "oppressor." If we feel we have been wronged by another, then we see ourselves as their victim. The victim-oppressor mentality also underlies feelings of guilt and remorse. When we self-blame, we continue with the delusion of duality—only this time, we are the oppressor. Rather than telling us how to overcome feelings of guilt and remorse, the gurus teach us how to overcome ego. When ego is overcome, then duality ends, and one no longer views the world in fragments, but rather as a perfect whole in which we are able to perceive the interconnectedness of all life. This leads to a state of true contentment and bliss, which is called *anand*.

197. Is there difference between the ego and the mind?

Gurbani distinguishes between the ego and the mind. The ego operates within the mind, but it is not the mind. The mind is the space where all thinking happens, including egotistical thinking. Gurbani teaches that in addition to controlling one's ego, we must learn to control other negative thought processes that inhibit spiritual progress. The five main ones identified by the Gurus are: *kaam* (lust), *krodh* (anger), *lobh* (greed), *moh* (attachment), and *hunkar* (ego or pride). Other negative emotions, such as fear, jealousy, or hatred, can also become barriers to spiritual growth. An out-of-control mind might be one that is in the grip of ego or any one of the other negative thought processes.

Guru Amar Das explains the importance of controlling the mind, in the following sabad:[277]

> Through deep deliberation one is able to see that without subduing the mind, no person attains success.
> The devotees grow weary roaming to holy places, but the mind is still not subdued.
> The Gurmukh (disciple) remains absorbed in the Truth (One Source), and thus his/her mind is subdued while they are alive.
> Nanak, in this way the filth (negative thoughts) that effects the mind is removed, and the mind's ego is burned away with the Sabad.

This sabad encapsulates a number of Sikh teachings: to achieve success in anything, one must learn to subdue (control) the mind; attending at pilgrimage sites does not further this goal and is a useless spiritual exercise; a subdued mind is one which is absorbed in (connected to) the truth; this can only be achieved while one is alive; and the negative thought processes that affect the mind, including ego, can be controlled through meditation.

---

[277] *SGGS* 650, "vin man marey koey na sijaee vekho ko liv laey. bhekhadhaaree teerathee bhav thake naa eh man maariaa jai. gurmukh eh man jeevat marai sach rahai liv lai. naanak is man kee mal iau utarai haumai sabadh jalai.
"ਵਿਣੁ ਮਨੁ ਮਾਰੇ ਕੋਇ ਨ ਸਿਝਈ ਵੇਖਹੁ ਕੋ ਲਿਵ ਲਾਇ ॥ ਭੇਖਧਾਰੀ ਤੀਰਥੀ ਭਵਿ ਥਕੇ ਨਾ ਏਹੁ ਮਨੁ ਮਾਰਿਆ ਜਾਇ ॥ ਗੁਰਮੁਖਿ ਏਹੁ ਮਨੁ ਜੀਵਤੁ ਮਰੈ ਸਚਿ ਰਹੈ ਲਿਵ ਲਾਇ ॥ ਨਾਨਕ ਇਸੁ ਮਨ ਕੀ ਮਲੁ ਇਉ ਉਤਰੈ ਹਉਮੈ ਸਬਰਦ ਜਲਾਇ ॥

198. What is kindness?

Kindness transcends all boundaries and allows us to see and feel beyond just ourselves. It compels us to treat others in the way we would want to be treated and results in a net increase in our collective happiness. In the Sikh faith, compassion and kindness are considered the foundations of faith. We cannot be genuinely spiritual beings if we are not kind to all those around us. As we become closer to Waheguru, we begin to see the goodness within every person and every living thing. This awakens within us the desire to stand with and assist all those in need.

Kindness has no limit, and there is never enough of it. One simply needs to look around and see the poverty, inequality, and suffering that is in close proximity. Sikhi teaches us to ask ourselves whether we are "kind enough." What more can we do to improve the lives of others?

199. What is the value of compassion?

The Sikh word for compassion is *daiya*. It is one of the five virtues referred to earlier (see question 5). *Daiya* is considered the fundamental quality a person must possess, one of the first building blocks of spirituality: "Of all righteous acts and pilgrimage to all the sacred places, the most acceptable is compassion for others."[278] Compassion unites us. It compels us to see ourselves in others and take the first step beyond the bounds of the ego. It allows us to see the light of the Creator in all beings.

A story about Guru Nanak evokes this idea of compassion. It is said that when the Guru turned eighteen, his father sent him away on a business trip with a sum of money and told him to make a "good bargain." On the way, Guru Nanak met some hungry and destitute people and decided to use the money his father had given him to purchase food and clothing for them. When he returned home, Mehta Kalu asked what kind of business he had done and how much profit he

---

[278] *SGGS* 136: aThasaTh teerath sagal pu(n)n jeea dhiaa paravaan - ਅਠਸਠਿ ਤੀਰਥ ਸਗਲ ਪੁੰਨ ਜੀਅ ਦਇਆ ਪਰਵਾਣੁ ॥

had earned. On learning how Guru Nanak had spent the money, Mehta Kalu became very angry. Guru Nanak defended his actions, saying that he had not only made a good bargain—but a "true bargain" since there could be no better investment in life than assisting those in need. In that same spirit, Sikhs operate a free kitchen or *langar* at all Sikh gurdwaras (places of worship), in which all people are welcome to enjoy a meal free of cost. *Langars* are also set up and funded by the Sikh community in places ravaged by natural disasters, wherever they occur in the world.

200. Why is it important to forgive?

Forgiveness is a divine quality that spiritual individuals aspire to adopt, born from the same place as faith and compassion. Faith in Waheguru means believing that every experience, no matter how negative, can help propel us forward on our spiritual journeys. Compassion means understanding that the transgressor is a fallible human, not unlike oneself.

Forgiveness helps the person who has been wronged and the person being forgiven. Forgiveness has, at its root, the concept of accepting the will of the Divine. Without compassion and forgiveness, one cannot advance spiritually. Without compassion, one holds on to the pain of an injury and continually relives it. The anger associated with the wrong continues to eat away, both physically and mentally, and can infect one's life and relationships. Although the person who inflicted the injury may have initiated the pain, the choice to end it lies within oneself. Forgiveness is an act of strength and empowerment that allows the pain to stop—so healing can begin. We must forgive because the alternative is to live in anger and resentment, which can be very destructive to oneself and those around us.

Accepting and overcoming what has happened and choosing to move forward without dwelling in hatred or vengeance is what forgiveness is all about. Many faiths, including Sikhi, refer to the Creator as the "forgiver." While recognizing the importance of forgiveness as the first step, imbibing the virtue of forgiveness can be more difficult. The Sikh faith teaches that we must accept Waheguru's will and work within it. Forgiveness flows from acceptance. We must play with the cards that life has dealt us and make the best of them.

The Gurus practiced humility, kindness, and forgiveness. Here is one noteworthy example. When Guru Amar Das was anointed the third Guru, the sons of Guru Angad (the second Guru), were envious. Dasu and Datu believed that one of them should have been made Guru. Legend has it that one day Datu kicked Guru Amar Das. However, in utter humility, the Guru righted himself and caressed Datu's foot, saying, "I am old, and my bones have grown very hard. I fear they have hurt your tender foot."[279]

There are limits to forgiveness in Sikhi. Forgiveness does not mean that we justify or enable wrongdoing. It does not mean forgetting an injury or harm has been perpetrated—or pretending it did not take place. The Sikh faith teaches that where a wrong has occurred, steps must be taken to ensure that it is not repeated, either to oneself or to others.

---

[279] Story about Guru Amar Das sourced from Kalgidhar Trust, https://barusahib.org.

CHAPTER 20

Making Hard Decisions— Moral Landscape

Every day, we are faced with challenging moral decisions that govern our behaviours and how we conduct our daily activities. Ethics is the philosophy of morality. Morals are a set of principles people live by to make sure they are making the right decisions. Morals guide one's judgment between doing what is right and wrong and what is and is not acceptable for them to do. They are learned from the time people are born, first from their parents and then from external forces and the society they keep. They are shaped by personal beliefs, ethics, social norms, cultural practices, and religious influences.

The Sikh moral scheme involves the cultivation of virtues such as honesty, integrity, courage, humility, love, compassion, kindness, and forgiveness. This chapter explores the Sikh community's moral compass to guide difficult ethical and moral decisions.

201. What is morality?

Making a morally sound decision is choosing wisely between what is right and wrong. A morally correct decision or action is that which does not cause harm to oneself or to others. A morally wrong decision is that which causes harm to oneself or to others. The Sikh faith identifies five

vices (lust, anger, greed, worldly attachment, and ego) as individual
failings. The Gurus refer to these vices as the five "thieves" that take
away our ability to be spiritually awakened individuals. Harm to the self
is falling into the trap of these five vices. Harm to others is acting based
on these vices. To overcome these barriers to spiritual development, Sikhs
are advised to live a life rooted in meditation, hard work, and selfless
service.

202. What is true righteousness?

Merriam-Webster's Dictionary defines righteousness as the quality of
being morally right and justifiable. Sikhs distinguish between *moral
righteousness* and *true righteousness.* The latter is defined as the state of
mind when one's consciousness is wholly merged the Truth and one's
actions align with living in accordance with the divine will. It is the
ultimate state for a Sikh. To achieve this state of true righteousness or
divine consciousness, one needs devotion, patience, and a diligent work
ethic.

In *Jap Ji Sahib,* Guru Nanak uses the striking metaphor of a
goldsmith to explain how to develop this state of mind:

> In the smithy of self-control with the patience of a
> goldsmith, make intellect the anvil, knowledge the
> hammer, dedication the bellows, and hard work the
> heat of the fire. In the crucible of love, mould Divine
> Consciousness, which is the true mint to construct
> honest thoughts. Blessed are those whose actions are
> guided by Divine Consciousness. O Nanak, this is the
> way the Merciful One grants bliss.[280]

---

[280] *SGGS* 8: jat paahaaraa dheeraj suniaar—ਜਤੁ ਪਾਹਾਰਾ ਧੀਰਜੁ ਸੁਨਿਆਰੁ॥

Duncan Greenlees wrote an analysis of this text:

> Guru Nanak, in a few strong phrases, has illuminated
> the distant paths ahead of us all, but he closes his great
> sabad by bringing us right back to the practical side of
> life, which is not an empty dream of philosophy but a
> hard fight for right. He provides us with a roadmap of
> the discipline needed before the aspirant can expect to
> tread the path of true righteousness to the very end.[281]

Greenlees also lists qualifications that make up that "austere discipline"
and that must first be acquired:[282]

- the self-control of body, mind, and desires
- perseverance, an effort, for the fickle and fainthearted cannot
  travel far
- purity, which must lie behind all correct thinking and so
  illuminate the mind with a sight of the truth
- the essential truths of all religions
- fearlessness, which is born only from reverence for and faith
  in God
- the austere fire of "renunciation and spirituality"
- The immortalizing love of God
- the Creator's name, which is the essence of the Guru's teaching

In Guru Nanak's quote about the goldsmith, the key words are "actions"
and "grace." The emphasis is on the right actions for the upward climb—
not works alone, not grace alone, but grace enabling works. All the forces
of nature allow a person of grace who strives to live according to God's
Word. Bhagat Kabir says, "With your hands and feet, do all your work,

---

[281]   Duncan Greenlees, *The Gospel of the Guru-Granth Sahib*, World Religion
Series (London: Theosophical Publishing House, 1975), 264.
[282]   Ibid.

but let your consciousness remain with the immaculate Creator."[283] Sincere efforts and noble deeds without a clear spiritual goal in mind achieve precious little. What is required is a constant meditation on Waheguru's name. That is the state of "true righteousness" that a Sikh strives for.

203. How do Sikhs maintain their practice when it conflicts with wider social norms?

Whether one is a practicing Buddhist, an Orthodox Jew, or an adherent to the Church of Jesus Christ of Latter-day Saints, living a spiritually informed existence will routinely bring one into conflict with the wider society. This is also the case with an amritdhari Sikh. From how they dress (unshorn hair and dastaar), to what they eat (generally vegetarian food), to what they avoid (alcohol and other intoxicants), to where they pray (gurdwara), to how they marry (*Anand Karaj* ceremony), amritdhari Sikhs continuously challenge surrounding social norms by their very existence.

Sikhs take their inspiration from their Gurus. Challenging the status quo is a value exemplified by the Gurus; they looked and spoke differently, and they also acted differently. Many of them were jailed, and some were executed,[284] for challenging existing social and political structures that oppressed women and other marginalized groups. The Gurus did not waver, and they refused to compromise their beliefs. They emphasized social activism with spiritual commitment. Practicing Sikhs

---

[283] *SGGS* 1376: haath paau kar ka`am sabh cheet nira(n)jan naal—ਹਾਥ ਪਾਉ ਕਰਿ ਕਾਮੁ ਸਭੁ ਚੀਤੁ ਨਿਰੰਜਨ ਨਾਲਿ॥

[284] Guru Nanak was imprisoned when the Mughal ruler, Babur, invaded India. Guru Hargobind was imprisoned because the Mughal emperor could not tolerate growing Sikh influence and power. Guru Arjan and Guru Tegh Bahadur were executed for refusing to renounce their beliefs. Guru Gobind Singh was fatally stabbed by Bahadarshah's assassin. Guru Gobind Singh's two youngest sons (aged seven and nine) were bricked alive.

are enjoined to be saint-soldiers (*sant-sapahi*)—people of firm belief and courage—whose day-to-day lives are guided by compassion and love.

The Gurus recognized that following a spiritually informed existence, including the Sikhi path, is not an easy road to travel. Guru Angad describes this is *Anand Sahib (Song of Joy)*:[285]

> Distinct is the way of the bhagats (spiritual devotees).
> Distinct is the way of life of the bhagats, who tread a most difficult path.
> They renounce avarice, greed, pride, and material attachments, and do not boast.
> Traveling on this path is like walking on a road that is sharper than a two-edged sword, and finer than a hair.
> But they, who shed their ego by Guru's grace, lose all desire for material wealth, and their aspiration merges with the Divine.
> Says Nanak, the path of the bhagats has always been distinct since the beginning of time.

The pressure to conform to societal or peer pressure can be overwhelming. For some, it becomes too much to handle, and they prefer to let go of their distinct outward appearance in order to fit in. This means that some Sikhs may cut their hair, remove their turbans, or start drinking alcohol. But many others hold tight to their practices and beliefs and refuse to conform to society's expectations.

The common thread among those Sikhs who choose to maintain their Sikhi practices and distinct identity in the face of overwhelming opposition is their deeply held belief in the teachings of the Sikh Gurus and their value of self-respect over social acceptance. They find peace when their outward identity reflects their inwardly held beliefs. Rather than being oppressive or restrictive, they see Sikhi practices as freeing

---

[285] *SGGS* 917: Bhagataa kee chaal niraalee; challaa niraalee bhagataeh keree bikham maarag chalanaa; lab lobh aha(n)kaar taj tirasanaa bahut naahee bolanaa...
ਭਗਤਾ ਕੀ ਚਾਲ ਨਿਰਾਲੀ ॥ ਚਾਲਾ ਨਿਰਾਲੀ ਭਗਤਾਹ ਕੇਰੀ ਬਿਖਮ ਮਾਰਗਿ ਚਲਣਾ ॥ ਲਬੁ ਲੋ ਭੁ ਅਹੰਕਾਰੁ ਤਜਿ ਤ੍ਰਿਸਨਾ ਬਹੁਤੁ ਨਾਹੀ ਬੋਲਣਾ॥

them from social bondage. A Sikh who does not feel the need to change their appearance or pick up social practices that are antithetical to Sikhi teachings in order to be liked or fit in is someone who values sincerity over social conformity. Their need to be truthful to who they are is greater than the need to be liked by others.

204. How do Sikhs handle violence and injustice?

The saint-soldier concept also guides Sikhs to come to the aid of others. Embedded in the enjoinder to "recognize all humans as one"[286] is the call to action if someone is being oppressed or harmed. The Sikh response to personal injury or insult is to forgive and take the moral high ground. This helps both parties heal and move ahead in life. Sikhs are, however, duty bound to intervene when violence or injustice is directed at others, particularly the weak, feeble, or disadvantaged. Guru Gobind Singh wrote, "When all other means of righting injustice have been tried and failed, it is legitimate as a last resort to turn to the sword."[287] The preamble to the 1948 United Nations Universal Declaration of Human Rights reads, "Whereas it is essential if a man is not to have recourse, as a last resort, to rebellion against tyranny and oppression, that human rights should be protected by the rule of law." Where human rights are being infringed upon or innocent people are being oppressed, the Sikh teachings are remarkably like the words contained in the preamble.

This enjoinder to stand up against oppression, even if that requires the raising of a sword, explains the disproportionately high participation of Sikhs during the two world wars. However, as saint-soldiers, Sikhs must temper their actions so that they are acting out of love and compassion

---

[286] Dasam Granth 51: maanas kee jaat sabai ekai pahichaanabo. ਮਾਨਸ ਕੀ ਜਾਤਿ ਸਬੈ ਏਕੈ ਪਹਿਚਾਨਬੋ॥

[287] Dasam Bani, verse 22: choon kaar az hameh heelte dar guzashat. halaal asat buradan ba shamsheer dasat—ਚੁ ਕਾਰ ਅਜ ਹਮਹ ਹੀਲਤੇ ਦਰ ਗੁਜ਼ਸਤ ॥ ਹਲਾਲ ਅਸਤੁ ਬੁਰਦਨ ਬ ਸ਼ਮਸ਼ੇਰ ਦਸਤ ॥

Jean Holm and John Bowker, eds., *Making Moral Decisions*, Themes in Religious Studies (London: Frances Pinter Publishers, 1994), 165.

rather than anger and hatred. The raising of the sword must be used only as a last resort to combat injustice and establish lasting peace and harmony. It is only to be done when other more peaceful methods, such as the raising of the pen or the voice, have failed.

205. Are blood or organ donations permissible in Sikhi?

Blood or organ donations are not covered in the Sikh scripture or the *Sikh Rehat Maryada* (code of conduct). However, these are considered acceptable and respectable means of serving others. Donating blood is an outstanding example of how many Sikhs perform practical and spiritual service. Sharing with others (*vand shakna*) is considered an important value in Sikhi. Assisting those less fortunate includes offering all resources or services possible—monetary, emotional, intellectual, spiritual, and practical. There is nothing more personal than helping alleviate another person's pain and suffering by donating one's blood or organs. This is also a form of honouring those whose blood was shed to protect our freedom and dignity.

Many gurdwaras and Sikh organizations across the world organize annual blood donation drives. In Canada, the World Sikh Organization led a blood donation initiative in 1985 to commemorate the innocent lives lost in the June 1984 Indian Army attack on Darbar Sahib (the Golden Temple) and the Sikh genocide during the first week of November 1984. The Sikh Nation group of British Columbia has made this an annual international event among Sikhs in November.

206. Does Sikhi prohibit stem cell research?

The Sikh faith does not preclude the use of human intelligence or technology to improve living conditions, preserve life, or improve someone's quality of life. Sikhi respects the sanctity of life and is against any avoidable loss of life. Stem cell research has its pros and cons, and there are divergent views on it among the world's population, including Sikhs. While stem cell research can potentially offer cures and therapies for previously incurable diseases, some Sikhs are concerned about the ethical implications of the destruction of the embryo in the process of harvesting stem cells.[288]

Most Sikhs also feel that scientific and medical experience should be valued, and any means adopted to improve or preserve it should be encouraged and is ethically acceptable if it does not harm any other form of life. In 2008, a Sikh woman received a lifesaving bone marrow transplant (adult stem cells) from a German woman. I am told the recipient is still alive and ever in debt to the technology and the donor who saved her life.[289] The operation created a lifelong bond between two people.

207. Are birth control or abortions permissible for Sikhs?

The Sikh faith has no injunctions against the use of contraceptives. Sikhi teaches respect for life and social responsibility. A common-sense approach to family planning is widely accepted by Sikhs. Birth control is considered a personal decision for a couple, and they can choose their preferred methods. Some families may prefer natural family planning to avoid any side effects of pills or medical devices.

Sikhi does not take any formal position on abortion. Though female infanticide is specifically prohibited in the Sikh code of ethics (*Rehat Maryada*), the *Rehat Maryada* is silent on abortion. While one can argue that by extension, gender-selective abortion is against Sikhi, it would be a stretch to argue that abortion in general is prohibited.

The Sikh faith teaches that life begins at conception. The *SGGS* says, "The Creator created the body from sperm, and protected it in the

---

[288] Jhutti-Johal, Jagbir. *Sikhism Today (Religion Today)*, Bloomsbury Publishing. Kindle edition, location 343.

[289] "Sikh Woman Gets Bone Marrow," Sikhnet.com (2007).

fire pit of the mother's womb for ten months."[290] (The reference to ten months versus forty weeks—280 days is the average length of human gestation—is based upon the Indian lunar calendar, which has 354 days, compared to the Gregorian solar calendar of 365 days.) Sikhi teaches that each one of us is given the freedom to decide for ourselves, and we are accountable for our actions, whether noble or immoral. "We are all judged by our deeds and actions," says Guru Nanak.[291]

There are divergent views among the Sikh community regarding abortion. Some Sikhs believe that abortion or deliberate miscarriage is morally wrong—even if there are fetal abnormalities. For them, the only exception might be if the mother's health is in danger or the fetus will not survive beyond birth. On the other hand, many (and likely the majority) of Sikhs believe that a woman has the right to choose and determine if she wants to carry a pregnancy to full term.

208. Can Sikhs use artificial insemination or in vitro fertilization (IVF)?

Sikhi also does not take any position on artificial insemination (IVF). Infertility is a fact of life. The Mayo Clinic estimates that, in the United States, 10 to 15 percent of couples are infertile. In Canada, the percentage of infertile couples is roughly 16 percent, a number that has doubled since the 1980s.[292] The World Health Organization lists similar statistics around the world. Infertility can cause a lot of suffering and mental agony for families.

In many communities, including Panjabi Sikhs, women may suffer from stigmatization, discrimination, and ostracism due to infertility.

---

[290] *SGGS* 481: bi(n)dh te jin pind keeaa agan kund rahaiaa. Dhas maas maataa udhar raakhiaa bahur laagee maiaa—ਬਿੰਦੁ ਤੇ ਜਿਨਿ ਪਿੰਡੁ ਕੀਆ ਅਗਨਿ ਕੁੰਡ ਰਹਾਇਆ॥ ਦਸ ਮਾਸ ਉਦਰਿ ਰਾਖਿਆ ਬਹੁਰਿ ਲਾਗੀ ਮਾਇਆ॥

[291] *SGGS* 7: karmee karmee hoi veechaar— ਕਰਮੀ ਕਰਮੀ ਹੋਇ ਵਿਚਾਰੁ॥

[292] Mayo Clinic, "Infertility," https://www.mayoclinic.org/diseases-conditions/infertility/symptoms-causes/syc-20354317; Government of Canada, "Fertility," https://www.canada.ca/en/public-health/services/fertility/fertility.html.

This stigmatization is not supported by Sikh teachings. Gurbani teaches us to accept the divine will. But because having children is highly valued in Panjabi Sikh society, the social pressure on couples to produce offspring may be deeply felt. It is thus not uncommon for Sikh families to turn to artificial insemination or in vitro fertilization (IVF):

- *Artificial insemination:* There are views both for and against the use of artificial insemination within the Sikh community. Not surprisingly, both sides quote Sikh values and ethics to support their views. Proponents say that Sikhi endorses having a family. Opponents argue that infertility is the will of Waheguru, and the couple should accept this divine will. They argue that adopting a child in need of a parent is preferable to producing a child in the face of infertility.
- *In vitro fertilization (IVF):* Sikhs consider the relationship between a husband and wife sacred. For some, artificial insemination of a woman with the sperm of a man who is not her husband raises ethical and moral questions. Jagbir Jhutti-Johal, a lecturer in Sikh Studies at the University of Birmingham, writes, "The insemination of a wife with the sperm of someone other than her husband could be viewed as only one step removed from adultery, and consequently an adultery-like stigma is attached to the process."[293] However, I am not aware of any Sikhs who have expressed such a concern. In my view, it would be a stretch to argue that using another man's sperm to artificially inseminate a woman's egg in a clinical setting would be considered adultery by any rational Sikhs.

209. Is genetic engineering appropriate?

The *Oxford Languages Dictionary* defines *genetic engineering* as the deliberate modification of the characteristics of an organism by

---

[293] Jagbir Jhutti-Johal, *Sikhism Today* (London: Bloomsbury Academic, 2011).

manipulating its genetic material. Technologically changing the genetic makeup of cells and moving them across species boundaries to produce new organisms is generally referred to as genetic engineering.

While there is no clear consensus among Sikhs on the subject, the Sikh faith firmly stresses the sanctity of life and the acceptance of Waheguru's will. As W. Owen Cole wrote in 2004,

> Sikhs have great respect for the natural form and believe it should not be tampered with. If a couple knows that there is a risk of passing on a genetic disorder, they should use contraceptive means to avoid it. Some consultants, however, think that this scientific [genetic engineering] knowledge is God-given and should be used to benefit humanity.[294]

While there is likely no moral objection in Sikhi to genetic research and advancement of scientific knowledge that benefits humanity, most Sikhs would likely agree that such practices must be ethically based and follow strict scientific rigor.

210. Is there a practice of shunning or excommunication among Sikhs?

A distinction needs to be drawn here between the teachings of the Sikh Gurus as contained in the *SGGS* and the code of conduct (*Rehat Maryada*) developed by Sikhs in the twentieth century to regulate the affairs of the Sikh community. The sacred Sikh writings do not address temporal affairs such as shunning or excommunication. The *Sikh Rehat Maryada* (code of ethics) stipulates that a violation of the code of ethics can result in disciplinary action. In the case of extremely grave violations,

---

[294] W. Owen Cole, *Understanding Sikhism (Understanding Faith)* (Edinburgh: Dunedin Academic Press, 2004). Kindle edition, location 1780.

shunning or excommunication from the community can also occur. The Sikh practice of shunning or excommunication is somewhat complicated:

- *Shunning*: Shunning refers to the practice of actively avoiding interacting with someone who is considered to have committed a grave social transgression. Depending on its cultural antecedents, the word may or may not have respectful tones. There are specific instances in which the Sikh code of conduct condones public shunning. For example, Sikhs are enjoined from having contact with those who commit infanticide and so-called honour killings.[295] The *Rehat Maryada* also contains an enjoinder for Sikhs to avoid interacting with people known as *Ram Raeeay*. They are the followers of Ram Rai. Ram Rai was the son of Guru Har Rai. Sikh historical accounts indicate that Ram Rai committed a grave transgression by changing a word of a sabad in order to appease Aurangzeb, the Mughal emperor.[296] The Gurus were of the firm view that the truth, which emanates from the divine light, should never be concealed, and the teachings of the Gurus should never be changed in deference to authority. Ram Rai acted in contravention to this teaching and was shunned by his own father, who ordered Ram Rai never to see him again and instructed Sikhs not to maintain any social or religious relationship with Ram Rai. The followers of Ram Rai disagreed with the Guru, and thus began the Sikh community's ongoing practice to refuse to have dealings with them.
- Excommunication: Excommunication implies a severe religious censure for an ethical transgression. It is akin to religious castigation. It is rare, but it does happen in the Sikh community. Sikhs have developed a practice to ensure due process is followed when excommunication is being considered. This includes giving the alleged transgressor a show-cause notice and providing them

---

[295] *Sikh Rehat Maryada*, chapter 10, section 16(l).
[296] *SGGS* 466: miTee musalamaan kee peRai piee kumi(h)aar. ਮਿਟੀ ਮੁਸਲਮਾਨ ਕੀ ਪੇੜੈ ਪਈ ਕੁਮ੍ਿਆਰ॥

with an opportunity to explain their transgressive behaviour. Usually, the heads of five *takhats* (seats of power) comprise the judicial bench which hears such cases.[297] If the transgressor fails to appear before the religious court or fails to resile from their behaviour, they may be excommunicated. There are many examples of Sikhs being served show-cause notices, including Emperor Maharaja Ranjit Singh and Surjit Singh Barnala, the chief minister (premier) of Punjab in 1987. Both of them were pardoned after admitting their shortcomings and penitence. Recently, a former Sikh cabinet minister was excommunicated by the Akal Takhat in 2017 when a rape charge was filed against him.[298] In another instance, it was used against a Sikh scholar who wrote a textbook that was considered to contain offensive comments about the authenticity of the *Guru Granth Sahib*.[299] He appeared before the Akal Takhat panel, admitted his error and penitence, and agreed to correct his writing.

The practice of excommunication is not without controversy. Some Sikhs believe it has been used for political purposes, to silence those who challenge the Sikh leadership, or to undermine academic freedom.

---

[297] Minor transgressions are handled at the local gurdwara level following a similar process of assembling a committee of five initiated Sikhs to render a decision.

[298] The Indian Express, October 6, 2017.

[299] globalsikhstudies.net, Amritsar, Jun. 27, 1994: "Pashaura Singh was declared guilty of five charges of blasphemy. Pashaura Singh had made a number of baseless observations in his Ph.D. thesis, 'The Text and Meaning of the Adi Granth, submitted to the University of Toronto in 1991... The unanimous verdict followed a detailed hearing of Pashaura Singh's case in an eight-hour non-stop session of the five high priests presided over by Prof. Manjit Singh at the Akal Takht Sahib on the 25th June 1994." Pashaura Singh admitted his shortcomings and penitence.

211. Is there a Sikh view on capital punishment?

There is no specific writing on capital punishment in the *SGGS*, and no evidence that the Gurus advocated capital punishment against criminals. However, Sikh philosophy is generally considered to be against capital punishment. The basic principles of the right to life, equality, and dignity are emphasized throughout Gurbani, which teaches Sikhs to view life as a sacred gift from the Creator. Waheguru is described as the "Generous Giver of Life,"[300] and all creation is said to emanate by the "divine command."[301] The Gurus taught forgiveness and the ability of each human being to change (rehabilitation). During Maharaja Ranjit Singh's rule, none of his subjects were executed, irrespective of how heinous the crime. Most Sikhs believe that while we have the right to make laws to incarcerate people for offenses against society, we do not have the moral right to take the life of another individual. Nevertheless, some Sikhs are in support of capital punishment.

212. Is there a Sikh view on honour killing?

The term "honour killing" does not exist in the Panjabi language. It is a term coined by Western sociologists to explain the murder of a person who has been deemed to have dishonoured the family unit or society at large. The Sikh faith does not support honour killings or any act of violence related to such thinking.

Honour-based violence is a phenomenon that continues in many parts of the world, particularly in regions where there is a strong traditional patriarchy. The concept is usually invoked in relation to perceived sexual transgressions by a female or against a female. Such violence is often aimed at women, but it can also be aimed at men who are deemed to have dishonoured a woman. The desire to protect or

---

[300] SGGS 882: kirapaa karahu dheen ke dhaate meraa gun avagan na beechaarahu koiee—ਕਿਰਪਾ ਕਰਹੁ ਦੀਨ ਕੇ ਦਾਤੇ ਮੇਰਾ ਗੁਣੁ ਅਵਗੁਣੁ ਨ ਬੀਚਾਰਹੁ ਕੋਈ॥

[301] SGGS 1: hukamee hovan aakaar hukam na kahiaa jaiee—ਹੁਕਮੀ ਹੋਵਨਿ ਆਕਾਰ ਹੁਕਮੁ ਨ ਕਹਿਆ ਜਾਇ॥

retain a person's honour is used to legitimize recourse to violence so that the person's standing can be restored. Men use honour systems and the imminent threat of violence as a way of maintaining social order. Cases where the murder of a male occurs alongside the woman occur when the victims are seen to be in an immoral sexual relationship that disrupts social norms. Despite all laws to protect the life and liberty of everyone, honour killings continue to take place, primarily in India, Pakistan, and Middle Eastern countries.

Many studies have been written on this subject. Navratan Singh Fateh's thesis "Honour Killing" for the master of laws degree from the University of Toronto (2012) is relevant to our discussion:

> The perpetrator in these crimes has no economic motivation and is purely fueled by the abstract desire to bring back the honour to the family by eliminating the family member who brought dishonour. The perceived dishonour is normally a result of the loss of control felt by the male members of the family on the sexual behaviour of a female member of the family.[302]

The Sikh faith prohibits honour killings. The Sikh Rehatnamas, said to have been written more than three hundred years ago during Guru Gobind Singh's time, forbade Sikhs from associating with anyone who killed their daughter (*kurimar*).[303] The *Sikh Rehat Maryada* states: "A Sikh should not maintain any relationship with the killer of a daughter."[304] Some cases of so-called honour killings have also surfaced in North America, including in the Sikh community. Though most Sikhs consider any type of gender-based violence to be morally reprehensible, the fact that it still continues means that much more needs to be done to address it. It is the moral and ethical duty of every Sikh to take a stance against

---

[302] Navratan Singh Fateh, "Honour Killing" (master of laws thesis, University of Toronto, 2012).

[303] Grewal J. S. *The Singh Way of Life: The Rahitnamas in History, Literature, and Identity* (New Delhi: Oxford University Press), 206–26.

[304] *Sikh Rehat Maryada*, chapter 10, article 16(l).

injustice. What could be more unjust than harming a young woman or man simply because of who they choose to love?

213. Are suicide or euthanasia acceptable?

There is no specific commentary on suicide or euthanasia in Gurbani or *Rehat Maryada*. However, human life is considered a precious gift from the Creator. Life provides an opportunity for self-realization and merging with the divine light. Suicide and euthanasia, or the active termination of one's own or another person's life, are not considered acceptable by many in the Sikh faith. Gurbani teaches Sikhs perseverance and acceptance of divine will. Guru Arjan says, "Pleasure and pain come by Your Will, O Beloved; they do not come from any other."[305]

When one is faced with chronic disease and unbearable pain, the Sikh approach is to get appropriate medical attention. This includes the use of prescription pain medication, mood stabilizers, appropriate psychological counseling, or therapy. To assist in maintaining one's mental health and to alleviate the experience of pain, Sikhs emphasize meditation on Waheguru and drawing on the *sangat* (congregation) for support. Family and friends should make every effort to assist the individual and guide them to appropriate mental health support services. It is important that they feel valued and loved and are given the tools to heal.

Sikhs believe that Waheguru is the giver and taker of life. Although it may be joyful or sorrowful, long or short, only the Creator has the right to control it. Most Sikhs are opposed to euthanasia, medically assisted dying, because they believe that birth and death should be left in the hands of Waheguru. Nevertheless, there are those who believe it may be acceptable in some situations. Even for those for whom active termination of life is not acceptable, in some dire situations where an unconscious individual is facing imminent death and life is being sustained only by

---

[305] *SGGS* 432: sukh dhukh teree aagiaa piaare dhoojee naahee jai—ਸੁਖੁ ਦੁਖੁ ਤੇਰੀ ਆਗਿਆ ਪਿਆਰੇ ਦੂਜੀ ਨਾਹੀ ਜਾਇ॥

artificial respiration, family members have consented to the removal of artificial respiration (the patient's breathing tube).

214. Can there be a "just" war?

There is a concept in Sikhi called *dharm yudh,* which loosely translates to "just war." A *dharam yudh* is a war fought in defence of a people's rights or in response to oppression or unjustifiable aggression. The goal is protection of human rights and liberties and justice for those who cannot stand up for themselves. Sikhs believe that a *dharam yudh* must be fought even if it cannot be won. However, it is to be a measure of last resort— when all other attempts to resolve the conflict have been thoroughly exhausted. The motive must not be one of revenge or hostility, and only the minimum force needed for success may be used. Torture, needless killing, and the mistreatment of others are strictly prohibited. Any Sikh participating in a *dharam yudh* must behave as a saint-soldier and "fear none, frighten none."[306] Civilians must not be harmed, and places of worship of any faith should not be damaged or desecrated. The army must be disciplined, and soldiers who surrender should not be harmed. There must be no looting, the territory must not be annexed, and property taken must be returned. Sikhs also believe that treaties and cease-fires must be honoured.

Sikh history is replete with examples where Sikhs were forced to take up arms to defend their very right to live and to protect the rights of others to freedom of religion and conscience. The Sikh belief that even soldiers aligned with the oppressive regime must be treated as human beings worthy of dignity and respect is best exemplified with the story of Bhai Ghanaiya (1648–1718). During Guru Gobind Singh's time, the Sikhs were forced out of their homes and hunted. During one particular battle between the Sikhs and Moghuls, Bhai Ghanaiya, a devout Sikh, was seen providing water and tending to the injuries of wounded soldiers

---

[306] *SGGS* 1427: Guru Tegh Bahadur, bhai kaahoo kau dhet neh neh bhai maanat aan—ਭੈ ਕਾਹੂ ਕਉ ਦੇਤ ਨਹਿ ਨਹਿ ਭੈ ਮਾਨਤ ਆਨ॥

on both sides of the battleground. Some Sikh soldiers complained to the Guru. When asked to explain his actions, Bhai Ghanaiya told Guru Gobind Singh that he was unable to distinguish between Sikh and Moghul soldiers as he saw them all as children of Waheguru. The Guru commended Bhai Ghanaiya for his compassion and provided him with resources so he could continue tending to the Moghul soldiers.

215. Do Sikhs practice restorative justice?

According to the Centre for Justice and Reconciliation, "Faith was a source of inspiration for many who constructed the institutions of contemporary criminal justice. It was also a resource for some of the early practitioners of restorative justice. Its influence on both groups continues."[307]

The Sikh community has, for centuries, practiced a form of restorative justice that focuses on restitution and rehabilitation, and it requires offenders to take responsibility and show remorse. The process is used more frequently in Panjabi villages and remote communities where reconciliation is given higher priority than incarceration. It requires consent of all parties before it can be initiated. The process involves the selection of five members within the Sikh congregation (picked by community members) who come together with the victim, community, and the offender. They are specifically selected to adjudicate a particular offense. The process involves allowing all affected parties the opportunity to share their views and for the offender to explain their actions and accept responsibility. The goal is to facilitate healing and rehabilitation. Where there is no remorse or responsibility accepted, there can be no healing. If deemed appropriate, there may be the imposition of *tankhah*, a penalty usually consisting of specific forms of community service. The offender performs the service for either the congregation, an alternative benefactor (charity), or both. The purpose of the activity

---

[307] Resorativejustice.org; RJ Library "Centre for Justice & Reconciliation," Washington, DC.

is to foster humility, accept responsibility, and restore the offender to the community if possible.

216. What is the Sikh attitude toward homosexuality and same-sex marriage?

The *SGGS* does not address the subject of sexual orientation—and neither does the Sikh code of ethics. The following verse in Gurbani refers to a marriage relationship: "Those who have one light (one soul working in unison) in two bodies, are called husband and wife."[308] Many Sikh scholars translate this verse to mean that Guru Amar Das was speaking about heterosexual marriages only. However, proponents of same-sex marriages argue that Sikhi places no preference on heterosexual relationships. They note that marriage in Sikhi is a union of souls, the soul is genderless, and the outward appearance of human beings (male or female) is a temporary physical state.

Sikh teachings mandate respect for all human beings, regardless of sexual orientation or gender identity. Nevertheless, the Sikh community is split on the issue of homosexuality and acceptance of same-sex marriages. This flows from cultural influences rather than religious teachings. The issue came to a head in 2005, when the Canadian Parliament was considering passing a bill legalizing same-sex marriage. Some members of the Sikh community sought the counsel of the Akal Takhat jathedar (head of the temporal authority for Sikhs). Giani Joginder Singh Vedanti spoke out against homosexuality and told Sikh-Canadian members of Parliament that they had a religious duty to oppose the same-sex marriage legislation proposed by the Canadian government.[309] Vedanti issued an advisory notice stating in part, "The basic duty of Sikh MPs in Canada should be to support laws that stop this kind of practice

---

[308]   *SGGS* 788: ek jot dhui mooratee dhan pir kaheeaai soi—ਏਕ ਜੋਤਿ ਦੁਇ ਮੂਰਤੀ ਧਨ ਪਿਰੁ ਕਹੀਐ ਸੋਇ॥

[309]   Brian Laghi, "Sikh Leader in India Denounces Same-Sex Marriage," *Globe and Mail*, January 18, 2005, https://www.theglobeandmail.com/amp/news/world/sikh-leader-in-india-denounces-same-sex-marriage/article974479.

[homosexuality], because there are thousands of Sikhs living in Canada, to ensure that Sikhs do not fall prey to this practice." His opinion had little impact on the four Sikh MPs or broader Sikh community. When the Parliamentary vote was held, two of the four Sikh MPs supported the same-sex marriage legislation, one abstained, and only one of them opposed the bill. The World Sikh Organization of Canada also stood steadfast and endorsed the bill in favour of same-sex marriage. Though this stance was not without controversy, the WSO continues to maintain its principled position for equality for all, regardless of sexual orientation.

Regarding support for 2SLGBTQ+[310] rights, as with the community at large, there seems to be a generational divide within the Sikh community—with greater support existing among younger Sikhs. A majority of Sikhs in Canada do not take issue with 2SLGBTQ+ rights as long as they do not infringe upon the right of each Sikh congregation to decide if they will allow such a marriage to occur within their own gurdwara. The Canadian *Civil Marriage Act*, Bill C-38 (SC 2005, c. 33) provides that protection.

The topic of sexuality is still not openly discussed in many Panjabi Sikh homes. Though homosexuality is becoming increasingly accepted, it is still widely misunderstood among Panjabi Sikhs. As such, it will take a concerted effort to provide widespread education to dispel myths about homosexuality and educate the Panjabi Sikh community about 2SLGBTQ+ people.

217. How do Sikhs view extramarital relationships?

Sexual relations outside of marriage are considered to be against Sikhi values. We are taught to look upon those younger than us as our children, peers as siblings, and our elders as parents. Guru Nanak writes, "O fool, having a relationship outside of marriage is like eating poison, and you will suffer in pain."[311]

---

[310] Two-spirited, lesbian, gay, bi-sexual, transsexual, queer (or questioning), plus.

[311] *SGGS* 1255: par dhan par naaree rat ni(n)dhaa bikh khaiee dukh paiaaa—ਪਰ ਧਨ ਪਰ ਨਾਰੀ ਰਤੁ ਨਿੰਦਾ ਬਿਖੁ ਖਾਈ ਦਖੁ ਪਾਇਆ ॥

The Sikh Gurus taught that a spiritual person must control lust, anger, greed, worldly attachment, and egotism.[312] Such behaviours are like a veil that does not allow an individual to recognize the truth and the presence of Waheguru within. Although all five of these vices are inherent to the human condition, they must be controlled to follow the spiritual path. The thoughts we harbor in our minds are the seeds that may eventually lead to action—and the real effort is to conquer the mind.

Guru Gobind Singh said, "Love your wife ever and ever so much that even in a dream you should not share the bed of another woman."[313] The message for Sikhs (male and female) is clear: it is not only lustful actions that are to be avoided, but thoughts and dreams as well. The primary tool Sikhs are to use to conquer lust and other vices is to meditate on the divine name (naam). By meditating on Naam, one endeavours to discover Waheguru's light within and to see it permeating throughout creation. In such a state, lust and the other vices of the mind fall away, and the individual is able to recognize the truth.

218. Is it acceptable to satirize religious leaders or beliefs?

Religious satire is probably as old as religion, and nothing I write here could bring it to an end. Nor should it end. Freedom of expression and freedom of religion are protected under the law, at least in most democratic countries. "Trenchant criticism, commentary, satire, and humour help build institutions in a free society," writes the Bar Association of India.[314] The only constraint is to refrain from commentary that incites violence or hatred.

---

[312] *SGGS* 194: kaam karodh lobh moh tajo—ਕਾਮ ਕ੍ਰੋਧ ਲੋਭ ਮੋਹ ਤਜੋ॥

[313] *Dasam Granth* 836–37: nij naaree ke saath neh tum nit baddaiyahu. par naaree kee sej bhool supane hoo(n) na jaiyahu—ਨਿਜ ਨਾਰੀ ਕੇ ਸਾਥ ਨੇਹੁ ਤੁਮ ਨਿਤ ਬਧੈਯਹੁ ॥ ਪਰ ਨਾਰੀ ਕੀ ਸੇਜ ਭੂਲਿ ਸੁਪਨੇ ਹੂੰ ਨ ਜੈਯਹ ॥

[314] *Times of India*, August 18, 2020: Bar Association of India comes out in support of Prashant Bhushan.

There are several instances in Sikh history of the Gurus performing acts that appear to be satirical in nature. They were not intended to ridicule a religion; they were meant to provide constructive criticism through common logic. Guru Nanak once traveled to a famous pilgrimage site and saw that Hindu pilgrims were performing a ritual of standing in the "holy" river and offering handfuls of water to the rising sun. He turned his back to the sun and began throwing water toward the west. The pilgrims ridiculed him for throwing water in the opposite direction. They asked what he was doing, and Guru Nanak replied, "I am watering my fields back home" and he continued throwing water. The pilgrims laughed and said he was being foolish. Guru Nanak replied, "Surely if the water you are offering the sun will reach your ancestors, then the water I am throwing should reach my fields, which are much closer."

Guru Nanak's objective was to make the pilgrims reflect on the deeper meaning of their rituals and whether they had merit. He was not openly offensive, and he did not condemn the pilgrims outright. They understood what he implied. As in this example, religious satire plays a role in inspiring thought, and if anything, it is an opportunity to confirm our beliefs or engage in dialogue to clarify misunderstandings. In cases where satire is found to be offensive, the response must be a thoughtfully argued rebuttal.

PART VII

Organization and Administration

CHAPTER 21

Governance

According to *Merriam-Webster*, *governing* is the "act or process of governing or overseeing the control and direction of something." Therefore, governance is how rules, norms, and actions are structured, sustained, and regulated—and how the faithful are held accountable. Let's not confuse religious governance with corporate organization. They are two different structures. Furthermore, each religion has its distinct structure or pyramid in how it governs itself.

The Sikh dharam, as discussed earlier, is congregational and not hierarchical. During the more than two hundred years of human Gurus from Guru Nanak to Guru Gobind Singh (1469–1708), there was no confusion about who the adherents relied upon for spiritual guidance or clarifications on social issues. This changed in 1708, when Guru Gobind Singh proclaimed the *Sri Guru Granth Sahib* as the eternal Guru of the Sikhs, to which Sikhs could turn for spiritual guidance. He also declared that the Panj Pyare (any five initiated and practicing Sikhs) could constitute a decision-making body and provide guidance in secular matters, such as leadership in social issues or assisting with interpretation of the Gurus' teachings. Since that time, the Sikh community has come up with its own governance practices in order to ensure continuity, authenticity, and adhesion of the Sikh community. This chapter provides answers to questions about how the Sikhs govern their own affairs and manage their institutions.

219. How do Sikhs govern themselves?

A Sikh religious leader, a *Jathedar*, is the head of a jatha, which is a group of larger than five people in Sikhi. This title is now being conferred on the heads of five *takhats* ("seats of power," explained below). Sikhs have had a very tumultuous history, and sometimes community decisions were made on the run. Until 1920, the heads of *takhats* were selected and appointed by the *Sarbat Khalsa* ("assembly of all Sikhs.") After the martyrdom of Guru Arjan in 1606, Guru Hargobind conceptualized a sovereign spiritual and temporal institute to govern Sikh religious and political affairs. To implement this, in 1608, he got a raised platform erected facing the Darbar Sahib, Akal Bunga, which is where there now stands a gorgeous building known as the *Akal Takhat Sahib* ("throne of the eternal.") Situated within the Darbar Sahib complex in Amritsar, it is the seat of Sikh temporal and spiritual authority.

From the sixth to the tenth Guru (1606–1708), the spiritual and temporal power remained vested in the Gurus. However, in 1708, rather than nominating a human successor to guruship, Guru Gobind Singh, the tenth Guru, divided the Guru's authority into two integrated domains: the spiritual and the temporal. He proclaimed the *Sri Guru Granth Sahib* (Sikh scripture) as the eternal Guru (Guru Granth), the spiritual authority, and passed on the mantle of temporal power to Khalsa (Guru Panth). This was in line with Guru Nanak's concept of *Sabad Guru,* the spiritual utterances in the *Sri Guru Granth Sahib*, as the eternal Guru.[315]

The *Sikh Rehat Maryada* (code of conduct) confers authority on Panj Pyare (initiated Sikhs) to decide issues of a religious, educational, social, and political nature by adopting a resolution (*matta*). However, subjects that affect the fundamental principles of the Sikh religion are addressed by the five *jathedars* in the form of Panj Pyare or by the Sarbat Khalsa (assembly of all initiated Sikhs) by adopting a joint resolution known as a *gurmatta*. For addressing spiritual and temporal issues, the Akal Takhat *jathedar* chairs all deliberations. The five recognized *takhats* are:

---

[315]   *SGGS* 942: sabad guru surat dhun chelaa. ਸਬਦੁ ਗੁਰੂ ਸੁਰਤਿ ਧੁਨਿ ਚੇਲਾ ॥

- *Akal Takhat Sahib*: As discussed above, the Akal Takhat institution was founded by Guru Hargobind, the sixth Guru, to address the spiritual and temporal concerns of the Sikh community. Thus, Guru Hargobind established the concept of Miri and Piri, representing the temporal and spiritual realms that Sikhs must balance in their daily lives. Since the time of the Gurus, the spiritual authority is vested in the *Sri Guru Granth Sahib*, the eternal Guru, and the temporal authority is entrusted to the Akal Takhat institution. The Sikh religion is a congregational religion.

- *Takhat Patna Sahib*: Patna is the capital city of Bihar state, in the northeastern part of India, where Guru Gobind Singh was born in 1666. This is also the place where the Muslim *peer* (also spelled *pir*, meaning "elder" or "saint") Bhikhan Shah tested the Guru's impartiality. It was built by Maharaja Ranjit Singh (1780–1839) and is historically recognized as the second *takhat* after the Akal Takhat Sahib.

- Takhat Kesgarh Sahib: This *takhat* is situated in Anandpur Sahib, a town in Punjab, India, initially named Nanaki Chak in 1665 by Guru Teg Bahadur, the ninth Guru of the Sikhs. The city was named to memorialize Guru Nanak's elder sister, Babe Nanaki (1464–1518) and honour his mother, Mata Nanaki (1598–1678). It later came to be known as Guru Ka Chak, and it is now called Anandpur Sahib. It is also where Guru Gobind Singh, the tenth Guru, held a mass *amrit* (initiation) ceremony and founded the Khalsa association in 1699. He declared it the birthplace of Khalsa and that of all *amritdhari* Sikhs. Guru Gobind Singh made this town his home base for most of his life.

- *Takhat Sachkhand Hazur Sahib*: Also spelled *Hazoor Sahib*, this *takhat* is located on the banks of the River Godavari in Nanded, in the state of Maharashtra, western India. This is where Guru Gobind Singh spent the last two years of his life and declared Guru Granth Sahib, the Sabad Guru (spiritual writings), as the eternal Guru of the Sikhs. Gurdwara Sachkhand Sahib stands on the spot where Guru Gobind Singh was cremated.

- *Takhat Damdama Sahib*: The fifth *takhat* is situated in a town called Talwandi Sabo, in Punjab, where Guru Gobind Singh rested for more than a year after fighting three battles at Anandpur Sahib, Chamkaur, and Mukatsar against the forces of the Mughal government as well as the Rajput, Hindu, hill states. It is here where he also, in 1705, dictated from memory the entire text of the *Aad Granth* and got it transcribed by Bhai Mani Singh, adding to the primal scripture compiled by the fifth Guru, Guru Arjan, the sabads of his father and spiritual predecessor, Guru Teg Bahadur. He had to get this new Granth prepared because the Dheermal family refused to part with the primal scripture (*Aad Granth*) that they had in their custody.[316] He added Guru Teg Bahadur's religious writings to complete the full version of the *Sri Guru Granth Sahib* that the Sikhs today revere and display in all gurdwaras or homes. The Aad Ganth, the primal version, is available in Kartarpur, near Jalandhar, for viewing. I saw it in 1978.

Since establishing the Shiromani Gurdwara Parbandhak Committee (SGPC) in 1925, commonly referred to as the "Sikh mini-Parliament," the SGPC has appointed heads for all *takhats*—though not without some controversies. Each takhat is currently managed by an appointed *jathedar* (head), including the Akal Takhat Sahib. Though all of them function independently for their day-to-day administrative affairs, for addressing the religious and social issues of the larger Sikh community, they work under Sri Akal Takhat Sahib's leadership to arrive at unanimous decisions.

---

[316] Dheermal was the eldest brother of Guru Har Rai, the seventh Guru. When Guru Hargobind, the sixth Guru, was relocating from Kartarpur to Kiratpur, he trusted his grandson Dheermal to take care of the *Aad Granth* in Kartarpur. Dheermal later refused to give the primal scripture to the Guru when his younger brother Guru Har Rai was anointed to be the seventh Guru.

220. What is the history of the Sikh Assembly, the Sarbat Khalsa?

What is the history of the Sikh Assembly, the Sarbat Khalsa The word *sarbat* means "all" or "everything," and Khalsa, as previously discussed, stands for the initiated Sikhs. Together, Sarbat Khalsa refers to an assembly of all initiated Sikhs. This was a biannual deliberative assembly of the Khalsa (similar to a parliament in a direct democracy). The tradition of Sarbat Khalsa goes back to 1708 when Guru Gobind Singh called the whole Sikh community to assemble in Nanded, Maharashtra, and conferred guruship on the *Sri Guru Granth Sahib*. When Sikhs asked when they would see the Guru again, he said, "Khalsa [an initiated Sikh who practices Sikhi in word and action] is my true form, and within such Khalsa, I abide."[317]

The Sarbat Khalsa continued meeting intermittently until 1920 when the SGPC was established to seize control of gurdwaras from managers appointed by the British. Sikhs could not tolerate such deliberate intervention in their places of worship, and bloody conflicts took place at some prominent historical gurdwaras. Finally conceding to the community's pressure, the colonial government enacted the Sikh Gurdwaras Act in 1925. It governs all SGPC affairs, including the appointment of *jathedars*. Unfortunately, this act diluted the Sarbat Khalsa concept, and the community is working hard to revive it, particularly as it relates to the selection of Jathedars.

221. Does anyone speak with authority for the Sikhs?

During the time of the Gurus, the Gurus spoke with authority for Sikhs. In 1708, Guru Gobind Singh delegated temporal decision power to the Panj Pyare (five initiated and practicing Sikhs). Decisions about the religious interpretation of the Sikh scriptures and conflicting social

---

[317] Amrit Kirtan, 291: Khalsa mero roop hai khaas. Khalse mai hao karon nivaas.
ਖਾਲਸਾ ਮੇਰੋ ਰੂਪ ਹੈ ਖਾਸ॥ ਖਾਲਸੇ ਮਹਿ ਹੌ ਕਰੌ ਨਿਵਾਸ॥

issues, if they cannot be settled locally, are referred to the Akal Takhat.[318] The head of the Akal Takhat then assembles Panj Pyare. These five comprise himself, the *jathedar* of the Akal Takhat, and four *jathedars* of other *takhats* (seats of authority) to make a decision. If other *jathedars* are unable to participate, then the head *granthi* (Sikh scripture reader and curator) of Darbar Sahib or any of the *takhats* are invited to join as members of Panj Pyare. Ethical decisions are issued as edicts (*aadesh*) for all Sikhs to follow, and decisions on social issues are issued as directives (*sandesh*).

Most issues are locally resolved by the congregation or through the Panj Pyare chosen from within the community. The prerequisite for selecting Panj Pyare is to be an initiated and practicing Sikh with an unblemished reputation. The *Sikh Rehat Maryada* (code of conduct) allows for an appeal of a local congregation's decision to the higher authority of the Akal Takhat jathedar.

222. Do Sikhs believe in a particular system of government?

Sikh values and history are consistent with the ideals of a secular democracy. A proper functioning democracy must be respectful toward all and help support and sustain a peaceful and harmonious multi-faith, multicultural society. To write fancy words in the constitution of a country is not enough. Instead, leadership is needed to practically implement democratic aspirations to their fullest. The Sikhi vision of a fair and just society is best expressed in this sabad written by Bhagat Ravidas:[319]

---

[318] *Sikh Rehat Maryada* (Code of Conduct) section XXVII.

[319] *SGGS* 345: Begum puraa sehar ko naau. Dookh a(n)dhoh nahee the Thaau. Naa(n) tasavees khraaj na maal. Khaug na khataa na tara javaal. ਬੇਗਮ ਪੁਰਾ ਸਹਰ ਕੋ ਨਾਉ ॥ ਦੁਖੁ ਅੰਦੋਹੁ ਨਹੀ ਤਿਹਿ ਠਾਉ ॥ ਨਾਂ ਤਸਵੀਸ ਖਿਰਾਜੁ ਨ ਮਾਲੁ ॥ ਖਉਫੁ ਨ ਖਤਾ ਨ ਤਰਸੁ ਜਵਾਲੁ ॥

Begumpura, the City without sorrow, is the name of the town
There is no suffering or anxiety there
There are no troubles or taxes or commodities there
There is no fear, blemish or downfall there
Now I have found this most excellent city
There is lasting peace and safety there, O siblings of Destiny
God's kingdom is steady, stable, and eternal
There is no second or third status; all are equal there
That city is populous and eternally famous
Those who live there are wealthy and contented
They stroll about freely, just as they please
They know the Mansion of the Lord's Presence, and no-one blocks
their way
Says Ravi Daas, the emancipated shoe-maker
Whoever is a citizen there, is a friend of mine.

Sikhi is enacted through an individual's actions every day; life is a test and a testament to one's commitment to Sikhi. In accordance with this, Sikhs are committed to ethical action in the public sphere, which means Sikhi functions through secular responsibilities. Meeting one's social obligations and working for the upliftment of society at large are cornerstones of Sikhi. Social reform is a strong element throughout Sikh teachings and practice. Sikhi lays stress on one's duties as a citizen, rendering service to the community.

A democracy is government for and by the people. In a democracy, everyone has a voice. One's views are based on one's values and ethics. For some, values may come from their respective religious beliefs. Secularism can be thought of as a way to balance these views in the public to ensure government is working for the people. Secularism, therefore, requires equality of all religions—without special favour to the religion of the majority or any faith designated as the state religion. Sikhi strongly supports through its practice individual freedom and freedom of religion. We, as a society, should not attempt to silence anyone's views, but we should also recognize that no single community is above another.

Each of us has an opportunity to voice and influence the decisions of a government, but the government also represents all of society and protects freedom and equality for each of us. As clearly stated by American executive Supreet Singh Manchanda in a 2004 post on SikhNet.com:

> Democracy is power in action—not of a few, but [of] all. It gives every constituent a chance to use their voice, to use their power. Democracy works as a method of peaceful self-governance for diverse groups of people.[320]

Sikhs are no strangers to democracy and understand that it demands absolute integrity on the part of citizens to succeed.

---

[320] Supreet Singh Manchanda, "Twenty Years Later: Milestones on the Path to Peace," Seeds of Healing, SikhNet.com (2004), para. 4, https://www.sikhnet.com/pages/seeds-healing.

CHAPTER 22

Gurdwara—Place of Congregation and Learning

Humans are, by nature, social animals. Social interaction is critical to human development. We live in a multi-faith society, and each group has built a place where the faithful congregate and collectively worship according to their religious beliefs. As a temple, synagogue, church, or mosque serves the spiritual and social needs of Hindus, Jews, Christians, and Muslims, respectively, a gurdwara is a place of congregation and worship for Sikhs. Each place of worship, regardless of faith, is considered a sacred sanctuary for followers of the respective religion. Therefore, it is advisable to adhere to relevant rules devised by each faith group to respect the sanctity of the places of worship.

This chapter will explain certain unique aspects of a gurdwara and how to conduct yourself if you happen to visit one.

223. What is a Gurdwara?

The gurdwara (literally "the Guru's door" or "gateway to the Guru") is the hub of Sikh community, spirituality, and culture. It is a place where Sikhs gather to meditate, congregate, celebrate, and commemorate.

A gurdwara is a central institution for Sikhs and serves multiple functions. It is a place of worship, a place of learning, a place for serving others, and a place for gathering. The physical structure becomes sacred once the *Sri Guru Granth Sahib* is installed, and the presence of the *SGGS* itself commands the utmost respect. The gurdwara is where Sikh families gather to pray, socialize, and discuss issues of importance to the community. Each gurdwara has a free kitchen that is open to all persons. Many gurdwaras also have a library, gym, community school, dispensary (more common in India), and computer lab.

Traditionally, the Darbar hall, the central hall in a gurdwara, has four doors, one in each direction, to symbolize being open to all people, regardless of their social, religious, cultural, or racial background. An inverted lotus dome tops most gurdwaras; the lotus is a symbol of spirituality and purity. A gurdwara can be easily identified from a distance because of its tall flagpole (the Nishan Sahib) with a yellow or saffron, and sometimes blue, flag proudly fluttering in the wind. The flag is a symbol of hope, identifying a gurdwara from a distance as a place of solace for all those in need.

224. Why is a Gurdwara important?

Although Sikhs can worship on their own in the privacy of their homes, they see *sangat* worship (in congregation) as having its own unique merits. Sikhs believe that congregational worship can assist in understanding Gurbani and achieving heightened spiritual awareness. The Sikh code of conduct recommends attendance at the gurdwara because a collective gathering helps the devotee grow spiritually by listening to *keertan* (singing sabads) and *katha* (verbal discourse of Sikh scriptures).[321]

Some Sikhs attend their gurdwara every day before they go to work or in the evening. Sikhs consider all days equal, and one specific day of the week is not holier than another. However, attending gurdwara on Sundays in North American society is common for most Sikhs since that fits most patterns of work. In Muslim countries, the weekly congregation may occur on a Friday. Gurpurb (celebrating the Gurus' birth or death

---

[321] *Sikh Rehat Maryada*, chapter IV(a).

anniversaries) and some specific festivals attract the largest *sangat* in gurdwaras.

225. How did the gurdwara concept begin?

Guru Nanak introduced the term *dharamsaal* (spiritual centre) as a place where Sikhs could congregate. The first *dharamsaal* that functioned under the personal guidance of Guru Nanak was established in 1521 in a newly established village, Kartarpur, on the banks of the Ravi River, now in East Punjab, Pakistan. Guru Nanak traveled extensively throughout Eurasia, talking to people of different faiths and emphasizing the oneness of God and the equality of all human beings. He encouraged people to build a *dharamsala* (congregation centre) where Sikhs could gather to hear the Guru's spiritual discourse and sing religious sabads in praise of Waheguru. The *dharamsaal* concept continued until Guru Arjan, the fifth Guru, built Darbar Sahib in Amritsar in 1601.

Guru Hargobind, introduced the term *gurdwara*.[322] The term derives from the words *gur* (meaning "Guru"—spiritual teacher) and *dwara* (a door or gateway), together meaning "the gateway through which the Guru could be reached" or "door to the Guru."

There are now thousands of gurdwaras around the world, including more than four hundred in North America. Malaysia is home to the first gurdwara built by diaspora Sikhs in 1881. Canada's first gurdwara opened in 1908 in Vancouver. England's first gurdwara was built a few years later, in 1911, in London, and in 1912, Sikhs built a gurdwara in Stockton, California. Since that time, gurdwaras have been constructed in every town and country where Sikhs live. The first gurdwaras did not have traditional Sikh architecture and were often converted homes, churches, or industrial buildings. In recent years, however, as Sikhs have begun building gurdwaras from the ground up, aspects of the traditional architecture have been incorporated.

---

[322] Bhai Kahn Singh Nabha, comp., Gur Shabad Ratanakar *Mahan Kosh: The Sikh Encyclopedia in Punjabi* (1930).

226. How do Sikhs worship in the gurdwara?

The main hall where congregants gather is called the Darbar hall. This is where the *Sri Guru Granth Sahib* is installed. The *SGGS* is positioned in the centre of the room, toward the far end as one enters. It is placed on a platform under a canopy (*chandoya*) and covered with fine cloth brocades (*rumallah*).

Anyone who enters the Darbar hall is expected to walk up to the *SGGS* and bow to the sacred scriptures with folded hands. The bowing is called "*matha tek*," which literally means to touch one's forehead to the ground by kneeling. Most people will donate a small sum of money (ranging from one to five dollars) as they matha tek. Others may offer groceries, which are needed to operate the free kitchen. Once the person has bowed, they go to the *prashad station* where they are given a sweet pudding made out of flour, sugar, butter, and water. The pudding is called prashad, and it must be taken with open hands. Some people choose not to eat the prashad because they are allergic to wheat or are diabetic. However, almost everyone will take it and give it someone else if they are unable to consume it themselves.

Once a person has taken prashad, they take a seat on the floor among the *sangat* (congregation). All in attendance sit on the floor, with women on one side of the aisle and men on the other. Sitting on the floor denotes equality and is considered appropriate for meditation. Gurdwaras can become crowded very quickly, and people often sit shoulder to shoulder and knee to knee. Thus, the separation of the genders is done to ensure that no one feels uncomfortable sitting so close to a stranger of the opposite sex. In some gurdwaras, particularly historical ones in India, there is no separation of the genders, and congregants sit wherever they please. If someone is physically challenged, they may sit on a stool or chair, provided that this seating is lower than the platform on which the *Sri Guru Granth Sahib* is installed.

227. Is there a special dress code for a gurdwara?

Some basic protocols must be observed by anyone entering a gurdwara. All visitors to a gurdwara must take off their shoes and cover their heads upon entering the gurdwara. Both are mandatory practices. Tobacco, intoxicants, and narcotic drugs are strictly prohibited on the gurdwara premises, including the parking lot. The lobby of the gurdwara will contain shoe racks for shoes and extra head coverings (*rumals*) in case someone arrives without their own. Aside from the head covering, there is no mandated dress code, except modesty. Given that one is going to be seated on the floor, you may find it more comfortable to wear loose clothing. It is expected that people will wear clothes that are not too revealing, such as short shorts, dresses or skirts that are above the knees, or low-cut, strapless, or spaghetti strap tops. Although many people choose to wear traditional Panjabi clothes (narrow trousers and a long tunic), these are not mandated. Western clothes are perfectly acceptable.

228. Who owns a gurdwara?

Most gurdwaras are owned by the charitable society set up by the local Sikh congregation strictly for that purpose. They are considered to belong to the local Sikh community and are run by a volunteer executive and/or board.

229. How are gurdwaras funded?

Most gurdwaras start with local Sikh community members donating money, material, and in-kind labor to build the structure. There are no rules regarding donations. People may donate one dollar to thousands of dollars, depending upon their financial capacity and the overall need for community service. Many devotees give material and in-kind labor to help build gurdwaras, but all this is voluntary. Sometimes seed money may be needed to buy the land or help fund construction. When the community is short on cash donations, congregants will offer to take out personal loans—repayable at a modest interest rate or on generous terms—to allow the building to be constructed.

Once the gurdwara building is complete, it will require ongoing funding to manage the overhead expenses. These include the running of the free kitchen, paying the salary of the granthi, and any cleaning or administrative staff who might need to be hired. All of this money is collected through donations that are made by attendees. There is no set amount for donation. Most attendees will donate money each time they attend the gurdwara. This amount will be nominal, usually ranging from one to five dollars. In addition, congregants donate larger sums throughout the year. Again, there is no set time when such donations are made—they depend on the persons' own financial means, and the needs of the gurdwara.

230. Do you have to pay a fee to be a member of a gurdwara?

Membership is not required to attend at a gurdwara, and anyone can attend any gurdwara, partake in the langar, and attend all activities and functions without paying anything. Some gurdwaras have membership fee requirements to be eligible to select or elect the executive. For most, residency in the area and regular attendance are all that are needed to become a member. In Canada, gurdwaras are registered under the applicable society acts and are governed by provincial and federal government legislations.

231. How do Sikhs show reverence to the Sikh scripture?

In Eastern cultures, kneeling is customary as a sign of respect. Bowing is also a sign of respect when people greet elders, teachers, or authority figures. To some extent, we also bow in Western culture. Kneeling happens in Christian churches, and it used to occur before royalty (Western traditions). We bow to the judge to pay respect as we enter a court. We bow when we enter a karate dojo, and we even bow to the karate master.

When Sikhs bow to the *Sri Guru Granth Sahib*, the act is more significant. It is a much deeper spiritual experience than a simple cultural exercise. We enter a place of worship with folded hands, kneel, and bring our foreheads to the floor before the *Sri Guru Granth Sahib*. This is called "matha tek." This symbolic act is a sign that the Sikh is leaving their ego at the feet of the Guru (*manmat*) and is willing to accept the Guru's teachings (*gurmat*). It is sign that we humbly surrender to the Guru and put our destiny in Waheguru's hands. Prostration expresses our love and submission to Sabad (the divine infinite wisdom) in the Sikh scripture. This physical act of bowing to the *Sri Guru Granth Sahib* is not like bowing before an idol at the altar because it is not so. Sikhs revere their Guru (the person and the Word as contained in the scripture), but they do not worship it. They are obliged to read the word, understand it, reflect on it, and live it in their daily life. That is true remembrance of the Name Divine. The Sikh Gurus denounced idol worship. Guru Nanak says, "The idol worshipers are fools. When idols disappear, who will carry you across the ocean of trials and turbulences in life?"[323]

The Sikh faith promotes living a life of truth, following the spiritual teachings in the Sikh scripture. Bowing before the *SGGS* humbles the mind and reduces the ego and intellect in front of the Guru. To emphasize this message, Guru Nanak says, "The Sabad [divine word] is the Guru, upon whom I lovingly focus my consciousness; I am Sabad's disciple."[324]

As you walk into the main hall in the gurdwara, you will notice someone waving the royal *chaur* (whisk) over the *Sri Guru Granth Sahib* in reverence. The *chaur* is traditionally made of yak hair mounted in a

---

[323] *SGGS* 556: paathar le poojeh mugadh gavaar. oh jaa aap ddube tum kahaa taranahaar. ਪਾਥਰੁ ਲੇ ਪੂਜਹਿ ਮੁਗਾਯ ਗਵਾਰ ॥ ਓਹਿ ਜ ਆਪਿ ਡੂਬੇ ਤੁਮ ਕਹਾ ਤਰਨਹਾਰ ॥

[324] *SGGS* 943: sabad guru surat dhun chelaa. ਸਬਦੁ ਗੁਰੂ ਸੁਰਤਿ ਧੁਨਿ ਚੇਲਾ ॥

decorative wooden or metal handle. The current trend is to use synthetic material. Waving the *chaur* is a sign of reverence, utmost respect, and devotion to the divine message in the Sikh scripture. The tradition traces its history back to the time of the Gurus. Historically, a yak tail hair tuft was whisked over members of royalty, notably the Mughal Dynasty, as a submission to their superiority over their subjects.

In 1606, as Baba Buddha was carrying the *Aad Granth* (premier scripture) over his head for installation in the Darbar Sahib (Golden Temple), Guru Arjan was whisking the *chaur* with love for and devotion to the Divine. Thus, it became a practice for Sikhs to follow. Sikhs feel privileged and humbled by getting an opportunity to wave the *chaur*. Anyone—man, woman, or child—can take turns performing this service.

232. What is the name for a Sikh congregation?

The word *sangat* originates from the Sanskrit word *sangh*, which means "company," "fellowship," and "association." In Sikhi, *sangat* stands for the body of men and women who meet religiously, especially in the presence of the *Sri Guru Granth Sahib*. Therefore, *sangat* is a congregation.

Two other expressions that carry the same meaning and everyday use are *Sadh-sangat* or *Sat-sangat* ("fellowship of the seekers of truth.") These words have been in use since the time of Guru Nanak. In one of the verses, he answers the question: How do we recognize *sadh-Sangat*? "Where the lovers of Truth hold communion with One Creator alone."[325] *Sangat* has also been commonly referred to as the Sikh companionship established in or belonging to a locality.

---

[325] *SGGS* 71: satasa(n)gat kaisee jaaneeaai. jithai eko naam vakhaaneeaai. ਸਤਿਸੰਗਤਿ ਕੈਸੀ ਜਾਣੀਐ ॥ ਜਿਥੈ ਹਰਿ ਕਾ ਨਾਮੁ ਵਖਾਣੀਐ ॥

233. Who may enter a gurdwara?

Anyone can enter the gurdwara, which is open to all visitors irrespective of their belief or nonbelief. All gurdwaras are constructed with four doors facing each direction to express the ideal that persons from all four corners of the earth are welcome. However, there is only one main entrance to the gurdwara, which is intended to express that everyone enters as an equal. All are welcome to enter a gurdwara and participate in services, irrespective of religion, skin colour, or gender.

234. What are the seating arrangements in a gurdwara?

All historical gurdwaras, including Darbar Sahib (the Golden Temple), attract thousands of visitors every day. There are no seating arrangements. After paying obeisance to *Sri Guru Granth Sahib* (the Sikh scripture), worshippers and visitors sit on the floor anywhere they can find a spot. There is no restriction on men and women sitting together. However, in most gurdwaras, particularly in Canada, the United States, and Europe, men and women sit separately. Though there is no religious requirement to divide men and women into separate sections, the impetus behind this custom is to encourage congregants to focus on spirituality rather than to be distracted by the proximity of a member of the opposite sex. It promotes a safe space, particularly for women, who may not feel comfortable with a strange male sitting in such proximity to them. Gurdwaras can get very crowded. There are no physical dividers or individual seats, and everyone sits cross-legged on the floor.

While men and women sit separately, it is important to note that both genders are still in equal proximity to the *Sri Guru Granth Sahib*. There are both practical and cultural reasons for this practice. Some people claim that it helps them concentrate on *keertan* (singing sabads) and/or *katha* (verbal discourse). With men and women sitting separately, devotees don't have to be apprehensive about being unintentionally touched by a devotee of the opposite gender.

People do have a choice of sitting together or in separate sections. Also, non-Sikhs visiting gurdwaras do not have to feel pressured to conform to the protocol and can comfortably sit together with their families.

235. What is prashad?

Parshad, also called *karah parshad*, is a sweet vegetarian pudding offered to all attendees, including visitors, after all Sikh religious ceremonies— whether in a gurdwara, a home, or any other venue. *Parshad* is prepared from four ingredients: three parts water, and one part each of whole wheat flour, clarified butter, and sugar. While preparing *parshad*, a person (male or female) recites sacred verses from the *SGGS*. The practice of consuming *parshad* goes back to Guru Nanak. The emphasis is equality of all.

A person receives *parshad* by cupping their hands together. Napkins are provided since *parshad* can be very buttery and sticky. The person distributing parshad is required to distribute the same quantity to all. However, for health reasons, you may ask for a small amount. *Parshad* is not a mystical communion that requires a commitment to or reaffirmation of the Sikh faith. Non-Sikhs sitting through the ceremony may choose not to accept the *parshad*, but they do not lose their religious identity by taking it.

236. What is the significance of the langar?

Langar is a term commonly used for the buffet-style free meal service in every gurdwara. I use the term *buffet* to simplify the concept for non-Sikh readers, but the concept of *langar* has a much deeper spiritual significance for Sikhs. In simple terms, the *langar* stands for equality of all people of the world, sharing, compassion, and humility.

The institution of *langar* was established by Guru Nanak, the founder of Sikhi, to break down caste and social barriers. It was popularized by

Mata Kheevi, the spouse of the second Guru. Mata Kheevi's service and commitment to equality was honoured by her being the only person mentioned in the *Guru Granth Sahib* for her service to humanity. When Sikhi was sprouting in the South Asian subcontinent, the caste system stratified society, especially Indian society. This system to some extent continues—though to a much lesser degree. In the sixteenth century, people from higher castes would sit on cots, chairs, and stools, and the "lowest castes" were separated and forced to sit at a little distance and on the floor. The Gurus always wanted Sikhs to practice egalitarianism and communal harmony. Sharing (*vand shakna*), as you will recall, is one of the three underlying principles of Sikhi.

Before the *langar*, the prerequisite for visitors is to remove their shoes, cover their heads, and wash their hands before taking a seat. Most gurdwara langar halls do not have tables or chairs; instead, everyone is seated on the carpet. However, in some gurdwaras in North America, particularly British Columbia and California, people dine on tables and in chairs. For those gurdwaras that abide by the Akal Takhat edict and do not have regular dining on tables and chairs, benches or chairs are still provided for individuals with physical challenges. Some gurdwaras serve you where you sit; at others, you take a plate and line up for volunteers to serve you. The meal is usually cooked by community volunteers and served to all visitors regardless of gender, religion, social, economic, and ethnic background. The food consists of lacto-vegetarian dishes (no meat, seafood, or eggs) donated by the *sangat* (congregation), including rice, vegetables, dal (lentil soup), *dahi* (yogurt), an unleavened flatbread, or *poori* (deep-fried bread), and dessert.

237. What do the large circles, swords, and spears in front of SGGS represent?

Some gurdwaras will have some metal ornaments placed in front of the *SGGS*. The circular article is called *chakar*, which represents the Divine that has no beginning or end. The swords and spears are two primary weapons that were used during the time of the Gurus. Both were used for self-defence and to defend the Sikh faith. They remind Sikhs of their duty to stand up against injustice and defend the defenceless. The double-edged sword represents a Sikh's responsibility to separate truth from falsehood. These artifacts may be placed separately or found combined in one object, which is known as the *khanda*.

238. What is khanda—and what is its religious significance?

The *khanda*, the Sikh emblem, also recognized as a Sikh coat of arms, consists of a circle representing the Divine that has no beginning or end. The double-edged broad sword that stands in the middle represents a Sikh's responsibility to separate truth from falsehood. The two curved swords represent Miri and Piri, the temporal (secular) and spiritual realms that each Sikh must balance in their daily lives. The present-day form of Khanda was developed in the early twentieth century. The emblem reminds each Sikh that they have a responsibility to balance their secular and spiritual lives while moving through life, separating truth from falsehood, all the while remembering that they are part of the Divine that has no beginning or end. Guru Gobind Singh, the tenth Guru, says, "At first the Creator created the double-edged sword [a metaphor for energy and primal power], and then created the whole world."[326]

239. What is the significance of the Sikh flag (the Nishan Sahib)?

As mentioned, the Sikh flag flies outside every gurdwara. It is a triangular piece of ochre, saffron, or blue-coloured cloth with the *khanda* emblem in the middle. The flagpole also has a *khanda* or spear on top and is usually covered with the same fabric as the flag.

---

[326] Dasam Granth 119: kha(n)ddaa pirathamai saaj kai jin sabh saisaar upaiaa. ਖੰਡਾ ਪ੍ਰਿਥਮੈ ਸਾਜ ਕੈ ਜਿਨ ਸਭ ਸੈਸਾਰ ਉਪਾਇਆ ॥

The use of the Nishan Sahib was introduced by Guru Hargobind in 1608 in Amritsar at Akal Takhat.[327] He installed two flags to represent the concept of *Miri* and *Piri* (temporal and spiritual). The flag representing the Piri (spiritual) aspect of Sikhi is slightly taller than the Miri (temporal), signifying the hierarchy of spirituality over temporal power. All other gurudwaras have one flag. It signifies the sovereignty of the Sikh religion and—in keeping with the Sikhi tradition of compassion and sharing—is an open invitation to all those who seek help, shelter, and food.

240. What is the significance of a pool near or around the gurdwara?

The pool built around or close to a gurdwara is called a *sarovar*, also spelled *sarowar*, a Punjabi word that means "sacred pool." These square or rectangular pools have steps descending to the water. Historically, the *sarovars* were built for water supply and were used for bathing. In modern times, some have become "pools of pilgrims," and some Sikhs perform a spiritual ablution called *Ishnaan*. The practice of pilgrimage or spiritual ablution is not consistent with Sikh teachings, but some Sikhs still choose to follow it.

Some Sikhs believe that the sacred water of some *sarovars* has curative properties because of the continual prayers in the vicinity. One of the most famous *sarovars* in the Sikh tradition is Darbar Sahib, Amritsar, which Guru Ramdas dug after becoming the fourth Guru in 1574. Guru Arjan, the fifth Guru, completed this large moatlike pool when he built Darbar Sahib. He said, "*Ramdas sarovar naatay, sabh utray paap kamaatay,*"[328] literally meaning that "by bathing in the sacred pool of Ramdas, all sins shall be washed away." The emphasis is not on ritual bathing in the pool but on taking a bath in the spiritual teachings of the

---

[327] Pieter Friedrich and Bhajan Singh, *Captivating the Simple-Hearted: A Struggle for Human Dignity in the Indian Subcontinent* (California: Sovereign Star, 2018), 61.
[328] *SGGS* 624: ramdaas sarovar naatai. Sabh utrai paap kamaatai. ਰਾਮਦਾਸ ਸਰੋਵਰ ਨਾਤੇ ॥ ਸਭਿ ਉਤਰੇ ਪਾਪ ਕਮਾਤੇ ॥

Gurus, meditating on *Naam* (the Divine Word), which will cure mental and physical illnesses and wash away sins.

Most historical gurdwaras in India have sacred pools. Amritsar, for instance, is home to five such *sarovars*. Besides that of Darbar Sahib, initially constructed in 1577 and lined with bricks in 1588,[329] *sarovars* can be found at the following gurdwaras (with construction dates): Santokhsar (1587–88), Ramsar (1602–03), Kaulsar (1627), and Bibeksar (1628). Perhaps the best known of these historical shrines is Gurdwara Ramsar, located south to southeast of Darbar Sahib. The *sarovar* at Bangla Sahib Gurdwara in New Delhi (dedicated to Guru Har Krishan, the eighth Sikh Guru) is another favourite historical place of significance for Sikhs. Sarovars are not common at Gurdwaras in North America and the UK.

241. Can a gurdwara provide sanctuary to refugees facing deportation?

In the words of the famed American lawyer Clarence Darrow: "You can only protect your liberties in this world by protecting the other person's freedom. You can only be free if I am free." The Sikh flag (Nishan Sahib) outside every gurdwara is a sign of welcome for any person needing help and sanctuary. Sikhs will not provide refuge to a criminal, but they may assist someone who is fleeing persecution.

Sikhism is characterized by the values of liberty, equality, and justice, discarding discrimination of all kinds on the grounds of caste, class, race, religion, gender, and social status. The Sikh Gurus stressed that religious, social, and political freedom was the birthright of every individual. Sikhi has had a rich history of striving to restore the rights of the oppressed. Sikhs strongly believe that all individuals, regardless of nationality, have the right to all fundamental freedoms and rights. As a result, Sikhs strongly oppose the deportation of individuals if they will be subject to human rights violations.

---

[329]   Goldentempleamritsar.org.

Sikhs hold the utmost respect for the rule of law and due process. Sikhs believe that no one can be above the law—and that we must all work within the framework of our just laws to seek protection for the vulnerable. In Canada, we had a case of a refugee claimant seeking sanctuary in a gurdwara in the mid-1980s.

CHAPTER 23

The Power of Ardaas

Prayer—a request, a supplication—is often equated with a time when one is in need of something, feeling afraid, or feeling overwhelmed. Prayer can also be about gratitude and thanksgiving. I often hear many Sikhs saying that they have been praying for a long time with no positive or meaningful results. However, in Sikhi, prayer is not to be directed outward to seek material things; it should be directed inward to obtain spiritual upliftment.

Since prayer is all about our relationship with the Divine, we need to ask ourselves, What kind of relationship do we have with the authority we are requesting to grant our petition? In our physical world, when we need something, we go to the person we think has the capacity or means to give us what we need. That person could be an employer, a banker, a spouse, or a friend. Similarly, when we pray or make a request of Waheguru to bless us and grant our wish, we must feel the physical presence of Waheguru, have faith in Waheguru, and create that personal relationship. Creating this relationship makes our minds noble and our hearts humble.

This chapter explores the power of prayer from a Sikh perspective.

242. What is the meaning of prayer for a Sikh?

The Sikh prayer is called *ardaas* (also spelled *ardās*), meaning "a request, a petition, or supplication." Sikhs believe that sincere *ardaas* with conviction is never fruitless. Guru Arjan attests to this and says, "The prayer of Waheguru's humble devotee is never offered in vain."[330] The prerequisites to a fruitful *ardaas* are as follows: firm faith in Waheguru's existence, in Waheguru's power to grant the request, and in the soundness, dignity, and effectiveness of the petition; love and reverence for Waheguru during *ardaas*; and a pure, receptive heart.

For Sikhs, prayer is a personal dialogue with the Divine Source, and it is a conversation that may be had for different reasons:

➢ for spiritual upliftment
➢ to seek spiritual guidance
➢ to seek help in accepting the divine will
➢ for help in hours of trial and tribulation, sickness, and pain
➢ to express gratitude
➢ for the well-being of others
➢ for the welfare of all humanity (*sarbat da bhala*)

Some people may also use prayer as an opportunity to seek material comforts, but Sikhi discourages such a narrow focus on prayer, particularly since the goal of an aspirant is to try to rise above attachment to material things.

In a public setting, *ardaas* is usually said/recited while standing with hands folded before the *Sri Guru Granth Sahib*. If the *Sri Guru Granth Sahib* is not present, then ardaas can be done in a similar reverential posture facing any direction. In a private setting, one may do ardaas while seated or standing. Amridhari Sikhs perform the *ardaas*, a personal prayer to God, at least twice daily (morning and evening).

Although Sikhs are free to recite any prayer during their ardaas,

---

[330] *SGGS* 819: birathee kadhe na hoviee jan kee aradhaas. ਬਿਰਥੀ ਕਦੇ ਨ ਹੋਵਈ ਜਨ ਕੀ ਅਰਦਾਸਿ ॥

there is a standardized ardaas that is done in public functions and services. The formal ardaas has, broadly speaking, four parts. The first three are standardized, and the final part is unique to the person or the occasion. In the first part, a Sikh remembers the Divine Creator and each of the Sikh Gurus, starting from Guru Nanak to the *Sri Guru Granth Sahib*. The second part of the ardaas remembers those Sikhs (women, men, and children) who have sacrificed their lives for the faith and stood for justice and the service of humanity. In the third part, the Sikhs recount the aspirational values, virtues, and characteristics of a Sikh, such as faith, humility, integrity, and courage. In the fourth part, the Sikh personalizes the ardaas to the situation and the issue they are confronted with. The ardaas ends with a supplication for the betterment of all humanity. The ending sentence of our ardaas is "*Nanak naam chardikala, tere bhaane sarbat da bhala*," which translates as "Nanak asks for Naam [divine name], which brings us happiness and positive spirit. With your blessings, may everyone in the world prosper, and may there be peace for all."

The Sikh ardaas is congregational in structure, but it is also equally that of the individual. It is non-isolationist in the sense that it is not for the individual or for the congregation alone; instead, it is for all of humankind. Sikhs perform an individual prayer for every occasion in life, whether happy or sad. An individual *ardaas* can be short or couched in a person's own words, according to their individual needs and feelings. In this case, no particular forms, prescribed words, techniques, or rhythms are needed. Only the mind must have full faith in and submission to Waheguru. "Grant me the strength to live by your will" is the most common adage recommended in the *SGGS*. "The Almighty is the one who knows, who acts, and [who] does what is right. So, stand before Waheguru and make your supplications," says Guru Angad."[331]

---

[331] SGGS 1093: aape jaanai kare aap aape aanai raas. tisai agai naanakaa khali keechai aradhaas. ਆਪੇ ਜਾਣੈ ਕਰੇ ਆਪਿ ਆਪੇ ਆਣੈ ਰਾਸਿ ॥ ਤਿਸੈ ਅਗੈ ਨਾਨਕਾ ਖਲਿਇ ਕੀਚੈ ਅਰਦਾਸ ॥

243. Why do Sikhs believe in the power of prayer?

There is a common Sikh saying, "In times of peace, I express gratitude. In times of pain, I pray. At all times, I meditate.[332]"

Sikhs consider prayer to be a powerful phenomenon. Prayer makes us stronger spiritually and mentally, and studies have shown its positive effects on mental and physical health.

Dr. Jeffrey Small's Twitter feed of October 16, 2011, talks about the power of our brain as follows:

> Medical studies are done as double-blind experiments (neither the doctor nor the patient knows if they are receiving the real treatment or a placebo) because the human mind has the incredible power to heal the body on its own. The placebo effect is often as powerful as many of the drugs we take to cure our illnesses. Give a patient a sugar pill and tell them it is a stimulant, and the patient's heart rate and breathing will increase. They'll report feeling more awake and fuller of energy. If the pill is red, the effect is even greater! The more confident a doctor is in delivering the pill, the stronger the placebo effect in the patient. Seen in this light, the mechanism behind faith healings can also be understood as the power of the human mind.[333]

Some Sikhs firmly believe that prayer is the cure for all diseases and illnesses and may go so far as to refuse medicine. However, the Sikh code of conduct does not prohibit taking medicine to cure an illness that has a clear medical solution. Waheguru's grace is no less if it works through the medium of medicine. Most Sikhs believe that medicine and prayer can very comfortably coexist.

---

[332] sukh velay shukrana, dukh velay ardaas, har valey simran—ਸੁੱਖ ਵੇਲੇ ਸ਼ੁਕਰਾਨਾ, ਦੁੱਖ ਵੇਲੇ ਅਰਦਾਸ, ਹਰ ਵੇਲੇ ਸਮਰਨ ॥

[333] Jeffrey Small on Twitter, https://www.twitter.com/jeffreysmalljr.

244. What is the relationship between prayer and meditation?

The purpose of prayer is to focus the mind. A sincere prayer is recited for protection from vices (lust, anger, greed, worldly attachments, and ego). It also inspires us to connect with the Divine. Meditation, on the other hand, is a vehicle that connects us to the Divine. In Sikhi, the process is called *Naam Simran*, and it is conducted through the repetition of Waheguru's name. It brings a practitioner into harmony with the divine order (*hukam*), accepting Waheguru's will in suffering and pleasure, ultimately leading to a state of blissful "equanimity" (sehaj). A Sikh must lead a life of faith and devotion and surrender to the will of Waheguru. Guru Arjan, the fifth Guru, says, "Sweet is Your Will, O Waheguru; Nanak begs the treasure of your Naam, the Naam of Waheguru."[334]

245. Who leads a Sikh congregation in prayer and sabad singing?

While any *amrithdari* (initiated) Sikh can perform the necessary services in the congregation, spiritually knowledgeable individuals known as *gianis, granthis,* and *raagis* usually perform this role in a gurdwara. Each has different qualifications. Despite equality of both genders being stressed in the Sikh scripture, there are few women *gianis* or *granthis* in gurdwaras.

- *Giani:* Also spelled *gyani*, is an honourific Sikh title for a learned individual who often leads the congregation in prayers. In the absence of *raagis* (sabad singers), the *giani* sings or recites the sabads. The Punjabi word *gian*, from the Sanskrit, means "knowledge," and a *giani* is thus an expositor or "explainer" of the faith, someone with spiritual and religious knowledge who can help the congregation to understand the sacred Sikh

---

[334] *SGGS* 394: teraa keeaa meetha laage; har naam padaarath nanak maange. ਤੇਰਾ ਕੀਆ ਮੀਠਾ ਲਾਗੈ ॥ ਹਰਿ ਨਾਮੁ ਪਦਾਰਥੁ ਨਾਨਕੁ ਮਾਂਗੈ ॥

scriptures and the history of the religion. *Giani* also refers to an academic degree in Punjabi literature.

The Sikh scripture explains *giani* as someone who is spiritually wise. By first posing a question, "What is the nature of the spiritual people [*gianis*]?" Guru Nanak then says, "They are self-realized; they understand Waheguru. By the Guru's grace, they contemplate Him; such spiritual people are honoured in Waheguru's court."[335] Guru Teg Bahadur, the ninth Guru, also describes the qualities of a *giani*: "They are neither afraid of anyone stating the truth [in the *Sri Guru Granth Sahib*], nor do they scare anyone. Listen, O my mind, call such a person a giani (spiritually wise)."[336]

The prerequisite to being a giani is an intensive course of study and evaluation at an academic or religious institute. A giani will have thorough knowledge of the spiritual teachings in the *Sri Guru Granth Sahib* and the ability to translate the words of the sacred text into simple, everyday language. Many *gianis* in the Sikh diaspora can communicate in the language of their adopted country, but this is not always the case.

- *Granthi:* The curator and reader of the *Sri Guru Granth Sahib* in a gurdwara is known as a *granthi*. This name is of Sanskrit origin, meaning a "relator" or "narrator." To be appointed as a granthi, one must be amritdhari (initiated) and a practicing Sikh as per the *Sikh Rehat Maryada* (code of conduct), be able to read the *Sri Guru Granth Sahib* with proper punctuation and pronunciation, and have knowledge of and the ability to perform religious ceremonies in the gurdwara. The ability to perform *keertan* (singing sabads) and *katha* (verbal discourse of the scriptures) are additional sought-after qualifications. Guru

---

[335] *SGGS* 24: pranavat naanak giaanee kaisaa hoi. aap pachhaanai boojhai soi. gur parasaadh kare beechaar. so giaanee dharageh paravaan. ਪ੍ਰਣਵਤਿ ਨਾਨਕ ਗਿਆਨੀ ਕੈਸਾ ਹੋਇ ॥ ਆਪੁ ਪਛਾਣੈ ਬੂਝੈ ਸੋਇ ॥ ਗੁਰ ਪਰਸਾਦਿ ਕਰੇ ਬੀਚਾਰੁ ॥ ਸੋ ਗਿਆਨੀ ਦਰਗਹ ਪਰਵਾਣੁ ॥

[336] *SGGS* 1427: bhai kaahoo kau dhet neh neh bhai maanat aan. kahu naanak sun re manaa giaanee taeh bakhaan. ਭੈ ਕਾਹੂ ਕਉ ਦੇਤ ਨਹਿ ਨਹਿ ਭੈ ਮਾਨਤ ਆਨ ॥ ਕਹੁ ਨਾਨਕ ਸੁਨਿ ਰੇ ਮਨਾ ਗਿਆਨੀ ਤਾਹਿ ਬਖਾਨਿ ॥

Arjan, the fifth Guru, appointed Baba Buddha, the first *granthi* at Darbar Sahib on September 1, 1604, and the position has continued since.

- *Raagi:* A person who sings sabads, the ritual called *keertan,* in *raags* (melodic format), is called a *raagi,* also spelled *ragi. Keertan,* also spelled *keertan,* which is derived from the root *kirat* ("praise,") is an integral part of the Sikh religion that involves different musical instruments. *Keertan* stimulates the subconscious mind to feel the divine presence during the singing. Guru Nanak, the founder of Sikhi, recited his own sabads as Bhai Mardana, his constant companion during his prolonged preaching odysseys, played *rabab* or *rubab,* a lute-like musical instrument originating from central Afghanistan. *Rabab* or *rubab* is an Arabic word—from *rūḥ,* meaning "soul," and *bab,* meaning "door or gateway," together symbolizing the ancient instrument as the "gateway to one's soul." These days, most of the *raagis* generally play a harmonium, also called a melodeon, a keyboard instrument much like a traditional pump organ but smaller and more portable. It produces music by blowing air through reeds that are tuned to different pitches.

246. Do Sikhs use a rosary for meditation?

The rosary or string of prayer beads is called *mala* in Punjabi. While beads are among the earliest personal ornaments, and ostrich shell beads in Africa date to 10,000 BCE, the exact origin of prayer beads is uncertain. Their use can be traced back to Hindu prayers in India sometime in the third century before the Common Era.

In the Indian subcontinent, mystics and savants have regularly used rosaries as a meditative tool. The typical use for the rosary appears to be to keep track of how many prayers have been said, with a minimal amount of conscious effort, which allows more significant attention to the prayer. There are references to the rosary in the Sikh scripture in different contexts, but its use is entirely a personal choice, and there is no religious mandate.

In Sikhi, the sincerity of prayer is more important than performing a ceremonial ritual to impress others. *SGGS* talk about those who use rosaries without devotional worship of Waheguru. The fifteenth-century saint Bhagat Kabir says, "Without real meditation on Waheguru's name, applying ceremonial ritual marks on the forehead, holding rosaries in the hands, and wearing religious robes are nothing more than empty rituals. Don't treat Waheguru like a toy and play games with the One."[337]

---

[337] *SGGS* 1158: maathe tilak hath maalaa baanaa(n). logan raam khilaunaa jaanaa(n). ਮਾਥੇ ਤਿਲਕੁ ਹਥਿ ਮਾਲਾ ਬਾਨਾਂ ॥ ਲੋ ਗਨ ਰਾਮੁ ਖਿਲਾਉਨਾ ਜਾਨਾਂ ॥

PART VIII

The Sikh Psyche

CHAPTER 24

Sikh Home and Sikh Homeland

Every person desires and has a right to have shelter over their head. Many international conventions, including the Universal Declaration of Human Rights, enshrine as fundamental the right to adequate housing. Unfortunately, despite this recognition, worldwide, more than a billion people lack safe and sufficient shelter. That number stands at more than 1.7 million people in Canada, and at least twenty-five thousand people are "chronically homeless."[338]

"Home sweet home." "Home is where the heart is." These well-known expressions indicate that home is somewhere desirable and that it also exists in the imagination as much as in a particular physical location. From historical origins in the Panjab region, in the northern part of the Indian subcontinent, the Sikh population has dispersed to pretty much every country in the world. Hence, Sikhs can identify with multiple homelands. Their homes and homelands can span national boundaries. This chapter explores Sikhs' sense of belonging and identifies their multiple ties to many nations, often to more than one "home."

---

[338] Office of the United Nations High Commissioner for Human Rights, *The Right to Adequate Housing*, Fact Sheet No. 21 (Geneva: OHCHR/UN-Habitat, 2014); Canadian Human Rights Commission, "Statement—A Fundamental Right: CHRC Welcomes National Housing Strategy Legislation," April 12, 2019, https://www.chrc-ccdp.gc.ca/eng/content/statement-fundamental-humnan-right-chrc-welcomes-national-housing-strategy-legislation.

247. Did the Sikhs ever have their own country?

For almost the first half of the nineteenth century, Sikhs had their own nation—with its own government and a specific territory. It was called "Sikh Khalsa Raj, Sarkar-a-Khalsa, or the Punjabi Sikh Empire." The Sikh Empire was a significant power in the Indian subcontinent. Established under the leadership of Maharaja Ranjit Singh, it was the only secular empire in the region. It was the collection of twelve autonomous Sikh *misls* (confederacies), and the empire existed from 1799 to 1849—not long after the death of Maharaja Ranjit Singh—when the British Raj annexed it.

By the 1830s, the Sikh Empire extended from the Khyber Pass in the west to western Tibet in the east and from Mithankot in the south to Kashmir in the north.[339] The religious demography of the Sikh Empire was 73 percent Muslim, 23 percent Hindu, 3 percent Sikh, and 1 percent other. The population was 3.5 million. The empire was the last major region of the Indian subcontinent to be annexed by the British Raj. To provide some historical context, compared to the Sikh Empire with 3.5 million people, the population of the United States in 1790 was 3.9 million, and Canada's population at the time of Confederation in 1867 was three million.

The foundations of the Sikh Empire can be traced to as early as 1707, the year of Emperor Aurangzeb's death and the start of the downfall of the Mughal Empire. Banda Singh Bahadur, a Sikh commander, defeated Mughal forces and established the Sikh Raj (kingdom) from 1710 to 1716. With the Mughal forces significantly weakened and demoralized, the Sikh army, assembled under the name Dal Khalsa, led expeditions against them and the Afghans in the west. This led to the growth of the military, which eventually split into different *misls*, semi-independent confederacies. Each of these confederacies controlled different areas and cities. For more than thirty years, from 1762 to 1799, the Sikh commanders of the confederacies became independent warlords.

---

[339] Mithankot is a city located on the west bank of the Indus River (now in Pakistan), a short distance downstream from its junction with the Panjnad River.

The formation of the empire began with the capture of Lahore, by Ranjit Singh, from its Afghan ruler, Ahmed Shah Durrani, in 1758, and the subsequent and progressive expulsion of Afghans from Punjab, by defeating them in the Afghan-Sikh wars, followed by the unification of the separate Sikh *misls*. Ranjit Singh was proclaimed the maharaja of Punjab on April 12, 1801 (to coincide with Vaisakhi, the Sikh New Year festival), creating a unified political state. Sahib Singh Bedi, a descendant of Guru Nanak, conducted the coronation. The Sikh Empire was divided into four provinces: Lahore, which became the Sikh capital, Multan, Peshawar, and Kashmir.

Ranjit Singh had risen to power in a very short period, from being leader of a single *misl* to finally becoming the maharaja (great ruler) of Punjab. He began to modernize his army, using the latest training as well as new weapons and artillery. To modernize his army on European lines, he first engaged some deserters from the army of the East India Company and then recruited French, Britons, Greeks, Italians, Americans, and Eurasians as well. After Ranjit Singh's unexpected death in 1839, internal bickering and political mismanagement weakened the empire.

After the assassinations of Ranjit Singh's first three successors, Ranjit Singh's son Duleep Singh came to power in September 1843, at the age of five. His mother, Rani Jinda, became regent on his behalf. Her growing power and influence were perceived as a threat to the British, and they imprisoned and exiled her. Duleep Singh was removed from Panjab and forced to surrender or "gift" the world's largest cut diamond, known as the Koh-i-Noor diamond, to Queen Victoria. Duleep Singh was raised in a Christian household in England. With no family or other support, his Sikh identity was erased, and he converted to Christianity at the age of fifteen. The threat posed by Duleep Singh to the British Raj meant that his life was lived under scrutiny—and his movements were tightly controlled. Duleep Singh was only permitted to return to India on two occasions: the first was to bring his mother out of exile to live with him in Britain, and the second time was to take her body to India for her last rites. Duleep Singh eventually converted back to Sikhi and died in Paris.[340] The Sikh kingdom was never reclaimed. (Source: Manjit Singh Sidhu, *History of Punjab*, Modern Publishers, Delhi, 2008)

248. What is Khalistan?

"Khalistan" is an ideal name given to an independent Sikh state that some Sikhs want to reclaim from India. As discussed in the previous answer, Sikhs had their own independent country until it was annexed by the British Empire (Raj) in 1849. Not long after Maharaja Ranjit Singh's death, his wife, Rani Jinda, was imprisoned, and their son Duleep Singh was apprehended by the British and taken to England in 1854.

Although the Sikh Empire died with the rise of the British Raj, the idea of Sikh independence was not discarded; it was merely mothballed. It lived on in the collective memory of Sikhs through their prayers. The words "*Raj Karega Khalsa*," often attributed to Guru Gobind Singh, literally mean "the Khalsa shall rule," which became the rallying cry for Sikh sovereignty during the persecution Sikhs endured under the Mughals in the eighteenth century. Later, in the wake of British dominance in Punjab, the words would become part of the Sikh daily prayer, and they continue to be recited today.

Leading up to the partition of India and Pakistan in 1947, there was considerable lobbying for some sort of autonomous area where Sikhs could "experience the glow of freedom." The fact that there had once been a Sikh empire with its own governing administration, a standing army, and identifiable borders fueled hope that Sikh independence, at least as a concept, could be resurrected.

In October 1971, the call for an independent Sikh nation—Khalistan—came from a seemingly unlikely source. Having grown dissatisfied with the prospects for real reform in Punjab from the Indian government, Jagjit Singh Chauhan, a London-based medical doctor who had served in the late 1960s as deputy speaker and finance minister for

---

[340] https://www.npg.org.uk/collections/search/person/mp18775/maharaja-duleep-singh.

the Punjab Assembly, abruptly proclaimed an independent Khalistan in a half-page advertisement in the *New York Times* and asked for United Nations recognition. The ad made a moderate splash—enough that Chauhan could get a hearing from a few American politicians and attract a certain amount of Sikh support, financial and otherwise.

After moving back to India for a few years in the late 1970s, Chauhan once again relocated to London in 1980, but not before hoisting the Khalistan flag on March 23, 1980, in Anandpur Sahib. By June 16 of that year, he had left the country and declared himself president-in-exile of the Republic of Khalistan. He continued his crusade with lukewarm support within the Sikh diaspora.

In 1982, Sikhs in Punjab launched a peaceful agitation for their religious rights and some regional autonomy. Meanwhile, government-directed police clamped down on a spreading civil disobedience movement, which would last for almost two years. They saw more than thirty thousand Sikhs arrested for exercising their right to peaceful protest. Unfortunately, this resulted in India sending armed forces into Darbar Sahib (the Golden Temple) and thirty-eight other gurdwaras, killing thousands of pilgrims on June 6, 1984. Sikhs revolted and called for an independent "Khalistan."

"Punjab was the arena of one of the first major armed conflicts of postcolonial India. During its deadliest decade, as many as 250,000 people were killed," [Preface xi], writes Malika Kaur.[341]

Does Khalistan still matter? To many, it does—and this remains an issue that must be decided by those most affected by the change it would augur: the people of Punjab.

---

[341]   Kaur, Malika. "Faith, Gender, and Activism in Punjab Conflict." *The Wheat Fields Still Whisper*. Palgrave Macmillan, 1st ed. 2019 (January 14, 2020).

249. When and why did Sikhs decide to migrate to different parts of the world?

Leaving the familiarity of one's home is not an easy decision to make. A common belief is that people relocate for economic opportunities or to join their families. However, many other factors may trigger a person's move from their place of birth to another country. Many people migrate to escape conflict, persecution, terrorism, or human rights violations. Some might move in response to natural disasters, adverse climate change, or other environmental factors. According to statistics released by the United Nations on September 17, 2019, "In 2019, the number of migrants reached an estimated 272 million."[342]

Let's examine Sikh migration to countries that today have a significant Sikh population. These are all English-speaking countries that share common cultural and historical ties. Above all, they are a beacon of democracy, much closer to the Sikh ethos. The listing is in order of population.

- *United Kingdom:* The relationship between the Sikhs and Britain has been tumultuous at best, and it has been impacted significantly by the effects of colonialism. The first known Sikh subject in Britain was taken there forcefully by the British, Maharaja Duleep Singh (September 4, 1838—October 22, 1893), son of Maharaja Ranjit Singh. From 1880 onward, Sikh soldiers from the Indian Army were regularly brought to London for various parades and displays. Sikh regiments paraded for Queen Victoria's Golden Jubilee in 1887, her Diamond Jubilee in 1897, and the coronation of King Edward VII in 1902. A small number of Sikhs started to arrive at the beginning of the twentieth century. The first gurdwara in London was built in 1911.

    Today, the United Kingdom has an established and thriving Sikh community. The Sikh population as per the 2011 census

---

[342]   United Nations, https://www.un.org/en.

was 432,429, comprising 420,196 in England, 2,962 in Wales, 9,055 in Scotland, and 216 in Northern Ireland. Early in 2020, the Sikh Federation UK estimated "approximately 700,000–800,000 ethnic Sikhs in the U.K."[343]

- *Canada:* Punjab was annexed by the East India Company and incorporated into British India in 1849. That offered an opportunity for Sikh soldiers to travel throughout the British Empire. In 1897, Captain Kesur Singh and a group of Sikh officers arrived in Vancouver, Canada, on the *Empress of India*. They were on their way to Queen Victoria's Diamond Jubilee celebrations in England. The legend goes that they fell in love with the Canadian landscape. After returning to India, they encouraged Sikhs to use their British citizenship right to come to Canada. By 1908, about five thousand Sikhs had moved to Canada. Most of them were British Indian Army veterans.

  These first immigrants faced institutionalized racism. In 1908, to restrict South Asian immigrants, a "continuous journey regulation" was adopted by the Canadian government. The regulation was challenged on several occasions, most significantly in 1914, when wealthy Sikh merchant Gurdit Singh Sirhali chartered the *Komagata Maru* to sail to Vancouver with 376 prospective immigrants (340 Sikhs, twenty-four Muslims, and twelve Hindus). The ship arrived at the Vancouver Harbor on May 23, 1914, but the voyagers were not permitted to disembark. They remained on the ship for two months while the legality of the continuous journey regulation was challenged in the courts. The Supreme Court of British Columbia upheld the legislation, and the *Komagata Maru* was escorted out of Vancouver Harbor on July 23, 1914. When the ship landed in Calcutta, twenty of its passengers were shot by British Indian police and troops as they tried to disembark.

  Between 1910 and 1920, only 112 Indian immigrants entered Canada. In 1944, the Canadian census shows that

---

[343] *Sikh Siyasat News*, January 26, 2020.

there were 1,756 Canadian Sikhs. In 1967, Canada changed its immigration criteria, establishing a points system by which specific attributes—education level and facility with English or French, for example—were stressed in determining suitability. Canada was facing a shortage of skilled labor, and it began to draw from the non-European work pool. Sikhs came by the tens of thousands. In 2022, the Canadian Sikh population is estimated to exceed 750,000. My own family has deep roots in Canada, mainly through my wife, Surinder Kaur. Her grandfather, Inder Singh Dhaliwal, came to Canada in 1904, and after living in Vancouver for a year, he moved to California.

- *United States of America*: On April 6, 1899, the *San Francisco Chronicle* announced the arrival of four Sikh men who were allowed to enter the United States. This is the first record of South Asian pioneers in California. As in Canada, they faced a hostile environment in California. The early Sikh settlers predominantly came from farming backgrounds from Punjab. Like Canadian Sikh immigrants, many of the early pioneers in the United States had served in the British Indian Army and police in India. Their primary route to California was via Canada. Although the United States does not track residents of Asian origin by religious faith, it is estimated that the United States is home to more than half a million Sikhs. In the 2020 US Census, the Sikhs were counted as a separate ethnic group.

- *Australia*: A former British colony, like Canada, Australia has a tumultuous history. Colonization had a devastating impact on the continent's Indigenous people, who have lived on this land for thousands of years. Captain James Cook's possession of the east coast of Australia for the British Crown in 1770 and his subsequent report inspired British authorities to establish a "penal colony" in 1788. It appears that some Sikhs arrived in the late 1830s. Like those of numerous other faiths, they were part of the penal transport of convicts to New South Wales, which consisted of Queensland and Victoria. The 1857 census shows that there were 277 Sikhs and Hindus (but mostly Sikhs) living in Australia. According to Sikh.com.au, which was created by Sikhs in Australia, "Beer Singh Johal and Narain Singh Heyer are identified arriving in 1895 & 1898, respectively."[344] The 2016 census identified 125,000 Sikhs living in Australia.

---

[344] Sikh.com.au.

CHAPTER 25

Health, Wealth, and Happiness

We live in a world where happiness is associated with economic well-being. However, if there were a direct correlation between the two, then every wealthy person would be happy—and everyone who is less financially well off would be unhappy. However, that does not appear to be the case. The link between wealth and happiness is good health. One can live without wealth, but it is impossible to survive without good health. Let us look around. In 2020, the COVID-19 pandemic put all of us on edge. Wealth was not the focus anymore; instead, health became our primary concern, though there is a correlation between good health and economic well-being.

Wealth alone can never make a person happy. Guru Arjan, the fifth Sikh Guru, writes, "Contentment is not found chasing after material wealth because we humans are never satisfied; those earning a thousand run after a hundred thousand, and those making a hundred thousand are chasing a million, and so on."[345] This chapter explores fundamental questions of wealth versus happiness in our lives.

---

[345] *SGGS* 278: sahas khaTe lakh kau uTh dhaavai. ਸਹਸ ਖਟੇ ਲਖ ਕਉ ਉਠਿ ਧਾਵੈ ॥

250. Life is short. Is it all right to enjoy life if you don't hurt others?

Life is short, and the right to enjoy life is a fundamental one. Research from the United Kingdom appears to confirm a direct relationship between enjoyment and length of life. A study of ten thousand people aged fifty to one hundred was conducted over nine years (2002–2011) by Professor Andrew Steptoe and his team at University College, London, as part of the university's English Longitudinal Study of Ageing. The researchers' study suggests that "those who enjoy life the most are three times more likely to live a little longer than those who enjoy it the least." The study also found that "one in six people in England aged over 50 were socially isolated,"[346] which implies that social interaction is essential to leading a happy and satisfying life.

The *SGGS* takes us on a pleasant journey of a different sort, which has the benefit of longevity—though that is not the target of life—and provides peace, happiness, and contentment. Guru Nanak says, "O mortal, you came here to earn a profit [spiritual gain]. What useless activities are you attached to? Your life-night is coming to its end."[347] The profit the Guru is talking about here is to make a spiritual gain and bring your life closer to the Creator. Thus, any activity you undertake should help you move closer to that destination, one step at a time. To achieve that goal, Guru Nanak provides a road map: "Surrender your mind and body to the Creator, your friend—this will give you the most exquisite pleasure."[348]

This does not mean you should withdraw from the world and lock yourself up in the basement or cellar, as my British friends call it. Surrendering your mind and body is to accept Waheguru's will and indulge in selfless service. It is identifying the individual will with the

---

[346] Hannah Richardson, "Enjoyment of Life 'Key to Living Longer,'" BBC News, October 15, 2012, para. 1 and second-last para., https://www.bbc.com/news/education-19926775.

[347] *SGGS* 43: praanee too(n) aaiaa laahaa lain. ਪ੍ਰਾਣੀ ਤੂੰ ਆਇਆ ਲਾਹਾ ਲੈਣਿ ॥ ਲਗਾ ਕਿਤੁ ਕੁਫਕੜੇ ਸਭ ਮੁਕਦੀ ਚਲੀ ਰੈਣਿ ॥

[348] *SGGS* 1410: tan man dheejai sajanaa aaisaa hasan saar. ਤਨੁ ਮਨੁ ਦੀਜੈ ਸਜਣਾ ਐਸਾ ਹਸਣੁ ਸਾਰ ॥

divine will. Laughing, dancing, and jumping around in happiness is part of life, and Guru Nanak addresses this as follows: "Dancing and bouncing around can be a feeling of intense excitement and happiness. O Nanak, the minds beholden to the fear and the presence of Waheguru are also filled with the love of Waheguru."[349]

Thus, the key to real happiness and enjoyment is not drinking, dancing, and indulging in potentially unethical activities. Instead, one strives to realize the divine presence within oneself while leading a purposeful life. Real happiness produces harmony through an integrated development of human personality and controlling impulses, desires, and thoughts. Absolute pleasure recognizes the Divine in all and how one is no longer separated from the Almighty. If divinity, progress, and truth are not realized in human existence, then the very purpose of one's life is defeated. Guru Nanak warns of unethical behaviour: "Living your life for eating, drinking, and laughing is useless."[350] The Guru emphasizes that real enjoyment comes from constant remembrance of the Creator and selfless service of humanity—all else is fleeting. With worldly pleasure comes pain, and true happiness is a state beyond any pleasure. Guru Amar Das, the third Guru of the Sikhs, cautions us to be vigilant: "Set fire to such rituals and ceremonies that lead you away from beloved God."[351]

Yes, life is short, but let's make the best of it. For Sikhs, making the best of it means focusing on the intangible joys that one experiences through meditation and living a Sikhi-informed life. The enjoyment of life comes from living in harmony, love, and restraint.

251. What is the state of sehaj?

There is a concept in Sikhi called "the state of *sehaj*," which is the state of realization and awareness of Waheguru.[352] People in the state of sehaj

---

[349] *SGGS* 465: nachan kudhan man kaa chaau. ਨਚਣੁ ਕੁਦਣੁ ਮਨ ਕਾ ਚਾਉ ॥

[350] *SGGS* 351: khaanaa peenaa hasanaa baadh. ਖਾਣਾ ਪੀਣਾ ਹਸਣਾ ਬਾਦਿ ॥

[351] *SGGS* 590: jaalau aaisee reet jit mai piaaraa veesarai. ਜਾਲਉ ਐਸੀ ਰੀਤਿ ਜਿਤੁ ਮੈ ਪਿਆਰਾ ਵੀਸਰੈ ॥

[352] Sikhnet.com: Can ordinary people experience a state of grace?

experience ultimate bliss and are content with their lives. They are aware of the presence of Waheguru's light within. This state is only possible through the practice of *Naam Simran* or *Japna* ("remembering Waheguru" or "calling Waheguru to mind") and by the grace of the Guru. Regardless of gender, social status, or ethnicity, grace is available to all people.

The Sikh Gurus taught that spirituality is not limited to any one group. The *Sri Guru Granth Sahib* is composed of verses from the Sikh Gurus, bards, and saints from many different backgrounds and castes. These include bhagats Ravidas and Kabir, who were from the "lowest" of the so-called castes for whom Hinduism taught that spirituality or redemption was impossible. Kabir wrote, "Whosoever sings or listens to the name of God with focused consciousness, there is no doubt, in the end, they will attain the highest spiritual status."[353]

Another belief that the Sikh Gurus contested was that spirituality was only possible for a priestly class or those who abandoned the world searching for Waheguru. The Gurus declared that there would be no priesthood in Sikhi, and any Sikh could lead services or address the congregation. Family life was encouraged, and the Gurus taught that abandoning one's family and renouncing the world to find Waheguru was, in fact, counterproductive.

All this having been said, the people who attain the state of sehaj live far more than just "ordinary" lives. They live according to spiritual discipline and are driven by a thirst to experience Waheguru. They live a life of service to the Creator and the world and inspire countless others. So, while "ordinary" folks can certainly experience Divine and the state of sehaj, the experience transforms them into something extraordinary.

252. What is happiness?

Before I answer this question, let's be sure to understand what exactly is meant by happiness. Defining happiness and how to attain it "has kept

---

[353] *SGGS* 335: koiee gaavai ko sunai har naamaa chit lai. kahu kabeer sa(n)saa nahee a(n)t param gat pai.
ਕੋਈ ਗਾਵੈ ਕੋ ਸੁਣੈ ਹਰਿ ਨਾਮਾ ਚਿਤੁ ਲਾਇ ॥ ਕਹੁ ਕਬੀਰ ਸੰਸਾ ਨਹੀ ਅੰਤਿ ਪਰਮ ਗਤਿ ਪਾਇ ॥

our best minds busy for as long as we have had the conscious faculty to dream, hope, or be disappointed," wrote I. J. Singh on SikhNet.[354] He continued:

> For happiness, Aristotle prescribed a triad of pleasure, honour, and self-sufficiency. Humans, he claimed, feel pleasure when they do "good," and they pursue honour to feel satisfied that what they do is good. This sounds [like] somewhat tautological and circular reasoning. But this is how we reassure ourselves that we are living up to the full potential of our virtues. Happiness then is the sense of living life to its fullest potential.

Correlations exist between happiness and social, economic, and personal milestones, but mixed results face us: wealth, beauty, and fleeting pleasure are unrelated to general happiness, as are severe illness or marriage. One must then reject the idea of collecting toys to ensure happiness, as many people do. Cultural psychobabble continues to bless us with "how to" books on happiness, but they seem to be of limited value. Just peruse *Psychology Today* to see the many ways, behavioural and pharmacological, that the human mind has invented to find happiness.[355] According to I. J. Singh, in 2013, Arthur C. Brooks, president of the American Enterprise Institute, wrote an op-ed in the *New York Times* in which he "boiled down our age-old debate on happiness to a few salient human requirements that make a stable 4-legged stool: *faith, family, friendship, and work.* Sounds simple, but, as with most matters that seem self-evident, the devil is in the details."[356]

Inspired by Singh's article, let's look at happiness from the Sikh perspective. The *SGGS* is, in its essence, a manual for living a happy life. The Gurus taught that true happiness does not come from material things; it is a state of being arrived at when one lives in harmony with

---

[354] I. J. Singh, "Chasing Happiness," SikhNet.com, December 12, 2014, para. 4, https://www.sikhnet.com/news/chasing-happiness.

[355] Ibid., paras. 5 and 8.

[356] Ibid, para. 13.

the universe. "While we see happiness in owning successful businesses, mansions, costly means of conveyances, food delicacies, flashy clothes, sightseeing, and indulgence in sexual relationships, these are false," says Guru Nanak.[357] In another verse, Guru Nanak says, "The great giver has given the intoxicating drug of falsehood. People are intoxicated, and they have forgotten death, and they have fun and are happy for a few days."[358] The *SGGS* teaches us that to get rid of this falsehood and enjoy everlasting happiness, we need to divorce the five vices: lust, anger, greed, emotional attachment, and ego. "Hundreds of thousands of princely pleasures are enjoyed if the true Guru [the Divine] bestows His glance of grace," says Guru Arjan.[359]

253. Is it necessary to believe in a religion to be happy?

Todd B. Kashdan, a psychology professor at George Mason University, has written extensively on religion and happiness. In his article on the topic written in 2015, [360] he cites the Chicago-based National Opinion Research Center's data collected on church attendance and happiness ratings from 34,706 people from 1972 until 1996. This study indicated that the more frequently people go to church, the happier they report their lives to be, but Kashdan writes about how this may not always be true:

---

[357] *SGGS* 16, 17, and 42: baabaa hor khaanaa khusee khuaar. ਬਾਬਾ ਹੋਰ ਖਾਣਾ ਖੁਸੀ ਖੁਆਰ॥ and many more *sabads*.

[358] *SGGS* 14: amal galolaa kooR kaa dhitaa dhevanahaar. matee maran visaariaa khusee keetee dhin chaar. ਅਮਲੁ ਗਲੋਲਾ ਕੂੜ ਕਾ ਦਿਤਾ ਦੇਵਣਹਾਰਿ ॥ ਮਤੀ ਮਰਣੁ ਵਿਸਾਰਿਆ ਖੁਸੀ ਕੀਤੀ ਦਿਨ ਚਾਰਿ ॥

[359] *SGGS* 44: lakh khuseeaa paatisaaheeaa je satigur nadhar karei. ਲਖ ਖੁਸੀਆ ਪਾਤਿਸਾਹੀਆ ਜੇ ਸਤਿਗੁਰੁ ਨਦਰਿ ਕਰੇਇ ॥

[360] Todd B. Kashdan, "Does Being Religious Make Us Happy?" *Psychology Today* (blog), October 7, 2015, https://www.psychologytoday.com/us/blog/curious/201510/does-being-religious-make-us-happy.

Ed Diener and his colleagues dissected a Gallup World Poll of 455,104 individuals from 154 nations. What they found was that in healthy nations (where basic needs are being met, where people feel safe walking home alone at night, etc.), there was no advantage to being religious—both religious and nonreligious people reported feeling respected and socially supported, and as a result, both reported being happy. But in unhealthy nations, religion offered an advantage in terms of an uptick in well-being. It ends up that your life circumstances influence the presence and benefits of being religious.

Kashdan concludes that these findings highlight how "clinging" to religion shouldn't necessarily be seen in a negative light. Happiness is fleeting, but the profound meaning is akin to a stable operating system for working through adversity and appreciating abundance. It is important to know that religion is only one path to well-being, and a path that, on average, provides only slight assurance that well-being is a given.

With this research in the background, I turn to the Sikh faith. Sikhs are no different than the people in the study referenced above. Ask Sikhs how they feel, and often the response is "Chardi kala"—in high spirits. For Sikhs, a happy life results naturally from practicing the three underlying principles of the Sikh faith I have talked about continually: Divine-remembrance, selfless service, and honest living. And, supporting the findings described by Kashdan, many Sikhs indeed turn to religion to find peace within when they are under stress or are facing a tragedy. This is a human and natural response. Faith is very personal, and only the practitioners know how happy they are. I can personally attest that religious belief is undoubtedly a source of my peace and happiness. Isn't that what counts?

CHAPTER 26

A Grab Bag of Questions

Over the years, I have been asked many, many different questions about my faith—by Sikhs as well as non-Sikhs. I always say, "There is no such thing as a stupid question." The previous twenty chapters covered questions that are relevant to diverse aspects of Sikhi—from Gurus and gurdwaras to Sikh customs, ethics, and politics. However, when I put this book together, I was left with a few "outlier" questions that resisted categorization but also demanded answers. They are collected in this final chapter.

254. How do Sikhs handle doubt?

Faith and doubt do not mix. It is one or the other; there is nothing in between. If a belief or practice does not feel right or does not make sense, we need to pay attention to why. Guru Nanak inspired people to question blind rituals and insisted that religion does not mean we leave critical thinking at the door. Faith must be accompanied by wisdom. "Why do you waver, O mortal being? The Creator shall always protect you. The One who created you shall also provide you nourishment for growth and survival," writes Guru Arjan, the fifth Guru.[361]

---

[361] *SGGS* 724: too kaahe ddoleh praaneeaa tudh raakhaigaa sirajanahaar. jin paidhais too keeaa soie dhei aadhaar. ਤੂ ਕਾਹੇ ਡੋਲਹਿ ਪ੍ਰਾਣੀਆ ਤੁਧੁ ਰਾਖੈਗਾ ਸਿਰਜਣਹਾਰੁ ॥ ਜਿਨਿ ਪੈਦਾਇਸਿ ਤੂ ਕੀਆ ਸੋਈ ਦੇਇ ਆਧਾਰੁ ॥

It is natural as human beings to have doubt, whether it is about the spiritual path one is on or even the very existence of God. When those doubts arise, it is important to examine them. The Sikh faith teaches that Waheguru is not an idea to be believed or not; it is an experience to be had. Waheguru can be felt and seen through meditation on *Naam* (God's name). Our spiritual path should bring us spiritual experiences and allow us to feel Waheguru's presence all the time. If this is not happening, then we should examine our practice to see where we could improve.

There will, however, be some things that we must temporarily take on trust and accept that we will come to understand them in due course. Trust is born from experience. Because my faith has been an enormously positive force in my life, when doubts arise, I continue with my practice and turn to the *Sri Guru Granth Sahib* with the firm belief that my doubts will be relieved.

255. Are there denominations or sects in Sikhism?

Sikhi is still a relatively young faith and does not have formally recognized denominations. However, several sects (*sampradayas*) do exist among Sikhs.

The *Namdharis* do not follow the Khalsa code of conduct and differ from the mainstream Sikhs in the belief that the succession of person-gurus did not end with Guru Gobind Singh; instead, they consider their sect leader as their Guru.

Another sect is Sikhi is the *Nihangs*. They dress in more traditional attire and are distinguishable by their blue robes, large swords and spears, and decorated turbans surmounted by steel quoits. A Sikh scholar, Dr. Balwant Singh Dhillon, says, "Etymologically, the word Nihang in Persian means an alligator, sword and pen but the characteristics of Nihangs seem to stem more from the Sanskrit word *nihshank,* which means without fear, unblemished, pure, carefree and indifferent to worldly gains and comfort. In its strictest sense, they observe the Khalsa code of conduct and do not profess any allegiance to an earthly master..."

Instead of saffron, they hoist a blue Nishan Sahib (flag) atop their shrines."[362]

There are also two religious groups that do not affiliate themselves with Sikhi, though they physically resemble Sikhs. The Sant Nirankaris and Radhaswamis are led by individuals who appear to be Sikhs (recognized by their turbans and unshorn hair), but they don't call themselves Sikhs. The Akal Takhat has excommunicated the Nirankaris, and their influence has diminished.

256. Will the Sikh faith change over time?

Sikhi is made up of philosophy, spiritual teachings, and cultural and religious practices. The *Sri Guru Granth Sahib* enshrines the faith teachings, and the *Sikh Rehat Maryada* enshrines the practices, customs, and traditions. The faith teachings will not change over time because it is forbidden to change the *SGGS*. However, the traditions and practices have changed and may continue to change over time. For example, to marry according to Sikh rites, it's now mandatory to walk around the *Sri Guru Granth Sahib* after each lav (vow) and acknowledge acceptance of the message in the spiritual verse by bowing down and touching the forehead on the floor. However, until the later part of the twentieth century, the couples did not walk around and sat still in front of the *SGGS* while the lavan (vows) were read.

257. Why is participation in religions, including Sikhi, declining?

In *Who Am I?*, Steven Reiss, a professor of psychology, identifies sixteen basic desires that motivate our behaviours and define our personalities. Writing about his book in *Huffpost* in 2015, he listed these desires as "acceptance, curiosity, eating, family, honour, idealism, independence, order, physical activity, power, romance, saving, social contact, status,

---

[362] Gopal, Navjeen: "The Indian Express," April 15, 2020.

tranquility, and vengeance."[363] He and his colleague surveyed one hundred thousand people of all backgrounds in North America, Europe, and Asia and found that everything that moves us—all human motives—expresses one or more of these sixteen basic desires.

Professor Reiss, discussing his latest book, *The 16 Strivings for God: The New Psychology of Religious Experience*, wrote: "Religion rises and falls in popularity depending on how well it satisfies our needs versus the secular alternatives. Four significant shifts in secular culture may be behind the decline in religious affiliation."[364] I quote from his article below and have added how these study conclusions relate to the Sikh community from my point of view:

➤ *Organized religion versus spirituality.* Historically, mysticism— or what some call "spirituality"—has been associated with disinterest in organized religion. More Americans than ever are saying that they are "spiritual but not religious."

• People seem to be shifting the search for meaning by looking within rather than to the heavens. This may be motivating a decline of interest in organized religion.

➤ *My take:* The Sikh faith teaches us to look within because that is where God resides. Guru Amar Das reminds us, "Oh my mind; you are the embodiment of the divine light—recognize your origin."[365] Although I have found no scientific study about the Sikh community, it is estimated that religiously nonaffiliated persons make up less than 10 percent.

➤ *Tribalism versus humanitarianism.* A common way of honouring one's ancestors is to embrace their moral code and religion. Historically, loyalty to the tribe and clan has motivated participation in organized religion.

---

[363] Steven Reiss, "Four Reasons for Decline of Religion," *Huffpost*, December 12, 2015, https://www.huffpost.com/entry/four-reasons-for-decline-_b_8778968.

[364] Ibid. Following quotes are also from this article.

[365] *SGGS* 441: man toon jot saroop hai aapanaa mool pachhaan. ਮਨ ਤੂੰ ਜੋਤਿ ਸਰੂਪੁ ਹੈ ਆਪਣਾ ਮੂਲੁ ਪਛਾਣੁ ॥

- The global economy may have significantly increased social contact among people from different cultures and religions. As we learn the similarities of people everywhere, I suggest that many of us may be less inclined to think of people like Hindus, Jews, Christians, Muslims, and Sikhs and more inclined toward thinking of people of faith as similar regardless of religious affiliation.

➢ *My take:* The trend among Sikhs is also toward globalization and interfaith activities.

➢ *Traditional versus nontraditional families.* Historically, organized religions have relied heavily on the family to raise religious children and recruit new church members. Today, we have a predominant family restructuring, with fewer than half of North American kids living in a traditional family. This change in family structure may be responsible for less successful religious training and recruitment of young people.

➢ *My take:* The percentage of traditional families among Sikhs is estimated to be around 90 percent. The Sikh community is sympathetic to children from single-parent families and makes an effort to assist them. As in Western society generally, with its high cost of living and emphasis on materialism, parents working opposite shifts or sometimes two jobs don't always have enough time to spend with their children. This may be one reason why some children grow up disconnected from faith and opt for other activities.

➢ *Trust versus the loss of confidence in institutions.* The internet has given us unprecedented access to information about our institutions, many times exposing their darker sides.

- As we learn more about our society and its institutions, we sometimes become painfully aware of hypocrisy and scandal. That may be a critical reason that confidence in many of our institutions, from businesses to schools to government, is below historical norms.

➢ *My take:* This cultural shift is relevant to the Sikh community as well. Language is the primary cause of disillusionment and youth not connecting to the faith. Almost all activities in gurdwaras are conducted in Punjabi, irrespective of location. Why would you attend a place of worship where you did not understand 70 percent of what was being said? Would I attend a school if I could not understand my teacher? I know that in Canada, Sikh youth would like to have part of the service in English. Efforts are underway in some gurdwaras to provide this service, which is a good sign.

As "seekers of truth," Sikhs must exhibit the practice of their faith through conviction and not merely by convention or ritual. Thus, the participation in Sikhi mandates a spiritually active approach to teaching through one's appearance and actions—a challenge we all share as members of humanity, no matter what religion we practice.

CHAPTER 27

Looking Back while Moving Forward

"[Generally] change in our society is incremental. Real change, enduring change, happens one step at a time," said the late Ruth Bader Ginsburg at her 1993 nomination hearing to become an Associate Justice of the US Supreme Court.[366] Her statement is entirely in line with the Sikh experience. It took hundreds of years for Sikhi to develop and prosper, one step at a time, from Guru Nanak to Guru Gobind Singh (1469–1708).

In this chapter, I reflect upon Sikhi's progress through the rearview mirror, being cognizant that if I stare too long, I will miss what is right in front of me and likely cause a devastating accident. Analyzing the current crossroads at which the Sikhs stand is not a trivial matter, and I will endeavour to examine internal and external challenges facing the Sikh community and assess whether we, as a community, are "walking the talk."

258. Looking back.

The Sikh spirit is wonderful! It does not need any proof. Sikhs are, in general, very hardworking and ambitious people. Despite many

---

[366] Joan Ruth Bader Ginsburg was an American lawyer and jurist who served as an associate justice of the Supreme Court of the United States from 1993 until her death in September 2020.

challenges, they have established themselves in virtually every part of the world. In many of those countries, members of the Sikh faith have achieved some degree of prominence. In Canada, a practicing Sikh, Jagmeet Singh, leads a major political party. Navdeep Singh Bains has been a minister of innovation, science, and industry. Harjit Singh Sajjan, formerly minister of defence, is currently the minister of international development of Canada. Tim Uppal, former minister of Democratic Institutions, was recently appointed deputy leader of the official opposition party of Canada. Madam Justice Palbinder Kaur Shergill serves on the British Columbia Supreme Court, and another Sikh, Sarbjit Singh Marwah, is a Canadian senator. In the United States, the attorney general of New Jersey, Gurbir Singh Grewal, is also a practicing Sikh. Sir Mota Singh was the first practicing Sikh appointed a British judge in 1982. Lord Justice Rabinder Singh is currently a British Court of Appeal judge and president of the Investigatory Powers Tribunal, and Inderjit Singh, the Lord Singh of Wimbledon CBE, is a member of the British House of Lords. Dr. Anarkali Kaur Honaryar is a human rights activist and politician. She was the first non-Muslim member of the National Assembly of Afghanistan and is a recipient of the UNESCO-Madanjeet Singh Prize for the Promotion of Tolerance and Non-Violence. The diaspora Sikhs have made inroads in all spheres of the world's political, economic, social, and financial institutions.

However, despite the obvious political and financial success of the Sikh community, the tenets of the Sikh faith are virtually unknown. Because Sikhs are not by nature proselytizing people, they have been largely content to operate in relative obscurity in terms of widespread knowledge of their faith. However, now more than ever, Sikhi has a vital role to play as the world struggles to find a unified way forward. Climate change, the COVID-19 pandemic, violence against women, and economic disparity are some of the greatest existential crises of our time. Sikhi teaches us to protect our environment, protect our sisters and daughters, and care for one another. Working for all of humanity's well-being is a tenet of the Sikh faith and something Sikhs pray for twice daily. Below, I examine some of the internal and external challenges facing the Sikh community that inhibit their ability to take a leadership role on the world stage.

259. What are the internal challenges for the Sikhs?

Two primary challenges faced by Sikhs are identical for all religions:

- remaining relevant in a world where material wealth takes precedence over the pursuit of spiritual enlightenment
- the universal shift away from organized religion due to skepticism and preference for individual spirituality.

There are additional challenges that are unique to the Sikh community. These include:

- *Failure in Sikh leadership:* There is no dearth of capable leaders and intellectuals in the Sikh community. The Shiromani Gurdwara Parbandhak Committee, the "mini-parliament of Sikhs," has lost the moral authority to manage Sikh institutions and guide Sikhs, due primarily to single political party control and its tainted process of electing/selecting the president and the executive committee. The process of handpicking candidates by the Shiromani Akali Dal (a dominant political party in Punjab) has completely undermined the whole purpose of establishing the SGPC in 1920. The recent Supreme Court of India's decision (September 20, 2022) to validate a separate Gurdwara Management Institution for Haryana has further eroded SGPC authority.

  In addition, the unorthodox removal and replacement of Akal Takhat Jathedars by SGPC has lowered the Akal Takhat Jathedar's independence. Dr. Dharam Singh, a Sikh scholar, says, "The religious leadership needs to realize that they are at present poor role models. The youth reject them and rebel against them. Implicitly, this rebellion is a reflection of their going astray from essential Sikh identity." Significant reform needs to occur with the structure, format, and workings of the SGPC if it is to regain credibility and assume the leadership role it was designed to take. There is also a need for every Akal Takhat Jathedar to ensure that they fulfill their role with integrity and wisdom and are guided by the teachings contained in the *Sri Guru Granth Sahib*. This requires independence from—rather than subservience to—politicians and political parties, including the Shriomani Akal Dal and SGPC. The Akal Takhat Jathedar must reflect the ideal of a saint-soldier: a fearless warrior who acts out of compassion and love rather than fear.

- *Proliferation of Derey (ਡੇਰੇ) and Babey (ਬਾਬੇ):* Baba (singular of Babey) literally means grandfather. However, Baba is also a generic term that refers to a religious leader who has their own personal following. *Dera* (singular of derey) is the generic name for the place where they hold religious services and meet with their congregants. These derey are usually located outside the influence and territory of the social space of a community. In Panjab, more than twelve thousand (Sikh and non-Sikh) derey have mushroomed, and the majority are no more than cults. Too often, these babey pray on innocent devotees who turn to them for spiritual guidance. Sadly, a failure of the Sikh leadership is partly to blame for the proliferation of these derey.

- Let's briefly examine why people are attracted to *derey* (ਡੇਰੇ) and *babey* (ਬਾਬੇ), most of which are no more than cults. These cult leaders claim they receive revelations directly from God. They have promotional teams within their derey to attract a vulnerable population. Rachel Bernstein, a cult-recovery therapist, says, "Cults are typically marketed as organizations that promote self-betterment, whether that means the promise of enlightenment or the skills to make all of your professional dreams comes true." She identifies a set of traits that make someone susceptible to joining a cult. "They want to better themselves either professionally or personally; they want a greater sense of community; and they're in a state of extreme state of vulnerability.

Having a well-grounded and practical approach is vital to counteract the influence and impact of these derey. It should be the responsibility and duty of the SGPC to develop educational programs to safeguard the collective interest of the community and guide people by disseminating information about Sikhi and providing them resources to improve their lives.

- *Lack of involvement of diaspora Sikhs:* More than five million Sikhs live outside of India. Despite concerted efforts by diaspora Sikhs to be included in the decision-making process, SGPC has failed to get them involved, thus limiting its intellectual and economic assets pool.
- *Lack of accessibility of the Sri Guru Granth Sahib*: Traditions and practices surrounding where, who, and how one can keep and read the *SGGS* have turned into social taboos that have no connection to Sikh principles. They have made the *SGGS* physically inaccessible to the average person. To be able to truly benefit from the teachings of the Gurus, one must be able to access the *SGGS* frequently. However, only the wealthy can afford the physical space in their homes dedicated solely to housing the sacred *SGGS*. Fortunately, electronic copies of the *SGGS* are now available, making it more accessible. However, this requires one to have access to a computer or smartphone. Further, due to the language of the original prose, many people are unable to understand the *SGGS* even if they do access a copy. There are dozens of inconsistent Punjabi interpretations of *SGGS* and several poorly written English translations. They are often more difficult to comprehend than the original *bani* itself. The English translations frequently rely on a Western paradigm, Christian terminology, or archaic language structures to interpret the teachings of the Gurus. These fail to accurately capture Sikh teachings. Sikh scholars need to focus on producing

accurate translations in multiple languages, which are easy for the layperson to understand.

- *Erosion of the Panjabi language:* Given the close nexus between Panjabi and Gurbani (Gurmukhi script), the declining use of Panjabi in Panjab is disheartening. The widespread use of Hindi or English in Panjabi homes has meant the diminishment of the Sikh community's ability to maintain its language. This, in turn, affects the ability of Sikh youth, even those raised in Panjab, to understand and follow the teachings of the Gurus as contained in the *SGGS*.

260. What are the external challenges for the Sikhs?

In addition to internal challenges, the Sikh community faces many external challenges. These include:

- *Political threat in India to Sikh identity and community*: Sikhs always have to be on guard for fear of annihilation by the government and a political structure that does not adequately protect minority religious rights and freedoms. "The growth of Hindu nationalism and the emergence of the BJP as the party of government poses a new threat to a distinct Sikh identity," write Professors Gurharpal Singh and Giorgio Shani.[367] Though the events of 1984 occurred more than thirty years ago, Sikhs continue to feel unsafe in a "modern India" in which divergence from the predominant religious traditions is not always viewed favourably.
- *The Sikh Gurdwara Act 1925:* British Empire annexed Panjab and the northwestern region of India in March 1849, ending the sovereignty of the Sikh Raj. Against the wishes of Sikh religious leadership, the government discreetly appointed pro-British *Mahants* (head priests or clerics) to manage many historical

---

[367] Singh Gurharpal and Giorgio Shani. 2022. *Sikh Nationalism: From a Dominant Minority to an Ethno-Religious Diaspora.* Cambridge University Press, UK (163).

gurdwaras. In 1920, Sikhs established the Shiromani Gurudwara Prabandhak Committee to educate the Sikh masses and prepare them to gain control of their religious places of worship. This led to a bloody struggle and the loss of hundreds of innocent lives, particularly at Nankana Sahib (the birthplace of Guru Nanak) in February 1921. The British India government enacted Sikh Gurdwara Act in 1925 to provide infrastructure for Shiromani Gurdwara Parbandhak Committee to exercise control over historical gurdwaras. While it is debatable whether this was necessary or even desired by the Sikhs of that time, there is clearly no justification for ongoing government control of Sikh institutions. The structure of the SGPC has become an albatross around Sikhs' necks. Politicians (irrespective of their political stripes) have exerted undue control over the SGPC elections and many other religious affairs of the Sikh community, and they have prevented the Sikhs from having a say in their own affairs. For example, the act is very clear about a five-year term limit for the board.[368] The current SGPC general body was elected in 2011. Despite demands from the Sikh community, no election date has been set by the government for almost eleven years.

- *Sikh identity in the diaspora:* Sikhs have faced numerous challenges in freely practicing their faith throughout the world, particularly in the Islamic States and some Western countries. A thriving population of 250,000 Sikhs in Afghanistan has been reduced to less than 150. In 2004, France passed a law banning religious symbols in schools. The Sikh "turban" (dastaar) was included in this ban, which has had an adverse impact on the ability of Sikhs to maintain a core part of their distinct identity. Quebec, a Canadian province, followed France and passed a law banning visible religious symbols by public servants in 2019. This Quebec law (Bill 21) has impacted dastaar-wearing Sikhs,

---

[368] Sikh Gurdwara Act 1925, section 51 Term of membership reads, "The members of the Board shall hold office for (five) years from the date of its constitution or until the constitution of a new board whichever is late."

kippah-wearing Jews, and hijab-wearing Muslim women in
Quebec. This case is heading to the Supreme Court of Canada
for a legal decision. In the United States of America, the Sikh
image is still associated with suspicion and fear because of the
misplaced identity and conflation of the Sikh dastaar with that
of Osama Bin Laden, the mastermind of the heinous 9/11 attack
on the World Trade Center in New York. This has resulted in
racist attacks on Sikhs, including the Oak Creek, Wisconsin,
massacre in which an assailant attacked congregants in a
gurdwara, killing six and injuring four on August 5, 2012.

- *Unfamiliarity by non-Sikhs*: In an April 2009 poll in *Maclean's*
magazine, only 12 percent of Canadians said they had a good
understanding of the Sikh faith. This is even more disheartening
when one realizes that Canada has one of the largest populations
of diaspora Sikhs and many Sikhs holding highly visible positions
of authority. While the diaspora Sikh community has worked
hard to improve its image, much more must be done to educate
others about our beliefs and who we are. Despite being the fifth
largest faith group globally, Sikhs are rarely included in any
textbooks about world religions. They are often overlooked by
less populous but better-known faith groups such as Bahá'í or
Taoism. The Sikh faith has universal and inclusive beliefs, but
most people know little about it.

261. Do we walk the talk?

Most people talk the talk (Sikhs and non-Sikhs alike), but they do
not walk the talk. We espouse beliefs and values, and we preach them
to others, but we fail to follow them ourselves. As Guru Nanak says,
"galee asee changeeyan, achari buriyaan—we are good at talking, poor
in action [we do not walk the talk].[369] We forget that such failings in

---

[369] *SGGS* 85—Gala(n)nee asee cha(n)geeaa aachaaree bureeaaeh - ਗਲੀ ਅਸੀ
ਚੰਗੀਆ ਆਚਾਰੀ ਬੁਰੀਆਹ ॥

behaviour ultimately result in loss of credibility and trust—two valuable commodities for a successful, meaningful, and contented life. "It's tough enough to compete with external forces without having to do battle with internal inconsistencies as well. Understanding how our actions either support or contradict our messages is critical to success, be it individual or organizational," writes Eric L. Harvey, the author of *Walk the Talk*.

Sikhi is a way of life. Being a Sikh means living your Sikhi every day. It means waking up in the morning and setting the intention to live the day in accordance with the Sikh values, such as Naam Japna (meditation and reflection on the One), vand shakna (sharing what we have with others), and kirat karni (earning an honest living). It means cultivating the five virtues or qualities of compassion (*daiya*); truth (*Satt or Sach*); contentment (*Santokh*); humility (*Nimrata* or *Gareebi*); and love (*Pyaar*). These qualities hold transformative power, and they are fundamental to human development, ethical living, and transcendence.

Living your Sikhi also means reflecting upon the day and determining if you have walked the talk. If the answer is no, then you must delve further into yourself and ask which one of the fives thieves—lust, anger, greed, attachment, or ego—swayed us from sticking to our Sikhi path. The five thieves lose their power over us when we cultivate positive qualities within ourselves.

Guru Arjan reminds us: "O mortal, you came to this earth to earn the profit of the One's Name. With what useless task are you engaged as your life is passing away?"[370]

---

[370]   *SGGS* 42: praanee too(n) aayaa laahaa lain. lagaa kit kufukhRe sabh mukdee chalee rain. ਪਰਾਣੀ ਤੂੰ ਆਇਆ ਲਾਹਾ ਲੈਇ ॥ ਲਗਾ ਕਿਤੁ ਕੁਫਕੜੇ ਸਭ ਮੁਕਦੀ ਚਲੀ ਰੈਇ ॥

EPILOGUE

The golden rule for leading a happy life is to "treat others as you would want to be treated in their place." We are all children of one Creator; hence, we are equal. None of us are superior or inferior to others by birth, gender, religion, race, or the colour of our skin. *"Manas ki jaat sabhe eke pehchanbo.* Recognize all humans as one," writes Guru Gobind Singh.[371]

Sikhi was the first world religion that supported gender equality and actively encouraged it. The Sikh scripture equalizes men and women. It talks about the strength of women:

> From a woman, a man is born; within woman, man is conceived [your mother]; to a woman, he is engaged and married [your wife]. From a woman, a woman is born [your sibling]; without a woman, there would be no one at all. Therefore, how could they be any less than men?[372]

This was written more than five hundred years ago in the *Sri Guru Granth Sahib.* It was revolutionary then, and it is still revolutionary! In Sikhi, women are equal to men in role, status, and power. As a father of two daughters and grandfather of four girls, this knowledge moves my soul.

The practice of religion must be a lived experience that uplifts us. The Sikh faith is a spiritual journey and a source of joy that one

---

[371] Dasam Granth: maanas kee jaat sabai ekai pahichaanabo. ਮਾਨਸ ਕੀ ਜਾਤਿ ਸਬੈ ਏਕੈ ਪਹਿਚਾਨਬੋ ॥

[372] SGGS 472: bha(n)dd ja(n)meeaai bha(n)dd ni(n)meeaai bha(n)dd ma(n)gan veeaahu. ਭੰਡਿ ਜੰਮੀਐ ਭੰਡਿ ਨਿੰਮੀਐ ਭੰਡਿ ਮੰਗਣੁ ਵੀਆਹੁ ॥

encounters daily. Let me take you through my journey to Sikhi. I grew up as a Sikh. I wore a dastaar growing up, and I served in the Indian Air Force with distinction. I came to Canada with my turban intact and even found a job with a turban more than half a century ago. Five months into my career, a lure of promotion made me psychologically weak, and I removed my turban. After almost a decade without my turban, on Vaisakhi Day 1981, my attitude changed.

To mark the occasion, I spoke in our gurdwara in Williams Lake, British Columbia, about the significance of the celebration. During my speech, I touched on many subjects, including the five articles of the Sikh faith. Since I was speaking in the gurdwara, I had donned a turban. Since several of our family's non-Sikh friends were in attendance, I decided to speak in English rather than Punjabi. As I spoke, I noticed John Bas, a devout Christian and a friend, listening attentively. After the speech, he approached me and said, "Gian, can we talk?"

"Why don't we eat first?" I replied, gesturing for him to join me downstairs in the langar hall, where a traditional Punjabi vegetarian meal was being served.

"Sounds good, but first, let's talk," he said.

"Sure. What's up?"

He paused for a moment and took a deep breath. "I've never seen such a phony as you, Gian."

The look on my face must have registered somewhere between amused and irritated. "Excuse me?"

"I can see your bracelet. That's fine," he said. "I can see your turban. But under the turban, I know your hair is cut. I know you trim your beard. I know you don't carry a *kirpan*."

"I'm sorry … what are you trying to say, John?"

"You've just given a very eloquent speech talking about how important these things are to your faith, and yet you don't even practice what you've just preached. If this were a church, my church, we would never have allowed you to speak."

I could have given him reasons why my actions did not match my words—solid explanations that could have served as a rationale. I could have told him that, since I was still teaching part-time at Cariboo College, I was concerned about how my students would perceive me. If I wore the five articles of my faith, would they still be able to relate to me and see past the trappings of my religion? In business, I could also have said that the turban and beard could hold me back and, in a worst-case scenario, impact my ability to provide for those I love. I could have said all of this, but I did not because he was right. I was a hypocrite—and the realization stung.

For a long time, I had known something was missing in my life. Regardless of my successes, I had felt unfulfilled, lacking, and hollow. I was a practicing Sikh, no question; every day, I had done my daily prayers for my entire life. We had placed the *Sri Guru Granth Sahib*, the Sikh scripture, in a dedicated room at home, and we read from it daily. However, I realized that by forgoing the five Ks (five articles of the Sikh faith: *kesh*, *kangha*, *kara*, *kashera*, and *kirpan*) and distancing myself from the beauty behind this most visible declaration, I had never fully embraced my own faith. This realization caused me mental pain and moral anguish. To this day, I remind myself, "Practice what you preach, Gian Singh." In 1981, after a soul-searching decade, I made my spiritual commitment and became an amritdhari Sikh.

I practice the Sikh faith because I believe in the truth of the *Sri Guru Granth Sahib* teachings. These teachings make me a better person. I am certain that other people of faith feel no differently about their own beliefs. Furthermore, as I understand it, religion is at its core about happiness and a state of "high spirits"—what Sikhs call *chardi kala*. If that is not the role of religion in our lives, we need to step back and figure out what is going wrong.

Guru Nanak taught that religious labels are meaningless if our actions and the content of our character are not virtuous. When we are born, we are simply human beings. Despite all the labels we may wear, we are all cut from the same divine cloth at our core. So, I would encourage you, dear reader, to look beyond religion and all other labels. Traditions and customs are an excellent way to stay connected to the transitory world around us, but getting caught up in superstitions makes a person weaker.

Another important lesson I would like to share from Guru Nanak's teachings is that religion must spring from compassion. Without love and compassion, religion is hypocrisy. Since God's light shines in all of creation, all of us are equal and worthy of respect. Religion must inspire us to experience that light and see it in others. If religion is a source of judgment, hatred, and division, then it hinders spiritual growth and is not being practiced correctly.

Human life is a gift and an opportunity to become one with the Creator. Guru Gobind Singh says, "Bravo to the soul of that person, who remembers the name of God on the lips and reflects [in their] mind on the war of righteousness."[373] In another exhortation, the Guru tells us, "Khalsa—a sovereign, a pure (an association of initiated Sikhs), should fight every day to conquer evil [vices like lust, anger, greed, worldly attachment, and ego]."[374] The Guru asks us to fight many battles. In these verses, the Guru is not glorifying war; instead, the battlefield referred to here is that of the mind, which is where the foremost never-ending battle occurs. In our minds, we must fight and conquer vices.

In conclusion, I would like to say that it has been a privilege to write this book. Opportunities for religious, social, and cultural dialogue are rare, and this book has become a vehicle for me to have a conversation with myself. I hope the many questions I have addressed will enrich your life with added knowledge about your neighbours. Encountering a lonely turban in your life someday may make you think about the background of this very identifiable group of friends and neighbours who pray for you every day. In this way, I hope to bring people of faith and nonbelievers alike together. The idea of empowering people started with Guru Nanak. In his dialogue with yogis (ascetics), he said, "See the camaraderie of all humanity as the highest order of yogis; by conquering your mind, you can conquer the world."[375]

My parting message for readers is to treat religion as more than just a label. I pray for prosperity for every one of you—and may Waheguru be in all your thoughts and actions!

---

[373] *Dasam Bani* 550: dhan jeeo teh ko jag mai mukh te har chit mai judh bichaarai. ਧੰਨਿ ਜੀਓ ਤਿਹ ਕੋ ਜਗ ਮੈ ਮੁਖ ਤੇ ਹਰਿ ਚਿਤ ਮੈ ਜੁਧੁ ਬਿਚਾਰੈ ॥

[374] Khalsa Rehat Nama—Bhai Nand Lal Ji—Khalsa so jo karey nit jung—ਖਾਲਸਾ ਸੋ ਜੋ ਕਰੇ ਨਿਤ ਜੰਗ ॥

[375] *SGGS* 6: aaiee pa(n)thee sagal jamaatee man jeetai jag jeet. ਆਈ ਪੰਥੀ ਸਗਲ ਜਮਾਤੀ ਮਨਿ ਜੀਤੈ ਜਗੁ ਜੀਤੁ ॥

ACKNOWLEDGMENTS

ਪੜੀਐ ਗੁਣੀਐ ਕਿਆ ਕਥੀਐ ਜਾ ਮੁੰਢਹੁ ਘੁਥਾ ਜਾਇ ॥

What is the point of reading, studying, and
discussing if one loses one's roots?
—Guru Amar Das (1479–1574), *SGGS*

Writing books is an art for some people who articulate their thoughts
so well that the books become bestsellers. For me, it was a challenge.
Writing became a passion a little late in my life, and this is my third book,
or should I say fourth, including one Punjabi *Angahe Raah* translation
of my first book (*An Uncommon Road*). As I embarked on this journey a
few years ago, my primary encouragement came from my children—my
daughters, Kamaljit Kaur and Palbinder Kaur, and my sons, Harjinder
Singh and Surjit Singh. My sons-in-law, Hardip Singh and Amritpal
Singh, and daughters-in-law, Amarjit Kaur and Sukhwinder Kaur,
played the quarterback roles. My biggest fans and my life's charm are
my ten grandchildren: Harneet Kaur, Manraj Kaur, Ravdeep Singh,
Mohnaam Kaur, Jasdeep Kaur, Jujaar Singh, Ajeet Singh, Kurbaan
Singh, Eimaan Singh, and Teja Singh. I am also now a great-grandfather
to Karmin Singh! I hope this book will inspire them to retain Sikh values
and inculcate them in their own children and grandchildren.

Like my previous three books, this one could not have been brought
to completion without the presence, affection, and support of my wife,
Surinder Kaur. She is my lifeline. Every time a scriptural reference
mystifies me, she has the answer for me. Thank you, partner!

I owe a ton of gratitude to two academicians and Sikh scholars who spent a significant amount of time reviewing the drafts. Dr. Gurnam Singh Sanghera, a former principal and visiting professor at the Centre for Studies on *Sri Guru Granth Sahib* at Guru Nanak Dev University, Amritsar, reviewed the first draft, and I truly appreciate his valuable input. I was fortunate to make the acquaintance of Professor (Dr.) Dharam Singh, an accomplished author and the former head of *Encyclopedia of Sikhism* at Punjabi University, Patiala. His scholarly critique and counsel immensely helped me improve the contextual material. Thank you, my friend, for devoting so much time—a precious commodity—to reviewing the manuscript and writing an insightful and descriptive foreword.

When I shared the manuscript with my dear friend Rev. Cannon T. Neil Vant, I was unsure whether he would have time to read it. He read it—and then he provided me with exceedingly valuable input about my comments on Christianity. Bless you!

Naomi Pauls of Paper Trail Publishing reviewed my first draft and provided excellent feedback. Although she was not familiar with the Sikh religion, she challenged me with questions on subjects that were unclear to her to make my answers more specific and reader friendly, particularly for non-Sikh bibliophiles. I am also truly grateful to Dr. Harjeet Singh Grewal, University of Calgary, and Dr. Paramjit Kaur of Guru Teg Bahadur, Khalsa College, Anandpur Sahib, for reviewing the manuscript to ensure accuracy of historical references, quotes from Gurbani, and Sikh ideology. Dr. Amritpal Kaur, former professor and dean of academic affairs at Punjabi University, Patiala, was kind enough to review it on a short notice and provide scholarly endorsement. Thank you!

I must say, I am blessed to have a family that takes a keen interest in reading and critiquing my writings. Love you all, my internal editorial board!

Thank you, Jeff Stevens, Jeff Miller, and the entire team at Archway Publishing (Simon & Schuster) for your professional support in editing and publishing the book and making it possible to share it with the world. Thanks to Kira Axsiom for the final proof-reading touch. Her meticulous attention to detail was nothing short of remarkable.

If you're like me, wanting to check the acknowledgments first to gauge the author's character, I hope I have passed the litmus test. Please delve into it and enjoy reading it! However, if you're reading this at the end, thank you. I hope the book was informative and that it deepened your understanding of Sikhi. If you have a question that has not been covered, I would love to hear from you! Drop me a line at gianssandhu@gmail.com.

—Gian Singh Sandhu

SELECTED GLOSSARY OF PANJABI TERMS

Aad Ganth	The premier Sikh scripture
Aadesh	Edict issued by the Akal Takhat Jathedar
Akal Purakh	God, Creator, Divine
Akal Takhat	A seat of Sikh temporal authority in Amritsar (literally, throne of the Timeless One)
Akhand Path	Uninterrupted reading of the *Sri Guru Granth Sahib* (Sikh scriptures) from beginning to end. It usually takes about forty-eight hours.
Akhar	Consonant—alphabet
Amrit	The nectar of immortality, prepared for initiating the Sikhs
Amritdhari	A person who has been initiated into the Sikh faith and abides by the Sikh code of conduct, including carrying all articles of faith at all times
Amrit Sanchar	Initiation ceremony (also called *Khande Ki Pahul*)
Anand	Spiritual bliss
Anand Karj	Sikh marriage rites—spiritual bliss or union
Ardaas/ardas	Prayer, request, petition, supplication
Atma	Soul, the spirit
Baba	Grandfather or wise elder. It is an honourific used to refer to someone who is deeply respected for their knowledge and leadership, regardless of age. The female term is *Bibi*.
Babey	Self-proclaimed "God-men" or cultlike figures
Bandi	Imprisoned
Bandi Chhor	Liberator

Bandi Chhor Divas	Day of liberation
Bani	Divine utterances; refers to spiritual writings in the *SGGS*
Bhagat	Spiritually enlightened person
Bhai	Brother, also used as an honourific title
Bhangra	Panjabi folk dance
Bibek Budh	Wisdom and discerning intellect
Bibi	An honourific prefix used for women in respectable positions
Brahmand	Universe
Char Sahibjaday	Refers to four sons of Guru Gobind Singh
Chardi Kala	High spirit—positive mental attitude
Chaur	A ceremonial whisk waved over the Sikh scripture
CE	Common Era
Chuni	Chiffon scarf a woman wears over her head
Darbar	Main congregation hall in a Gurdwara, court
Darbar Sahib	Most revered place of worship for the Sikhs (also known as the Harmandir Sahib or Golden Temple)
Dastaar	Turban
Dasvandh	Donating one-tenth of net earnings to charity
Daiya	Compassion
Dera	It is a generic name for a place where *Babe* or self-proclaimed "messengers of God" hold religious services and meet with their congregants. These deras are usually located outside the influence and territory of the social space of a community.
Dhad	An hourglass-shaped percussion instrument native to Punjab
Dhadi	Minstrel or bard
Dhadi Jatha	Balladeers, a group of ballad singers
Dhol	An oval-shaped drum played with bamboo sticks from both sides
Dholki	Smaller version of dhol (oval-shaped drum), played with hands from both sides

Dhun	Unstruck sound of meditation, melody of Gurbani sabad singing
Dharam	A spiritual path or practice that informs daily living; divine order, duty, righteous action
Dharamsaal	A religious sanctuary (precursor to the Gurdwara), a place to congregate
Divas	Day, celebration day
Ek / Ik	One
Faqir	An ascetic Muslim monk
Gatka	Sikh martial art
Ghalughara	Holocaust, genocide
Gian	Spiritual wisdom or knowledge
Giani	One who has spiritual wisdom
Gidha	Popular Panjabi folk dance performed by women
Golak	A receptacle in which donations made in the Darbar Hall are kept
Granthi	A person who reads the *Sri Guru Granth Sahib* and is well versed in Sikh philosophy and history (must be Amritdhari)
Grehsiti Jiwan	Family or married life
Gurbani	The sacred teachings of the Sikh Gurus and of other spiritually enlightened individuals (as contained in the *SGGS*)
Gurdwara	Sikh place of congregation and worship, gateway to Guru
Gurmukhi	Punjabi script standardized by Guru Angad, the second Guru
Gurpurb	Celebration of Sikh Gurus' anniversaries
Guru	Divine teacher, deliverer or liberator from darkness (ignorance) to light (enlightenment) spiritual master
Guru Granth Sahib	The Sikh scripture, the final and eternal Guru of the Sikhs
Gurmatta	Joint resolution passed by Sarbat Khalsa
Gurmukhi	From the Guru's mouth (the script in which the *Sri Guru Granth Sahib* is written)
Harmonium	Melodeon, pump organ
Hola Mohalla	Mock fight, a Sikh festival that follows the Holi festival

Hukam/Vaak/ Hukamnama	A sabad from the *SGGS* opened at random. It is taken as the Guru's command, divine order
Janam Sakhi	A hagiographical account of the Guru's life
Janaiyu	A sacred religious thread worn by Hindu males
Jatha	An assembled group, often for a particular purpose
Jathedar	A term used for heads of Takhats, leader of a group, community, or a nation
Ji	Suffix connoting respect
Jivanmukti	A state of liberation while living
Jot	Light (eternal light)
Joti Jot	Immersion in eternal light
Jot Saroop	Luminescence of light
Kashera	Cotton undergarment (one of five articles of the Sikh faith)
Kakkars	Sikh articles of faith
Khanda	Sikh emblem
Kangha	Wooden comb (one of five articles of the Sikh faith)
Karm/Karma	Measure, action
Karra	Iron or steel bracelet (one of five articles of the Sikh faith)
Kateb	Abrahamic scriptures (Torah, Bible, and Quran)
Katha	Verbal explanation/discourse of Gurbani and Sikh history
Katha Vachak	A scholar delivering spiritual writing or history discourse
Kaur	Princess, queen/sovereign
Kabit	Poem or couplet
Kesh	Uncut hair (one of five articles of the Sikh faith) that must be covered with a dastaar
Keski	Smaller dastaar worn by men or women
Keertan/Kirtan	The singing of Gurbani
Kesdhari	A Sikh who does not trim their hair or wear a turban
Khalsa	An initiated Sikh who abides by the *Sikh Rehat Maryada*, the Sikh code of conduct
Khalsa Panth	The collective body of initiated adherents of the Sikh faith
Khand	Domain
Khanda	Sikh emblem
Kirpan	Sword (one of five articles of the Sikh faith)

Kirt Karna	Earning one's livelihood through honest means
Kurta Pajama	Long tunic and narrow pants (traditional Panjabi attire commonly worn by Sikh men and women)
Kutha	Meat of animal slaughtered through a painful or ritualistic manner
Langar	Community kitchen in a Gurdwara
Laav	Sikh matrimony vow (single)
Lavaan	Plural laav (vows)
Lorhvand	Needy recipient (the person for whom the service is rendered)
Mahurat	Omen
Mala	Rosary, prayer bead
Milni	A pre-wedding family introduction ceremony
Manant	Offerings made on fulfillment of a desire
Manji	Area, region, diocese, bed, or platform
Manji Sahib	An elevated platform where the *SGGS* is placed
Matta	Resolution
Mela	Festival
Miri	Temporal power or sovereignty
Misl	A small, independent principality or confederacy
Mool	Basic, main, root, or chief
Mool Duar	Navel
Mool Mantar	Seed formula, the first verse in the *Sri Guru Granth Sahib*, which serves as a kind of a creed
Mukti	Liberation from the cycle of birth and death, reincarnation
Naam	Name (spiritual word)
Nagar	Town
Nagar Keertan	Sikh procession singing sabads on public roads. Sometimes referred to as a parade
Naam Japna	Remembrance of Divine name, embarking on a quest for self-actualization through meditation
Nimrata/Gareebi	Humility
Nirankar	God, formless Creator
Nishan Sahib	Sikh flag

Nitnem/Nitname	Daily routine and habit
Paathi	A person who reads the *Sri Guru Granth Sahib*
Palki	Canopy under which the *Sri Guru Granth Sahib* is installed
Panj Pyare	Five beloved Amritdhari (initiated) Sikhs who represent the first five Sikhs initiated in 1699
Panth	The Sikh community as a whole
Parbhat Pheri	Early morning rounds
Parmatama	Supreme soul
Parshad/Karah-Parshad	A sweet pudding-like dish made out of three parts water, and one part each of flour, sugar, and clarified butter. It is served to all who enter the Darbar hall in a gurdwara.
Patase	Sugar puffs
Piri	Spiritual sovereignty
Pyar	Love, respect
Raag	Musical measure/modes, peculiar musical scales meant to be sung in melodic format at different times of the day
Raagi	Sikh sabad singer, musicians
Rabab / Rubab	A lute-like stringed musical instrument
Rehat Maryada	Sikh code of conduct and daily practices
Rehatnama	Code of conduct
Sabad/Shabad	Spiritual writings in the *SGGS*
Sadh Sangat/Sat Sangat	Fellowship of the seekers of truth
Sahib/Saheb	Sahib is a vital term meaning utmost respected "sir" or grace
Sahijdhari	A non-initiated Sikh who evolves slowly
Sahijpath	Gradual or slow reading, reading of the *SGGS* from beginning to end with no time limit
Saka	A heroic historical event
Sakhi	Historical account
Salwar Kameez	Long tunic and pants (traditional Panjabi outfit worn by many Sikh women)
Sanchar	Ceremony
Sangat	Sikh congregation, company, fellowship, an association
Santokh	Contentment

Sanskaar	Accumulative or residual proclivities of past births
Sarangi	A bowed, short-necked string instrument
Sarb-sanjha	All-inclusive, accessible to all
Sarbat Da Bhalaa	Redemption for the entire world
Sarbat Khalsa	Assembly of all initiated Sikhs
Sardarni	Honourable, madam
Sarovar	A sacred pool built within a Gurdwara precinct
Satt / Sach	Truth
Sati	The Hindu ritual of burning a widow on her husband's funeral pyre
Seva	Selfless service
Sevadar	A person who serves others
Simran	To remember, to meditate, continuous recitation of Naam
Singh	Sikh middle or last name (lion)
SGGS	*Sri Guru Granth Sahib*, the sacred Sikh scriptures
SGPC	Shiromani Gurdwara Parbandhak Committee, the Sikh administrative body
Singh	Lion (denoting initiated Sikh male)
Singh Sahib	Honourific designation meaning "Your Honour or "the Honourable"
Sri	Prefix used as a sign of reverence or respect
Sri Guru Granth Sahib	The sacred Sikh scriptures that are the eternal Guru for the Sikhs
Tabla	A combination of two small drums
Takhat	Throne
Tankhahnama	Sikh penal code
Tan, Man, Dhan	Body, mind, and wealth
Taus	A bowed string instrument
Ujarj Jao	May you displace from here!
Vaak	A randomly opened sabad from the *SGGS* (considered the Divine directive for the event)
Vaar	Ballad

Vaisakhi	The founding of the Order of the Khalsa and the first of the month of Vaisakh celebrated annually by Sikhs around the world (also known as Khalsa Sirjana Divas)
Vand Shakna	Sharing of one's earnings with others (particularly the needy)
Varn Vand	Social classification in Hindu scriptures: Brahmins (priests, scholars and teachers); Kshatriyas (rulers, warriors, and administrators); Vishayas (agriculturalists and merchants), and Shudra (laborers and service providers, the "untouchable"). The Sikh faith does not believe in this classification.
Vasde Raho	May you prosper and stay here forever!
Ved	Hindu scriptures
Waheguru	God, Divine, or Creator (also spelled as Vahiguru)
Yogi	Ascetic (someone who denounces the world)
Yug	Era of time

BIBLIOGRAPHY AND FURTHER READING

Archer, John Clark. *The Sikhs in Relation to Hindus, Moslems, Christians, and Ahmadiyyas: A Study in Comparative Religion.* Princeton, NJ: Princeton University Press, 1946.

Barker, Phil. "Guilt and Shame." In *Beyond Intractability*, edited by Guy Burgess and Heidi Burgess. Boulder, CO: Conflict Information Consortium, University of Colorado. Posted July 2003. https://www.beyondintractabiity.org/essay/guilt-shame.

Beall, Stephen Michael. "A Universal Humanism?" January 2019. https://www.researchgate.net/publication/330465557_A_Universal_Humanism.

Benham, W. Gurney. *The Book of Quotations.* Philadelphia: J. B. Lippincott, 1914.

Bhamra, Rajinder Singh. *Sikhism and Spirituality.* Bloomington, IN: Xlibris Corp., 2015.

"British Historian: Punjabi Books Were Burnt to Reduce Literacy Rate of Punjabis." *Daily Sikh Updates*, 2018. http://dailysikhupdates.com/british-historian-claims-punjabi-books-burnt-reduce-literacy-rate-punjabis/amp.

Canadian Heritage. "The Sikh Heritage Museum of Canada Receives Support from the Canada History Fund." Press release, July 26,

2018. https://www.newswire.ca/news-releases/the-sikh-heritage-museum-of-canada-receives-support-from-the-canada-history-fund-689235561.html.

Chahal, Devinder Singh. *Sabd Guru to Granth Guru: An In-Depth Study.* Laval, QC: Institute for Understanding Sikhism, 2004.

Chawla, Janet. "The Mythic Origins of the Menstrual Taboo in the Rig Veda." Matrika. 1992, http://www.matrika-india.org/Research/MythicOrigins.htm.

Cole, W. Owen. *Understanding Sikhism (Understanding Faith).* Edinburgh: Dunedin Academic Press, 2004,

Cunningham, Joseph Davey. *History of the Sikhs: From the Origin of the Nation to the Battles of the Sutlej.* Reprint ed., 1994. New Delhi: D. K. Publishers, 1990.

Dhillon, Balwant Singh. *Early Sikh Scriptural Tradition: Myth and Reality.* Amritsar: Singh Brothers, 1999.

Dhillon, Dalbir Singh. "Evolution of Institutions and Ethical Doctrines." Chapter 3 in *Sikhism: Origin and Development.* New Delhi: Atlantic Publishers & Distributors, 1988.

Dhillon, Harish. *The Sikh Gurus.* New Delhi: Hay House India, 2015.

Dhillon, Iqbal Singh. *Folk Dances of Panjab.* Delhi: National Book Shop, 1998.

Durkheim, Émile. *The Elementary Forms of the Religious Life,* translated by Joseph Ward Swain. Glencoe, IL: Free Press, 1954. Original work published 1912.

Eck, Diana L. "What Is Pluralism?" The Pluralism Project, Harvard University. https://pluralism.org/about.

Eliade, Mircea. *A History of Religious Ideas. Volume 1: From the Stone Age to the Eleusinian Mysteries.* Chicago, IL: University of Chicago Press, 1978.

Fateh, Navratan Singh. "Honour Killing." Master of Laws thesis, University of Toronto, 2012.

Friedrich, Pieter, and Bhajan Singh. *Captivating the Simple-Hearted: A Struggle for Human Dignity in the Indian Subcontinent.* California: Sovereign Star, 2018.

Gordon, General Sir John J. H. *The Sikhs.* Edinburgh and London: William Blackwood & Sons, 1904.

Greenlees, Duncan. *The Gospel of the Guru-Granth Sahib.* World Religion Series. London: Theosophical Publishing House, 1975.

Grewal, J. S. "The Singh Way of Life: The Rahitnamas." In *History, Literature, and Identity: Four Centuries of Sikh Tradition.* New Delhi: Oxford University Press, 2015.

Gulati, Devinder Singh. "What Is Naam in Sikhism?" Quora.com, August 31, 2017.

Gupta. Hari Ram. *History of the Sikhs. Volume 1, The Sikh Gurus (1469–1708).* 2nd rev. ed. New Delhi: Munshiram Manoharlal, 1984.

Holm, Jean, and John Bowker, eds. *Making Moral Decisions: Themes in Religious Studies.* London: Frances Pinter Publishers, 1994.

Jhutti-Johal, Jagbir. *Sikhism Today.* London: Bloomsbury Academic, 2011.

Johnston, Hugh, "Group Identity in an Emigrant Worker Community: The Example of Sikhs in Early Twentieth-Century British Columbia." *BC Studies*, no. 148 (Winter 2005–2006): 3–23. https://ojs.library.ubc.ca/index/php/bcstudies/article/view/1772/1817.

———. *The Voyage of the* Komagata Maru: *The Sikh Challenge to Canada's Colour Bar.* 3rd ed. Vancouver, BC: UBC Press, 2014. Original work published 1979.

Kashdan, Todd B. "Does Being Religious Make Us Happy?" *Psychology Today* (blog), October 7, 2015. https://www.psychologytoday.com/us/blog/curious/201510/does-being-religious-make-us-happy.

Kaur, Madanjit. "The Creation of the Khalsa and Prescribing of the Sikhism." In *Advanced Studies in Sikhism: Papers Contributed at Conference of Sikh Studies Los Angeles* (195–213), edited by Jasbir Singh Mann and Harbans Singh Saron. Irvine, CA: Sikh Community of North America, 1989.

———. "Guru Granth Sahib Sanctified as Guru." In *Advanced Studies in Sikhism: Papers Contributed at Conference of Sikh Studies Los Angeles* (121–37), edited by Jasbir Singh Mann and Harbans Singh Saron. Irvine, CA: Sikh Community of North America, 1989.

Kaur, Malika. "Faith, Gender, and Activism in Punjab Conflict." *The Wheat Fields Still Whisper*: Palgrave Macmillan, 1st ed. 2019 (January 14, 2020).

Kertzer, Morris N., and Lawrence A. Hoffman. *What Is a Jew? A Guide to the Beliefs, Traditions, and Practices of Judaism that Answers Questions for Both Jew and Non-Jew.* New York: Macmillan, 1993.

Khokhar, Kulwant Singh. "Anand Marriage—Development and History." *Global Sikh Studies*, 2005.

Kirby, William T. "Tattoo Removal." In *Lasers and Energy Devices for the Skin*, 2nd ed. (74–93), edited by Michael P. Goldman, Richard E. Fitzpatrick, E. Victor Ross, Suzanne L. Kilmer, and Robert E. Weiss. Boca Raton, FL: CRC Press, 2013.

Kirste, Imke, et al. "Is Silence Golden? Effects of Auditory Stimuli and Their Absence on Adult Hippocampal Neurogenesis." *Brain Structure and Function*, December 2013. doi:10.1007/s00429-013-0679-3.

Kovach, Bill, and Tom Rosenstiel. *The Elements of Journalism: What News people Should Know and the Public Should Expect.* London: Atlantic Books, 2001

Leadem, Rose. "9 Ways to Focus a Wandering Mind (Infographic)." *Entrepreneur*, May 6, 2018. https://www.enterpreneur.com/amphtml/312812.

Leidner, Gordon. "Lincoln's Honesty." Great American History. https://greatamericanhistory.net/honesty.htm.

Leonard, Karen. *Making Ethnic Choices: California's Punjabi Mexican Americans (Asian American History and Culture).* Philadelphia, PA: Temple University Press, 1992.

Littleton, Catherine A. "Restructuring Sexual Equality." *California Law Review* 75 (1987): 1279–1337.

Manchanda, Supreet Singh. "Twenty Years Later: Milestones on the Path to Peace." Seeds of Healing, SikhNet.com. 2004. https://www.sikhnet.com/pages/seeds-healing.

Mandaiker, Arjun. "The History of the Tabla." Desiblitz.com. N.d. https://www.desiblitz.com/content/history-tabla.

Mansukhani, Gobind Singh. "Sikh Ethics." All About Sikhs, January 27, 2014. https://www.allaboutsikhs.com/sikh-literature/ books-boss/sikh-ethics-gobind-singh-mansukhani.

Marshall, Michael. "The Secret of How Life on Earth Began." BBC, October 31, 2016, http://www.bbc.com/earth/ story/20161026-the-secret-of-how-life-on-earth-began.

Mathumohan, N. "Reading Sukhmani Sahib." *Abstracts of Sikh Studies* 5 (2003), 59.

Mayell, Jaspal Singh Dr. "Punjabi Language is 5500 Years Old," Amritsar, Singh Brothers, 2017.

McCabe, Des. *The 5 Minute Guide to Sikhism*. New Activity Publications, 2012.

Muldoon, Sylvan J., and Hereward Carrington. *The Projection of the Astral Body*. York Beach, ME: Samuel Weiser, 1973. Original work published by Rider & Co., London, 1929.

Nabha, Bhai Kahn Singh, comp. *Mahan Kosh: The Sikh Encyclopedia in Punjabi*. 1930.

Neki, J. S. *The Spiritual Heritage of Punjab*. Amritsar: Guru Nanak Dev University, 2000.

Osho. *Meditation: The First and Last Freedom*. Osho Media International, 2010.

Parks Canada. "Government of Canada Recognizes National Historic Significance of Residential School System," Press release,

September 1, 2020. https://www.newswire.ca/news-releases/government-of-canada-recognizes-the-national-historic-significance-of-the-residential-school-system-and-former-residential-school-sites-861320160.html.

Parrinder, Geoffrey. *Perspectives on Guru Nanak*. Patiala: Punjabi University, Patiala, 1990.

Perry, Robert. "12 Remedies for the Wandering Mind." Circle of Atonement, https://www.circleofa.org/library/12-remedies-for-the-wandering-mind.

Pincott, Fredrick. In *Guru Nanak in the Eyes of Non-Sikhs*, edited by Sarjit Singh Bal. Reprint ed. Chandigarh: Panjab University, 1995. Original work published 1969.

Prill, Susan E. "Sikhi and Sustainability: Sikh Approaches to Environmental Advocacy." *Sikh Formations 11,* no. 1 (2015): 1–20.

Rahi, Malkiat Singh. *Guru Granth Sahib in the Eyes of Non-Sikh Scholars.* Chandigarh: Singh Legal Foundation, 2003.

Reiss, Steven. "Four Reasons for Decline of Religion." *Huffpost,* December 12, 2015. https://www.huffpost.com/entry/four-reasons-for-decline-_b_8778968.

Rich, Albert II: "Gender and Spirituality: Are Women Really More Spiritual?" Senior honours thesis, Liberty University, Lynchburg, Virginia, 2012.

Sahni, Ruchi Ram. *Struggle for Reform in Sikh Shrines,* edited by Ganda Singh. Sikh Ithas Research Board, 1969.

Sandhu, Gian Singh. *An Uncommon Road: How Canadian Sikhs Struggled Out of the Fringes and into the Mainstream.* Vancouver, BC: Echo Storytelling Agency, 2018.

Sarna, Navtej. *The Book of Nanak.* New Delhi: Penguin Books India, 2003.

SikhNet Inspirations. *What Is Naam? Deep Explanation (Part 1)* [Video]. https://www.sikhnet.com/videos/what-naam-deep-explanation-part-1.

Sidhu, Gurbachan Singh. *A Brief Introduction to Sikhism*, 5th ed. 2003.

Sidhu, Gurmeet Singh. *Beyond Otherness: Sikhism: New Mystical Experience and Interfaith Dialogue.* Chennai: Notion Press, 2015.

Sidhu, Gurmukh Singh. *Sikh Religion and Islam: A Comparative Study.* Mullanpur Mandi, Punjab: Guru Nanak Charitable Trust, 2001.

Sikh Welfare Foundation of North America. Guru Nanak Dev to Guru Gobind Singh Ji.

SikhWomen.com. "Why Do Sikhs Wear a Turban and What Does It Mean?" http://www.sikhwomen.com/turban/sikhs.htm.

Singh, Avtar. *Ethics of the Sikhs.* Reprint ed. Patiala, India: Publication Bureau, Punjabi University, 2009. Original work published 1970.

Singh, Baldev, PhD. *Gurmat: Guru Nanak's Path of Enlightenment.* India: Khalsa Tricentennial Foundation of North America, 2015.

Singh, Dharam. *Guru Nanak: Contemporary Concerns and Response.* Amritsar: Singh Brothers, 2019.

Singh, Gurharpal, and Darshan Singh Tatla. *Sikhs in Britain: The Making of a Community*. London: Zed Books, 2006.

Singh, Gurharpal and Giorgio Shani. *Sikh Nationalism: From a Dominant Minority to an Ethno-Religious Diaspora*, Cambridge University Press, UK, 2022.

Singh, Gurnam. "Sikh Music." Chapter 32 in *The Oxford Handbook of Sikh Studies*, edited by Louis E. Fenech and Pashaura Singh. New York: Oxford University Press, 2014.

Singh, Inder Jit. "Chasing Happiness." SikhNet.com, December 12, 2014. https://www.sikhnet.com/news/chasing-happiness.

———. *Sikhs and Sikhism: A View with a Bias*. New Delhi: Manohar Publishing, 1994.

———. *Sikhs Today: Ideas and Opinions*. Ethnicisland.com, 2012.

———. *The World According to Sikhi*. Ontario: Centennial Foundation, 2006.

Singh, Jagjit. *The Sikhism: Culture, History, and Religion*. Amritsar: Chattar Singh Jiwan Singh, 2008.

Singh, Jaswinder. "Discovering Divine Love in the Play of Life." *Journal of Contemporary Sikh Studies* (2000).

Singh, Khushwant. *A History of the Sikhs (Set of Two Volumes)*, 2nd ed. Oxford: Oxford University Press, 2004–5. Original work published 1963.

Singh, Kirpal. *Janamsakhi Tradition: An Analytical Study*. Amritsar: Singh Brothers, 2004.

Singh, Navroop. "Guru Nanak Dev Ji's Visit to Rome, Italy, in the Year 1520." Post on Gurmat Discussion Forum, September 12, 2013. https://gurmatbibek.com/forum/read. php?3,29281,29281#msg-29281.

Singh, Neutral. "Polygamy and Sikhism." Sikh Philosophy Network. June 1, 2004. https://www.sikhphilosophy.net/threads/ polygamy-and-sikhism.534.

Singh, Nikki-Guninder Kaur. *The Name of My Beloved: Verses of the Sikh Gurus.* San Francisco: Harper, 1995.

———. "Sikh Art." Chapter 34 in *The Oxford Handbook of Sikh Studies*, edited by Louis E. Fenech and Pashaura Singh. New York: Oxford University Press, 2014.

Singh, Pashaura, and Louis E. Fenech, eds. *The Oxford Handbook of Sikh Studies.* New York: Oxford University Press, 2014.

Singh, Patwant. *The Sikhs.* New York: Knopf Publishing Group, 2000.

Singh, Patwant, and Harinder Kaur Sekhon. *Garland Around My Neck: The Story of Puran Singh of Pingalwara.* Amritsar: UBS Publishers' Distributors, 2001.

Singh, Puran. *The Spirit Born People.* CreateSpace, 2017. Original work published 1928.

Singh, Ranbir. *The Sikh Way of Life.* 3rd ed. New Delhi: India Publishers, 1982.

Singh, Sarbjinder. *Divine Revelation.* New Delhi: Sikh Foundation, 2008.

Singh, Satbir. *Sada Itihaas [Our History]*. 12th ed. Jalandhar, India: New Book Co., 2011.

Singh, Trilochan. *Sikhism and Tantric Yoga*. London: International Institute of Sikh Studies, 1977.

————. *The Turban and the Sword of the Sikhs*. Amritsar: Chattar Singh Jiwan Singh, 1976.

Smetanin, P., D. Stiff, C. Briante, C. E. Adair, S. Ahmad, and M. Khan. "The Life and Economic Impact of Major Mental Illnesses in Canada." Toronto: RiskAnalytica for the Mental Health Commission of Canada, 2011.

Tatlay, Santa Singh. *Gurbani Tat Sagar,* parts 1–6. Punjabi books available at SikhBookClub.com.

Tolle, Eckhart. *A New Earth: Awakening to Your Life's Purpose.* New York: Viking, 2005.

Toynbee, Arnold. Foreword to *Selections from the Sacred Writings of the Sikhs*. Translated by Trilochan Singh. Macmillan, 1960.

Tuli, Pritpal Singh. *Sikh Traditions and Festivals*. Amritsar: Chattar Singh Jiwan Singh, 2013.

United States Centers for Disease Control and Prevention. "Influenza (Flu): 1918 Pandemic." https://www.cdc.gov.

Uzoka, Azubike. *Growing Up, Growing Old: Chronicle of an Ordinary Life*. iUniverse, 2011.

Ward, Keith. *The Big Questions in Science and Religion*. West Conshohocken, PA: Templeton Press, 2008.

Williams, Caroline. "7 Ways to Tame Your Wandering Mind and Achieve Better Focus." *New Scientist*, May 17, 2017. https://www.newscientist.com/article/2131286-7-ways-to-tame-your-wandering-mind-and-achieve-better-focus.

World Health Organization. "Mental Disorders Affect One in Four People." Press release, October 4, 2001. https://www.who.int/whr/2001/media_center/press_release/en.

Sikh Scripture and Code of Conduct

Khalsa, Sant Singh, trans. *Sri Guru Granth Sahib* [English translation]. 5 vols. SikhNet, 1972. Also available as an audiobook from storytel.com.

Macauliffe, Max Arthur, trans. *The Sikh Religion: Its Gurus, Sacred Writings and Authors*. 6 vols. New Delhi: S. Chand, 1985. Original work published 1909.

Sikh Rehat Maryada (Code of conduct). English version available on SikhiWiki: Encyclopedia of the Sikhs. https://www.sikhiwiki.org.

Singh, Gopal, trans. *Sri Guru Granth Sahib* [English translation], 9th ed. 4 vols. World Book Centre, 1993.

Singh, Manmohan, trans. *Sri Guru Granth Sahib* [English translation]. 8 vols. 1962–69.

Singh, Prof. Sahib, trans. *Sri Guru Granth Darpan* [Sikh spiritual writing] [Punjabi translation with commentary and word meanings]. http://www.gurugranthdarpan.net/darpan.html.

INDEX

ABOUT THE BOOK

Who Are the Sikhs? is teeming with knowledge, references, and answers to 300 frequently asked questions about Sikhi (the Sikh Faith) and its socio-religious and politico-economic affairs. The author traces the origin or road map of the Sikh faith and identity, and delves into the who, why, what, when, and where of the Creator and the Creation, including evolution. Sikh beliefs, ethics, and practices are eloquently described.

The question-and-answer format makes it easier for a reader to choose a topic and find a quick answer. It's ideal for conversation students, researchers, interfaith couples, multicultural communities, and anyone who wants to know Sikhs. The book embodies both simplicity and scholarly details. The author depicts Sikh philosophy, theology, ideology, and relevance to contemporary life in a common phraseology, making it simpler for the average reader to comprehend. He also shows how susceptible and uncharted trails (such as abortion, test-tube babies, surrogate mothering, artificial insemination, etc.) can be approached and strategized through Gurbani, the spiritual utterances in the Sikh Scripture.

ABOUT THE AUTHOR

 GIAN SINGH SANDHU is an author, educator, entrepreneur, and social activist. Leaving behind an exceptional career in the Indian Air Force, he immigrated to Canada in 1970. He spent most of his life working in the forest industry and a short stint teaching at the college level. Gian Singh is the founding president of two Gurdwaras (Sikh places of congregation and worship) and the World Sikh Organization of Canada (a leading human rights advocacy group). His visionary leadership won him the regional Entrepreneur of the Year award in 1994 and the nomination for the 'Entrepreneur of the Year National Award in the same year. He is a recipient of the Order of British Columbia (OBC), the highest civilian award, and the Queen's Golden Jubilee Medal for Community Service. Gian Singh has authored and co-authored several books listed on the publication page. In addition, he has written over 200 scripts on Sikh heritage. On top of his writing passion, the former CEO and president of a group of forest companies is presently the President & CEO of the Guru Nanak Institute of Global Studies (www. gurunanakinstitute.ca), a non-profit post-secondary education and research institute. He resides with his wife, Surinder Kaur, in Surrey, British Columbia, Canada.

CPSIA information can be obtained
at www.ICGtesting.com
Printed in the USA
BVHW041242020423
661605BV00001B/2